Romania After Ceauşescu

Romania
After
Ceauşescu

The Politics of Intolerance

TOM GALLAGHER

EDINBURGH UNIVERSITY PRESS

This book is dedicated to the men and women of Asklepyos, the medical and social aid charity in Cluj which, without ethnic or religious distinction, has brightened the lives of thousands and which provides a model of democratic organisation that political parties of Romania could well emulate.

© Tom Gallagher, 1995

Edinburgh University Press Ltd
22 George Square, Edinburgh

Typeset in Plantin
by Bibliocraft, Dundee, and
printed and bound in Great Britain

A CIP record for this book is
available from the British Library.

ISBN 0 7486 0613 0

Contents

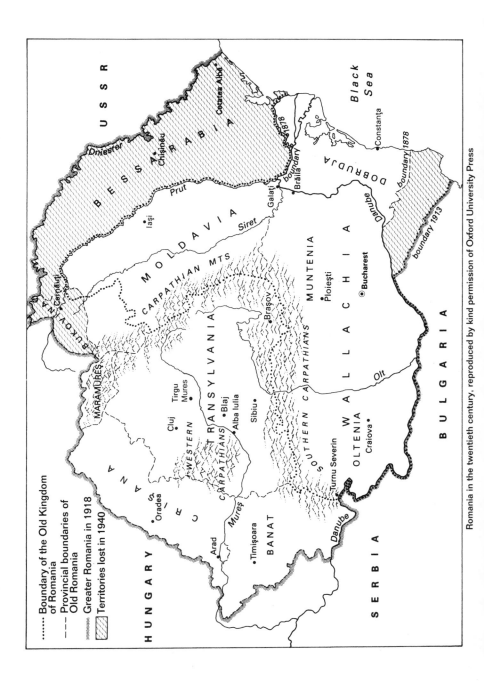

Romania in the twentieth century, reproduced by kind permission of Oxford University Press

Boundary of the Old Kingdom of Romania

Provincial boundaries of Old Romania

Greater Romania in 1918

Territories lost in 1940

Acknowledgements

It is customary to list the friends and acquaintances who provided information, hospitality, criticism and other forms of assistance during the four years in which I was working on this book. But I shall leave out a good many names, since printing them in the current uncertain circumstances of Romania would be a poor way of returning their thoughtfulness and generosity. Among those to whom I owe very special thanks are Iosif and Elena, Alin and Corinna, Viorel and Alina, Dan and Marton as well as Dodo, Tibi and Istvan.

Others who have taken a public stand in the politics of contemporary Romania, either through their scholarship or as a result of their roles in the media and in trying to foster inter-ethnic co-operation, can be acknowledged more openly.

Carol Harsan, an indefatigible journalist and no mean poet, provided much raw material about events at Cluj which enabled me to make sense of developments in that city earlier than I might have done; Doina and Nicolae Harsanyi patiently described the growth of civic politics in Timişoara when we met in Tallinn; in a number of extended conversations, Smaranda Enache from 1990 to 1993 described each stage of the unequal contest in her native Tirgu Mureş between advocates of Romanian-Hungarian co-existence and elements of the old nomenklatura; irrespective of later events which placed us on divergent paths, I remain grateful to Eva Blenesi, formerly of the Fidesz Party, for introducing me to the Balvanyos summer camp in 1991; two Hungarian residents of Cluj, Eva Cs. Gyimesi and Peter Banyai, deserve thanks for helping me to appreciate the intricacies of politics in the Hungarian community. Finally, I am indebted to the staff of the Institute of History in Cluj (a group of scholars who maintained their integrity and high scholarly standards) for many stimulating conversations, in particular to Gheorghe Cipaianu, Gheorghe Iancu and Liviu Tirau. They are unlikely to agree with all the conclusions reached here, but nevertheless they helped me to appreciate several of the nuances in inter-ethnic relations in in Transylvania.

Foundations which faciliated this research deserve to be warmly thanked, for without their assistance it would have taken even longer to complete. They include the Nuffield Foundation which gave me a research award in 1990 and another two years later (in conjunction with Dr Dennis Deletant); the Soros Foundation in Cluj which in 1992 provided me with one years subscription to the daily bulletin of the ARPRESS news agency; also the Westminster Foundation for Democracy which, through the good offices of Diana Warwick, Sue Chudleigh and Tracey Jarvis, funded an open media project in Cluj which I helped draw up in 1992.

Finally, I would like to express my thanks to Dr Francisco Veiga for his generosity with materials and to Dr Dennis Deletant of the University of London for his quiet encouragement and practical assistance during the years I have been working on this project; and to James O'Connell, Professor Emeritus of Peace Studies at Bradford University, for facilitating my research trips trips in 1990–3. Needles to say, any mistakes or inaccuracies that are found in the book are my own responsibility.

Introduction

Whatever the future holds in store for Romania, that country is likely to be linked in the popular imagination with the tyranny of Nicolae Ceauşescu for many years to come. The suffering which the most exacting of the Warsaw Pact's tyrants inflicted upon his own people evoked a generous response from west European citizens after it became relatively easy to enter Romania at the end of 1989. The bravery of young protesters, who defied Ceauşescu's soldiers and secret policemen during the communist regime's final bloody moments, captured the imagination of the rest of Europe, and the television coverage of the gun-battles in Bucharest and Timişoara was one of the defining moments of the 1989 revolutions in eastern Europe. The practical help which hundreds of British medics, teachers, social workers and craftsmen have brought in order to rebuild shattered lives and offer purpose and hope to ordinary Romanians is a rare example of western Europe reacting to the problems of the east in a disinterested manner.

However, the efforts of foreign volunteers have often been hampered by officials groomed by the Ceauşescu regime whose power was challenged but not broken. The people's revolt of 1989 was quickly smothered by these political insiders who managed to carry out an internal coup, disposing of Ceauşescu in the process. The dictator – hurriedly executed along with his wife and co-ruler Elena Ceauşescu on Christmas day 1989 – was blamed for the abuses of previous decades while the system that produced him was largely overlooked. Many of the authoritarian features of the Ceauşescu years have been retained in a modified form within the shell of a newly-minted democracy. Unsupervised political activity is still regarded with hostility. The state refuses to allow the autonomous bodies making up the nascent civil society to check its power over ordinary citizens. The Securitate, the secret police of communist times, continues to shadow anti-government forces, though its name has been changed and its image freshened up. Membership of the government elite still offers opportunities for enrichment, as a flawed privatisation of some state assets has enriched former members of the communist establishment. Parliament and the media can discuss abuses of power, but they have little leverage over the reluctant democrats in charge of Romania. As for local government, it is controlled in all important respects by the centre, which was true in Romania long before the onset of communism.

Only the naive or recklessly optimistic expected that the legacy of the Ceauşescu regime could be swiftly buried. But the extent to which continuity rather than change has been the dominant motif in Romania in the half-decade since 1989 has come as a surprise even to to the more knowing who did expect change to be slow and incomplete. The durability of techniques of political control and manipulation associated with Ceauşescu's rule suggests that his nationalistic and centralised dictatorship was far from being an abberation.

In Yugoslavia, Slobodan Milosevic, another ambitious and unscrupulous Communist Party official, has emulated Ceauşescu by using nationalist rhetoric and imagery to gain control over the ruling party and turn many of his fellow citizens against minorities – or else co-ethnics of liberal views – who are dubbed as the enemy within. Both Milosevic and Ceauşescu insisted that they were able correctly to interpret and uphold the popular will of the nation. Their brand of nationalism denied individualism and disempowered intermediate institutions designed to set curbs on what the state could do to its citizens. Citizens hitherto defined by jobs, education, character and ideas, as well as nationality, were increasingly reduced to one dimension as the climate of insecurity turned nationalism into a state religion. This top-down nationalist mobilisation went much further in Yugoslavia than in Romania; in 1991 it culminated in war and the disintegration of the country, enabling powerful ethnic elites in Serbia and Croatia to push citizens in the direction of complete ethnic polarisation.

Ceauşescu might have engineered an ethnic conflict between the Romanian majority in Transylvania and the Hungarian minority which had ruled the province up to 1918, if his ruinous economic and social policies had not also turned the bulk of the Romanian-speaking population against him. Romanians and Hungarians joined forces in the cities of Timişoara, Cluj and Tirgu Mureş to challenge the dictator's claim to rule over them. But, in no more that three months, Tirgu Mureş was to witness the first serious inter-ethnic collisions in post-communist eastern Europe as the Romanian officials, appointed on ethic criteria in what had until recently been an overwhelmingly Hungarian city, engineered a collision between Romanians and Hungarians.

The ruling National Salvation Front of Ion Iliescu, Romania's President since 1989, had already gone back on a promise to provide a comprehensive package of minority rights. Within a few weeks it was using nationalism to manage change on its own restrictive agenda, and with increasing boldness it has allowed officials associated with the xenophobic policies of the pre-1989 years to step back into the limelight. Some have been given key jobs in sensitive ministries, and in 1993 one was even placed in charge of state television, the electronic media being a key weapon for indoctrinating the populace along nationalist lines. The National Salvation Front has changed its name several times, and is today know as the Party of Romanian Social Democracy. But it remains a nationalist party run by ex-communist apparatchiks who emphasise nativist themes and criticise the wholesale adoption of western economic and political models. In the past, nationalism had appealed to unsuccessful citizens and declining social groups, and so it is in Romania today. It offers a sense of belonging to a wider national family via an emotional solidarity that democracy has rarely been able to replicate. Citizens grouped into an electorate simply do not possess the strong group identity or sense of belonging that members of national communities possess.

Participation in the electoral process may acquire a significance after a period of authoritarian rule or in the wake of attempts to stifle democracy. But democracy normally lacks emotional artefacts like land, religion, language or customs which enable nationalism to renew itself and issue powerful emotional appeals.

Democracy everywhere invites groups to separate and to compete for resources. Differences are heightened – difference of interest, culture, religion and national identity – and these become defined in a party-political sense. In a country like Romania, with pre-existing ethnic divisions, it was difficult to avoid these differences being expressed in terms of sharp party rivalry. Nationalists invoked memories of cultural subordination in the past to oppose concessions to once powerful minorities. A sense of insecurity and permanent grievance among minorities either caused them to leave, in the case of most German-speakers, or to cultivate a siege mentality in the case of not a few Hungarian speakers.

The emphasis on ethnic values means that a government or an opposition-in-waiting is less likely to be judged by its performance in safeguarding the material interests of citizens or upholding basic rights. Politics based on ethnic identity gives rulers more scope to be anti-democratic, corrupt, or unbalanced in their behaviour and not to need to pay a price at the ballot-box because the sources of legitimacy for the state do not place strong enough emphasis on civic values or economic competence. States influenced by a civic rather than an ethnic definition of democracy usually possess institutions such as a constitutional monarchy, parliment, civil service or judiciary which elicit widespread consent. Political institutions which in Germany, Spain, Britain or the USA may command high levels of respect are pitifully weak in eastern Europe. Hence the temptation for politicians to seek legitimacy or consent from citizens by appealing to ethnic characteristics.

After all, national programmes are among the easiest to understand, and it has not proven hard to construct populist manifestoes that offer answers by the application of appropriate national solutions while identifying a range of national enemies responsible for current misfortunes. In its most extreme manifestations, nationalism promotes racial hatred or prejudice; it propagates racial superiority or exclusiveness and it encourages discrimination, an official and/or societal, against ethnic minorities and all those who cannot be easily assimilated.

In countries like Hungary, the discontented have withdrawn from political participation rather than assemble behind demagogues. It has one of the lowest percentages of ethnic minorities in Easter Europe. But in Yugoslavia, whose ethnic distinctiveness was recognised by the communists who divided the country into federal republics and autonomous provinces very roughly matching the ethnic distribution of the population, nationalism was manipulated by the elites in dispute at the end of the 1980s over the nature of the state and the distribution of power within it.

Yugoslavia after 1991 may be described as an example of an elite-directed national conflict; Czechoslovakia, the other federal state in the region, broke up one year later as a result of conflicts between rival territorial elites over economic policy and the distribution of resources. In both countries, the antagonism at societal level was less strong than among elites competing for states or control of resources, or bent on acquisition of a monopoly of power. Communities which for centuries devised informal strategies to cope with ethnic group differences and regulate conflict were often powerless to stop ethnocentric elites splitting them up into rival groups and forcing them to take sides in disputes which did not really affect their own interests. Thus it is difficult to see who, other than small groups in Slovakia, or the other various war zones of the former Yugoslavia, benefited from the disintegration of the federal states of which they were part.

The communist era robbed local communities of whatever means they had previously enjoyed to determine their own affairs. In the absence of local democracy, they were unable to nominate trusted representatives from their own ranks who could act on their behalf in dealing with the central state. Instead, unaccountable communist elites acquired skill in manipulating ordinary citizens, techniques which they employed in the post-communist era especially if a power vacuum ensued.

The most effective survival strategy has been to stir up ethnic differences and give them a value which they lacked previously. Not all former communists intent upon remaining in politics have embarked on this course, even in countries already troubled by ethnic problems; by no means all ultra-nationalists have links with former party elites: some ultra-nationalists have sprung from apolitical backgrounds, others retained conservative nationalist outlooks even under communism, and several figures known for their ethnocentric outlook may even have had a background in liberal opposition politics. Governments claiming a reformist orientation have also sought to divert attention away from severe economic problems by raising emotive nationalistic questions. This is a phenomenon not unknown in western Europe, where mainstream government and opposition parties have dabbled with xenophobic and anti-immigrant parties because hard economic times mean that they can no longer court their voters with policies based on growth and welfarist principles.

Erich Fromm, the social psychologist, identified various social types who are uncomfortable with freedom, illiberal in their attitudes, and happiest with a centrally-directed, strong state which lays down how they should think and behave. These types exist in all societies, but the stress on conformity and discipline in behaviour and though patterns that was a feature of communist rule perhaps made authoritarian-minded citizens more numerous than elsewhere. Certainly, the experience of two generations of rigid state paternalism has created large groups of citizens ill equipped to cope well with the demands on an open and competitive society where individuals have far greater responsibility for their own lives, where the rules are more complicated and the risks for the unenterprising correspondingly greater than they were under communism.

Certainly, populist leaders wishing to build a minimalist democracy that pays only lip-service to individual freedoms have been able to exploit authoritarian sentiments and the desire for the return of a strong state. Those using the politics of intolerance in eastern Europe to make public careers may not all be driven by authentic nationalist feelings, but they nevertheless see the manipulation of nationalism as the easiest way to create an electoral following.

Perhaps there may be certain similarities between communism and nationalism which enable ambitious office-holders from the pre-1989 era to adapt successfully to competitive politics. Both are systems of ideas and norms built around an impersonal force – the nation or the working class – which becomes the sole focus of loyalty on society. There is a stress on unity behind individuals able to define the collective will in societies based on doctrinaire nationalist or communist principles. The emphasis on uniformity of thinking leaves little room for autonomous institutions enabling the individual to lead a social life independent of the state. States based on such totals doctrines, that can assume the form of secular religions, rarely acquire the means to regulate conflict; the power wielded by individuals whose skill as manipulators, or as contestants in power struggles, enables them to direct the collective will, faces none of the limitations generally found in pluralist systems. Coercion and violence is often necessary to enforce uniformity behind an ideology which can be a mask for the same abuse of power and the misallocation of resources. Political successions often come about as a result of power struggles in which violence may be used rather than form contests in which aspirants are judged on meritocratic grounds. Nationalism and communism mobilise support by identifying 'national' or 'class' enemies that threaten the very survival of the state.[1]

There is much to learn about the use and abuse of nationalism in politics through studying the recent Romanian experience. The defence of national values has been at the core of politics as the country has switched from constitutional monarchy to right-wing dictatorship and finally to communist rule. After a brief flirtation with communist internationalism, Romania evolved a distinctive brand of national communism after slipping out of Moscow's orbit in the 1960s. Many of the officials who achieved career fulfilment by merging national communist ideology continue to enjoy positions of influence in post-communist Romania. The story of their brief disgrace and swift rehabilitation is a fascinating one and is a sad commentary on the failure of the 1989 Romanian revolution to promote genuine or long-lasting liberalism. Instead, highly-placed and seasoned political operators have managed change on their own nativist terms. The hope that the power of the chauvinist intellectuals had been decisively broken in Romania lasted for only a matter of months in 1990. Romania provides a salutary example of how it is possible to use nationalism to delay the passage of a country from a closed to an open political system. A study of the flourishing nationalist press in Romania, whose circulation almost certainly exceeds that of any other country in the region (including Serbia), reveals the mentality and arguments inimical to the progress of a healthy democracy. The anti-western, anti-democratic and anti-minority views propagated by best-selling weeklies like *România Mâre* denote a fundamentalism which has taken hold in countries as far apart as Algeria, India and parts of the former Soviet Union as a result of a backlash of modernisation based on secular, capitalist or federalist ideas. In the 1930s, Romania figured prominently in the European backlash against the rationalism, political utilitarianism and individualism of the nineteenth century known as fascism. If the post-communist settlement based on market economics and limited association with western institutions produces a backlash among citizens who have failed to benefit from these changes, it is likely that Romania will again be at the forefront. The country lies on the religious fault-line between western and eastern Christianity which since the end of the Cold War has been a source of renewed friction in the Balkans. With Yugoslavia and Czechoslovakia having broken up in 1991–2, Romania is one of the last major beneficiaries of the Versailles settlement to remain intact. A study of its flawed and incomplete transition from authoritarian rule and the way that past models influence present governing arrangements is essential for understanding the role that nationalism is playing in eastern Europe in the 1990s.

To understand why Romanian democracy is being influenced by nationalist values, it is necessary to examine the first experience with democracy in Romania that lasted from independence down to 1938. Although in key respects it was a record of failure due to the absence of internal cohesion, stable economic growth and social justice, the length of the constitutional epoch meant that it was bound to have an impact on the post-1989 politics whose practitioners had no domestic example of governance to draw upon other than the discredited communist one. The reluctance of the political elite to encourage the growth of civil society, the tradition of state dominance over citizens, the acceptance of arbitrary political behaviour, the weakness of an autonomous middle-class based on commerce, and the influence of intellectuals and the state of bureaucracy in politics can only be properly understood by examining pre-communist politics, above all the turbulent inter-war period.

The years from 1938 until the imposition of communism in 1947 were full of controversial and tragic events which reverberate in Romanian politics today. The breach between the Hungarian minority and the rest of the population acquired an intensity lacking before, which the temporary influence enjoyed by the Hungarians in the first phase of communist rule deepened farther: the reluctance of many Romanians to grant substantial minority rights to Hungarians after 1989 can only be understood by exploring the turbulent events of the 1940s and early 1950s. Similarly, the ability of post-communists to define the new political agenda on their minimalist terms is best understood by examining how, from a weak base, Romanian communists were able to impose the power of the state down to village level, no other government having ever succeeded in doing this.

Chapter 2 examines how Romanian communists looked for legitimacy beyond Marxism, mobilising the past to achieve this goal. The ability of Romanian communism to acquire autonomy from its Soviet overlord is studied not least because it places in context the bid by the current Iliescu regime to establish an autonomous relationship with the West through the use of similar tactics.

Chapter 3 examines the crucial first quarter of 1990 and shows how the National Salvation Front consolidated itself in power by embracing national values and encouraging ultra-nationalistic forces in Transylvania where it was troubled by the strength of opposition to its rule. The violent collision between Romanians and Hungarians in the city of Tirgu Mureş is reconstructed since it cast a pall over inter-ethnic relations for a considerable period. Particular attention is paid to the role of the state authorities in this episode, since it lead to a rupture in previously good relations with Hungary and swung Transylvanian Hungarians decisively into the opposition camp.

Chapter 4 examines the nature of the post-1989 transition from totalitarian rule. It is argued that an agenda of limited change has been pursued by reluctant democrats who have bowed to prevailing circumstances rather than voluntarily renouncing authoritarian behaviour and embracing pluralism.

The ruling NSF has emerged as a champion of Romanian national interests and a guarantor of stability in the midst of serious regional instability. It has sought legitimacy by promoting nationalist values from the pre-communist period when diverting the public attention from the the abuses of the communist era, the one in which it was formed. The past has been mined for contemporary political advantage even at the expense of inter-ethnic peace. In the midst of mounting economic difficulties, the process of placing ultra-nationalists in positions of power and influence has continued. Deteriorating economic conditions and the malfunctioning of a political system that is only superficially democratic are creating a sense of impotence and frustration that poses a threat to the maintenance of inter-ethnic peace.

Chapter 5 examines the record of the democratic parties which currently offer the best chance for Romania to break free of a political environment shaped by nationalist and authoritarian values. It examines their achievements, particularly in establishing close links with the Hungarian minority party, identifies the obstacles that need to be overcome if their relevance is to grow, and pinpoints miscalculations that have added to the difficulty of their task. In particular, it examines the weak strategy devised for dealing with ultra-nationalists; indeed, a large part of the chapter focuses on the electoral battle in Cluj during 1992 which exposed the way that the local state along with the media and the armed forces were ready to join forces to secure victory for the nationalists at the expense of moderate reformers who threatened their interests. It is argued that what happened in Cluj then could be repeated at a national level with catastrophic results for Romania's democratic prospects and perhaps even for the stability of the region.

Chapter 6 profiles the ultra-nationalist parties which are primarily responsible for ensuring that national values enjoy a central place in the new Romanian democracy. On current trends, they have as much chance as the democratic opposition of replacing Iliescu and his supporters in office.

Romania is able to sustain two expanding nationalist parties based on differing wings of the power structure installed by Ceaușescu and never completely dismantled. The origins and rise of these parties are examined along with their ability to acquire power and influence via the media, sectors of local administration, and the privatisation process. The ideology of Romanian chauvinism is examined to see how much continuity and change there is with Ceaușescuism. The social groups they appeal to, their electoral record, and intra-nationalist rivalries are assessed along with their potential to consolidate earlier gains.

The conclusion examines the prospects for a resolution of inter-ethnic conflict. It examines what elements in Romanian political culture can help to span the ethnic divide, and it looks at the role of external factors in influencing the direction of Romainian politics. Finally, it examines possible future scenarios for Romania if nationalism continues to be a determining feature politics after 1989.

NOTES

1. See Zagorka Gulubovic, 'Nationalism and Democracy: The Yugoslav Case', *Journal of Area Studies*, 3 (1993).

Chapter 1

Romania's First Experiment with Democracy

Democracy destroys the unity of the Romanian nation, dividing it among political parties, making Romanians hate one another, and thus exposing a divided people to the united congregation of Jewish power . . .

This argument alone is so persuasive as to warrant the discarding of democracy in favour of anything that would ensure our unity . . . For disunity means death.

Corneliu Zelea Codreanu[1]

Since the First World War, the view that without nationalism democratic government is impossible is one that has enjoyed widespread validity. Transnational alternatives to the nation-state, such as the European Union have struggled to create a new set of over-arching loyalties that will move citizens beyond national allegiances, but without conspicuous success. The break-up of dynastic empires in eastern Europe, the decolonisation of Africa and the collapse of Soviet power in Eurasia resulted not in new multi-national political units but in the creation of a plethora of nation-states. Governing arrangements that denied the national principle had been discredited by autocratic long-distance rule from Vienna, Moscow, Istanbul or the colonial capitals of western Europe. After 1989, nationalism once again asserted its claim to be a precondition for and main carrier of democracy.[2] But at key moments in the recent past it has also been the main enemy of democracy, the extreme variant known as fascism almost banishing democracy from Europe in the 1930s.

Nationalism is almost a universal condition. Its appeal has traversed the globe from western Europe to distant Oceania in little more than a century. What counts is the kind of nationalism that nationalists wish to put in place and the means they use to achieve their purpose.[3] The long age of nationalism has witnessed a continual struggle between a civic and inclusive nationalism willing to define citizenship broadly and an ethnic and exclusive variety that insists upon the superiority of a particular ethnic group. The experience of eastern Europe makes it clear why the more intransigent form of nationalism has always had greater appeal in that part of the world and why in our decade, the 1990s, its most determined advocates threaten to unleash instability and violence that will surely not be confined to a region which twice this century has plunged mankind into two catastrophic general wars.

THE REVOLT AGAINST BACKWARDNESS

From the fourteenth century onwards, most east European states lost their independence and were absorbed in three large empires which after 1500 dominated nearly all of the region – the Hapsburgs, the Ottoman and the Russian empires. Thereafter, much of the region suffered steep economic and social regression.[4]

The contrasting evolution of society in parts of western Europe made countries like France and England a source of inspiration for those in the east intent on overcoming despotism and foreign rule. States evolved which enjoyed long-term independence and experienced economic progress. Ethnic, religious and linguistic communities in western Europe underwent a process of gradual integration lasting 200–300 years. It was an incomplete process, as shown by the rise of separatist and regional movements in supposedly homogeneous western European states in the second half of this century. But, gradually, membership of one nation-state became the chief basis for political identity. Dynasties like the post-1688 British royal houses, or modernising states like the post-1789 French one, expanded central authority to the provinces. A sense of patriotism grew up that was based on attachment to the ruling dynasty, to a set of governing ideas or to success in war, or economic and territorial expansion overseas.

Whereas the formation of states was gradual in the west and often preceded a developed sense of nationalism, it proved a late and sudden event in eastern Europe, with national identity being imposed hurriedly on the populations of the states that succeeded multi-national empires. The absence of self-rule and autonomy and the lack of striking economic progress meant that claims to nationhood were not based on concrete economic achievements. Instead, the emphasis was placed on culture or religion as pillars of national identity. A common language, culture and history became a substitute for a modernising state on the west European model. Herder and the other eighteenth-century German Romantics gave impetus to the cult of the nation's past and to the philosophical, historical and literary efforts which laid the foundation of national culture.[5]

National movements grew out of language movements. Cultural and political elites sought to escape backwardness by emphasing cultural uniqueness. Pan-German and Pan-Slav movements emerged imbued with a sense of national mission. The past was invoked and suitably rearranged to establish inalienable rights to land and national existence. Intellectuals came to think of their language group as a nation and they tried with varying success to spread language-based national awareness to the lower strata of the population.[6]

THE ROMANIAN EXAMPLE

Romania's national awakening was based in large part on an eighteenth-century language movement which popularised the view that the Romanians spoke a language closely related to Latin and were direct ancestors of the Romans. Beforehand, they had been known as Wallachs, a people spread over the principalities of Wallachia and Moldavia (under Turkish control from the sixteenth-century) as well as Transylvania, which was ruled by the Hapsburgs from the 1700s.

Uniate clergymen were the first great advocates of the Romanian cause. The Uniate Church was Orthodox in its rites but accepted the spiritual authority of Rome. It had been promoted by the Hapsburgs to weaken the influence of the Orthodox faith on their territory, and its championing of a distinct Romanian spirit was just one of the unexpected outcomes that have arisen from great-power meddling in the area over the next 300 years. Uniate clergymen succeeded in popularising the theory of Daco-Roman continuity which insists that the modern-day Romanians are the descendants of two noble races, the Dacians and the Roman legions who defeated them after an arduous struggle, and that their descendants have permanently inhabited the territories where Romanian speakers were in a majority by the eigtheenth-century. At a time when the Romanians were widely seen as a subject race with no case for having political rights, Gheorghe Sincai, Samuil Micu and Petru Maior devised a history with the aim of raising consciousness and establishing a claim for equality of treatment. As Uniate theology students in Rome, they had been inspired by the monuments of the Roman Empire, especially the famous column of Trajan and its connection with ancient Dacia, once the name of their homeland. John C. Campbell has described as well as anyone, how these priests were moved to promote nationalism in the Romanian lands:

> It was but natural that they, the representatives of a people which had for centuries suffered from an inferiority of status and an inferiority complex, should jump to the conclusion that they were the direct descendants of the noble Romans, rightful owners of a heritage since filched from them by the barbarians. Hence their proclamation of the Roman origin and Latin character of the modern Roumanians, and the uncritical acceptance of

the theory by intellectuals and popular leaders in Transylvania and in the Principalities as well. The importance of this for Roumanian nationalism was manifold. It provided an immeasurable stimulus to the consciousness of nationality. The Roumanian would no longer be willing to be merely the despised 'Wallach'; he was of nobler stock than his Magyar and German superiors. The Roumanians were no longer a 'geschichtloses Volk' but were the inheritors of a great imperial civilization. With all the nations of Europe under the influence of the German Romantics, digging into their past in search of forgotten civilizations, certainly none could match these claims. Closely connected with this new pride of 'race' and flowing equally from the theory of Latin origins was the idea of being a chosen people with a mission. The modern Roumanians, so went the argument, are the standard bearers of Latin civilization, which during the centuries of barbarian migrations they were able to defend in the fastnesses of the Carpathians. They are, therefore, pure-blooded Romans, more so than the Romance peoples of the West, who have been corrupted by other strains; they are an island of Latinism in a sea of Slavic and Turanian barbarians, their mission to serve as an eastern outpost of Latin culture.[7]

The Romanian grammar written by Sincai and Micu in 1780 was the first attempt to depict Romanian as a Latin tongue, with Latin roots and inflection. In contrast to most of the language reform movements of the region which emphasised the vernacular, the Romanian authors sought to re-Latinise the language by purging from it words with a non-Latin origin and by substituting the Latin for the Cyrillic alphabet.[8] This linguistic struggle was of more than esoteric importance. In eastern Europe, the rise of nationalism has focused around such linguistic issues. Intellectuals strove to create a uniform national literary language upon which could be built a national culture.[9] The Latin revivalist movement quickly spread from Transylvania to Wallachia where it struggled to overcome the Greek influence that had overlain the Romanian-speaking population of that principality. Intellectuals remained in the ascendancy long afterwards in Romania and its neighbours owing to the absence of a strong economic bourgeoisie able to lay down material norms and values.

In the late eighteenth-century, and again after 1918, the rise of national awareness was accelerated in eastern Europe by international developments – war, revolution and diplomacy – which were used by nationalists to acquire autonomy and eventually statehood. The French revolution of 1789 was a crucial event given the way it undermined the traditional order upon which dynastic rule rested in eastern Europe. The uprising against royal, aristocratic and clerical privilege sought to replace absolutism with the rights and liberties exercised by free citizens who had ceased to be royal subjects. But it was the belief that the world belonged not to tyrannical rulers but to oppressed peoples which had the greatest impact on the Europe of kings and emperors. The revolutionary order in France exposed the weakness of absolutism by defeating invasion attempts mounted by states terrified that the radical contagion might spread to their realms. Resistance triumphed by mobilising national sentiment.

The word 'nationalism' was not in common use during the revolutionary period, but a leader emerged who recognised the emotional force contained in nationalism. Napoleon, the first real populiser of modern nationalism, appealed first to French nationalism and then to the desire of subject peoples to be liberated from absolutist rule, while his real goals were to found an empire and a dynasty.[10] The power and prestige that could flow to whoever could plausibly claim to interpret the collective national will was something not lost on future ambitious men ready to use the emotions generated by nationalism ultimately to gratify their urge for personal power. But the role of nationalism as a liberating force that was a main carrier of democracy quickly reasserted itself after the return of absolutist rule to Europe in 1815. Nervous rulers saw nationalism and democracy as a combined evil threatening their survival. The Concert of Europe became the first of several universalist assaults meant to contain nationalism.

One of the first corners of post-Napoleonic Europe where the established order was challenged was in Wallachia.[11] Tudor Vladimirescu, a small landowner from Oltenia in the west of what was still a Turkish-controlled principality, led an uprising of peasants in 1821 that was more social than national in origin. It overlapped with an overtly nationalist rebellion launched by Greeks in Moldavia, the second Romanian principality in Turkish hands. Romanians were unwilling to enlist under the banner of Greek nationalism. Vladimirescu's rising ended when he was killed by the Greeks, such internecine feuding revealing how difficult it was for nationalists to co-operate against an imperial overlord.

Vladimirescu's revolt, though a failure, was followed by a decline in Greek influence in Wallachia which enabled Romanian national feeling to spread. Romanian nationalism had obtained an authentic hero around whom a cult of the martyr quickly grew up. Vladimirescu had also involved the common people in his adventure, something that later nationalists would find it difficult to do, however often they invoked the name of the Romanian peasantry and claimed to be acting on their behalf.

The dynastic alliance against the forces of revolution survived until 1848; the revolutions that spread across Europe in that year showed how rapidly the nationalist message was spreading. But some of the problems in the way of fulfilling the goals of nationalism were also exposed; the absence of homogeneous ethnic communities living in defined areas produced friction and rivalry among nationalist movements that enabled multi-national empires to resist this most serious challenge so far to their authority.

Transylvania in 1848–9 was a prime example of a territory in revolt against imperial rule, where conflicting nationalists thwarted each other's efforts. Hungarian nationalists under Louis Kossuth were ready to grant citizenship to the non-Hungarians who dwelt among them. However, Kossuth refused to recognise the existence of a Romanian nation; the non-Hungarians were viewed as cultural inferiors whose best hope lay in merging with the superior Hungarian nation. Later, his long exile enabled Kossuth to see that he had been wrong, but denying the Romanians a national personality contributed to the defeat of his rising and began a cycle of recrimination and rivalry between two peoples sharing Transylvania that has yet to exhaust itself.

In 1867, Hungary achieved self-government – and control of Transylvania – as a result of an arrangement which turned the centralised Hapsburg Empire into a dual monarchy. The Romanians, although numerically in the majority in Transylvania, were denied autonomy. Hungarian leaders reflected the influential belief, one that originated in post-1789 France, that local diversity and autonomy was a reactionary obstacle to progress and that government must be centralised. In an age when a belief in the hierarchy of nations was widespread, the Hungarians felt it was their vocation to absorb the backward lesser peoples in their midst and raise them to a higher cultural plane. Of course, this view was resisted by many Romanians who, by the 1860s, believed themselves to be the direct heirs of a great civilisation, that of ancient Rome.

Romanian nationalism had evolved through a long and successful campaign on the part of intellectuals to convert other sections of the population to their national ideals. This was also true of Italy where, in little more than twenty years, the peninsula was unified by armed force, great-power politics and Italian revolutionary action, backed by Piedmontese statecraft.[12] Given the perceived cultural and historic links between Italy and the Romanians, the Risorgimento had a big impact on a people whose leaders viewed them as an outpost of Latin civilisation in the east. The triumph of German unification in 1871 was perhaps even more important. The idea that membership of the nation should be based on common ethnicity, one first propagated by the German Romantics a century before, received powerful endorsement. It was one that had influenced east European nationalists, some of whom endeavoured to create a mono-ethnic state in regions where the population was far more ethnically diverse than in Bismarck's Germany.

A Romanian state was slowly taking shape as German and Italian independence was confirmed. It was based on the principalities of Wallachia and Moldavia which in 1859 elected Alexandru Ioan Cuza as their ruler. Turkey, the former imperial overlord, recognised him in 1861, and, when he resigned in 1866, Turkey was pressurised by France into accepting

Prince Charles of Hohenzollern-Sigmaringen as hereditary ruler of an independent Romania. Finally in 1878, the complete independence of Romania was recognised by the European powers at the Congress of Berlin, and, three years later, Prince Carol, a member of the Catholic wing of the Prussian royal house, assumed the title of King Carol I.

NATIONALISM DEFINES INDEPENDENT ROMANIA

Nationalism became the primary state policy of the new Romania. Attempts were made to Romanise minorities by ensuring that Romanian was the only official language of instruction. Whatever government ruled usually styled itself the leader of the national liberation movement, which made any opposition to its rule seem unpatriotic.[13] But Romanian independence had been accomplished by none of the stirring events that gave the Italian Risorgimento such an heroic aura. Instead Romanian politicians had proven to be skilled negotiators in their dealings with the great powers; they were effective in preventing the substitution of Russian rule or overlordship for that of the Ottoman Empire at a time when the Balkans were a cause of diplomatic conflict and fierce international rivalry.[14] To preserve a fragile independence and forestall outside attempts at domination, Romania's leading intellectuals promoted a sense of patriotism via the new universities being founded, the school system, and the army. The Romanian Academy was created in 1867 with the declared purpose of collecting as many documents as possible and storing them in one place in order to facilitate research on the unity of origin, language and culture of the Romanian people, thus helping to legitimise their right to national sovereignty.[15]

The Romanian historic 'catechism' lays down that all of the land surrounding the Carpathian mountains has been inhabited since prehistoric times by the same basic ethnic group: first the Dacians, then the Daco-Romans, and finally their descendants the Romanians.[16] This people retreated to the forests in times of adversity and withstood the pressure from Hungarians, Germans and others who settled in the area.

Establishing the Romanian people's place in history and its continuity on ancestral land were nation-building tasks that required less effort than economic and social modernisation; the skills as propagandists for the national cause that politicians had already displayed in their subtle negotiations with the great powers were directed inwards to people who had retained a parochial identity hardly extending beyond their own village, family or valley. Ion C. Brătianu, founder of the political dynasty that would dominate political life in the first two generations after independence, was able to trace a Romanian tradition of freedom back to what were seen as the nation's origins when the Dacians first fought against and then intermingled with the conquering Romans. He claimed that the Romanian people had inherited a freedom-loving tradition from republican Rome which explained 'the miracle that a nation of ten millions could preserve the traditions of democracy faithfully and clearly. It is a nation of ten million people which is more Roman than the Romans themselves!'[17]

The search for an exalted pedigree was meant to rank Romania above its neighbours. Writing in 1935, the philosopher Emil Cioran put such myth-making neatly in perspective:

> the myths of a nation are its vital truths. They might not coincide with the truth; this is of no importance. The supreme sincerity of a nation towards itself manifests itself in the rejection of self-criticism, in vitalization through its own illusions. And, does a nation seek the truth? A nation seeks power.[18]

Successive Romanian political systems evoked a heroic past as compensation for a prosaic reality where it would be hard to detect the liberal and democratic features that Brătianu claimed to be features of the Romanian collective personality down the ages. During the entire span of the constitutional monarchy (1881–1938), Romania either enjoyed an extremely narrow franchise, or else elections were shamelessly manipulated with only one or two exceptions. The vote was confined to the tiny urban middleclass drawn largely from the professions and the civil service. A civil code based on the French *Code Napoleon* laid the basis for a centralised state in which local government was denied any power of initiative.[19]

The control thus established over local officials gave whichever was the ruling party a telling advantage in elections.[20] The peasantry were spectators in elections where rival programmes counted less than the ability of parties to mobilise support behind a personality or a political clan. Social reform was not on the agenda of the Romanian state, except briefly during Prince Cuza's time, and the way in which land was distributed then did not improve the conditions of the rural population. After independence, peasants were gradually made aware that their own leaders were as unconcerned with their welfare as their predecessors, even though they were fellow countrymen. There was no concept of citizenship, denoting a sense of obligation on the part of both the ruler and the ruled.[21] The gap that had existed between the Romanian masses and representatives of political power under foreign rule was reproduced under native rulers. But unlike the phanariots, Romanian politicians could use nationalism to prevent alienation assuming revolutionary proportions. The nation was the underlying theme of political life and every government styled itself as the national movement pursuing the historic mission of the Romanian nation. Liberty was defined as essentially meaning collective freedom from foreign domination rather than liberty of the individual. Nicolae Bălcescu had argued in 1848 that 'the question of nationality is more important than liberty. Until a people can exist as a nation, it cannot make use of liberty. Liberty can easily be recovered when it is lost but not nationality.'[22] For over a century, such a restricted definition of liberty, which said little about the internal nature of government, would be relentlessly inculcated into the population via an education system dominated by nationalist themes.

Romania held aloof from its neighbours. The most powerful one, Russia, was viewed with suspicion and resentment. The treatment of the country as a Russian dependency, Czarist attempts to block or delay Romanian independence, and the annexation of Bessarabia with its large Romanian-speaking population, permanently soured relations between two states that had divergent interests despite their common attachment to the Orthodox religion. Hungary, despite its maltreatment of the Transylvanian Romanians, was regarded with less hostility than Russia by influential statesmen like Dimitrie Sturdza, prime minister in the 1890s.[23] The nationalist fixation with Transylvania in the seventy-five years after it joined Romania in 1918 might easily suggest that it was a perennial concern. But Sturdza was far from being alone among pre-1914 leaders in publicly disavowing the conquest of Transylvania or even autonomy for the province. Instead, Romania asked for an end to Hungarian attempts to Magyarise the Romanian-speaking majority in Transylvania. Assistance for Romanian schools in Transylvania was provided, but an indication of government priorities was the donation of much larger sums of money for the education of Romanian speakers living in the southern Balkans and known as the Aromânii, the Macedo-Romans, or the Vlachs.[24] The exact motives for the large expenditure on the widely-dispersed Vlachs was never clear, but to prevent their complete absorption by the Slav peoples (and the Greeks) in whose states they dwelt may have been regarded as reason enough at the time. Romania was opposed to any move that could lead to a union of the Slav races under Russian sponsorship which it saw as a threat to its own existence. Many leaders were prepared to endorse the view of the King (expressed in 1910) that 'we belong to the Balkans neither ethnographically nor geographically nor any other way'.[25]

According to one source, the Romanian national doctrine included several negative stereotypes of the foreigner: besides the Russians, the Turks were seen as pagan occupiers, the Poles were arrogant foes who in medieval times had had designs on Romanian land, and the Hungarians were perennial oppressors of Romanians.[26] In addition, a preoccupation arose with the Greeks and the Jews, viewed as 'internal foreigners' who had penetrated Romanian economic and social life from the eighteenth-century onwards.[27] But in 1829 Greek influence had been curbed by the ending of phanariot rule even though the greatest families of the nobility (*boierime*) were mostly of Greek extraction.[28] However, Jewish influence increased in the economy in the decades after independence.During the second half of the nineteenth century, Russian Jews moved in increasing numbers into Hapsburg lands as well as the Romanian principalities. In 1859, about 118,000 Jews lived in Moldavia and 9,200 in Wallachia. By 1899, the number had increased to 210,000 in Moldavia and 68,000 in Wallachia.[29] Opposition to the Jewish presence was expressed by Romanian intellectuals already under strong nationalist influence. Jews were discriminated against under the 1866 constitution, which laid down that the only foreigners who could become citizens were those belonging to the Christian faith. Jews were also prevented from buying rural property (the constitution of 1991 also preventing foreigners from buying land). Such restrictions helped to shape the particular character of the Romanian Jewish population and its relations with other inhabitants of Romania:

> They tended to congregate in the large cities, particularly in Bucharest and in Iaşi where they took up occupations such as that of merchant and small trader. In the countryside they could be found as stewards on large estates, as owners of inns selling alcoholic drinks, and as moneylenders – occupations that could bring them into conflict with the peasant population.[30]

Intellectuals directed their fire at the Jews for supposedly undermining Romania's social structure based on the patriarchal and rural values of the village world.[31] Demographic pressures and a growing shortage of cultivated land were perhaps more threatening to existing rural social values: the population grew from 4,800,000 in 1880 to 7,300,000 in 1913, the increase being mainly on the land where 'expropriations, enclosure, and foreclosure created what socialist commentators called neo-serfdom'.[32] A century later, in newly independent countries of east Africa and South-East Asia, anger at the meagre rewards arising from independence would make convenient targets of immigrants who had enjoyed economic success in their new homelands and who could be branded as alien exploiters. In Romania's case, it was only pressure from the great powers at the 1878 Congress of Berlin which compelled her rulers to grant its Jewish population equal citizenship.[33] This was one of the first examples of inter-governmental pressure in Europe to safeguard the rights of a minority. But the government never fully complied with the treaty, and the rising tide of nationalism kept the Jewish question very much alive.

Mihai Eminescu, whose brilliance earned him the accolade of Romania's national poet, was preaching uncompromising nationalism in poems that he wrote in the 1880s. For Eminescu, the nation, 'in the truest meaning of the term', meant the peasant class, 'the most positive class of all, the most conservative as to speech, costume, and custom, the bearer of a people's history'.[34] He denounced foreigners, and influential Romanians governed by foreign examples, for betraying Romania's rural values and allowing the country to be turned into an economic and cultural colony. Romanians who turned their backs on their heritage deserved no pity, as these lines in his poem, *Doina*, make clear:

> If any shall cherish the stranger
> May the dogs eat his heart
> May the weeds destroy his house
> And may his kin perish in shame.[35]

Romania's experience of invasion and subjugation during the last eighty years have given these lines an intensity they might otherwise never have acquired. Nationalists were also inspired by his belief that the supreme law was 'the consummation of the nation and country by every means and in every way, even if the means and the way do not conform to civilization and humanitarianism'.[36]

Eminescu's harsh words about the Jews – 'foreigners of a non-Christian persuasion who could not merge with our people' – would also be remembered and retold.[37] Jewish interests were attacked by land-hungry peasants unlikely to have heard of Eminescu in a rural uprising which shook the Romanian state to its foundations in 1907.[38] The revolt quickly assumed a general agrarian rather than an anti-Semitic character and was directed against large tenant farmers and absentee landowners.[39] It spread right across the country before being put down at an estimated cost of 10–11,000 lives.[40] The repression may have been the price of averting military intervention from both Vienna and St Petersburg which might have endangered Romanian independence.[41] The fact that such moves were seriously contemplated shows how conditional Romanian sovereignty remained.

It would take the triumph of communism in Russia after 1917 before a meaningful agrarian reform was drawn up and carried through. Meanwhile, anti-Semitism had assumed proportions sufficient to lay the basis of a lucrative political career for A. C. Cuza, professor of political economy at the University of Iaşi from 1901 and the founder of the National Democratic Party in 1911. A deputy without interruption from 1911 to 1938, he was the most consistent upholder of anti-Semitism in the press, in university and political life, and at public rallies for well over half a century.[42] An atheist and socialist in his early life, he shifted towards right-wing nationalism, being hostile to economic liberalism and democracy, a trajectory that would be emulated with even greater success by several ex-communist nationalists in the 1990s.[43] All the major questions of politics and economics blended into the Jewish question for this mediocre but influential demagogue. Significantly, he was joined in the first successful promotion of national populism in Romania by the accomplished historian, Nicolae Iorga. Iorga insisted that the economic domination of the Jews contradicted 'the exclusive right of free Romanians to control the country's socio-economic organisation'. Later, Iorga was prepared to respect Jews who contributed to Romanian culture and tolerate them when they did not compete with ethnic Romanians.[44] He was even prepared to deny that the rural question had a simple explanation bound up with the Jewish presence, as when he wrote:

> There is no doubt that our peasantry is the most backward of all in Europe; in no other country, not even in Turkey has the peasantry been left so far behind as the peasantry in the Romanian kingdom. No one in particular can be held responsible for their status; there are just so many factors, that to determine accountability would be a totally lost cause.[45]

But after the 1907 peasant rebellion, Iorga, along with Cuza, attempted to lay the blame on the Jews. It would not be the last time that nationalists, embarrassed by violent internal disagreements that undermined deeply-held tenets about the fundamental unity of Romanians, looked for an external source upon which to pin the responsibility.[46]

In the decades before 1914, Romanian education expanded thanks to the reforms of an energetic education minister, Spiru Haret;[47] one by-product was a growing surplus of graduates in the professions. The public service was too small to absorb the surplus, and professional disappointment meant that a growing number of lower-middle-class intellectuals were ready to believe the explanations of Cuza and the early Iorga that Romanians were being prevented from putting their talents at the disposal of their country because of the grip on large areas of national life exercised by foreigners, particularly Jews.

Pre-war Romania was able to absorb the first stirrings of radical nationalism. The country had been the most stable in the Balkans; constitutional government had not been interrupted by military revolts or assassinations of government leaders as was the case in neighbouring states. Governments had peacefully replaced one another in office after corrupt but usually orderly elections. There were no restive minorities that withheld their loyalty from the state. However, the First World War would radically alter Romania. After the country intervened on the Allied side in 1916, nearly all of it was swiftly occupied by German-led forces. Although Romanian troops fought well, the preservation of a Romanian state and its ability to benefit from the peace treaty were largely the outcome of great-power confrontations in which Romania counted for very little.

GREATER ROMANIA AND THE FAILURE OF STATE-BUILDING

After 1918, the pre-war 'Old Kingdom' or *Regat* more than doubled its size and its population. The southern Dobruja was acquired from Bulgaria, Bessarabia from Russia (which had annexed it in 1812), and the Bukovina from Austria. But it was at the expense of Hungary that Romania made its largest territorial gains. Pre-war Hungary lost seventy-one per cent of its territory, while Romania's size increased by 209 per cent. The 102,286 square kilometres acquired from Hungary at the 1920 Treaty of Trianon was actually an area larger than that left to Hungary itself. It comprised the whole of the principality of Transylvania, the eastern half of the Banat, part of the mountainous area of the Maramures in the north, and below that the Crisana, consisting of the western slopes of the Bihor mountains and a strip of lowlands at their foot.[48]

Romanian nationalists had acquired nearly everything they had desired, and the new state was christened *Romania Mâre* or Greater Romania. However, Ion-Ionel Brătianu had caused a major conflict at the peace conference by wishing the boundary with a truncated Hungary to be at the Tisza river, which would have meant the annexation of solidly Hungarian territory.[49] R. W. Seton-Watson, a champion of the Romanian cause, criticised Brătianu's stance: he 'should have recognised that by a "world conjuncture" never likely to recur Romania had obtained her maximum programme, and that only a policy of far-sighted moderation and toleration would enable her to preserve what she had not won unaided'.[50]

Romania had benefited from a desire on the part of the western allies to punish their chief adversaries, of which Austria-Hungary was second only to Germany. The unpredictable menace of bolshevism in Russia also persuaded the Allies to inflate the size of states on her western borders – principally Poland and Romania in the hope of creating bastions of the west in eastern Europe.[51] A settlement influenced by the desire to punish the vanquished and quarantine revolutionary Russia inevitably violated the principle of self-determination upon which the Versailles Treaty system was supposedly based. The historian Benjamin Neuberger has claimed that in the peace treaties, the principle of self-determination was only consistently applied where it weakened enemy states, but was disregarded where its consequences would have been unfavourable to the allies (for example in South Tyrol, the Austrian province ceded to Italy after 1918).[51]

Ethnic groups were too intertwined for a set of national states each inhabited by a homogeneous population to emerge. Between one-fifth and one-quarter of the population of eastern Europe were still national minorities after 1918. A League of Nations was established, one of whose aims was to settle disputes between its member states and offer some security for minorities. But its authority proved to be purely moral, and most states refused to recognise an authority which infringed their own sovereignty. The inability of national minorities to obtain satisfactory treatment in states which wished to fulfil the national principle by assimilating or expelling them prevented the post-First World War settlement from becoming a stable or a permanent one. Balkan and Danubian countries which proclaimed themselves to be national states were usually multi-national ones. Bitter conflicts between stateless nationalities and ones which had a state behind them poisoned relations between different countries in the region and allowed outside powers to exploit the situation. Romania, as perhaps the chief beneficiary of the Versailles settlement, found itself increasingly vulnerable as the threat of conflict and war hung over the Balkans.

Minorities comprised twenty-eight per cent of Romania's population. The rulers of *Romania Mâre* faced the problem of integrating regions and peoples at different stages of development into membership of a centralised state. The most nationalistic politicians, grouped in the National Liberal Party which dominated politics down to 1928, characterised Romanian unification as an inevitable process sanctioned by certain iron laws of history. But it was soon clear that no serious preparations had been made in Bucharest for unification and that the prevailing instinct was to rule the new territories by the centralised methods under which the ethnically homogeneous *Regat* had been administered. In devising the architecture of the new state, Brătianu and his allies showed that they were influenced by ethnic nationalist criteria. The nation-state belonged primarily to the 'historic' or state-building nation which had a mission to construct the new political order in its own image. Romania thus became another of Europe's *Staatsvolk*, a people who are culturally and politically pre-eminent in a state, even though other groups are present sometimes in significant numbers. Drawing upon the experience of post-1918 eastern Europe, one commentator has written that 'there is a tendency on the part of such people to equate the entire country with their own ethnic homeland and . . . to perceive the state as the particular expression of their own ethnic group'.[52] Adoption of Romanian nationality was seen as a necessary criterion for exercising full citizenship. Hungarians or others who insisted that their nationality was not Romanian while displaying total loyalty to the Romanian state and performing their duties as citizens were regarded as outsiders or even intruders.[53]

Romanian nationalists preaching the official position, that people of Daco-Romanian origin had settled the lands of Greater Romania first, were fully prepared to argue that later settlers were intruders on their national lands.[54] The Brătianu government refused to sign the Paris treaty guaranteeing certain basic rights for minorities, the Prime Minister arguing that 'the minority Treaty was an attempt to weaken the unified nationalist character of the Romanian state'.[55] Romania only signed when a more amenable government was formed, but the machinery for monitoring minority rights was not a serious deterrent for governments embarking upon building a single nation-state in the multi-national territories which they now ruled. The 'natural', 'organic' or 'spontaneous' growth of nationalism in earlier times was replaced by 'a government-engineered mechanistic campaign of "nation-building"' in the 1920s and 1930s designed to reinforce the claim of ascendant nationalities over the mixed territories they occupied.[56] However much the process might be described as a natural historic evolution by intellectuals whose task was to make the present stay in harmony with a mythic past, the state took precedence over the nation. In the words of Josef Pilsudski, the architect of a Poland which had even more minorities within its boundaries than Romania, 'it is the state that makes the nation not the nation that makes the state'; by this political definition, the new east European political entities were less 'nation-states' than 'state-nations'.[57]

It is wrong to assume that a consensus existed among Romanian leaders about minority policy and the centralising nature of the new state. In pre-war times, Transylvanian Romanians had been the main targets of the assimilationist strategy towards minorities pursued by Hungary, ones later to be adopted with varying degrees of intensity by the states that emerged from the ruins of the Hapsburg empire. But after 1918, some of their leaders were reluctant to treat the large Hungarian minority in the way that their own people had been treated by Budapest because it was recognised to be a futile strategy.

Magyarisation had failed in the Transylvanian countryside and had had only limited effect in the towns, its most lasting result being to instil a strong sense of solidarity among Transylvanian Romanians. For protection against Hungarian state injustice, the Romanian National Party (RNP) (founded in 1881) had looked to the emperor in Vienna rather than across the Carpathians to Bucharest for redress. This party was committed to a system of autonomy for the territories of the Danube basin under a supranational federal government. Neither from the Hapsburgs nor from the Romanian state was practical assistance forthcoming, but a moderate and able group of leaders emerged from among the Transylvanian Romanians who, as a people, were far less socially polarised than their brethren in the

Regat. The absence of a native Romanian nobility in Transylvania and the tendency for political leaders to emerge from the most educated sections of the small landowning peasantry, gave the region's politics a different flavour from that of southern Romania. This was clear from the Grand National Assembly held at Alba Iulia in Transylvania on 1 December 1918 as the defeated Hapsburg empire was lurching towards final collapse. The event was organised by the RNP and its leader Iuliu Maniu who had displayed leadership by transporting Romanian contingents in the Austrian forces back to Transylvania amid chaotic conditions, thereby increasing the likelihood of a peaceful transfer of authority in the region. Some 1,228 delegates from various districts of Transylvania, along with representatives from church and national organisations, assembled in Alba Iulia before a crowd of 100,000 Romanians.[58] The assembly passed a resolution calling for unification with the *Regat*, but important conditions were attached. Transylvanian autonomy was to be respected, the union was to be based on representative government, and a guarantee of civil liberties and political and civil rights was to be granted to 'the co-existing peoples'.[59] Paragraph 1 of Article 3 of the Alba Iulia declaration today, as in the past, is quoted far more often by Hungarians than Romanians:

> All of the peoples have the right to public education, public administration, and the administration of justice in their own languages, provided by individuals chosen from among their own members. All peoples will receive rights of representation in the government of the country and in the legislative organ in accordance with their numbers.[60]

In November 1919, the moderate Transylvanian agenda emerged at the forefront of national policy when one of the few honest elections seen in inter-war Romania resulted in a clear victory for the RNP which was in alliance with the Peasants Party based in the *Regat*. It was the first election fought under manhood suffrage (women were unable to vote in competitive elections until 1989), and a coalition government was established with the RNP leader Dr Alexandru Vaida Voevod as premier and Ion Mihalache as agriculture minister. The government stood for a distribution of large estates to the peasantry to be accompanied by comprehensive socio-economic reforms and a channelling of investment to the villages, as well as a programme of administrative decentralisation. Before anything could be done, King Ferdinand (who had succeeded his uncle as king in 1914) dismissed the government and new elections were organised whose outcome contradicted the previous ones.[61] Agrarian reform was carried out but without the major infrastructural investment and other reforms needed to make it a success; the aim was to prevent another rural explosion, this time under the influence of the Russian revolution. The ruling elite remained ignorant of peasant feeling, and its deep-seated fears showed how little its members believed in one of the cherished national myths, namely that Romanians are an organically united people, resistant to destructive foreign influences.

A centralised system of government was imposed on the country without local conditions being studied and local opinion being consulted as to the suitability of this approach. The Alba Iulia declaration was hailed as a historic milestone, but Romania's rulers felt under no obligation to incorporate its clauses relating to decentralisation or minorities into the new 1923 constitution. In 1925, the country was divided into seventy-one prefectures: prefects appointed by Bucharest enjoyed absolute control locally. Municipal organs were unable to defy their writ even if they had the force of local opinion behind them. The mayors in the larger towns were also government appointees, and the notaries who administered the villages were appointed by the prefects.[62]

Italy was proving to be an important cultural influence on the new Romania (France even more so), and Bucharest followed the example of Italy after unification by imposing the laws and officials of one part of the country over the greatly enlarged territory irrespective of huge variations in economic development, social conditions and ethnic ties. In both countries, the fears of regionalism and its possible effects in undermining national strength were not far from the surface. Romania (even accounting for its minorities) was linguistically more united than Italy, where only two to three per cent of the population had Italian as their first language at the time of unification; according to Denis Mack Smith, to most Italians the 'national language' would have been unintelligible and the word 'Italy' was unknown.[63] In the 1860s, a revolt against Piedmont, which had imposed its laws and administration on the rest of the country, led to 100,000 troops being sent to control a revolt against northern rule.[64] The *Regat* never had any need to take such drastic action in Transylvania after 1918, but the political elite would undoubtedly not have hesitated if the need had ever arisen.[65]

Against the background of the triumph of centralism in Italy, Lord Acton, the great nineteenth-century liberal historian, writing in 1862, opposed the elevation of nationalism as the core organising principle of new states. He argued for a more plural approach:

> The presence of different nations under the same sovereignty is similar in its effects to the independence of the Church in the State. It provides against the servility which flourishes under the shadow of a single authority, by balancing interests, multiplying associations, and giving to the subject the restraint and support of a combined opinion. . . .The co-existence of several nations under the same State is the test, as well as

the best security of its freedom. It is also one of the chief instruments of civilisation; and, as such, it . . . indicates a state of greater advancement than the national unity which is the ideal of modern liberalism.

If we take the establishment of liberty for the realisation of moral duties to be the end of civil society, we must conclude that those states are substantially the most perfect which . . . include various distinct nation-alities without oppressing them. Those in which no mixture of races has occurred are imperfect; and those in which its effects have disappeared are decrepit. A state which is incompetent to satisfy different races condemns itself; a State which labours to neutralise, to absorb or to expel them, destroys its own vitality; a State which does not include them is destitute of the chief basis of self-government.[66]

These words had special pertinence for Romania in the 1920s and 1930s and indeed for nearly all east European states which twice this century have been given the task of rebuilding their political institutions after long periods of warfare or dictatorship. Even in post-1918 Czechoslovakia, the one state in the region where democracy enjoyed long-term success, rigid centralism prevailed. Initial plans to create a political system that would reflect the ethnic diversity of the state were quickly replaced by thinking based on the French model of centralised rule.[67]

THE FAILURE OF REFORM AND PRESSURE ON MINORITIES

Both inter-war Hungary and the Soviet Union were unwilling to recognise post-Trianon Romania, and claims to Transylvania and Bessarabia were frequently reiterated. However, it was the chronic disunity of the Romanian political elite rather than minority demands or the subversive activities of irredentist neighbours that destabilised *Romania Mâre*. Escalating conflict between parties intent on controlling the machinery of an unreformed state that was ill-equipped to cope with weightier responsibilities and new social demands soon caused disquiet. The ability of the king to protect his subjects against the machinations of politicians – always rather ephemeral – had ended with the death of Romania's first king, Carol I, in 1914. The image of the king as father of his people wore increasingly thin and was shattered during the era of misrule inaugurated by King Carol II not long after he ascended the throne in 1930. The decline in the prestige of the monarchy became evident as early as 1922 when the RNP boycotted the coronation of King Ferdinand and Queen Marie, even though it was held at Alba Iulia, the scene of the 1918 unity declaration. The Liberals, then in power, were closely linked to domestic commercial, industrial and banking interests. Economic policies sprang from a strong nationalistic outlook.

Liberalism is normally associated with a free movement of goods and investment; however, the Romanian Liberals feared that this would keep

Romania a weak agrarian state at the mercy of foreign capital and unable to provide the means for its own defence.[68] But policies meant to foster native industry depressed peasant living standards.[69] While prominent intellectuals like Nichifor Crainic and Lucien Blaga extolled the peasant world as the fulcrum of Romanian spirituality, the priorities of nearly every government were firmly urban and linked to the appetites of the oligarchy and urban middle class. A few statistics are sufficient to reveal how enormous the urban–rural divide was in Romania. The number of Romanian students in higher education as a percentage of the population was greater than that of Czechoslovakia and even Germany.[70] Yet illiteracy at the beginning of the 1920s was officially forty-five per cent, (the actual figure probably being much higher).[71] While the inter-war Bucharest bar numbered more lawyers than the Paris bar, Romania's ratio of rural doctors to rural population was no better than India's, i.e. 1.1 per 100,000.[72]

An artificial education system which emphasised nationalism and valued disciplines like law and the classics over ones able to foster economic and social development encouraged political extremism among graduates in the 1930s frustrated at their lack of success. But beforehand there had been a hopeful interlude between 1928 and 1930 when a government held office committed to economic and social policies that corresponded to the needs and interests of the peasants who formed a majority of the population.[73]

The Liberals faced a growing challenge after 1926, the year in which the RNP in Transylvania and the Peasant Party in the Regat merged to become the National Peasant Party (NPP). The deaths of the Liberal strongman Ion-Ionel Brătianu and King Ferdinand followed in quick succession in 1927, opening up a political vacuum that was filled by the victory of the NPP in 'genuinely free elections' held at the end of 1928.[74] The new prime minister, Iuliu Maniu, was the only Romanian politician with a significant mass following. His government was the first to be free of *Regateni* domination, and it entered office with high expectations.

Maniu's patriotism was unquestionable given the pivotal role he had played in the unification events of 1918, but it was an enlightened and inclusive nationalism as shown by decentralising measures which he attempted to introduce. In 1929, a bill was drawn up to restore the historic provinces abolished in 1922, one that envisaged self-government in the regions.[75] In 1930, the first village and county elections to self-governing bodies were held. In these, the national minorities gained representation in proportion to their numbers.[76] A competent minority statute was drawn up with the co-operation of the Saxons but not the Hungarian minority.[77] However, these measures (which had caused the Liberals to boycott parliament for over a year) were revoked when the austere Maniu resigned in October 1930, having been offended by King Carol II's matrimonial irregularities. Maniu has been criticised for being an ineffectual moralist, resigning over a secondary issue, instead of mobilising the forces of democracy against a king who soon showed himself ready to sacrifice democracy and the wider national interest for his own personal designs.[78] Maniu had been thwarted in his attempts to assist agriculture by the collapse of world grain prices in the midst of the world depression and the swift onset of protectionism.

Political attitudes hardened in line with the fall in living standards brought about by the depression. In the early 1930s, Romania saw the value of its main crops fall by seventy per cent and the total value of its exports cut by half.[79] Using 1929 as a base year (100), money wages declined to 61 in 1931 and only reached 92 in 1939. State employees were sometimes unpaid for months, and conditions for the peasantry were particularly desperate.[80] Against such a background, militant nationalism flourished and safeguards for minorities were eroded. The economically active middle class in Transylvania, drawn largely from the Saxon, Hungarian and Jewish communities, found itself under challenge from the state. Firms which displayed shop-signs in non-Romanian languages were taxed, and a twelve per cent surcharge was levied on firms which kept their books and accounts in languages other than Romanian.[81] The co-operative movement, strong in Transylvania, initially proved effective in combating the state's anti-minority policy. In 1932, a drive to remove minority officials got under way, in consequence of which large numbers were dismissed. C. A. Maccartney has claimed:

> there seems to be no question that it is next door to impossible for a member of the minority to enter the Romanian public services today. Here and there there may be an exception: a skilled workman might get some technical post for which no Romanian could be found – a Bulgarian might get into the gendarmerie, a Saxon might be given a small post in a purely Saxon district. Family influence might even place a Magyar in some corner where the Romanian nationalist press did not notice him. But broadly speaking, the younger generation of the minorities must renounce all hopes of a State career.[82]

State encroachments were felt particularly keenly by the Saxons of southern and central Transylvania who had enjoyed important aspects of self-government since their arrival in the thirteenth-century. But Saxon privileges that medieval rulers could tolerate proved intolerable for Romanian nationalists building the state-nation. In 1938, the centuries-old institutions of local self-government which shaped Saxon identity were abolished on Bucharest's orders – the so-called Saxon National University (Nations-Universität) and the community of the Saxon judges (Sieben-

Richter-Waldungen).[83] In 1934, the last remaining Saxon burgomaster had been replaced by a Romanian, a bitter loss owing to the very keen interest the Saxons had taken in their own local government: 'to be without a single burgomeister of their own nationality was an experience that the Saxons had not undergone in their 800-year history'.[84]

The Saxons had been organised in autonomous and self-regulating communities that were not necessarily subordinated to a ruler. Their city and regional government had never given way to a demand for territorial sovereignty. They had shown loyalty to imperial and national authorities provided that their individual safety and religious and economic rights were respected. They occupied an intermediate status between politically subordinate autonomy and territorial statehood that could have served as a prototype for dealing with minority questions while leaving existing state boundaries intact. However, the loss of their civic institutions, which had provided equilibrium for the community through a long and chequered history, led to a fatal imbalance, not a few Saxons throwing in their lot with the Nazi German cause and unleashing a set of circumstances which, by the 1990s, had led to the virtual disappearance of a community once nearly 800,000 strong.[85]

Conditions also declined for Romanians and non-Romanians alike in the

Table 1.1 Minorities, 1930.

	Number	Percentage
Romanian	12,981,324	71.9
Hungarian	1,425,507	7.9
German	745,421	4.1
Russian	409,150	2.3
Ukrainian	582,115	3.2
Serb, Croat, Slovene (Yugoslav)	51,062	0.3
Bulgarian	366,384	2.0
Czech and Slovak	51,842	0.3
Jewish	728,115	4.0
Turk and Tatar	176,913	1.0
Gypsy	262,501	1.5
Gagau	105,750	0.6
Other	170,944	0.9
Total	18,057,028	100.0

Source: Joseph Rothschild, *East-Central Europe between the Two World Wars*, University of Washington Press, Washington 1974, p. 284.

Bukovina, under Austrian rule from 1775 to 1918. In the land reform, the principal beneficiaries were non-peasant applicants – civil servants, doctors and politicians – who enjoyed preferential links with the state. Romanian speakers were a minority and a Ukrainian party was able to return three deputies to Bucharest. But this was whittled down to one in 1933 as a result of an electoral law which laid down a threshhold of two per cent of the nationwide vote before a party could obtain parliamentary representation. The Ukrainian party had to co-operate with several small democratic parties before it could obtain any representation.[86] But attempts at assimilation of minorities did not always proceed to plan, as the reaction of land colonists, mostly ex-soldiers from the Romanian army (many of whom initially knew little about farming), shows:

> We were sent here to make this land Roumanian, but living among the Ukrainians, and learning farming from them, we are, many of us, speaking only the Ukrainian language. In fact, we are fast becoming Ukrainians ourselves.[87]

If the Hungarian minority was treated with more sensitivity than the others, this probably had to do with the existence of a neighbouring state of co-nationals which had not come to terms with the loss of the greater part of its territory in 1918–20. A liberal Romanian historian is able to point out that, excepting the Baltic states, Romania was the only east European country which gave the minorities educational autonomy.[88] The same source mentions that in Transylvania, for a population of fewer than 1,500,000 Hungarians, there were fifty-two daily papers and more than 200 periodicals published in Hungarian. Nicolae Iorga, prime minister in 1931–2, insisted that:

> We have no plan to transform a good Hungarian or a good German into a hypocritical Romanian, because we do believe that those who abandon all their past and sell their soul in exchange for some advantages will be, for the nation which is supposed to receive them, not a profit but a poison.[89]

Moves which Constantin Anghelescu, minister of religion and education from 1933 to 1937, directed against the minority schools network, suggest that in other influential quarters assimilation was favoured.[90] Between 1920 and 1940 a total of forty complaints by the Hungarian minority in Romania were submitted to the League of Nations.[91] The council of the League devoted more than fifteen per cent of its meetings to minority questions in 1923, a percentage which grew progressively, reaching over fifty per cent in 1933.[92]

The 1923 constitution guaranteed 'citizens, without any distinction of

ethnic origin, of language or of religion ... liberty of conscience, education, press, and free association, all rights established by law'.[93] However,
documents even as venerable as constitutions have proven unreliable as
guides to the actions or intentions of political leaders. In the 1930s, as
political warfare intensified, ethnic Romanians found that the constitution
offered little protection against the arbitrary behaviour of some of their
rulers. Where minority conditions eased, it was often the result of an
influential political leader exercising discretionary powers on their behalf.
The best-known example is Nicolae Iorga, the powerful and complex personality whose scholarly energy made him the intellectual giant of inter-war
Romania. After breaking with the anti-Semite Cuza in the early 1920s, he
abandoned hardline nationalism. As prime minister in 1931–2, he chose a
Saxon as under-secretary for minorities in the office of the prime minister, a
Hungarian theologian becoming special adviser to the official.[94] There was
a genuine attempt by Iorga to improve relations with the Hungarians and
Saxons. Perhaps he realised that a state as weak as the pre-war Romanian
one did not have the capacity to assimilate minorities and, to echo Lord
Acton's words that 'a State which labours to neutralise, to absorb or to
expel them, destroys its own vitality'.[95]

Communications between the different parts of Romania were difficult
and slow and undoubtedly impeded national integration. The rail and
road system was too inefficient to distribute food for domestic needs
and agricultural production destined for export.[96] Indeed, the inter-war
Romanian state proved deficient in many of the ways that states normally
sought to establish their integrity and authority: as well as an inadequate
system of transport and communications, *Romania Mâre* proved incapable
of providing adequate defence, civil order, a reliable system of justice, a
reasonably equitable taxation system, and a framework for industry and
commercial activity. The national interest was reduced to safeguarding
territorial gains and realising the historic Romanian mission.[97]

ANTI-DEMOCRATIC INTELLECTUALS

The emphasis upon controlling territory rather than improving the conditions of citizens or the quality of the state machine may have stemmed from
the dominance that intellectuals had acquired in Romanian public life.
They had recorded and restored distinctive histories and embellished or
invented past glories during the period when the nation became conscious
of its existence and its mission. The productive middle classes, engaged
in commerce and industry, were not able to wrest the political advantage
from intellectuals. The dominant role that some of the minorities exercised
in business affairs meant that in Romania economic acumen did not
automatically translate into political influence. Joseph Rothschild has been

struck by the direct involvement of so many intellectuals in Romanian politics and their ability to acquire 'symbolic capital' through 'the prestige of their work as well as the reputation of their militant patriotism'.[98]

As nationalism was promoted sometimes with religious intensity by prominent intellectuals, Transylvania acquired an importance in the national consciousness which it had lacked before 1918. The region was described as one that had preserved the very core of Romanian nationhood during the long stretches of history when Romanians had been unable to control their own collective fate. The ability of Romanians to preserve what was intrinsic to their race and character in the forests and mountain retreats of Transylvania was seen as establishing their supremacy over neighbours and temporary conquerors: 'only a superior culture could endure regardless of the severity and extent of its political subjugation'.[99]

Undoubtedly, Transylvania assumed such an important place in Romanian nationalism because next door in Hungary there were nationalists even harder at work showing how it had been crucial for the preservation of the Hungarian national ideal. The 800-year sway exercised by Hungarian rulers over a region which had been the only part of Hungary not to be occupied by the Turks in the seventeenth-century made its recovery a primary aim of Budapest state policy after the 1920 Treaty of Trianon. The loss of historic real estate of this magnitude meant that doctrinaire nationalism shaped the politics of inter-war Hungary. Generally, these were more stable than Romanian politics. Perhaps the mission to recover territory felt to have been unjustly taken engendered more solidarity among key political groups in Hungary than the desire to preserve territorial gains which had occurred relatively unexpectedly and for which Romanian officials had made no serious preparation. But, in both states, the prospect for democracy declined as the quarrel over Transylvania intensified: there was no shortage of Romanian or Hungarian intellectuals who insisted that democracy was a suspect political philosophy because it exposed internal weaknesses or encouraged a spirit of compromise that was prejudicial to the national interest.

It is difficult to identify many outstanding Romanian intellectuals from the inter-war period who consistently defended democratic government as an appropriate form for Romania; Constantin Stere and Virgil Madgearu are two distinguished but increasingly isolated examples. However, there were a number of prominent intellectuals who acquired a considerable reputation by identifying a national mission, defining the national soul, or discussing the relationship between Romania and its neighbours and, above all, with the west. Nicolae Iorga's prodigious output as a historian had been shaped by a defence of Romanian national values and Romanian specificity. It evoked an idealised past that was agrarian, patriarchal and without class conflict.[100] Nichifor Crainic and Nae Ionescu were two philosophers who defined an essentially Romanian spirituality which they traced back to the village world shaped by the religious values of the Orthodox Church. Crainic lived in Romania from 1889 to 1972 and his ideas influenced both the radical right and the ethnocentric communism of the Ceausescu period. He believed that the Romanian village had assisted nation-building by its ability to screen out foreign influences and keep alive a fundamental spirituality deriving from Byzantine orthodoxy. To survive, Romania had to remain faithful to its traditions and avoid becoming contaminated by western values which would only bring dissolution and ruin in their wake.[101] If Romania followed such a path, she could obtain her second independence – that of the spirit – to reinforce the political independence obtained after 1877.[102] Crainic had no doubt that democracy was unsuitable for Romania because of its association with western bourgeois civilisation. He could see no difference between capitalism, socialism and communism, and he condemned each of them for their origins in Renaissance rationalism, the Enlightenment and the French Revolution. For Crainic, mankind could be differentiated on the basis not of class but of race and culture.[103] The Daco-Roman origins of the Romanians and their deep-rooted Orthodox faith gave them a cultural inheritance that made them unique and would ensure their survival. But in the 1930s, as democracy faced assaults from governing systems making a total claim on people's allegiances, Crainic modified his attitude to the west. His admiration for Italian fascism prompted him to switch his attention from the Byzantine east to Rome where a new anti-rationalist western spirit could now be detected. In 1936, influenced by the Italian corporate state, he elaborated his own form of state-managed economic system which he called 'ethnocracy'; all aspects of economic life – from agriculture and commerce to the liberal professions – were to be autochthonous: thus the role of minorities, especially the Jews, was to be reduced if not curtailed altogether.[104]

The march of events in the 1930s showed that cultural nationalists like Crainic, who argued that liberal democratic impulses from the west were incompatible with Romania's innate traditions, enjoyed far greater influence than their counterparts in other south-east European states. Already in 1934, a new law required every business in Romania to have Romanian staff to the extent of at least eighty per cent in each of the groups into which the Act divides persons.[105] Beforehand, the government received many resolutions from various trade and professional organisations demanding ethnic quotas or restrictions. Perhaps the most original was the demand of Romanian chimney-sweeps that members of the minorities should not be admitted to their calling given the belief that a chimney-sweep 'can

see everything, hear everything, go freely anywhere'.[106] The seriousness
with which this proposal was put forward indicates how far it was seen as
necessary for national values to animate even the most prosaic aspects of
everyday life.

It was intellectual unemployment, stemming from the failure of graduates (especially from law faculties) to obtain steady employment, which
fuelled demands for ethnic quotas in commercial employment and the
professions.[107] R. W. Seton-Watson observed 'the growth of a half-baked
intellectual proletariat', one that another scholar observed was intent on
'placing itself at the service of the state to reinforce its own position'.[108]
Democracy held out little appeal for the growing army of graduates with
poorly-paid state jobs or else only unemployment to look forward to,
especially after the onset of the great depression. Mircea Eliade, the young
philosopher, spoke for many in his generation when he complained in
1936 that 'democracy may be full of charm and comfort, but so far . . . it
has not made us into a strong State, nor has it made us conscious of our
greatness . . . If by leaving democracy Romania becomes a strong State,
armed, conscious of its power and destiny, history will take account of that
deed.'[109]

EXTREMISM AND WAR

Romania retained the trappings of parliamentary rule down to 1938, but
it was a caricature of western-style democracy in which elections were
'arranged' in advance and the state felt itself under no obligation to act
responsibly towards ordinary citizens. No culture of compromise or parliamentary accommodation emerged in inter-war Romania. Increasingly,
advocates of political change were animated by a total and violent break
with past arrangements rather than their reform. Given the chasm that
separated the rhetoric of a state which insisted that Romania was a beacon
of enlightenment in eastern Europe from the sad reality, it is not altogether
surprising that a radical right-wing movement was able to acquire a mass
following as prospects for reforming the corrupt parliamentary regime
faded completely in the 1930s.

The Legion of the Archangel Michael, better known by the title of its
political section, the Iron Guard, insisted that western political forms were a
gimmick meant to subjugate Romania and prevent it from realising its own
creative destiny.[110] The Jew was the mortal enemy of Romania because
of his identification with the debased products of the west – anti-Christian
communism as well as liberal democracy.[111] Under a visionary leader,
Corneliu Zelea Codreanu, a law graduate and son of a schoolteacher, the
Iron Guard mobilised impressive support without stimulus or assistance
from Germany or Italy. Codreanu emerged from the provincial world

of a small Moldavian town determined to cleanse the country of alien urban influences. He would be the first of several nationalist saviours who sought to mobilise the countryside against the city and who would receive his strongest backing from frustrated members of the professional classes suspended between urban reality and a mythic peasant world to which it was impossible to return though it offered emotional fulfilment.

Local conditions strongly favoured the radical right. Codreanu was of mixed race (with Slavic or German forebears) and he came from a border area (not an unusual background for an ultra-nationalist ready to place himself at the head of a national movement, as events would prove again after 1989).[112] While the Iron Guard was not derivative of western fascism, its anti-Semitism and obsession with Orthodoxy suggests that it was influenced by the Slavophile chauvinist movements that flourished in Russia prior to 1917. Bessarabia, adjacent to Codreanu's native Moldavia, had been a stronghold of the anti-Semitic Black Hundred movement distinguished by its 'anti-liberal and anti-capitalist . . . xenophobia, aggressive nationalism . . . [and] myth of decadence and national rebirth'.[113] One of its leading figures, Vladimir Mitrofanovich Purishkevich, was a landowner with ethnic Romanian ties who had founded his own 'Union of the Archangel Michael' at the turn of the century.[114]

But however much the Iron Guard purveyed conspiracies, prejudices and Orthodox sentiments that had been long in circulation in Russia – the seedbed for much of the nationalist right in eastern Europe – it came across to growing numbers of frustrated Romanians as an authentic movement promising national rebirth and spiritual restoration. Adherents joined for idealistic reasons impressed by Codreanu's efforts to improve the lot of the peasantry and who admired the discipline and dedication which were signally lacking in any political party. The Iron Guard also attracted the sons of Aromani immigrants from Greece who had been resettled in southern Dobruja when Romania acquired this territory from Bulgaria in 1918. These hardy shepherd peasants were meant to hold an outpost of greater Romania thinly populated with ethnic Romanians.[115] The Bucharest political elite which had masterminded this wholesale transfer of populations at a time when Greece needed to find room for 2,000,000 Greeks received from Turkey, could not easily have imagined that the Aromani or Vlachs could become a destabilising element in the affairs of Greater Romania. But within the Iron Guard they provided an aggressive hard-core prepared to slay all who stood in the way of the movement.[116]

Two prime ministers were assassinated by the Iron Guard in the 1930s, but its most celebrated victim was Nicolae Iorga, killed in 1940, having two years earlier complained about Codreanu: 'Who is this young man who is saluted by the youth of this country, who have forgotten their old teachers?'[117] At its apogee in 1938, the Iron Guard had 34,000 'nests' and a membership running into several hundred thousands. It has been claimed that one-fifth of Romania's 10,000 Orthodox priests belonged to it: 'they found in it a capacity for social mobilisation and dynamism lacking in Orthodox Christianity'.[118]

Until the 1930s, large-scale political violence had been absent from Romanian public life. Since then, those who have found it difficult to accept that Iorga, the great sage of Romania, was slain by fellow nationalists, have emphasised the Macedonian origins of a great many Iron Guard gunmen as if to argue that it was not really a Romanian phenomenon.[119] However, it is all too easily forgotten that Romania's national bard, Eminescu had given powerful endorsement for actions much later undertaken by Codreanu's men when he wrote: 'a political crime committed by a private person ceases to be a crime when it is based on higher views and dictated by the clean notion, even if it be mistaken, of saving the state'.[120] Guardists proclaimed Eminescu as their 'grand precursor', and their movement's propensity for extremism was well known by 1937 when it made a powerful impact in the December general election. Officially it secured sixteen per cent of the vote, but it is widely recognised that it achieved a much larger percentage, revealing of the huge inroads it had made into Romanian society.[121] The King, who had cleverly used his office to divide the political parties, placed his government in the hands of two smaller right-wing nationalist parties, led by Professor Cuza, the veteran of Romanian anti-semitism and Octavian Goga, a Transylvanian poet formerly of liberal instincts.[122] It would have been difficult if not impossible for the King to reach an accommodation with the Iron Guard, who saw Carol II as the epitome of the ills afflicting Romania.

If Codreanu could not be bought or marginalised like the party leaders, he had to be destroyed; following the collapse of the forty-four-day Goga–Cuza government in February 1938, the King imposed a royal dictatorship. On 24 February 1938, a new corporatist constitution was approved by 4,289,581 votes to 5,843 in a referendum where voting was open and compulsory. The independence of the judiciary and the autonomy of the universities had been suspended a few days previously, and all political parties were dissolved by law.[123] Two months later, the Iron Guard was suppressed and Codreanu arrested. A treason trial followed and Codreanu was condemned to ten years in prison. But, in November 1938, it was announced that, along with twelve of his followers, he had been 'shot while trying to escape'.[124] One month later, the King organised his own political party, the Front of National Rebirth. It adopted many of the Legionary themes such as work, patriotism, religion and personal dignity.[125] In modern Romanian history, it is not unknown for a victorious movement to incorporate part of its defeated opponent's programme if, by doing so, it can plausibly lay claim to national unity.[126]

Although nationalist concerns were increasingly centred on Transylvania, the region was largely unaffected by escalating political violence and was not one where the Iron Guard made strong inroads.[127] One reason for its relative failure may be religious. The Uniate Church, which owed its spiritual allegiance to Rome while retaining the Orthodox or Eastern rite, was the faith of nearly 1,500,000 Transylvanian Romanians (1930 census figures): adherence to a faith widely seen as a carrier of western values may have insulated them from a movement like Codreanu's, which was heavily impregnated with eastern Orthodox mysticism. Moreover, the warfare between the Guard and its opponents was largely an ethnic Romanian feud. Transylvania's minorities, including the Jews, were unaffected. The Hungarian minority remained non-militant and detached from active politics. Between 1920 and 1940, rather than lobbying energetically for its own interests at home (or resorting to terrorism like Croat nationalists), its leaders complained to the League of Nations about Romanian ill-treatment.

The anti-minority stance of the Transylvanian politician, Dr Vaida Voevod, worried all the minorities in the 1930s, especially those with economic interests. From being a Romanian deputy in the pre-war Budapest parliament who had dismissed a 'Greater Romania' as 'tavern fantasy' and fought instead for Transylvanian autonomy within the Hapsburg empire, Dr Vaida's views hardened considerably in the 1920s.[128] During the depression, he sought to appeal to the educated sons of Transylvanian peasants by demanding that the minorities cede economic opportunities to them. C. A. Maccartney has described the background to this:

> The state could not afford to employ nearly all the ex-students, and most unhappily, the sudden growth of the number of persons grimly determined to lead bourgeois lives, coincided with a moment when no accumulation of capital was taking place which would have enabled them to find shelter in new or enlarged enterprises.[129]

While in charge of a government from January to November 1933, Dr Vaida tried to introduce measures which would have confined state employment, and other areas of the labour market deemed of national importance, to ethnic Romanians.[130] He may have been taking to its logical conclusion the influential view that the interests of the state and the dominant nation were as one. However, he was obstructed by the Liberals, who did not wish to see such a nationalist card falling into rival hands; and, within his own party (the NPP), he failed, at its 1933 congress, to muster a majority for his plans. Vaida then seceded with his followers and made an alliance with Goga's Christian National Party around the slogan 'Romania for the Romanians'. His programme was the archetypal chauvinist one which did great harm to majority–minority relations in the whole region during the 1930s:

> the application of the national principle in all state and private enterprises; reinstatement of the Romanian church in its calling as 'creator and judge'; alteration of the constitution to'anchor the national idea and the structure of the life of the State'; securing the predominance of Romanian labour; the removal of 'foreign elements' from economic life by checking lists of Romanian citizens and expelling foreign skilled labour.[131]

Divisions among Romanian parties, each claiming to possess the nationalist mantle, impeded the realisation of such a draconian programme, even though the atmosphere was increasingly conducive to populist appeals. Recourse to nationalism by most of the leading players in Romanian politics intensified political warfare and left the country gravely weakened as nationalist ambitions and rivalries on a continental scale unleashed a second general war in Europe in 1939. Despite the inglorious end of *Romania Mâre*, it would remain an inspiring beacon for Romanians fifty years later when another opportunity arose to experiment with representative institutions. The limited public involvement in politics, the inadequacy of political structures, and the abuse of power that marked that earlier period would give little pause for thought. The search for indigenous models and examples to guide the country into the future proved stronger than the need to guard against repeating mistakes which, if taken far enough, might only make democracy a parenthesis between different forms of authoritarian rule.

NOTES

1. Corneliu Zelea Codreanu, 'A Few Remarkson Democracy', quoted in S. Fischer-Galati (ed.), *Nation, Man and State in Eastern Europe*, Pall Mall, London 1970, p. 327.
2. Eugene Kamenka, 'Nationalism: Ambiguous Legacies and Contingent Futures', *Political Studies*, 41, No. 4 (1993), p. 85.
3. Michael Ignatieff, *Blood and Belonging: Journeys into the New Nationalism*, BBC/Chatto, London 1993, p. 189.
4. Ivan T. Berend, 'The Cultural Identity of Central and Eastern Europe', *New Hungarian Quarterly*, Vol. 28, No. 107 (Autumn 1987), p. 27.
5. Philip Longworth, *The Making of Eastern Europe*, Macmillan, London 1992, p. 140.
6. H. Seton-Watson, *Nations and States: An Enquiry into Nationalism*, Weidenfeld & Nicholson, London 1975, p. 148.
7. John Campbell, *French Influence and the Rise of Roumanian Nationalism*, Arno Press, New York 1970 (Ph.D. originally submitted to the History Department of Harvard University in 1940), pp. 22–3.

8. Berend, op. cit., p. 31.
9. Campbell, op. cit., p. 25.
10. Hans Kohn, *Nationalism: Its Meaning and History*, Van Nostrand, New York 1965, pp. 28–9.
11. Vlad Georgescu, *A History of the Romanians*, IB Tauris, London 1990, examines the creation of the Romanian national state and is a rare example of a recent work in English by a Romanian historian not warped to suit the requirements of the Romanian communist state. This section of the chapter makes use of Georgescu as well as Barbara Jelavich, *History of the Balkans, Volume 1: Eighteenth and Nineteenth Centuries*, Cambridge University Press, Cambridge 1983.
12. Seton-Watson, op. cit., p. 106.
13. P. Sugar and I. Lederer, *Nationalism in Eastern Europe*, University of Washington Press, Seattle WA 1969, p. 51.
14. Jelavich, Vol. 1, op. cit., p. xi.
15. C. Stefanescu, 'The Romanian Academy Adrift', *Radio Free Europe Research*, Vol. 13, No. 29 (22 July 1988), p. 9.
16. The word 'catechism' is used by Paul Michelson whose foreword to Ştefan Paşcu's *A History of Transylvania*, Wayne State University Press, Detroit MI 1982, shows the importance of historiography in forging national identity in Romania.
17. Juliana Geron Pilon, *The Bloody Flag: Post-Communist Nationalism in Eastern Europe*, Transaction Publishers, New York 1992, p. 54.
18. Leon Volovici, *Nationalist Ideology and Anti-Semitism: The Case of Romanian Intellectuals in the 1930s*, Pergamon Press, Oxford 1991, p. 187.
19. Lawrence Graham, *Romania: A Developing Socialist State*, Westview Press, Boulder CO, 1982, p. 13.
20. Jelavich, Vol. 1, op. cit., p. 294
21. Trond Gilberg, *Nationalism and Communism in Romania*, Westview Press, Boulder CO and Oxford 1990, p. 11.
22. Maurice Pearton, 'Nicolae Iorga as Historian and Nation-Builder', in Dennis Deletant and Harry Hanak (eds), *Historians as Nation-Builders*, Macmillan, London 1988, p. 164.
23. R. W. Seton-Watson, *A History of the Roumanians: From Roman Times to the Completion of Unity*, Cambridge University Press, Cambridge 1934, pp. 376–8. A powerful case is made for the view that the Romanians in pre-1918 Hungary enjoyed much greater civil, religious, economic and educational rights than minorities in Romania, Prussia or Russia during the same period in Sandor Biro, *The Nationalities Problem in Transylvania, 1867–1940*, East European Monographs Series, Columbia University Press, New York 1992, passim.
24. Seton-Watson, *A History of the Roumanians*, pp. 383–4.
25. Ibid., p. 436.
26. Volovici, *Nationalist Ideology*, p. 4.
27. Ibid., p. 5.
28. Eugen Weber, 'Romania', in H. Rogger and E. Weber (eds), *The European Right: A Historical Profile*, University of California Press, Berkeley CA 1974, p. 501.
29. Barbara Jelavich, *History of the Balkans, Volume 2: Twentieth Century*, Cambridge University Press, Cambridge 1983, p. 26.

30. Ibid.
31. Volovici, *Nationalist Ideology*, p. 4.
32. Weber, 'Romania', p. 508.
33. Georges Castellan, *A History of the Romanians*, East European Monographs, Boulder, CO 1989, pp. 139–40; Jelavich, Vol. 2, op. cit., p. 26.
34. Volovici, *Nationalist Ideology*, p. 13.
35. Mark Almond, *The Rise and Fall of Nicolae and Elena Ceaușescu*, Chapmans, London 1992, p. 31.
36. Weber, 'Romania', p. 507.
37. Volovici, *Nationalist Ideology*, p. 13.
38. Eminescu died in obscurity in 1889. His posthumous recognition was slow to get under way. R. W. Seton-Watson's encyclopaedic 596-page *A History of the Roumanians*, has not a single reference to Eminescu.
39. Seton-Watson, *A History of the Roumanians*, p. 386.
40. Weber, op. cit., p. 508; Daniel Chirot, *Social Change in a Peripheral Society: The Creation of a Balkan Colony*, Academic Press, New York 1976, pp. 150–5.
41. Seton-Watson, *A History of the Roumanians*, p. 388.
42. Volovici, *Nationalist Ideology*, p. 22.
43. Cuza and his contemporary equivalent, C. Vadim Tudor both held senior posts in the Romanian Senate which gave some cover of respectability to their extremist views.
44. Volovici, *Nationalist Ideology*, p. 5.
45. Radu Ioanid, 'Nicolae Iorga and Fascism', *Journal of Contemporary History*, Vol. 27 (1992), p. 469.
46. In July 1994, the Romanian Information Service (successor to the Securitate) issued a report which emphasised alleged Soviet and Hungarian involvement in the December 1989 revolt. This can only have been issued with high-level backing, and it made claims that had only hitherto been made by the chauvinist press.
47. Francisco Veiga, *La mística del ultranacionalismo (História de la Guardia de Hierro Rumania, 1919–41)*, Univ. Autonomia de Barcelona, Barcelona 1989, p. 37. Perhaps because his educational efforts strengthened national unity, Haret was the only pre-communist Romanian politician commemorated with a postage stamp in the communist era.
48. C. A. Maccartney, *Hungary and Her Successors: The Treaty of Trianon and Its Consequences, 1919–1937*, Oxford University Press, London [1937] 1965, p. 251.
49. Jelavich, Vol. 2, op. cit., p. 124.
50. R. W. Seton-Watson, *Transylvania: A Key Problem*, The Claric Press, Oxford 1943, p. 7.
51. Raymond Pearson, *National Minorities in Eastern Europe, 1848–1945*, Macmillan, Basingstoke 1983, p. 136.
52. Benyamin Neuberger, 'National Self-Determination: Dilemmas of a Concept', in *Nationalism in Europe, Past and Present*, University of Santiago de Compostela 1994, p. 40.
53. Walker Connor, *Ethnonationalism: The Quest for Understanding*, Princeton University Press, Princeton, NJ 1994, p. 375.
54. G. Schopflin, 'Rumanian Nationalism', *Survey*, Vol. 20 (Spring–Summer 1974), p. 100.

55. E. Illyes, *National Minorities in Romania: Change in Transylvania*, Columbia University Press, Boulder CO and New York 1982, p. 89.
56. Pearson, *National Minorities*, p. 223.
57. Ibid.
58. Castellan, *A History of the Romanians*, pp. 161–2.
59. Jelavich, Vol. 2, pp. 157–8.
60. Illyés, op. cit., p. 87.
61. Jelavich, Vol. 2., pp. 161–2; Joseph Rothschild, *East-Central Europe between the Two World Wars*, University of Washington Press, Washington DC 1974, p. 296.
62. Jelavich, Vol. 2, p. 163; Julius Rezler, 'Economic and Social Differentiation and Ethnicity: The Case of Eastern Europe', in Peter Sugar (ed.), *Ethnic Diversity and Conflict in Eastern Europe*, ABC-Clio, Santa Barbara CA 1980, pp. 311–12.
63. Denis Mack Smith, 'Regionalism', in E. R. Tannenbaum and E. P. Noether (eds), *Modern Italy: A Topical History since 1861*, New York University Press, New York 1974, p. 127.
64. Ibid., p. 48.
65. Ibid., p. 136.
66. Lord Acton, 'Nationality', quoted in Hans Kohn, *Nationalism: Its Meaning and History*, Van Nostrand, New York 1971, pp. 124–5.
67. Jan Obrman, 'Havel Challenges Czech Historical Taboos', RFE-RL *Research Report*, Vol. 2, No. 24 (11 June 1993), p. 47.
68. Henry L. Roberts, *Rumania: Political Problems of an Agrarian State*, Yale University Press, New Haven CT 1951, pp. 128–9.
69. For details, see Jelavich, Vol. 2, p. 164
70. Rothschild, *East-Central Europe*, p. 320.
71. E. Garrison Walters, *The Other Europe: Eastern Europe To 1945*, Dorset Press 1988, p. 226.
72. Rothschild, *East-Central Europe*, p. 320.
73. Keith Hitchins, *Conştiinţa Naţională Si Actiune Politica La Românii Din Transilvania, 1868–1918*, Editura Dacia, Cluj 1992, p. 179.
74. Rothschild, *East-Central Europe*, p. 301.
75. Paul Shoup, 'The National Question and the Political Systems of Eastern Europe', in S. Sinanian et al., *Eastern Europe in the 1970s*, Praegar, New York 1972, p. 126.
76. Illyés, op. cit., p. 278, n. 5.
77. Shoup, 'The National Question . . .', p. 127.
78. H. Seton-Watson, *Eastern Europe, 1918–41*, Cambridge University Press, Cambridge 1945, p. 212.
79. H. Hessell Tiltman, *Peasant Europe*, Jarrolds, London 1936, p. 107.
80. Weber, 'Romania', pp. 545–6.
81. Rezler, 'Economic and Social Differentiation', pp. 311–12.
82. Maccartney, *Hungary and Her Successors*, p. 296. Powerful evidence for these claims is found in the second part of Biro, *The Nationalities Problem in Transylvania*.
83. Illyés, op. cit., p. 93.
84. Maccartney, op. cit., p. 293.
85. See Georges Castellan, 'The Germans of Rumania', *Journal of Contemporary History*, Vol. 6, No. 1 (1971).

86. The above information was obtained from Hessell Tiltman, op. cit., p. 141.
87. Hessell Tiltman, op. cit., pp. 150–1.
88. Andrei Pippidi, 'Nation, Nationalisme et Démocratie en Roumanie', *L'Autre Europe*, part 26–27 (1993), p. 154.
89. Ibid.
90. Illyés, op. cit., pp. 74–5.
91. Ibid., p. 75.
92. Xosé M. Nunez Seixas, 'National Minorities in Central and Eastern Europe and the Internationalisation of Their Rights', in *Nationalism and Europe, Past and Present*, University of Santiago de Compostela 1994.
93. Pippidi, op. cit., pp. 152–3.
94. Illyés, op. cit., p. 77.
95. Kohn, *Nationalism: Its Meaning and History*, p. 163.
96. Hessell Tiltman, op. cit., p. 115.
97. Stephen Fischer-Galati, 'Introduction', in Joseph Held (ed.), *Democracy and Right-Wing Politics in Eastern Europe in the 1990s*, Columbia University Press (East European Monographs Series), Boulder CO and New York 1993, p. 2.
98. Rothschild, *East-Central Europe*, p.186.
99. Gilberg, *Nationalism and Communism*, p. 21.
100. Hitchins, *Conştiinţa Naţională*, p. 211.
101. Ibid., p. 222.
102. Ibid., p. 223.
103. Ibid.
104. Ibid., p. 224; for a further exploration of Crainic's ideas, see Katherine Verdery, *National Ideology Under Socialism: Identity and Cultural Politics in Ceausescu's Romania*, University of California Press, Berkeley CA 1991, pp. 47–8.
105. Maccartney, op. cit., p. 327.
106. Ibid.
107. H. Seton-Watson, *Eastern Europe*, 1918–41, pp. 144–5.
108. R. W. Seton-Watson, *Transylvania: A Key Problem*, p. 9; Veiga, *La mística del ultranacionalismo*, p. 33.
109. Mac Linscott Ricketts, *Mircea Eliade: The Romanian Roots, 1907–1945*, East European Monographs, Boulder CO 1988, p. 901.
110. Weber, 'Romania', p. 530.
111. Stephen Fischer-Galati, *20th Century Romania* (2nd edn), Columbia University Press, New York 1993, pp. 53–4.
112. Veiga, *La mística del ultranacionalismo*, p. 138.
113. Walter Laqueur, *Black Hundred: The Rise of the Extreme Right in Russia*, Harper Collins, New York 1993, p. 290.
114. Laqueur, op. cit., p. 23.
115. Bernard Newman, *Balkan Background*, Robert Hale, London 1944, pp. 65–6.
116. Weber, op. cit., pp. 543–44, Veiga, op. cit., p. 144; Veiga writes that the Aromani in the Iron Guard regarded themselves as a kind of elite: 'They felt themselves to be "more Romanian than the Romanians" who, according to them, had been influenced by the Slavs. The Aromani felt themselves to be less adulterated descendants of Roman soldiers . . .' (Veiga, op. cit., p. 146).
117. Michel Sturdza, *The Silence of Europe*, Watchtower Books, Boston MA 1968.
118. Veiga, op. cit., p. 173.

119. The world-renowned philosophers, Mircea Eliade and Emil Cioran, were prepared to dismiss the Iron Guard as an alien intrusion in the Romanian body politic after the war even though their close links with it in the 1930s would have clearly suggested that this was not the case. See Volovici, op. cit., p. ix.

120. Weber, op. cit., p. 540.

121. Fischer-Galati, *20th Century Romania*, p. 57.

122. Goga had been a member of the RNP before eventually founding his own National Agrarian Party in 1932. As well as espousing anti-Semitism, he campaigned to restrict minorities' access to higher education and made enthusiastic visits to Rome and Berlin. See Veiga, op. cit., p. 110.

123. Rothschild, op. cit., p. 311.

124. Veiga, op. cit., pp. 255–60.

125. Jelavich, Vol. 2, op. cit., p. 207.

126. A telling example occurred in 1990 when the recently-elected National Salvation Front borrowed the free-market rhetoric of its opponents even though during the spring election campaign it had been denounced as an economic sell-out.

127. Veiga, op. cit., pp. 96, 115.

128. Walter Kolarz, *Myths and Realities in Eastern Europe*, Lindsay Drummond, London 1946, p. 177.

129. Maccartney, op. cit., p. 325.

130. Ibid., p. 326.

131. Ibid., pp. 328–9.

Chapter 2

The Legacy of Communism

The fate of Romania and the other states born at Versailles showed that twenty years of statehood behind arbitrarily-drawn frontiers had failed to greatly improve personal security or enhance the economic progress of the peoples of eastern Europe. Inter-state rivalry had weakened the states which had sprung from the Versailles settlement and made them vulnerable to the totalitarian regimes that enabled German and Russian power to spread across much of east-central Europe. If the new states had realised that their fragility and provisional nature required mutual co-operation and the acceptance of arbitration for managing disputes, the fate of the peoples living under the post-1918 'national states' might not have been so awful. However, the new states were unwilling to empower a body like the League of Nations to arbitrate effectively between them, and it thus proved wholly unsuccessful as an instrument for preventing war.

Romania, under Brătianu, briefly aspired to join the great powers, but the shortcomings of the state machine and Romania's geo-political weakness exposed this as a bombastic goal before the dust of Versailles had settled. Thereafter, the country tried to protect itself by manoeuvring among the powers and building an alliance system to safeguard its territory. Nicolae Titulescu, foreign minister in the mid-1930s, pursued vigorous diplomacy along these lines, but his work was undermined by the rise of totalitarianism and by the internal divisions battering Romania. Carol's kingdom was a laughing-stock by the end of his reign, its chief ally, France, having crashed to a humiliating defeat in 1940. The ruthless way that Hitler and the Soviets then carved up the country and the refusal of the western allies to defend free institutions in Romania after 1945 may, in no small way, have stemmed from the disorderly and corrupt image which Romania presented to the outside world.

Efforts by Carol to remain aloof from the world conflict collapsed in June 1940 when Stalin issued an ultimatum to cede Bessarabia and the northern half of the Bukovina to the Soviet Union. Resistance would have been futile, but a far heavier blow fell two months later when Hungary demanded the return of Transylvania (and Bulgaria the return of southern Dobruja). The failure of bilateral negotiations led to German and Italian arbitration and the so-called Vienna Award of 30 August 1940 by which Hungary regained approximately two-fifths of her 1918–20 territorial losses to Romania.

The Vienna Award spelt the end of Carol's personal dictatorship. He abdicated and left his teenage son, Michael, to reign over an uneasy Romanian army-Iron Guard coalition. In a span of three months, Romania had lost one-third of her land and her people, of whom about half were ethnic Romanians.[1] Despite changing hands in previous centuries, Transylvania had never been partitioned in such a piecemeal fashion. Over 1,000,000 Romanians were placed under Hungarian rule while about 500,000 Hungarians remained under Romanian rule; about 200,000 people left the Hungarian zone to take refuge in the south while 160,000 Hungarians left the part of Transylvania still in Romanian hands.[2] The resulting dispossession and suffering, memories of which were kept alive under Ceauşescu, were to be exploited by vote-seeking nationalists in the 1990s. Some were ready to ascribe collective guilt to Transylvania's Hungarians even though most were bystanders in the whirlwind that tore the region asunder. Indeed, Hungarian wartime documents published in Romania in 1986 reveal that the occupying authorities were often not well regarded by local people who shared their nationality; one revealed that:

> The native Magyars are discontented with the Hungarian regime because of the harsh measures taken by the authorities in all domains and because they are regarded as second-class citizens, all the main posts and most of the managerial positions having been taken by Hungarians from old Hungary'.[3]

Local Hungarians disappointment at the behaviour of their so-called liberators mirrored Transylvanian Romanian resentment at the way in which officials from the *Regat* had exploited the new province of Transylvania for their own benefit after 1918.

In the 1990s, the 1940–4 dictatorship of General Ion Antonescu has its admirers among Romanians who felt that post-communist reconstruction needed to be along firmly nationalist lines. Indeed, the war years have provided abundant ammunition for future polemics between nationalists convinced that Romania should choose a political model from among its own traditions, and for whom Antonescu is a fitting role model, and liberals who feel that the country's disastrous experience for most of the time since 1918 leaves it no option but to emulate states whose success with representative government had been much greater.

The first years of the Antonescu regime were disfigured by unchecked anti-Semitism, much of which had official blessing. From September 1940 to January 1941, Antonescu ruled in tandem with the Iron Guard which established a 'National Legionary' regime in which violence against Jews rose sharply. A Legionary uprising against Antonescu failed, but not before a Bucharest pogrom against Jews which claimed 124 lives.[4] On 29 June 1941, shortly after Romania entered the war on Hitler's side, a pogrom occurred in Iasi, the base for the anti-Semite A. C. Cuza since the turn of the century. It was carried out by the Romanian army and civil authorities with the help of German units present in the city, and almost 12,000 Jews were killed.[5] As Romanian troops reoccupied Bessarabia in the months following the German invasion of the Soviet Union, general massacres of the Jews were carried out; Bessarabian Jews, especially the intelligentsia, had long been considered by public opinion to be Communist and Russian sympathisers.[6] In September 1941, Antonescu ordered the deportation of those who had survived the killings to an improvised camp in a region of the western Ukraine known as Transnistria that had been awarded by Hitler to Romania.[7] Out of some 150,000 Jews deported there, only about 55,000 survived until 1944.[8] The Jews in southern Romania avoided a similar fate thanks to the intercession with Antonescu of the chief rabbi, Alexandre Safran, and leading Romanians from the Queen Mother downwards. A German order to deport the Jews of the *Regat* to concentration camps was disregarded by Antonescu. Jews who escaped from north Transylvania (most of the 150,000-strong community there was deported to Auschwitz in 1944) were given shelter in independent Romania, which became one of the few safe havens for Jews in occupied Europe. Understandably, nationalists intent on rehabilitating Antonescu made much of this years later. His earlier policy of state-led onslaughts on Romanian Jewry is disregarded and the ability of far more Jews to survive in partitioned Romania than in Hungarian-occupied Transylvania is offered as proof that Antonescu's rule was one of tolerance, at least in the harsh circumstances of the moment. Certainly in 1945 the Romanian Jewish community was the largest one in mainland Europe after the Soviet Union; however, out of over 650,000 that had lived under Romanian rule at the start of the war, only 350,000 or so were left.[9]

Antonescu committed himself wholeheartedly to the German cause. Romania stayed in the war after all of Bessarabia had been recaptured and, by 1943, with the war clearly going against the Axis, the Romanian casualty rate was approaching 500,000.[10] Despite the hatred between them arising from the 1940 frontier revision, Hungary and Romania were fighting on the same losing side. Hitler extracted more soldiers and resources for his war in Russia from each state in turn by threatening to modify the Vienna accord to the disadvantage of one or the other.[11] In the event, of the two reluctant allies, it was Romania which managed to break free of this vicious circle. On 23 August 1944, Antonescu was overthrown in a plot hatched by senior army officers and politicians in which the young King Michael played the key role. This was one of the decisive events of the Second World War which opened all of south-eastern Europe to the Soviet Red Army.[12] Romania declared war on Hitler soon afterwards, and 15 Romanian divisions fought alongside the Soviet Red Army, liberating north Transylvania and going on to fight in Hungary and Slovakia. Having suffered hugely fighting for Hitler, the Romanian army now suffered a further 150,000 casualties fighting against him.[13]

If Romania had been allowed to control its own affairs after 1944, there are grounds for thinking that it might have broken free of the cycle of despotism and instability that had plagued it for the past thirty years. Michael was a brave and democratically-minded sovereign aware of his public responsibilities and was thus a complete contrast to his father. The most popular politician in the country was the veteran Iuliu Maniu, now regarded as the 'greatest living Romanian' and someone who, significantly, continued to reject vindictive nationalism despite the carve-up of Transylvania.[14] In the nationalistic 1920s, he had swum against the tide even within his own party by publicly supporting a Danubian or south-east European confederation in which states could pool their sovereignty in order to overcome narrow nationalism and start to harness the abundant human energies of the region for peaceful purposes.[15] However, even although the National Peasant Party was the most popular party in the country (with the nationalist bloc associated with Antonescu in disarray), Romania was to be denied the chance of building the regional political and economic confederation which in western Europe would create such a profound transformation in fortunes over the next thirty years.

COMMUNISM AND CO-INHABITING NATIONALITIES

Outwardly, a retreat from nationalism took place in south-eastern Europe as shown by the signing of friendship treaties between former adversaries, by the shelving of territorial claims, and by the codification of minority rights; attempts were also made to integrate the different economies. But none of this was a voluntary process on the part of chastened leaders who, like their west European counterparts, at last realised the folly of narrow nationalism. Instead post-nationalism was imposed by the Soviet Union as it sought to brand a communist order on the whole of eastern Europe. The world was told that, under Soviet auspices, enduring peace and friendship were being established between formerly divided peoples.[16] However, it soon emerged that the new doctrine of internationalism under which eastern Europe was to be ruled put Soviet state interests first. The new post-war boundaries were not based on internationalist criteria but on long-term Soviet historical and national interests. Bessarabia and north Bukovina, seized in 1940, were swallowed up into the Soviet Union. Romania was required to pay huge economic reparations to Moscow for Antonescu's role in the German invasion of Russia even though this act had not been sanctioned by the Romanian people. Also, Stalin quickly placed Romania in the hands of a communist party dominated by members of the ethnic minorities and individuals from outside the state, something bound to strain inter-ethnic relations further.

Romania was probably the east European state where the strategy of divide-and-rule and plunder of territorial resources which lay behind the facade of internationalism was carried out most flagrantly.[17] Ruthless measures may have been necessary given the tiny social base enjoyed by the Romanian Communist Party (RCP). With less than 1,000 members (which means that its support was negligible among all ethnic groups, including those minorities which challenged the Romanian national outlook on Transylvania), the RCP had not been in a position to mount any serious wartime resistance, and the claim – afterwards consistently made – that it had played a crucial role in the 23 August 1944 coup was simply groundless.[18] Before the war, the RCP had endorsed the Comintern line of supporting the claims of discontented minorities in the Danubian-Balkan region, particularly Hungarians in the various parts of the Hungarian state allocated to other states after 1918.[19] Nowhere else in the region had the party been so weak and alien in the 1930s, and in no other east European state did it have so little genuine popular support.[20] Yet, by 1947, the RCP (now renamed the Romanian Workers Party: RWP) was on the verge of becoming a dominant elite with steps already being taken to demolish completely the old social and political order that had existed before Sovietisation.

It was not unduly difficult to suppress the inter-war parties or pressurise political chiefs into acting as tame figureheads (particularly Liberal ones). By the end of 1947, the King had been compelled to step down from the throne. How to solve the Transylvanian question without fuelling resentments that might jeopardise Soviet influence in the region proved to be a greater challenge, and it was one the Soviets never met despite a skilful attempt at defusing the question in the mid-1940s.

Despite the terrible fate of the Jews of northern Transylvania, the province remained far more multi-ethnic than other disputed territories such as the Sudetenland and parts of Prussia where defeated populations were driven out. The 1,500,000 Hungarians did not accompany the Hungarian army on its retreat in 1944. Although the history of the occupation still has to be properly written, there is not compelling evidence to suggest that local Hungarians actively collaborated withe the occupying forces of Admiral Horthy (Hungary's ruler until 1944), especially in carrying out repressive acts against Romanians.[21] Romanians in the 1990s can be found who are prepared to recall exemplary acts of courage by Hungarian neighbours who placed themselves in the line of fire in villages where the occupiers had lined up local Romanian dignitaries such as the priest, the bank manager and the local gendarmerie chief to be shot. But feelings understandably ran high in 1944–5, and clashes between Romanian nationalists and Hungarians led to the Soviet military command taking over the administration and banning officials from the Romanian government from entering Transylvania.[22]

On 9 March 1945, all of Transylvania was restored to Romanian jurisdiction days after the appointment of a communist-controlled government under Petru Groza.[23] It is likely that the timing of the announcement was meant to strengthen the hand of communists whose power-grab had elicited mounting opposition over the winter. What Stalin's overall intention was remains unclear, however; it may be that the province's strategic role as the gateway to central Europe from the Russian plains made it prudent to have Transylvania attached to a state which geo-politically was then firmly under the Soviet thumb.[24] There may also have been a perceived need to balance the ascendancy minorities then enjoyed in the RCP with a gesture to satisfy Romanian opinion. At the same time, Hungarian state alienation needed to be avoided if Moscow was to have compliant satellites in eastern Europe. Hungary recognised the Romanian borders at the Treaty of Paris in 1946, but the desire of its communist delegates to prevent the loss of all of Transylvania was an early indication that the retreat from nationalism imposed from the east did not come naturally.[25]

In 1945, a Hungarian university, as well as a theatre, opera house and radio station, were opened in Cluj. A network of Hungarian schools was reestablished, under state control, and state-run newspapers, cultural groups and publishing houses promoting the Hungarian language followed. Finally, in 1952, a Hungarian Autonomous Region (HAR) was set up which covered the areas of Transylvania – a long distance from the Hungarian frontier – where the greatest concentration of Hungarians was to be found. One source argues that Soviet national minority doctrine was the model for this experiment. The HAR was based on a format adopted in areas of the Soviet Union with a mixed population.[26] While remaining subject to the laws of Romania, it had its own administrative organs and was responsible for its own public order, the enforcement of laws, local economic and cultural activity, and a certain degree of economic and financial administration. Leaving aside Yugoslavia, Transylvania was the only part of eastern Europe subjected to Soviet national minority doctrine.

The first attempt to settle the minority question by compromise was being carried forward by a regime which was simultaneously sweeping away personal liberties. This era of surface harmony was bound up with Petru Groza, a prosperous Transylvanian lawyer and landowner, partly educated in Budapest, whose range of interests had resulted in agreeable contacts with diverse Hungarians. He was an anomalous figure whose wealth and social standing enabled him to act as a camouflage for the RCP as its grip on the country tightened.[27] Prime Minister for some years and chairman of the largely honorific state council from 1952 until his death in 1958, his period in the limelight coincided nearly exactly with the span of the moderate minority policy enacted in 1945. He appears to have had a genuine internationalist outlook and was committed to ending the traditional feud with Hungary, seeing it as pointless and mutually harmful.[28] But most Romanians were unlikely to react equably to the unprecedented concessions made to Hungarian speakers, especially as they coincided with assaults on those of their institutions which had been important symbols of nationhood. Even among Romanian RCP members there were mixed feelings about the nationality policy. On 13 June 1945, Lucreţiu Pătrăscanu, the minister of justice, had delivered a speech in Cluj in which he indicted those allegedly walking free on the city's streets who had been guilty of Horthyite crimes during the occupation, and he declared the Romanian language to be the correct one for all the Romanian territory.[29] Pătrăscanu, an able lawyer, was a home communist who seemed dangerously wayward, having not spent any part of his career in Moscow. His nationalism was distinctly premature in an era of communist internationalism, and not long afterwards he was purged.

In retrospect, the minority policy scripted by Moscow appears another example of an external power placing Romanians and Hungarians on a future collision course so as to advance its own interests. For each Hungarian who looked at the 1945–52 period as the only stage after 1918 when their cultural rights were properly safeguarded, there were rather more Romanians who had grounds for viewing it as a time of relentless terror and oppression. The later decades of communist power would prove far more damaging to the structure of Romanian society and to the economy, but the first decade of communist rule was characterised by a ferocious attack on all institutions and individuals that were seen as representing even a residual threat to the new order. Landowning peasants and wealthier urban groups were divested of their property by outright seizure, currency adjustments and punitive taxations. Members of the old elite were thrown out of their homes or else were obliged to share them with social inferiors (gypsies were billeted with Saxons in Transylvania as part of a levelling-down strategy, one that was a bitter blow to a group that had insulated itself from other communities).[30] The ruling RWP demonstrated its ruthlessness by placing on trial in 1947 the seventy-four-year-old leader of the NPP, Maniu and sentencing him to life imprisonment (he died in Sighet jail in 1953). Its flimsy legitimacy would be challenged as long as Maniu, and other NPP leaders remained at liberty.Records discovered in the Cluj Communist Party archives in the 1990s reveal that the NPP did much better in the rigged election of 19 November 1946 than official results suggested. The party received forty-two per cent of the vote in Cluj county as against the thirty-three per cent that went to the Democratic Popular Bloc composed of the RWP and fellow travellers, this being the best that could be achieved by the RWP even with the might of the state machine and Soviet occupying forces behind it.[31]

The NPP had always been closely linked to the Uniate (or Greek Catholic) Church of Romania which, ever since the eighteenth century, had acted as the custodian of Romanian national identity in Transylvania. For a revolutionary elite determined to stamp its will on the country, the dissolution of this church was a clear necessity. In the absence of a native Romanian nobility, the Uniate church had provided leadership and encouraged the brightest and most public-spirited members of the common people to improve themselves. It could be contrasted with the Orthodox Church which, in all matters not strictly spiritual, tended to support and obey the state rather than critically monitor its actions.[32] It was on Moscow's orders that the Uniate Church was disbanded after October 1948, similar action being taken against this church in the Ukraine and other parts of the Soviet empire.[33] All of its bishops refused to lend their names to this action and, one by one, they died in state custody (the last to survive, Iuliu Hossu, dying in 1970 just after being made a Cardinal by Rome). The suppression of the Uniates was meant to cut the links between ethnic Romanians and the Vatican and between Romanian national identity and Catholicism at a time when a massive denational-isation campaign was underway. Romanians were told that neither their language nor their culture was Latin but Slavic and that perhaps there was no real Romanian nationality at all. The role of Russia in Romanian history was upgraded and placed in a wholly benevolent light.[34] An attempt was even made to suggest that Wallachia and Moldavia were different nationalities, which struck at the very heart of the Romanian nation.[35]

The RWP's minuscule presence in Romanian life necessitated wholesale purges before opposition to its rule could be suppressed. Certain minor-ities also suffered as badly as ethnic Romanians. The German-speaking population, already more than halved in number by the decision of com-munities in north Transylvania, Bessarabia, the Bukovina and Dobruja to leave Romania, was subject to deportations and the wholesale confiscation of property.[36] The German Catholics of the Banat (known as the Swabians) suffered badly following Yugoslavia's 1948 decision to defy Moscow's edict and follow a separate communist path. To prevent contagion from national communism in Belgrade, a fifty-kilometre-wide zone on the frontier was evacuated: it is estimated that over 30,000 Swabians, along with Serbians, Romanians and Hungarians, were deported to the inhospitable Baragan plain near the Black Sea.[37]

Of course, Hungarian property-owners joined other 'exploiters' in prison after 1948, but there is little doubt that the internationalist ideal which supposedly lay at the heart of the communist message was attractive to Magyar workers and intellectuals in Transylvania. Hungarian nationalism had not enhanced their lives and had even placed them in jeopardy as a result of the 1940–4 occupation. To embrace Romanian nationalism was not an option that at that stage they were required to choose. Internationalism seemed to offer healthier options for creating a new identity that would enable them to live in peace with the other co-inhabiting nationalities (the term 'minorities' was frowned upon between 1945 and the late 1950s).

One western source has claimed that, at the start of the 1950s, the opinion of a large majority of Romanians was that the RCP consisted of a gang taking orders from the Russians which was directed by the Hungarians, Jews and – worse – Hungarian Jews, whose troops were drawn from the gypsies.[38] This is an oversimplification which fails to take account of the fact that the majority of new recruits to the RWP as it became the party of state were in fact Romanians. Leaving aside the difficulty of determining what a large majority thought about anything in the unfree early 1950s, the 'victim complex' certainly took root among Romanians, particularly intellectuals. It would be exploited by the chauvinist press after 1989 as it sought to revive anti-Semitism by dwelling on cases where noted Romanian intellectuals like Lucien Blaga were replaced by Jews of vastly inferior talent but who were committed to Marxism-Leninism.

Such charges were most frequently made by publicists who had been arch-collaborators of the regime in its ultra-nationalist phase after 1970. The origins of Romanian national communism can be traced as far back as 1952 when G. Gheorghiu-Dej, an ethnic Romanian, emerged as the undisputed leader of the party and the government after an uneasy period of power-sharing between communists from Jewish and Hungarian backgrounds as well as Romanian ones.

Gheorghiu-Dej was a working-class home communist who had spent the 1933–44 years in prison. He blamed the terror of the early communist years on the 'Muscovites' led by Ana Pauker who had returned with the Red Army, even though he had been party leader from 1946 onwards.

It was Gheorghiu-Dej who was also behind the execution of the national and reform communist, Patrascanu, in 1954.[39] But he slowly began to promote national values, less out of a commitment to genuine patriotism than as a means of securing absolute control over the party.[40] He found a base among the new party recruits, the bulk of whom could not have been Marxist and whose indoctrination was likely to have been superficial and of short duration.[41] The leadership may have sensed that it could best control or motivate a party dominated by ambitious young cadres of peasant background by depicting industrialisation and modernisation in nationalist terms.

NATIONAL AUTONOMY STRENGTHENS COMMUNIST ORTHODOXY

Stalin had encouraged the 'ethnicisation' of eastern European communist parties just before his death.[42] The new Russian leader, Khrushchev's repudiation of his predecessor and his own de-Stalinisation process, undoubtedly disturbed Gheorghiu-Dej and other Orthodox Stalinists who were only prepared to allow cosmetic liberalism. It was the desire of the elite around Gheorghiu-Dej for self-protection which placed Romania on a course of greater autonomy. The vital year in which this policy began to take shape was 1956. The Hungarian revolution of that year revealed the fragility of communist rule that relied mainly on Soviet power against a hostile population.[43] Romania had proven especially helpful in quelling the uprising. Two years later, as a sign of trust in a reliable ally, Soviet troops were withdrawn from Romania.[44] But, starting in the early 1960s, Romania began to champion the principle of non-interference by Moscow in the affairs of other communist states, and it refused to take Moscow's side in the escalating Sino-Soviet split. Khrushchev's attempt to turn Romania into a cheap supplier of agricultural produce for the Comecon zone was repulsed and the leadership decided that the only way to defend their hegemony was to opt for rapid industrialisation, with an emphasis on heavy industry.[45] So Romania's decision to promote national values and economic self-sufficiency stemmed from a desire by its rulers to defy pressure from whatever source to lift totalitarian controls.

Communist Romania's bid to achieve autonomy from Moscow was accomplished by a series of small steps and calculated moves.[46] The boldest moves were undertaken in relation to cultural life. Russian and Soviet interpretations of Romanian history were abandoned in the early 1960s. A return to national traditions and even some cultural contacts with the west were permitted. Great figures of the Romanian past were rehabilitated to one degree or another: Iorga in history, Brancusi in sculpture, Blaga in philosophy, even Goga in poetry, and Titulescu in diplomacy. The plays of Eugène Ionesco began to be staged in Bucharest as the works of a great

Romanian playwright.[47] At least owing to their economic nationalism, the pre-war Liberals were rehabilitated and the noted historian, Constantin C. Giurescu, minister of information in Carol II's dictatorship and imprisoned for years by the communists, was allowed to resume his career.[48]

In redefining itself as the leading patriotic and nationalist force in the country, the RWP was seeking to bury its earlier image of being not only un-Romanian but anti-Romanian.[49] By 1966, the pre-war party's stance of referring to Romania as a 'typical multinational state', created on the basis of 'occupation of foreign territories' was repudiated.[50] Besides appropriating the legacy of past cultural giants, an easy way to demonstrate patriotism was to show that the RWP was no longer biased *towards* ethnic minorities regarded as antagonistic to national values. From the second half of the 1950s, Jews were permitted to emigrate to Israel so that by the late 1980s, the Jewish community that had been a problematic as well as a creative element in Romanian life numbered only a few tens of thousands of people.[51] Many communist officials of Jewish descent also participated in this emigration, rendering the Romanisation of the RWP easier to accomplish. But it was the curtailment of various measures of autonomy to the Hungarians which was perhaps the clearest sign of the party's readiness to court nationalism.

It is worth recalling that the post-1945 minority policy had been imposed by the Soviet Union. Its involuntary nature and the fact that it occurred against a background of assaults on Romania's national heritage reduced the likelihood of a proper historic reconciliation, comparable to the burying of Franco-German enmity over Alsace-Lorraine.[52] Authoritarian regimes are rarely capable of overcoming inter-state or communal tensions of this kind, and their rulers often prefer to keep them alive so as to make opposition seem unpatriotic and therefore reduce challenges to their rule. So it proved in Romania.

Gheorghiu-Dej's motives for curtailing minority group rights were not necessarily shared by those in the population with strong views on the Hungarian question. In the party's eyes, cultural and political autonomy (even of the limited kind enjoyed by the HAR) simply did not go together with the political standardisation which the RWP required in areas of public life. Moreover, the solidarity shown by Hungarians in Transylvania to the 1956 uprising in Budapest caused alarm in the RWP.[53] There were Romanians who risked their lives by identifying with this anti-communist revolt, and there were no shortage of Hungarian RWP cadres prepared to cross into Hungary to restore the authority of the party, so Romanian reactions to the Hungarian events should not be viewed in simplistic terms. Nevertheless, it is clear that leaders wedded to centralism viewed as a troubling anomoly the autonomy enjoyed by a minority whose co-ethnics across the border had engaged in a bloody insurrection. The merging of Hungarian with Romanian schools, already under way before 1956, was stepped up after that year.[54] The apex of the Hungarian educational structure itself was chopped down in 1959 when the Bolyai university was summarily amalgamated with its Romanian counterpart, the Babes university.[55] The secretary of the RWP central committee, Nicolae Ceauşescu, was sent to Cluj to enforce the decision. A series of meetings was organised urging the intensification of Romanian-Hungarian brotherhood and the condemnation of hostile and unsound attitudes.

After 1989, the reconstitution of Bolyai university was a key demand of politically-active Hungarians. They argued that the merger had resulted in the systematic erosion of Hungarian-language teaching in higher education and that what remained on paper was a Byzantine device to fool the outside world that equal treatment was continuing.[56] However, the circumstances in which the minority had acquired cultural autonomy meant that most ethnic Romanians were unlikely to see it that way; unfortunately, the only government in Romanian history which permitted the Hungarian minority to view itself as a 'co-inhabiting nationality', deserving of its own cultural institutions, was one most lacking in popular legitimacy in Romanian eyes.

The enforced university merger in Cluj proved to be a staging-post in the rise of Nicolae Ceauşescu, who succeeded Gheorghiu-Dej as Romania's leader upon the latter's death in March 1965.[57] Ceauşescu was an ambitious and energetic communist of peasant background who had been a party member since the 1930s. In 1965, sixty-four per cent of party members were under forty years of age, while ninety-nine per cent had entered the party after 1945.[58] It was Ceauşescu who had moulded a party of career-orientated workers of peasant background, overwhelmingly Romanian in composition, while in charge of party organisation in the early 1960s. From the outset, it was clear that nationalism was to be encouraged because it was seen as a way of motivating people to carry out party policy.[59] Already in April 1964, the party's central committee had issued a ringing declaration of independence from Moscow which the new leader was intent on building upon. It asserted that no centre is authorised to issue instructions to other parties, to depose or install party leaderships, to excommunicate or liquidate whole parties, or to determine what is sound doctrine. Every party enjoying power was entitled to decide for itself how to reach socialism.[60]

The cautious liberalisation and de-Russification of cultural life witnessed at the end of the Gheorghiu-Dej era was stepped up. There were even signs that Ceauşescu might be ready to emulate the communist model of Tito's Yugoslavia in which an autonomous foreign policy was matched by internal reform, greater contact with the outside world, and efforts to encourage solidarity between different ethnic groups. Ceauşescu's image as a reform-minded Marxist ruler received a tremendous boost through his defiance of the Soviet Union in August 1968 when the latter sent in Warsaw Pact forces to crush the Czechoslovak experiment in pluralist communism. But little-noticed at the time was the fact that Ceauşescu had never endorsed 'the Prague spring' nor stated that it was worthy of emulation in his own country. His quarrel with the Soviets stemmed from their readiness to use force to determine how fraternal countries should order their internal affairs. Ceauşescu the nationalist rather than Ceauşescu the embryonic democrat had been galvanised into taking a stand.

The RWP realised more clearly than its non-communist predecessors that nationalism generates power and legitimises those who don its mantle. Through imposing the power of the state down to the most remote village and utilising mass communications to project the view that the party was completing the age-old struggle for Romanian independence, the RWP was able to acquire an unprecedented hold over the minds of many citizens.

The RWP was renamed the Romanian Communist Party in 1965. New party statutes released in May abandoned all reference to the 1917 Russian revolution or to the fatherland of the proletariat, hitherto the ultimate source of legitimacy for all communist regimes. It was expressly stated that it was the patriotic duty of all party members to defend the fatherland and its frontiers.[61] At the July 1965 party congress, a further reassessment occurred. The leading role was transferred from the working class to the socialist nation, causing one authority to remark that instead of Lenin's exhortation that communists should establish a society that is 'national in form and socialist in content', the Romanians had opted for a society that is 'socialist in form and nationalist in content'.[62] Henceforth the Romanian nation was at the centre of all major pronouncements, Ceauşescu arguing that the nation was 'an irreducible element of international life with its own character and autonomous essence'.[63] Article 2 of the new 1965 constitution referred to the minorities as 'resident nationalities', the term 'resident' implying to one observer that 'the nationalities have no fundamental right to be considered fully-fledged Romanians but are merely tolerated'.[64] Another observer, writing in 1966, was already convinced that it was Bucharest's intention to assimilate the Hungarians 'by quiet but unrelenting pressure'.[65]

In 1968, the Hungarian Autonomous Region (greatly diluted by administrative changes in 1960) was abolished completely.[66] The process of treating the minority as a distinct entity was at an end.[67] In 1972, Ceauşescu proclaimed that 'each co-existing nationality will for a long period keep its characteristic traits' but he went on to add that 'we have to work without pause for the goal of social and national homogenisation in our country'.[68] The regime's increasing determination to create 'one working people' that was alike in all essential aspects was an ill omen for the minorities as well as for the Romanian people as a whole. The state showed itself intent on socialising the people into a new set of loyalties while severing older, often very deeply-rooted, attachments.[69] The obsession with heavy industry, the demolition of historic town centres culminating in the razing of much of old Bucharest in the 1980s, the gearing of the education system around preparing young people for industrial tasks, and the plan to relocate or 'systematise' much of the rural population in 'agro-industrial' complexes are well-known outcomes of this totalitarian vision.

CEAUŞESCU MOBILISES THE PAST

The emphasis on homogenising the population and reducing social differences emerged after Ceauşescu had transferred power from the party to himself and a personal retinue dominated by his wife. The past was then interpreted to justify this personal dictatorship; history was seen as a process leading to the triumph of a higher form of society being installed by the *Conducator* (the Romanian word for 'Leader', officially adopted by Ceauşescu in the 1970s). Ceauşescu was described as the practical reincarnation of all ancestral bravery and wisdom from the Dacian kings onwards to Romania's feudal princes and the more recent fighters for national independence: by continuing the independence struggle he was fulfilling their historic mission and writing new pages of historic greatness that would be seen as such long into the future.[70]

To turn history into an arm of state policy, a decree was issued in 1974 which declared that 'those historical art treasures produced over the course of thousands of years on Romanian soil as a result of literary and artistic creativity and scientific and technical research' were to be part of the Romanian national heritage and therefore state property.[71] The archive, manuscript collection and libraries of the Transylvanian Hungarian and Saxon towns were commandeered by the state. Between 1971 and 1975, the State Archives forced some parishes to hand over their ecclesiastical and secular historical documents along with registers of births, marriages and deaths, some of which dated from the sixteenth and seventeenth centuries. A refusal to comply was punishable by law but, without access to such materials Transylvanian historical scholarship became increasingly difficult. The aim, according to one source, was to deprive the minorities of the documents of their own past which could still act as a source of national consciousness.[72]

Romania was not the only eastern European country where some form of historic legitimacy was looked for beyond Marxism, but East German communist attempts to link the regime with Martin Luther and the Reformation and Bulgaria's bid to revive memories of a seventh-century Bulgarian empire paled into insignificance compared to what happened under Ceauşescu. In 1980, Romania announced the 2050th anniversary of 'the first centralised and independent Dacian State'. In 1988, the commemoration of the seventieth anniversary of Romanian unification was seen as 'the embodiment of historical law' which 'owed nothing to agreements reached around the negotiating table'.[73] Even the much disputed Vlad Tepes (Vlad the Impaler), who was the prototype of Bram Stoker's Dracula, was reappraised as a progressive prince who followed a foreign policy similar to that pursued by the RCP.[74]

At the 1974 ceremony in which Ceauşescu was inaugurated as President, he was shown carrying a sceptre dating back to Vlad the Impaler's time. The leader was seeking a mystic populist appeal based on historic symbols stretching from the regal to the revolutionary. The ruler's appropriation of history may have reached its climax in 1986. In the weekly *Contemporanul*, of 18 July, the poet Victor Tulbare exalted in verse Ceauşescu's spiritual kinship with Horea, the leader of the 1784 Transylvanian peasant uprising; Stephen the Great, Prince of Moldavia (1457–1504); Nicolae Balcescu, leader of the 1848 revolution in Wallachia; Prince Dimitrie Cantemir of Moldavia (1710–11); Mihai Eminescu (1850–89), Romania's national poet; and Prince Michael the Brave (1593–1601), who briefly unified for the first time the principalities of Wallachia, Moldavia and Transylvania under his personal rule.

> He [Ceauşescu] descends from Horea's bones, from Stefan's breath
> From Balcescu's light and from Cantemir's thought;
> He is a dream out of Eminescu's dreams, and he descends from that
>   Michael who
> Wanted a sole abode for his people under eternal stars.[75]

George Kennan, the veteran American diplomat, wrote in 1967 that 'there is today no such thing as 'communism' in the sense that there was in 1947; there are only a number of national regimes which cloak themselves in the verbal trappings of radical Marxism and follow domestic politics influenced to one degree or another by Marxian concepts'. Ceauşescu's economic goals and his desire to bury society under a totalitarian edifice, were clear examples of Marxism-Leninism at its most doctrinaire, but the national symbols and rituals were acquired from different sources, both indigenous and external. The Byzantine tradition, with its emphasis upon compliance with dogma and orthodoxy as laid down by powerful rulers, should not be overlooked.[76] The radical right-wing movements of inter-war Europe also proved a rich seam to mine. It is no coincidence that the writers behind the most flagrant aspects of nationalist myth-making in the 1980s, re-emerged in the 1990s as unabashed promoters of the anti-Semitism and conspiracy theories associated with 1930s Romanian fascism. Any Italian or German visitor to Romania, able to recall the style of fascism in their own countries, would have seen some striking parallels. Ceauşescu, like fascist leaders before him, stressed the absolute precedence of the national community over the individual and the need for a ruthless and disciplined vanguard to take action on its behalf. Mussolini's 1932 essay on the role of the state would have fitted quite neatly into Ceauşescu's own vision of it:

> The State . . . makes [citizens] aware of their mission, urges them to unity; its justice harmonises their different interests . . . The State hands down to future generations the memory of those who laid down their lives to ensure its safety or to obey its laws; it sets up as examples and records for future ages the names of captains who enlarged its territory and of the men of genius who made it famous. Whenever respect for the State declines and the disintegrating and centrifugal tendencies of individuals and groups prevail, nations are heading for decay . . .[77]

Inter-war Romania produced an original fascist theoretician called Mihail Manoilescu whose thinking on the need for a strong autarkic state imposing its will on society through rapid industrialisation and an undemo-cratic corporate state came to fruition more obviously in Ceauşescu's time than in that of Carol or Antonescu.[78] Ceauşescu's Romania, like the major fascist states before it, stressed the existence of potential enemies and a host of undefined dangers. Only the unification of the people around the *Conducator* 'could forestall enemy forces, be they neighbours plotting to infringe on Romania's territorial integrity or more distant powers who have 'no business' in interfering in Romania's affairs'.[79]

Ceauşescu's leadership style stressed the organic links between citizens and their ruler, aligned against 'others' be they ungrateful minorities or neighbouring states.[80] Family, local and religious loyalties needed to be discarded so that they did not get in the way of the higher necessity to defend the state and its historic mission. Ceauşescu's role as the historic embodiment of the nation's greatness was regularly commemorated at 'Cîintarea României' (Song to Romania) festivals in the 1980s at which actors dressed as figures from history offered Ceauşescu bread and salt and anointed him as their successor.[81] If Ceauşescu had observed certain restraints in the promotion of his personality cult, it is possible that he could have retained at least a limited popular base for his regime. Economic improvements and defiance of the Soviet Union had brought genuine popularity in the 1960s. According to the well-placed dissident, Sylviu Brucan, the regime 'enjoyed stability so long as the 'unwritten social contract' between the Communist Party and the working class was strictly observed', one that 'assumed the party's obligation to ensure workers a decent standard of living'.[82] There was no familiarity with, or ready acceptance of, opposition party politics among the social groups created by the communist state, as the first post-communist election of May 1990 showed only too clearly. Many citizens were far more comfortable with a paternalistic state that directed society from above and protected national security.

The new working class that became the dominant social formation in Romania as a result of the breakneck industrialisation that reduced rural overpopulation was a product of the Marxist-Leninist state and had no earlier traditions to draw on. Industrial production was expanding faster than most other Warsaw Pact states in the decades after 1965, due in large part to the determination to create a society receptive to national Stalinist indoctrination.[83] But Ceauşescu frittered away the advantages that made Romania a relatively easy state to control, one facing few of the popular challenges that had shaken communist rule elsewhere. His ambition to turn Romania into a powerful industrial state that was a force in international relations eventually collapsed in the 1980s. The nature of the regime, with its emphasis on obsolete heavy industry and resistance to any information or views that questioned its dogmatic truths, precluded successful modernisation. Mihai Botez, an exiled social scientist, wrote that 'it lacks the ability to identify real needs and rational goals, perpetrating instead a fantasy world, and it is subject to a higher probability of error than other Communist regimes'.[84]

Romania was reduced to being a closed society, subject to intense repression, international isolation, and cultural decline. Ceauşescu's determination not only to service the interest of, but also quickly to pay off, large foreign debts in order to demonstrate his independence, caused untold suffering for his people. As the economy foundered and living standards fell, the state was ever more reluctant to tolerate unsupervised individual behaviour and keen to assert its leading role. Its totalitarian aims had been clearly set out in 1975 when 'multi-lateral development' was proclaimed as state policy. Its primary objectives were: the unification of a diverse population into 'one working people'; the reduction and elimination of disparities in economic development between the various regions; the elimination of differences in living standards and life-styles between city and countryside; and the achievement of equal occupational opportunity.[85] Henceforth there was no corner of society in which the state could not interfere. Thus, in 1986, Ceauşescu proclaimed the foetus 'the socialist property of the whole society. Giving birth is a patriotic duty . . . Those who refuse to have children are deserters, escaping the law of natural continuity'.[86] The military language was appropriate: drastic means were used to prevent abortions or the use of contraception, women being subject to compulsory gynaecological examinations at workplaces and police stations. International horror greeted the barbaric way in which the state sought to regulate the most intimate aspects of personal behaviour.

The other aspect of state policy which created a stir abroad was the treatment of the Hungarian minority by the regime. Reports of measures being taken to rob the minority of its cultural identity, isolate it from any contacts in Hungary, and disperse economically-active Hungarians beyond Transylvania reached the west in the 1980s. Some of these were exaggerated as when it was implied that Hungarian villages were being systematically demolished, but enough could be substantiated to provoke indignation over the fate of a group whose defenders proclaimed it to be the largest stateless minority in the whole of Europe.[87]

An ethnic group which obstinately clung to a language and culture whose promoters in earlier centuries had, according to official propaganda, brought misery and hardship to ethnic Romanians, was bound to feel exposed. Hungarian education was pushed to the fringes of the state curriculum as Ceauşescu applauded the fidelity of the Romanians for standing by *their* language and culture in the midst of foreign domination, his speeches clearly suggesting that such staying power was only possible for a superior culture and language.[88]

Ceauşescu refused to recognise the Hungarians (and indeed other minorities) as belonging to other nations. He claimed that because a nation had been created by centuries of 'living together', Hungarians, Germans and other groups were part of the Romanian nation.[89] Therefore, special measures to preserve their cultural identity were unnecessary, especially since state policy after 1975 was wedded to the goal of 'social and national homogenisation'.

The policy of reducing Hungarian education was stepped up in the 1970s; Hungarian schools were systematically attached to Romanian schools as mere sections which, in turn, were gradually phased out.[90] By the 1980s, Hungarian graduates were being routinely assigned to jobs in regions remote from their own ethnic communities. A 1984 ministry of education internal directive required all enrolling students to sign a 'contract' obliging them to accept whatever position the government 'guarantees' them after graduation.[91] Obviously, the dispersal of young professionals denied the Hungarian community the services of people who could act as leaders and spokesmen for its interests. Isolation from the outside world also weakened its cohesion: since 1974, decree law 224 had made it illegal to accommodate friends and relations from abroad in private houses unless they were immediate family. Of Romania's ethnic groups, Hungarians were by far the likeliest to have relatives abroad and they were obviously the most affected. Decree law 408, issued in 1986, prohibited even the holding of conversations with foreign visitors in private homes. The screw was then greatly tightened during what remained of the 1980s. In 1987, a ban on importing publications from Hungary was publicly imposed (though unofficially long in effect). By that year, the use of minority languages had been discontinued in all official communications, including court proceedings. From 1988, parents were actively forbidden to give their children any name that could not be translated into Romanian. From 1989, all place-names cited in newspapers, even those of the minorities, could be written only in the Romanian version.[92]

Owing to the way in which the government manipulated past injustices committed by Hungarians on Romanians, mutually antagonistic images were revived. In 1986, a book was published which revived memories of wartime suffering experienced by Romanians at the hands of Hungarians. *Horthyist Fascist Terror in North-Western Romania, September 1940–October 1944* provided statistical information on the repression carried out by occupying Hungarian forces in minute detail. For each county, an inventory of murders, tortures, beatings, arrests and desecrations of churches was provided.[93] The publication in 1986 by the Hungarian Academy of Sciences of a three-volume *History of Transylvania* produced a furious reaction from Bucharest. The initiative was attacked as 'unscientific' and 'nationalistic' even though it did not 'really try to disprove the theory of Daco-Roman continuity' and was critical of the Magyarisation policy of the Hungarian government before 1918.[94]

Inter-state relations suffered as Hungary slowly abandoned the line rigorously maintained by its post-1956 ruler, Janos Kadar, of not raising the treatment of its co-nationals in neighbouring states. On 27 June 1988, at least 40,000 people marched on the Romanian embassy in Budapest in protest at plans to demolish thousands of villages in Romania. This was the largest demonstration seen in Hungary since 1956 and it had the tacit approval of the authorities who, in a volte-face, were seeking to generate popularity by identifying with public concerns about the fate of Transylvanian Hungarians.[95] Romania responded by immediately closing down the Hungarian consulate in Cluj.

Long after the autonomy guarantees provided in 1945 began to be dismantled, Hungarians had tried to accommodate themselves to Romanian realities. In 1978, P. Boder, a television editor, had declared at a meeting of the Council of the Working People of Magyar Nationality that

the Hungarians in Romania love their homeland. The Hungarians in
Romania are patriots of this country. We have never played truant or
shirked responsibility either in history or in revolution – or in work either.
The leadership of the party and country may rely on us; the Romanian
nation may have full confidence in us . . .[96]

However, Boder found it impossible to live a Hungarian life in Romania
and, by the 1980s, along with thousands of other Hungarian-speakers, he
had resettled in Hungary. By now, the prospect of living under an internationalist regime in which cultivation of a Transylvanian identity would
not be incompatible with membership of a communist commonwealth of
nations had been shattered. Transylvanianism was regarded as a dangerous
concept that questioned the unity and integrity of the Romanian nation.
A common Transylvanian identity, even though it was composed of
different elements, meant that indeterminate numbers of Romanians and
Hungarians felt stronger affinity to Transylvania than to people of their
own speech from centres of power on the edges of the region.[97] Possession
of such a sub-state loyalty was undoubtedly stronger among Hungarians
than Romanians whose institutions standing for a Transylvanian outlook
– the Uniate Church and the *NPP* – had been swept away after 1946. But
the challenge posed by Transylvania to a regime intent on homogenising
the entire population helps to explain the relocation of migrants from the
Regat and outlying parts of Transylvania to the major cities of the province.
Within a relatively short period in the 1970s and 1980s, the demographic
profile of cities like Tirgu Mureş, Cluj and Oradea, ones that had been
strongly Hungarian in character, began to be altered. The demolition of
Hungarian districts to make way for high-rise flats to accommodate the
newcomers was described by Hungarian dissidents as a covert form of the
'systematisation' policy.

   In the early 1980s, the threat to the preservation of Hungarian identity
had produced a dissident movement among Transylvanian Hungarian
intellectuals. Nine issues of a *samizdat*, or underground magazine, called
Ellenpontok (Counterpoints) were produced.[98] Its authors sought to defend Hungarian culture by appealing to the doctrine of human rights
in the light of the fact that Romania had signed the 1975 Helsinki
accords with their strong human rights safeguards. Arrests and beatings followed before most of the dissidents were expelled to Hungary.
But a New York-based Hungarian Human Rights Foundation, formed
in 1976, was able to monitor state policy towards the Hungarian minority down to a minute level which showed that the ability of the
totalitarian state to screen Romania off from the outside world had its
limits.[99]

   Generally, the Hungarian intellectuals who condemned infringements of minority rights declined to protest about forms of oppression that enveloped the entire population.[100] Such introspection would continue after 1989, hampering efforts to create durable alliances among exponents of democracy.

One Romanian dissident with a broader vision was Mrs Doina Cornea, a lecturer in French at Cluj who, in 1982, began smuggling letters to Radio Free Europe, describing the awful state to which Ceauşescu had reduced the country. The Securitate, or secret police, were soon able to trace the letters back to their author, and in 1983 her university superiors terminated her employment without any voice being raised in her support. But she continued to smuggle out letters on themes such as truth, the need for a spiritual renaissance, inter-ethnic relations, and on the role of youth. She expressed solidarity with the workers in the city of Brasov who had staged a revolt in 1987, and she also condemned the policy of systematisation: on both sides of her family, Doina Cornea's grandparents had been peasants. She argued in her letter that the rural world of villages and small settlements was an inalienable part of the Romanian heritage which was given in trust to each generation. Her letter, written in July 1988, was signed by fifteen other Cluj residents. This was just one of several addressed directly to Ceauşescu, and such impertinence led to her being placed under house arrest from 1987 to 1989, the Securitate being reluctant to take more drastic action given the prominence she had acquired.

Besides, the secret police could find no evidence that Cornea's gesture had struck a chord with the wider community in Cluj. Most people's lives centred around queuing to acquire the minuscule food ration or else devising means to obtain food from the private holdings in land unsuited for collectivisation where they might have a relative or friend. One month before Mrs Cornea's letter on systematisation was written, the monthly food ration for each adult in Cluj was 750g of sugar, 0.5l of cooking oil, 2kg of potatoes, 0.5kg of wheat flour and 1kg of macaroni. Bread was rationed to 300g per day, but meat and dairy products were not formally rationed since there was nothing to ration.[101]

Nicolae Ceauşescu was swept from power in the final days of 1989 following mass demonstrations in Timisoara and Bucharest that provided an opportunity for party and military officials to move against him. There was no difficulty in understanding why ordinary citizens pushed beyond endurance had taken to the streets, but the motives which high state officials had for deserting Ceauşescu are more complex and evoked mounting controversy, as continuity with the past was seen to be an important element of the new political order. The violence of the change-over led to over 1,000 deaths as loyalists in the security forces mounted fierce resistance. This was all in marked contrast to the peaceful collapse of communist power witnessed in other Warsaw Pact states during the last months of 1989. Ceauşescu railed against foreign conspiracies on 21 December but, while no evidence has been found to back up this typical claim, it is clear that external events – as in each of the major turning-points of Romanian history after 1900 – played a contributory role in securing a change of regime.

The reform course launched by Mikhail Gorbachev in the Soviet Union after 1985 helped to determine the fate of the Romanian tyranny. It indirectly highlighted Romania's isolation, Ceauşescu emerging as the most vocal opponent of reform in the Soviet bloc. His fate was perhaps sealed by the effective abandonment of the Brezhnev doctrine in the late 1980s: henceforth the USSR was not prepared to intervene to prop up threatened communist regimes. Ironically, a regime which had enjoyed misplaced regard in the west because of the autonomy it had acquired from Moscow in the 1960s became doomed as soon as Moscow allowed the same degree of autonomy, and more, to other Soviet bloc states.

A beleaguered Ceauşescu was no longer able to invoke nationalism to demand fresh sacrifices or insist upon discipline from his subjects. The fall of the regime produced an exhilarating moment when the authentic voice of freedom-loving Romanians could be heard calling for 'libertate'. But it had taken a huge effort of will for tens of thousands of people to defy a dictatorship that showed itself capable of great viciousness when cornered. Civil society was weak or non-existent, since unsupervised group behaviour had been disallowed. None of the religious or civic institutions which had facilitated the re-emergence of democracy in other dictatorial European states from Spain to Poland existed in Romania.

How to create a workable democracy when a totalitarian party had monopolised all public space for nearly fifty years was bound to be a huge problem. The communist state had confiscated private property, instituted the state ownership of the economy, obliterated the market and monopolised employment. Independent social organisations were not tolerated, not even autonomous churches. The principle of the unity of political power was insisted upon. It was difficult to see how such a legacy could be erased, and soon many Romanians could be found who were prepared to say that they would be old men or women before the system had been decisively broken.

How to replace politics based on ethnic identity with a representative democracy based on a civic state would prove even more of a challenge. The impact of xenophobic communism could not be lightly erased. Nor could the tradition of dominance of the collective over the individual or of state over society which, in some respects, was already in place in Romania before the arrival of communism.

To some, it was an ill omen when Ceaușescu, his wife and a few aides were blamed for the faults of an entire system, the presidential couple being swiftly executed on Christmas Day 1989. But it would not prove so easy to erase his influence. The ex-communists of the hastily-formed National Salvation Front, which in the closing days of 1989 filled the power vacuum and assumed governmental responsibilities, had acquired their political training during the era of national communism. Like Ceaușescu, they had seen how nationalism could be used to extract obedience and delegitimise opposition. In the difficult period of readjustment that lay ahead, it was asking a lot to assume that rulers whose actions showed them to be reluctant democrats in certain respects would resist the nationalist temptation.

NOTES

1. Joseph Rothschild, *East-Central Europe between the Two World Wars*, University of Washington Press, Washington DC 1974.
2. Laszlo Kurti, 'Transylvania, Land Beyond Reason: Toward An Anthropological Analysis of a Contested Terrain', *Dialectical Anthropology*, 14 (1989), p. 29; Robert Lee Wolff, *The Balkans in Our Time*, Harvard University Press, Cambridge MA 1974, p. 43.
3. Ion Ardealanu et al., *Horthyist Fascist Terror in North-Western Romania*, September 1940–October 1944, Meridiane Publishing House, Bucharest 1986, p. 169.
4. See Alexandre Safran, *Resisting The Storm: Romania, 1940–47: Memoirs*, (ed ited and annotated by Jean Ancel), Yad Vashem, Jerusalem 1987.
5. Safran, *Resisting the Storm*, pp. 67–8.
6. Ibid., p. 78.
7. Radu Ioanid, *22* (Bucharest), 9 February, 1994.
8. Safran, *Resisting the Storm*, p. 28.
9. Ibid., p. 27.
10. H. Seton-Watson, *The East European Revolution* (3rd edition), Methuen, London, 1961, p. 87.
11. H. Seton-Watson, *Nations and States*, p. 182.
12. H. Seton-Watson, *The East European Revolution*, p. 89.
13. Hitchins, *Rumania . . .*, pp. 473, 475, 504.
14. Chapters 11 and 12 of Reuben H. Markham, *Rumania Under the Soviet Yoke*, Meador, Boston MA 1949, profile both the king and Maniu and describe the standing in which they were held at home in the mid-1940s.
15. Marin Nedelea, *Prim-Ministrii României-Mari*, Viața Românea̧sca, Bucharest 1991, p. 80.
16. R. R. King, *Minorities Under Communism: Nationalities as a Source of Tension among Balkan Communist States*, Harvard University Press, Cambridge MA 1973, pp. 74–5.
17. R. V. Burks, 'The Rumanian National Deviation: An Accounting', in Kurt London (ed.), *Eastern Europe in Transition*, Johns Hopkins University Press, Baltimore MD 1967, p. 99.
18. For an ethnic breakdown of the RCP's limited membership, see Graham, op.

cit., pp. 30–1 and Michael Shafir, *Romania, Politics, Economics and Society*, Pinter/Reinner, London and Boulder CO 1985, pp. 25–7; Burks, op. cit., p. 95, claims that the party had a mere 884 members in 1944.

19. D. Chirot, 'Social Change in Communist Romania', *Social Forces*, Vol. 57, No. 2 (1978), p. 460.

20. Ibid.

21. Ultra-nationalists, keen to place many charges at the door of Transylvanian Hungarians, have so far not made this one.

22. H. Seton-Watson, *The East European Revolution*, p. 203.

23. King, *Minorities Under Communism*, p. 41.

24. H. Seton-Watson, *Nationalism and Communism*, Camelot Press, London 1964, p. 103.

25. Stephen Borsody, *The New Central Europe: Triumphs and Tragedies*, East European Monographs, Boulder CO 1993, pp.178–9; King, op. cit., p. 40.

26. J. F. Brown, *Nationalism, Democracy and Security in the Balkans*, Rand Books, Santa Monica CA 1992, pp. 101–2.

27. Markham, op. cit., pp. 214–17, cites claims that Groza's wealth was acquired by dubious means when he joined the People's Party which was in government briefly in the early 1920s.

28. Joseph Rothschild, *Return to Diversity: A Political History of East-Central Europe since World War II*, Oxford University Press, New York and Oxford 1989, p. 109.

29. Vladimir Tismaneanu, 'Ceauşescu's Socialism', *Problems of Communism*, January–February 1985, p. 86.

30. Robert Lee Wolff, *The Balkans In Our Time*, p. 45.

31. Vasile Vese, 'The Advance of Communism in Romania – A Case Study of the City of Cluj', paper presented at the University of London, 28 April 1994. Nationally, Maniu's party was given only thirty-two of 432 seats in parliament, 366 going to the ruling bloc. Markham, op. cit., p. 393.

32. For collaboration of the Orthodox Church with the communist state, see Shafir, *Romania*, pp. 151–3.

33. A full account of the suppression of the Uniate church is contained in the monthly journal of the restored Uniates, Viaţa Crestina, Vol. 4, No. 20 (90), October 1993.

34. See Michael J. Rura, *Reinterpretation of History as a Method of Furthering Communism in Rumania*, Georgetown University Press, Washington DC 1961, passim.

35. Chirot, op. cit., p. 489.

36. See Georges Castellan, 'The Germans of Rumania', *Journal of Contemporary History*, Vol. 6, No. 1, (1971).

37. Castellan, op. cit., p. 71.

38. Claude Karnoouh, *L'Invention du Peuple, Chroniques de Roumanie*, Editions Arcantère, Paris 1990, p. 32.

39. Tismaneanu, 'Ceauşescu's Socialism'.

40. Vladimir Tismaneanu, *Reinventing Politics: Eastern Europe from Stalin to Havel*, The Free Press, New York 1992, p. 84.

41. Burks, op. cit., p. 102.

42. Tismaneanu, *Reinventing Politics*, p. 45.

43. R. R. King, *The Romanian Communist Party*, Hoover Institution Press, Stanford, CA 1980, p. 130.

44. Brucan's explanation of why this happened provides detail not found elsewhere. See Sylviu Brucan, *The Wasted Generation: Memoirs of the Romanian Journey from Capitalism to Socialism and Back*, Westview Press, Boulder CO 1993, pp. 55–6.
45. See J. M. Montias, *Economic Development in Communist Rumania*, MIT Press, Cambridge MA and London 1967, pp. 38–96.
46. P. Lendvai, *Eagles in Cobwebs: Nationalism and Communism in the Balkans*, Macdonald, London 1970, p. 294.
47. Burks, op. cit., p. 105.
48. See Paul E. Michelson, 'The Master of Synthesis: Constantin C. Giurescu and the Coming of Age of Romanian Historiography, 1919–1947', in Stephen Fischer-Galati (ed.), *Romania Between East and West*, Columbia University Press (East European Monographs Series), Boulder CO and New York 1982.
49. Lendvai, op. cit., p. 280.
50. King, *Romanian Communist Party*, p. 123.
51. King, op. cit., p. 133.
52. G. Schöpflin, 'Rumanian Nationalism', *Survey*, Vol. 20 (Spring-Summer 1974), p. 100.
53. Mary Ellen Fischer, *Nicolae Ceauşescu: A Study in Political Leadership*, Reinner, Boulder CO 1989, pp. 57–8.
54. King, op. cit., p. 130.
55. Details in Adam T. Szábo, 'A Hungarian University in Transylvania', *New Hungarian Quarterly*, No. 123 (Autumn 1991), p. 160; and Shafir, *Romania*, p. 160.
56. Details in *Arguments in Favour of Reviving Hungarian Higher Education in Romania*, The Bolyai Society, Kolozsvar 1991.
57. For Ceauşescu's background, see Fischer, op. cit., chapters 1 and 2.
58. Burks, op. cit., p. 103.
59. King, *Romanian Communist Party*, p. 127.
60. Burks, op. cit., p. 104.
61. Ibid., p. 105.
62. Schöpflin, 'Rumanian Nationalism', p. 92.
63. Ibid., p. 94.
64. G. Schöpflin, 'National Minorities under Communism in Eastern Europe', in Kurt London (ed.), *Eastern Europe in Transition*, Johns Hopkins University Press MA 1967, p. 131.
65. Burks, op. cit., p. 106.
66. Fischer, op. cit., pp. 112–13.
67. Burks, op. cit., pp. 102–3.
68. Pippidi, op. cit., pp. 136–7.
69. Schöpflin, *Politics in Eastern Europe*, Blackwell, Oxford 1993, p. 95.
70. A description of how the profession of history was turned into a propaganda arm of the dictator is provided by Vlad Georgescu, *Politică Şi Istorie*, Humanitas, Bucharest 1991.
71. Illyes, op. cit., p. 142.
72. Ibid., p. 144.
73. *România Liberă*, 16 November 1988, quoted in Mihai Sturdza, 'Distortions Mark 70th Anniversary of Romanian Unification', *Radio Free Europe Research*, Vol. 13, No. 52 (30 December 1988), p. 18.

74. See George Cioranescu, 'Vlad the Impaler – Current Parallels with a Medieval Romanian Prince', *Radio Free Europe Research*, Vol. 2, No. 5 (31 January 1977).

75. Dan Ionescu, 'Rewriting History', *Radio Free Europe Research*, Vol. 13, No. 38 (19 September 1988), pp. 20–1.

76. See Andrei Brezianu in *Romania: A Case of Dynastic Communism*, Freedom House, New York 1989, p. 9.

77. Quoted in Kohn, *Nationalism*, p. 174.

78. Chirot, 'Social Change . . .', p. 493; Philippe C. Schmitter, 'Reflections on Mihail Manoilescu and the Political Consequences of Delayed Development on the Periphery of Western Europe', in K. Jowitt (ed.), *Social Change in Romania, 1860–1940*, California University Press, Berkeley CA 1977, pp. 72–117.

79. Sturdza, 'Distortions . . .', p. 19.

80. Gilberg, *Nationalism and Communism*, p. 11.

81. See Anca Giurchescu, 'The National Festival "Song to Romania": Manipulation of Symbols in the Political Discourse', in C. Arvidsson and L. Blomqvist, (eds), *Symbols of Power*, Almqvist & Wiskell, Stockholm 1987; and Francisco Veiga, *Els Balcans: La desfeta d'in somni*, Eumo Editorial, Girona 1993, p. 59.

82. Brucan, op. cit., pp. 126–7.

83. Chirot, 'Social Change . . .', p. 471.

84. Georgescu, *A History . . .*, p. 273.

85. Sam Beck and Marilyn McArthur, 'Ethnicity, Nationalism and Development', in Sam Beck and John W. Cole, *Ethnicity and Nationalism in South Eastern Europe*, University of Amsterdam, Amsterdam 1981, pp. 53–4.

86. Doina Pasca-Harsanyi, 'Women in Romania', in N. Funk and M. Mueller (eds), *Gender Politics and Post-Communism: Reflections from Eastern Europe and the Former Soviet Union*, Routledge, London 1993, p. 46.

87. The most sober and well-documented account in English of the Hungarians' position in the Romania of the 1980s is Schopflin and Poulton, *Romania's Ethnic Hungarians*, Minority Rights Group, London 1991.

88. Trond Gilberg, 'State Policy, Ethnic Persistence and Nationality Formation in Eastern Europe', in Peter Sugar (ed.), *Ethnic Diversity and Conflict in Eastern Europe*, ABC-Clio, Santa Barbara CA 1980.

89. Fischer, op. cit., p. 241.

90. Lászlo Hamos in *Romania: A Case of Dynastic Communism*, pp. 99–100; Schopflin and Poulton, op. cit., pp. 12–13.

91. Hamos in *Romania: A Case of Dynastic Communism*, p. 102.

92. Ibid., pp. 102, 106, 108.

93. See Ion Ardealanu et al., *Horthyist Fascist Terror in North-Western Romania, September 1940–October 1944*, Meridiane Publishing House, Bucharest 1986.

94. Judith Patacki, 'A History of Transylvania: A Book with its Own History', *Radio Free Europe Research*, Vol. 12, No. 13 (3 April 1987); Kurti, 'Transylvania . . .', p. 21.

95. See Patacki, op. cit.

96. Kurti, 'Transylvania . . .', p. 35.

97. See G. Schöpflin, 'Transylvania as a Political Question', *Planet*, No. 62 (December–January 1988–9).

98. Kurti, 'Transylvania . . .', pp. 31–2.
99. Ibid., p.41.
100. Shafir, *Romania*, p. 174.
101. The experiences of this Romanian dissident are taken from her annotated letters and smuggled communiqués. See Doina Cornea, *Scrisore Deschise si Alte Texte*, Humanitas, Bucharest 1992.

Chapter 3

1990: Inter-ethnic Violence Disturbs a Free Romania

> In the course of three-quarters of a century, to the sound of incessant proclamations trumpeting 'the socialist friendship of peoples', the communist regime has managed to neglect, entangle, and sully the relationship among those peoples to such a degree that one can no longer see the way back to the peaceful co-existence of nationalities . . . .'
> Aleksander Solzhenitsyn[1]

The events of 1989 which culminated in the overthrow of and execution of Nicolae Ceauşescu and his co-ruler Elena Ceauşescu remain confusing five years later. The full story has yet to emerge of events which contained elements of a hastily improvised coup d'état and spontaneous popular revolt in which thousands of Romanians showed themselves ready to risk everything, whatever the odds, to topple their oppressive rulers.[2] Reconstructing the action-packed final weeks of 1989 would take more space than is available here. The story has been exhaustively related elsewhere.[3] But attention will naturally be paid to aspects of the violent political changeover which had an important influence on the subsequent political evolution of Romania.

The Ceauşescu state possessed more aspects of a totalitarian dictatorship than any of the other east European party-states. To proceed towards democracy from the starting-point of totalitatian dictatorship, without any transitional phase or the supervision of external bodies such as those which oversaw the introduction of democracy in post-war Germany or Japan, was a formidable undertaking. The more intense the authoritarian experience, the greater is the presence of an administrative class, one that is by its very nature disinclined to give up the instruments upon which its power and privileges are based. Such was the case in Romania.

Ceauşescu undermined his rule by increasingly reserving privileges for an entourage based on his own extended family, thus exposing sections of the political elite to some of the hardships and inconveniences that were the daily lot of most citizens. His neglect of the welfare of the mainline bureaucracy may help to explain why the response to his order that popular protests be firmly dealt with was not carried out with more zeal in Timişoara after unrest flared up there on 17 December 1989. For several days, hundreds of people had been gathering outside the church of Hungarian Reformed minister Lászlo Tökés to protest against plans to transfer him to a remote village. He had defied the authorities by criticising abuses of power in his sermons and calling for ethnic solidarity. By 15 December, Romanians and Serbs had joined the protest, and on the following day 5,000 protesters gathered in front of the RCP headquarters. Shootings began on the evening of 17 December; a determined stand by the security forces against anti-regime demonstrators would probably have produced a death toll far exceeding the official casualty rate of just over 1,000 killed, making the 1956 Hungarian uprising or the Tiananmen Square repression of June 1989 appear minor police operations by comparison. But the spontaneous popular uprising in Timişoara – and later Bucharest – was followed by an internal putsch which Ceauşescu was incapable of quelling. A range of political insiders who initially called themselves moderate communists wedded to socialist legality formed a National Salvation Front (NSF) on 22 December, the day that Ceauşescu effectively acknowledged the collapse of his rule by fleeing with his wife – by helicopter – from the Central Committee building of the RCP in Bucharest. The struggle within the regime has been seen as a clash of two sets of authoritarian values: orthodox communists and some reformers in the Gorbachev mould versus the brand of doctrinaire personal communism personified by Ceauşescu.[4] The aim of those who overthrew and subsequently executed Nicolae Ceauşescu was to abolish the personal rule of the discredited chief executive and not to change fundamentally the system of government by pressing forward with revolutionary changes. The idea of ordinary citizens taking control of the streets must have been unsettling for orthodox communists used to seeing themselves as the vanguard who carried out the popular will, and it may have been the desire to prevent anti-communist protesters building up a momentum which made them a force in their own right that caused insiders to act in the way they did. The first television broadcast made by the NSF leadership on 22 December assiduously avoided the use of the word 'revolution'.[5] Two days later, on 24 December, Virgil Magureanu read a communiqué of the NSF that triumphantly embraced the term when he declared that 'the revolution had won'.[6]

The NSF placed itself at the head of the revolutionary movement the better to contain it. The rhetoric of revolutionary change was embraced while the goal of a limited restructuring of the political order was not lost sight of. A thirty-nine-strong NSF council included army officers, students and intellectuals who had participated in the revolt, but the hard core were people who had been communists right up until the collapse of the regime: Ion Iliescu, Petre Roman, Silviu Brucan, Corneliu Manescu, General Victor Stanculescu, Alexander Birladeanu and Dan Martian. The NSF council expanded to 145 members in the last days of December but power remained in the hands of Ion Iliescu as Chairman of the Council and interim President of the Republic and Petre Roman as Prime Minister of an interim government. In the last days of December 1989, the NSF succeeded in consolidating its authority. The old structures of the RCP were taken over as committees of the NSF were set up in workplaces and at the level of each county, municipality, town, and commune. An instruction issued on 12 January 1990 by the NSF Council and signed by Ion Iliescu stipulated that these bodies at the central and territorial level 'function as bodies of state power'.

Relatively few Romanians had heard of fifty-nine-year-old Ion Iliescu. Educated in Moscow for five years in the early 1950s, he had been minister of youth and secretary of the party's central committee in charge of ideology until 1971, when his rapid progress up the party hierarchy was abruptly stalled after he registered some respectful dissent from Ceauşescu's increasingly doctrinaire policies. After 1971, Iliescu held a series of minor party posts: secretary in charge of propaganda in the Timis county party committee and then first secretary of the Iási county party committee. In the early 1980s, he became Chairman of the State Committee for Water before being further pushed into obscurity by being assigned a job in state publishing.[7]

Petre Roman, the forty-three-year-old lecturer who would be his political partner as crucial decisions were taken over the next two years was the son of Walter Roman, a former Spanish Civil War veteran who, until his death in 1983, had been a member of the RCP central committee and the director of the party's publishing house, Editura Politica. Roman was fluent in Spanish and French, and he held a doctoral degree from the Polytechnical School in Toulouse.[8]

Iliescu and Roman stood by the ten-point programme issued by the NSF on 22 December. It stipulated the introduction of a democratic, pluralist form of government and the abolition of the leading role of a single party; the holding of free elections; the separation of powers; the elimination of centralised economic management and the promotion of initiative and skills in all economic sectors; the restructuring of agriculture and the promotion of small-scale production; the reorganisation of education; the observance of the rights and freedoms of ethnic minorities; the reorganisation of trade and the halting of food exports; and the conduct of foreign policy 'in the interest of the people'.[9] The emphasis was on technocratic measures to put the country back on its feet. There were few clues in the early stream of NSF pronouncements about how conflicts would be dealt with or how the range of interests clamouring for attention would be accommodated. Iliescu and Roman emerged from a world in which there were no rules for peaceful resolution of conflicts because socialism had led to the abolition of all but the most secondary of disputes. Iliescu's statements emphasising the need for national unity suggested that he was uncomfortable with the idea of diverging interests, free-wheeling debate, and the legitimate right of opposition groupings to question the basis of his decisions; given the political background from which he had sprung, his difficulty with putting pluralistic rhetoric into practice is hardly surprising, but the presence of reluctant democrats at the helm proved a cause of acute instability in the first years after the 1989 uprising.

Events would also reveal that Iliescu found it difficult to abandon the long-standing state tradition of using nationalism in order to win popular backing. But the nationalist character of the NSF only became apparent when it faced overt competition from groups that denied its right to rule. Initially, the multi-ethnic character of the groups that had risen up against Ceauşescu raised hopes that nationalism would not be a defining characteristic of the new Romania.

Such hopeful signals prompted Hungary to recognise the new Romanian government on 23 December 1989, the first country to do so. Six days later, Hungary's Gyula Horn was the first foreign minister to visit Romania and see Iliescu. Thus Hungary rendered Iliescu important assistance as he sought to legitimise his authority before the outside world.

Hungary had sound reasons for following this course. She was more aware than any other country of how deeply Romanian-Hungarian relations (both at inter-state and inter-group level) had been damaged by decades of hostile propaganda from Bucharest to which millions of Romanians had been subjected. Speedy recognition of the Iliescu government at least helped to diminish the perception that Hungary was ever ready to exploit Romanian vulnerability in order to pursue territorial claims against her neighbour. Indeed, the mistrust and fear with which Hungarians entering Romania with medical supplies and food aid were greeted in the last days of 1989 revealed how effective chauvinistic state propaganda had been in moulding popular attitudes.[10] However, such corrosive feelings melted into the background as the opening of a new decade was accompanied by hopeful declarations that a fresh chapter in Romanian–Hungarian relations was being initiated. In mid-January, the Hungarian ministers of education and culture visited their Romanian counterparts and agreement was reached that Budapest could provide materials to meet the educational needs of the Hungarian minority. Already on 11 January 1990, a trade agreement had been signed between the two countries which removed restrictions on the sale of Hungarian books and newspapers in Romania.

Inter-state co-operation was accompanied by a number of agreements at municipal and association level. Municipal officials from the Hungarian city of Pecs and from the interim governing council in Cluj signed a twinning agreement in January, and there were other cross-border initiatives and declarations of friendship.

The early statements of the provisional government in Bucharest could only have strengthened the resolve of Romanian citizens keen to repair inter-ethnic relations at home and renew links with Hungary.

On 5 January 1990, a declaration on the status of the national minorities in Romania was released by the NSF which raised hopes that concrete steps would be taken to deal with minority concerns and undo much of the damage of the Ceauşescu period. A key passage, later much quoted, declared that:

> The revolution in Romania, an historic act of the entire people, of the Romanian nation and of the national minorities, attests to the unity and solidarity of all the homeland's sons who have wished freedom and authentic democracy. The bloodshed in common has shown that the policy of national hate-mongering based on a chauvinistic policy of forced assimilation as well as the successive attempts to defame neighbouring Hungary and the Hungarians in Romania, could not succeed in breaking the confidence, friendship and unity between the Romanian people and the national minorities.
>
> The National Salvation Front solemnly declares that it shall achieve and guarantee the individual and collective rights and liberties of all the national minorities.[11]

Individual and collective rights were to be enshrined in the new constitution of the country, and the declaration also promised that a ministry of national minorities' would be created to 'provide the appropriate institutional framework for the exercise of the minorities major rights, the use of their mother tongues, the promotion of the national culture and the safeguarding of ethnic identity'.[12]

One day before, on 4 January, a decree law on local government had laid down that in areas of Romania inhabited by ethnic minorities, decisions of the local state would be made known to citizens in their own language as well as in Romanian. Broadcasting in Hungarian and German, curtailed in the 1980s, was also allowed to resume. Within a very short time, radio stations in Bucharest and in the main Transylvanian cities were devoting about twelve hours a week to transmissions in Hungarian, and regional television broadcasts in Hungarian would not be long in following.

Attempts also got under way to restore teaching in Hungarian to the school curriculum in Tirgu Mures and Cluj. This involved removing Romanian pupils from schools which had previously been Hungarian, a policy in the hands of a Hungarian member of the government, Attila Palfalvi, one of two deputy ministers of education.[13]

The government's readiness to allow the Hungarian minority to play a full role in state affairs seemed to be confirmed by the appointment of well-known Hungarians to prominent official positions. Karoly Király, remembered as a rare Marxist dissident under Ceauşescu, was given a top post on the NSF's national council; when the membership of what was Romania's de facto unelected parliament was announced on 23 December, László Tökés and Geza Domokos were included.

It is worth noting that the various decisions made in the two weeks after 22 December 1989 which seemed to anticipate a new era in the treatment of minority affairs were made in a hurried and confused atmosphere and involved a relatively small number of people. What has become known about Iliescu and Roman's stance towards minority questions suggests that they were not motivated by a sense of guilt or remorse about the ill-treatment of Hungarians or a desire to make reparations to them. It is more likely that minority concerns figured more prominently on the NSF policy agenda earlier rather than later because Hungarians had organised themselves into a political body which soon showed that it was able to speak on behalf of a large section of the Hungarian population.

The Hungarian Democratic Forum in Romania (HDFR) emerged on 25 December 1989. It was set up by Geza Domokos, the director of the Kriterion publishing company which handled the state's falling output of books published in Hungarian. Domokos's job had allowed him a degree of contact with Hungarian intellectuals open to few other members of the minority before 1989. It was likely also to have brought him into contact with Ion Iliescu, whose last job during a period of semi-disgrace in the 1980s had been in state publishing. Both men had known each other in their youth, a friendship which Iliescu would warmly refer to long after relations between their respective political organisations had cooled. Such interpersonal contacts should not be discounted when seeking explanations for why certain political decisions were taken in the first transitional period. The restrictions placed on personal and group contacts – encounters that would have been regarded as innocuous in other Soviet bloc countries – invested friendships between individuals drawn together by shared professional or family links with a certain intensity. The political alliance between Ion Iliescu and Petre Roman, which began to founder one year after they first came to prominence, had been cemented in the restricted professional circles in which the scientific publisher and future president had first come into contact with the physics lecturer whom he would appoint as Prime Minister.

None of the new Romanian parties had effectively taken shape when Domokos launched the HDFR on 25 December 1989. Iliescu was not yet likely to be receiving submissions about the treatment of minorities which conflicted with the agenda based on introducing group rights that Hungarians had drawn up. His record between 1990 and 1993 suggests that he did not hold rigid views on minority questions and that his policy approach was subordinate to the overriding demands of political survival.

It was not until January 1990 that political parties began to register officially with the authorities; as for chauvinistic groups,they kept a low profile as long as feelings of public revulsion against Ceauşescu and the toll of deaths and wounded that had accompanied his removal from power ran high.

Domokos's early statements sought to reassure Romanians of the unthreatening intentions towards them of those who spoke on behalf of the Hungarian minority. At a meeting of the NSF national council on 4 January, he declared that 'all reasonable citizens of Magyar nationality . . . dissociate themselves from stupid actions directed against the representatives of the dictatorship's repressive arms', a reference to the killings of locally-billeted members of the security forces that had occurred in the Szekler counties towards the end of December 1989.[14] On 11 January, Domokos assured Romanians that the HDFR 'sets out to achieve the rights of the Hungarians with due respect for the territorial integrity and sovereignty of free and democratic Romania'; he then went on to point out that 'a future society cannot be built by simply correcting or amending the relations compromised by the Ceauşescu dictatorship between the Romanians and the national minorities and that a new vision [was] required . . .'.[15]

However, even before the magnitude of the task involved in gaining widespread acceptance of specific minority rights became obvious, warnings were being expressed about the difficulties that Hungarians could expect to face in seeking to accomplish their goals.

Andras Süto, Romania's foremost writer in Hungarian warned in January 1990 that 'decades will be needed before the wounds are healed and the nationalism fostered by the dictatorship is buried in the common soil'.[16] László Tökés warned on 19 January that 'a proportion of the Romanian intelligentsia, namely the Romanian teachers, take a rather sharp attitude of opposition to the return of schools and . . . to the recognition of collective Magyar rights, and the representatives of the Romanian educational officials continue to make the old mentality prevail . . .'. But Tökés was still sanguine enough to believe that 'sooner or later, co-operation will become unavoidable'.[17]

Somewhat more doubtful was Mihai Sora, a pre-1989 dissident from Timisoara who, not long after being appointed minister of education, expressed his support for the reintroduction of Hungarian into schools but warned that the main thing was the attitude of society and its openness, about which he had serious doubts.[18]

In Cluj, the failure of *Puntea* (The Bridge), a magazine published in both Romanian and Hungarian and dedicated to inter-ethnic co-operation, revealed a lack of enthusiasm for a publication which stressed what both of the ethnic groups sharing Transylvania's principal city had in common.[19] Perhaps too much can be read into the failure of a single magazine to remain in business when the great bulk of publications launched in the first months of 1990 were destined to have an equally short life. But at the very moment that *Puntea* was failing to attract readers, Cluj was also witnessing the first serious inter-ethnic dispute which sprang from the attempt to remove Romanian pupils and teachers from schools which had previously been wholly Hungarian.

The decision to reintroduce Hungarian-language teaching and to split schools had been taken at the start of 1990. Attila Palfalvi, the minister responsible, speedily sought to implement it. But in Cluj, when Romanian pupils found themselves moved to the old RCP training school, many took to the streets in peaceful protest along with their parents and teachers. Following an announcement by Palfalvi that the Hungarian section of the city's university would reopen as a separate institution in the autumn and that teaching would be carried out in Hungarian and German, a League of Romanian Students was formed to prevent the reorganisation of higher education along ethnic or linguistic lines.[20] Similar protests arose in Tirgu Mures, but, unlike Cluj, resentment at the way that Hungarians sought to overcome their grievances in education merged with other issues to quickly create sharp tension in that city.

The Hungarians concerned had miscalculated by taking the initiative in a sensitive area like secondary education where any rapid restoration of the pre-Ceausescu status quo could only be achieved by placing Romanians at a disadvantage. The reaction of those Romanian pupils and teachers most directly affected was probably little different from that of their counterparts in democratic countries where education everywhere has proven to be a sensitive political issue capable of thrusting normally passive citizens into the political arena if their entitlements seem under threat. Also, it is worth bearing mind that sharp intra-Romanian disputes arose over how to undo communist injustices where one group of citizens had been seen to benefit at the expense of another set. The clearest example was the bitter dispute over church property between the Romanian Orthodox Church and the Uniate (or Greek Catholic) Church which broke out once the latter were able to worship freely. The Orthodox authorities had held on to Uniate churches for much longer than local Romanian teaching authorities had been in charge of Hungarian schools, and they were equally reluctant to restore the status quo ante. So the reaction of Cluj pupils and adults to Palfalvi's precipitate action should not be viewed as automatic proof of inter-ethnic tension looking for an outlet. Inter-ethnic and intra-Romanian disputes over property instead denote an acute sense of insecurity and an inability to find mechanisms for resolving these disputes through compromise or negotiation.

Palfalvi was moved from his post on 27 January 1990 for 'taking decisions that separated Magyar tuition from Romanian tuition in such a way as to create tension between the Romanian population and the Magyar population in some Transylvanian settlements'.[21] But important ammunition had been given to beneficiaries of Ceauşescu's nationality policies who continued to hold many of the posts that they had acquired during his assimilationist drives of the 1970s and 1980s. They had lain low during the weeks in which anti-Ceauşescu fervour had swept different parts of the country. But officials threatened by an abandonment of pre-1989 policies in Transylvania were not slow to use their access to the media, and the other channels they had for influencing public opinion, in order to generate fear about Hungarian intentions. The stereotypical image of the arrogant and insensitive Hungarian, which had been reinforced by years of emphasising the oppressive aspects of Hungarian control over pre-1918 Transylvania, began to be revived. Time would quickly show that the dramatic examples of co-operation between two historically rival peoples, which made the Romanian revolution such an uplifting event, had barely scratched the surface of suspicions, ones both artificially induced or based on actual memories and perceptions.

By the first weeks of February 1990, the first clear signs of a Romanian counter-mobilisation in Romania had emerged with the formation of the Vatra Românească Union (Union of the Romanian Hearth). This self-proclaimed cultural organisation quickly revealed itself to be a radical nationalist pressure group able to call upon formidable resources in order both to block Hungarian demands and to depict them as threatening the territorial survival of Romania.

The evolution of the NSF from January 1990 onwards was likely to have shown Ion Iliescu that many Romanians remained strongly nationalistic in outlook and that it was a view he could not afford to ignore. As the NSF spread out from Bucharest, it absorbed the local RCP organisation in most parts of the country. Thus, in ethnically-mixed parts of Transylvania, the

NSF included former party activists who had first risen to prominence as a result of steps taken by Ceauşescu to marginalise the Hungarian population, actions which the NSF had condemned in its earliest statements. The NSF clearly found itself in a contradictory position. If it was prepared to honour its promises to Hungarians, this would be at the expense of state and party officials whose co-operation the NSF needed in order to extend its authority across the whole country. Ingenious compromises might have been able to satisfy Romanian office-holders in no hurry to vacate their posts and Hungarians who felt it was time to seek amends for recent injustices suffered at their hands. However, the Romanian political experience, both under Ceauşescu and indeed in earlier times, had not prepared citizens or their political rulers for such compromises. Even in east European states with longer and more encouraging democratic experiences than Romania, the painful exit from communism after 1989 revealed little aptitude for using the techniques of bargaining and negotiation to overcome conflicts.

The fragile consensus between the communist insiders and the dissidents and newly politicised elements who had briefly found themselves on the same side of the barricades in the anti-Ceauşescu revolt had collapsed by 24 January 1990, when outraged protesters took to the streets to denounce the NSF. They had been infuriated by a change of policy signalled at a meeting of the NSF's Council on 23 January when it was announced that the NSF would take part in the election as a political organisation. Having previously declared that it would serve only as an interim government until free elections were held, the NSF now declared its intention to be a challenger in these elections which were due in April 1990, Iliescu claiming that 'pressure from below' had influenced the decision.[22] He referred to discussions that 'we had with numerous workers, with miners in the Jiu Valley, in Maramures, with workers in large works in the capital', at which 'the Front as such was requested to declare openly that it would participate in the elections'.[23] In the communist era similar gatherings had been convened to provide legitimacy for party and state decisions, and the revival of such a practice helped raise fears that continuity as much as change was a hallmark of the Iliescu regime.

So, a month after being formed, the NSF had been transformed from political caretaker to active contestant for power. The suspicion that dissidents without a party background and members of newly-created parties had about the communist pedigree of NSF personalities were greatly reinforced by this volte-face. In response, the leaders of the emerging opposition based on the 'historic parties' issued a statement on 23 January maintaining that the Council's decision was in flagrant contradiction of its earlier promises expressed in its December programme. 'Through this decision', read the statement, 'the NSF has lost its neutrality and capacity of provisional administrator of power and its credibility before the public opinion. There can be no free elections and equitable conditions for all political formations when the NSF has a monopoly in a clearly totalitarian way on all state levers.'[24]

A series of street confrontations took place between 25 and 29 January 1990 which gave the NSF the upper hand against its opponents, but only after it was prepared to use methods that rested uncomfortably with its self-proclaimed mission of bringing democracy to Romania: calls were made on television for workers to rush to the centre of the city to protect the government. Unarmed opponents were beaten up on 28 January, and the offices of the best-known opposition parties (the National Liberal and the National Peasant Parties) were stormed on 29 January.[25]

On 6 February, the NSF registered as a political party, and it was later announced that Ion Iliescu would be its candidate for Romania's presidency. Against a background of international concern about what had just occurred, the provisional government made some concessions to its opponents. The NSF council, from which well-known anti-communists had resigned, was replaced by a Provisional National Unity Council (PNUC) in which the NSF's declared opponents in the approaching national poll were included. But it soon emerged that two-thirds of the 250 member-body was made up of NSF members or supporters.

The PNUC was a fractious consultative assembly whose delegates from the provinces gave the NSF a comfortable majority. Nearly all of them had, previously, been active in the RCP in their localities.[26] The collapse of the revolutionary front of December 1989 meant that Iliescu was thrown back on the support of former RCP stalwarts, whose outlook in several parts of Transylvania has already been discussed. This development was hardly reassuring for Hungarians who pinned their hopes on minority rights arising from the accomplishment of a genuine democratic revolution in Romania. Nor could the HDFR gain assurance from the way in which inflammatory television broadcasts had succeeded in producing a violent confrontation between citizens. The events of late January showed that the agencies of manipulation and political control which had enabled Romania to be dominated by unscrupulous leaders had not perished with Ceauşescu. Iliescu's reluctance to yield political power or to allow that power to be shared among interests he could not control, also revealed important continuities with the past. His autocratic leanings (albeit small-scale when compared with his predecessor's appetite for power), were bound to have repercussions for a large minority group like the Hungarian one which wanted to run important aspects of its own affairs while still remaining attached to the Romanian state. This Hungarian aspiration conflicted with the unitary character of the Romanian political system present ever since a Romanian state had taken shape after 1859.

The NSF's desire to become the country's leading political force and its reliance on former Ceauşescu loyalists to secure it a majority in hastily-arranged elections meant that the Romanian political situation had been radically transformed for the second time in a month.

Little-noticed amid the pre-electoral turmoil in Romania was the exodus of the Saxons of Transylvania. In Ceauşescu's time, about 12,000 a year had left for West Germany after the Bonn government agreed in 1978 to pay 10,000 Deutschmarks per head for each German allowed to leave. In December 1989, there were still 200,000 ethnic Germans left in Transylvania. But, in 1990, it is estimated that half that number left, abandoning Romania for good once the borders were opened.[27] The tenacity which had enabled them to withstand invasion from Mongols, Turks and Tartars, ever since King Geza II of Hungary had invited them to defend the eastern borders of his kingdom in 1143, had been crushed by the misfortune which befell the community during the communist dictatorship. Few Saxons believed that the conditions which enabled them to lead an autonomous, self-regulating existence for centuries could be restored after the devastation of the previous forty years. One teacher from Sibiu expressed what may have been a prevailing feeling in 1990: 'you can restore buildings – even rebuild those that the communists demolished – but you cannot change a population corrupted by forty years of communist dictatorship'.[28]

The exodus of a community which could, with the support of a protective German government, have acted as a powerful advocate of minority rights, was a disquieting comment on the new Romania and its prospects. The implications were unlikely to be lost on Hungarians, who would have cause to feel keenly the disappearance of a group which might have acted as a balancing force between themselves and ethnic Romanians.

The first sign of Hungarian minority concern with the NSF came on 27 January 1990 when the HDFR's provisional executive publicly disagreed with those who did not wish minority rights to be one of the NSF's priorities. Disappointment was also expressed with an address made by Iliescu on 25 January in which the HDFR was left with the impression that the Hungarian minority had been 'exclusively responsible' for tensions in some Transylvanian towns.[29]

In his broadcast, Iliescu had declared that 'many disquieting phenomena have been brought to our attention recently from certain Transylvanian counties in connection with separatist trends which cause tension between citizens of Romanian and Hungarian nationality'. Iliescu declined to specify what these 'separatist trends' were. Nevertheless, the very fact that the country's leader was referring to their existence one month after the fall of Ceauşescu can only have been encouraging to anti-Hungarians in Transylvania looking for ways to block the granting of minority rights.

The last time a high-ranking public official had referred to separatism was on 21 December 1989, when Ceauşescu had warned that street demonstrations were part of a separatist plot instigated from abroad. Hatred of the dictator proved greater than xenophobic leanings on that occasion. But Iliescu – who was emerging as a skilful political broker – would have been aware that in a situation fraught with uncertainty, nationalism remained one of the most powerful means of mobilising the masses. It is probably no coincidence that he embraced the language of Romanian nationalism within a few days of the NSF's decision to seek electoral approval. He may even have concluded that not to use the nationalist card would have made him vulnerable to competitors (and possibly to rivals within the NSF itself). Surveying the Balkans in the early 1990s, especially in light of events in the former Yugoslavia, one Belgrade-based sociologist has made the following comment:

> the leaders who refuse to be swept away from the competitive political scene have no other choice but to revert to nationalism. Extremism is forced upon leaders by the competitive forces and those who are not ready to accept nationalistic ways will be ruthlessly displaced by those who are.[30]

The emerging gulf between the government and the HDFR was reflected in statements issued by minority leaders from the end of January onwards. On 29 January, Geza Domokos told Iliescu that 'if decisions damaging to the rights of the Hungarian minority continued to be made', the HDFR 'would leave the NSF'. He also stated that he expected the NSF to consult with the HDFR before and not after a decision such as the removal of Palfalvi was made.[31]

On 22 February, Karoly Király expressed his disappointment at the failure of the government to send representatives to a sitting of the PNUC commission on national minorities.[32] Later, thirteen organisations representing minorities in Romania responded in similar aggrieved fashion owing to the failure of the PNUC secretariat to place their concerns before the full plenum of the PNUC.[33]

An unmistakeable sign that the Hungarian minority no longer possessed the ear of the government came on 6 February when the NSF published the programme with which it intended to obtain a mandate in forthcoming elections. Its references to minority interests were perfunctory, and there was nothing about collective rights for minorities.[34] As the NSF evolved from being a caretaker government leading the country through a difficult period to being an active contestant for power, there was mounting evidence that not only was the minority question decreasing in importance but also Iliescu and his colleagues were retreating from the declarations that they had allowed to be published in the name of the provisional government in the first weeks of the transitional period.

Perhaps surprisingly, in the light of the outspoken views which he would hold later, Pastor Lászlo Tökés, the best-known Hungarian minority figure, retained a conciliatory attitude to the NSF in several of his public statements even as its character changed. On 31 January, he told Rompres, Romania's state news agency, that the NSF was the only force capable of running the country and that he would continue to support it provided that its programme of democratisation for the nationalities was fulfilled.[35] A little earlier, he had criticised Palfalvi, the dismissed education minister, for having used autocratic methods when trying to convince Romanian teachers about the need for the separation of schools;[36] and in mid-February he was expressing the need for patience, declaring his own willingness to wait five years before Magyar schools in Transylvania were refounded.[37] It is interesting that these moderate statements were made to Romanian sources. But universities needed to be relaunched in 1990.

By early March 1990, Tökés's statements were growing markedly sombre. On 3 March, Budapest radio reported him saying that 'nationality differences could sharpen dangerously in Romania . . .The Bucharest government is doing nothing to resolve the nationality problems, and none of the December promises in this connection have been realised.'[38] At the same time, the HDFR and eleven other minority groups publicly objected to the appointment as minister of Transylvanian affairs of Adrian Moţiu, who was soon to emerge as a leading spokesman of Vatra Româneaşca.[39] Meanwhile, school strikes, marches and the collection of 50,000 signatures in a petition demanding the reinstatement of the Hungarian Bolyai university revealed that Hungarian political leaders were switching to direct protests as their channels of communication with the NSF leadership began to dry up.[40] An HDFR statement released on 17 March 1990 revealed the deep frustration that lay behind the collapse of a relationship that had seemed to promise so much for majority-minority relations at the start of the year:

> We note with sorrow that there are forces for which the revolution ended with the declaration of the democratic rights of the majority . . .The HDFR has to note that . . .both the PNUC and the government can be criticised as they have taken no attitude towards the interpellations advanced, the reports synthesised, and the information items that were illustrative of disturbing events.[41]

Some efforts were made to stop Romanians being swept into the ultra-nationalist camp. On 30 January, Radio Timişoara broadcast an open letter to the nation drawn up by a Hungarian group that included Tökés which sought to assure Romanians that, by guaranteeing the rights of the minority, they would not lose their own rights, and that the undoing of the Ceauşescu regime's educational policies could not be termed separatism.[42] However, a divisive history in which advances by one group were commonly seen as being gained at the expense of another and the fact that there were Romanians who had obtained career fulfilment through the Ceauşescu state who indeed stood to lose if the HDFR's claims were met, eroded the credibility of such appeals. Hungarians placed far more emphasis on trying to secure their core demands as quickly as possible than upon seeking to explain their motives to their Romanian fellow citizens. Sandor Balazs, a leading campaigner for the restoration of Bolyai university in Cluj, admitted in February that Hungarians appeared impatient, but he pointed out that 'the reason for impatience was that the Magyar nationality had already been deceived twice, and that they did not want history to repeat itself'.[43] The reference to being deceived twice concerned the measures drawn up to deal with minority questions by both the Romanian inter-war and communist governments.

Silviu Brucan, a former NSF spokesman emerging as an influential commentator, declared on 20 March 1990 that 'the Magyar minority wants to eliminate at a stroke every harmful effect of the assimilation campaign which began in the Ceauşeascu period . . . the Romanians simply do not understand demands of this kind, and they evaluate all this as extremist'.[44] Brucan's comment, clearly suggesting that many Romanians and Hungarians had irreconcilable views about Ceauşescu's nationality policy and what, if anything, should be done about it, were expressed one day after inter-ethnic clashes had broken out in Tirgu Mureş; the potential for a violent collision had become apparent from the start of the month. Videotapes of Valtra Româneaşca rallies in Tirgu Mureş, Cluj and Alba Iulia in late February and early March had shown large indoor audiences being addressed by speakers who denounced the Hungarian minority as irreconcilably hostile and bent on gaining control of Transylvania, with the crowds chanting threats against specific Hungarian leaders.[45]

The Romanian broadcasting media gave plenty of attention to protests over the fate of educational institutions in Tirgu Mureş, involving rival groups of Romanians and Hungarians, which lasted until mid-March; its coverage often reflected ultra-nationalist positions, something that the government belatedly admitted in the wake of fighting in Tirgu Mureş.[46] The first Romanian protests over Hungarian schools had been in Cluj, but it should not have been a surprise that it was Tirgu Mureş where ethnic differences flared up into violent conflict.

Tirgu Mureş (Maros Vasarhely in Hungarian) is a city which had been overwhelmingly Hungarian in its character and demography down to the

1960s. (According to Romanian census figures, 74.27 per cent of the city's population in 1948 was Hungarian, 73.74 per cent in 1956.)[47] Until 1968, it had been the capital of the Magyar Autonomous Region set up in the pre-nationalist phase of communist rule to bolster the view that the collective personality of Romania's largest minority was recognised by the Romanian state. Under Ceauşescu, the arrival in Tirgu Mureş of Romanians from the adjoining counties and from as far away as Moldavia led to the proportion of Hungarians dropping to little more than fifty per cent. The state's industrialisation drive led to the 'Romanisation' of other Transylvanian cities, where in 1966 largely Hungarian- and German-speaking minorities made up 35.3 per cent of the urban population (32.1 per cent of Transylvania's population overall).[48] But the process was much more hurried in Tirgu Mureş than anywhere else in Transylvania.

By the end of the 1980s, many of the city's Hungarian population keenly felt their relegation and believed that they were at the cutting edge of Ceauşescu's assimilationist drive. Meanwhile, the Romanian newcomers who lived in new settlements ringing the city had not had time to establish any level of familiarity with longer-term inhabitants. Many came from districts in which there had been few non-Romanian inhabitants, and the state's ringing insistence on the need for citizens to share a common identity based on Romanian culture and appreciation of past Romanian glories hardly encouraged newcomers to respect longer-established inhabitants who spoke a different language for which they strove to obtain official protection following the collapse of the Ceauşescu state.

In Tirgu Mureş, it quickly emerged that those who wished to modify an existing state structure and others who wished to dismantle it completely were possibly more evenly matched than anywhere else in Romania. Local officials who had benefited from Ceauşescu's policy of discriminating against Hungarians were disinclined to cede positions of authority to leaders of the Hungarian community, and there was less turnover in personnel in the administration of Tirgu Mureş and the county of Mureş than in other ethnically-mixed regions. The replacement of Romanian officials by Hungarians in the overwhelmingly Hungarian-speaking counties of Harghita and Covasna to the east of Tirgu Mureş may only have heightened fears among the city's recently-constituted political elite about the fate that awaited them unless they mobilised to protect their interests.[49] Tirgu Mureş's specificity may explain why the city's Romanian elite adopted its own survival strategy rather than follow the lead of the NSF which, upon becoming a political party, was destined to enjoy less success in the Mures area than in almost any other part of Romania.

Serious violence erupted in Tirgu Mureş on 19 March after minor affrays had occurred on 16 March. Widely differing accounts of events were given by local Romanian and Hungarian spokesmen. Moreover, government statements offered explanations that were at variance with one another: causal factors seen as crucial in initial statements were played down in later ones and received little credence in the official parliamentary report into the disturbances published on 23 January 1991.[50] It may well be impossible to arrive at a thorough, reliable account of what happened in Tirgu Mureş and there is not even agreement about the number of dead and injured in days of fury which wrecked community relations and gave the city the unenviable reputation of being the first place in post-communist eastern Europe where inter-ethnic conflict spilled over into fatal violence.

Reports filed by foreign journalists in the city indicate that serious violence first occurred on 19 March when a demonstration organised by Vatra Româneaşca turned into a siege of the HDFR offices. The Hungarian writer, Andras Süto, was badly beaten by a Romanian crowd as he left the building supposedly under the safe escort of Colonel Judea, chairman of the city council.[51] The hostile crowd was reinforced by Romanian villagers from Hodac and Ibanesti, fifty kilometres north of the city. In a region where public transport is even more inadequate than in other parts of the country, villagers were bussed in and out of the city on two consecutive days. The parliamentary enquiry into the disturbances found that mayors and public functionaries had been involved in transporting demonstrators to Tirgu Mureş on both days. Young Romanians from these villages apprehended in rioting revealed that they had been promised exemptions from local taxes imposed by a local mayor. This reveals the power that unscrupulous Romanian officials can exert over a society in which the voices of authority still command unquestioning obedience.[52]

Despite the events of 19 March, 20,000 people assembled for a peaceful rally on the 20th to protest at the previous day's violence. Romanian flags were waved as a gesture of loyalty, and citizens from both ethnic communities mingled in the crowd. However, more fighting occurred after anti-Hungarian crowds assembled and were reinforced by the returning villagers; some of the Romanian organisations represented at a peace rally had their offices ransacked by nationalist crowds.[53] Hungarians began to retaliate on this day and, reinforced by defenders who arrived from outlying districts, including a large number of gypsies, they began to gain the upper hand. At this point, army units responded to a call to end the fighting, which subsided in the city on 20 March leaving three dead and 269 injured according to the official figures.

Despite being unable to control events in the city, a statement was issued in the name of the government on 21 March which was categorical about what forces lay behind the Tirgu Mureş violence. It referred to

Hungarian celebrators of the 152nd anniversary of the 1848 revolution on 15 March as producing 'open attacks against the nationalist sentiments of Romanian people' with 'the state of tension and violent acts'escalating in following days.[54] The celebration of an event in which Hungarian nationalists had demanded constitutional reforms, liberal legislation and national independence for Hungary without taking into account the similar nationalist demands of the non-Magyar peoples was bound to be resented by Romanians ready to view it as part of the unchecked 'superiority complex' of those Hungarians in their midst. But the political aspects of the celebrations were not stressed, and efforts were made to include Romanians and be respectful to Romanian symbols. The government statement also claimed that the anniversary 'was misused by citizens of the Hungarian Republic who crossed the border en masse and who hoisted the Hungarian flag on various buildings and at wreath-laying ceremonies, displaying anti-Romanian slogans'.[55] On the same day, it was reported that Petre Roman, in a message to the Hungarian prime minister, blamed 'instigators from outside' for the riots: 'we should have expected the Hungarian government to call its own citizens to order [and] to refrain from . . . interfering in Romanian affairs'.[56]

Petre Roman later claimed that on 15 March tens of thousands of Hungarians crossed the border into Romania in thousands of vehicles.[57] This claim was denied by the injured Andras Süto, who contended that relatively few visitors joined the 1848 celebrations, and very few indeed in Tirgu Mures.[58] The 1991 parliamentary report appeared to support Süto's explanation, since it made no mention of Hungarian visitors as a determining factor behind the violence. However, it did emphasise the fact that certain elements of the Romanian media depicted the 15 March celebrations as irredentist. Specific mention was made of *Cuvîntul Liber*, the Tirgu Mureş daily newspaper, reflecting the views of threatened Romanian interests in the city. On 15 March, it published an anti-Romanian statement made by Hungarian émigrés in the USA which dated from the Ceauşescu era but whose publication date was altered to make it appear as if it had been recently drawn up. Elsewhere, Süto had accused the chairman of the city council, Colonel Judea, of playing an active role in disseminating this pamphlet.

The 1991 parliamentary report criticises the HDFR for not explaining the nature of its 1848 celebrations more thoroughly, but it found that the accusation made in parts of the Romanian media that the HDFR was engaging in an irredentist act had no basis in fact.[59] However, President Iliescu, in his first statement on the Tirgu Mureş violence, made on 20 March, had emphasised the background to the violence as an important contributory factor. 'The Romanian citizens,' he declared, 'expressing their position in connection with some previous actions, resorted to regrettable actions . . .'.[60]

A Hungarian minority response to the initial government explanation for why the violence occurred and who was to blame came on 22 March from Karoly Király, who was also a deputy chairman of the PNUC. He argued that 'the national hatred was aroused by the chauvinist propaganda of the Romanian mass communications media'. Furthermore, he claimed that the government was trying to evade its own responsibility and was practically placing the guilt on the national minorities and foreign citizens.[61]

Unidentified foreigners in the service of the Ceauşescu regime had been accused of responsibility for much of the violence meted out to his opponents during his final days of power. Perhaps it is not surprising that both the Romanian media and leading officials advanced external interference as a contributory factor for the violence which occurred in March 1990 when once again the Romanian state was seen to be badly malfunctioning.

An admission that mass media coverage (including that of the state television service) had been misleading, not to say inflammatory, came in governing statements on 23 and 24 March. On 24 March, a government communiqué 'dissociated itself from the mass media accusations against the Magyar nationality population in Harghita and Covasna counties regarding tendencies of separatism . . . considering them as groundless, and it denied news items linking Hungarian state citizens with planned instigations of violence.[62] On 24 March, Bucharest radio reported that the government had expressed its displeasure over the fact that Free Romanian Radio and Television (the name then given to the service to distance itself from the propagandistic one that existed under Ceauşescu) did not properly reflect the government's position (concerning events in Tirgu Mureş) at a time when that was absolutely necessary, given the existing tension in that area.[63]

Besides the role of the media, another source of criticism which the government had to deal with was the failure of the army and police to respond swiftly to the violence. There were even reports that some locally-based members of the security forces had been responsible for increasing violence. Helsinki Watch, the human rights watchdog, charged that the police made feeble efforts to prevent villagers returning on the second day and in some cases waved their buses through road-blocks supposed to halt them.[64] Numerous appeals by sixty to seventy trapped HDFR members for local police to come and rescue them proved of no avail; they arrived four hours after the first calls for assistance, by which time the mob had ransacked the building.[65]

On 22 March, Gyula Horn, the Hungarian foreign minister, had complained that Romanian police and military had been 'watching passively' as the situation deteriorated.[66] Shortly afterwards, eight local youth groups in Tirgu Mureş, drawn from both communities, had asked for a judicial investigation to 'identify and bring to justice the civilians, military and police officials who helped orientate the violent attacks or [who] stood idly by without defending those attacked'.[67] When the issue of the military's role came up at a press conference on 24 March, Iliescu's reply was evasive: 'we were reproached for not having taken measures of strength. Meaning what? Resorting to military occupation of the country?'[68] On 31 March, Petre Roman claimed that the army's low profile stemmed from 'attempts to use the army against the people before 22 December'. Afterwards, 'it was decided that the army should only interfere to give protection to government and party headquarters, and I can tell you that the military will never resort to force the way they do in western countries . . .'.[69]

In the same press conference, Roman admitted that the army might have intervened more quickly, but what he said amounted to an admission that defenceless Romanian citizens facing violent attack could not rely on the protection of the army. Ironically, eighteen months later, it was inaction by the security forces that resulted in Petre Roman being forced out of office as gangs of workers took over the capital, an incident that, like the Tirgu Mureş events, remains shrouded in mystery despite official investigations.

During much of 1990, a power vacuum would exist within the armed forces which meant that they played little part in any of the sudden upheavals that punctuated the political change-over in Romania, of which the Tirgu Mureş events (however serious) were only one example. In February 1990 the minister of defence had been forced to resign following the creation of a pressure group among officers which aimed to democratise the armed forces and remove officers implicated in acts of repression. The new minister, General Victor Stănculescu, kept a low profile during the events in Tirgu Mures. His statement of 19 March that 'the army was firmly determined . . . to defend the integrity of a free country' gave little clue as to what its role should be in the face of civil disorders like those in Tirgu Mureş, but it echoed similar comments made by his political superiors.[70]

President Iliescu declared on 25 March that 'the current serious political and ethnic conflicts create the impression that Transylvania may become a serious subject of discussion . . . . We want to state most categorically that Ardeal and its belonging to the Romanian homeland cannot be a subject of negotiation with anyone . . .'.[71] These views were echoed by the Romanian deputy premier, Gelu Voican Voiculescu, upon his arrival in Tirgu Mureş on 22 March to set up a commission of enquiry into the recent disturbances. Addressing a public rally in the city, he declared ambiguously that 'we ourselves will defend the country's integrity and never allow anybody to steal a piece of our fatherland's land'.[72]

Such statements by leading officials could have been construed as feeding the insecurity of those Romanians who had already been inflamed by nationalistic comments in the broadcasting and print media; or they might have sprung from a perceived need by NSF officials to demonstrate their own patriotic credentials as they prepared to campaign for votes in elections scheduled for 20 May. Whatever the explanation, the government managed to persuade unnamed members of the HDFR and Vatra Româneaşca to form a local committee that worked alongside the government committee looking into the events. Several meetings were held at which agreed statements were issued condemning violence, deploring action that led to local casualties and material damage, and appealing to the media 'to employ all available means to extend this state of quiet that we need so much'.[73]

Meanwhile, the main commission, which included one Hungarian and several high-ranking members from the former regime's law enforcement agencies, sought to produce a report based on its findings within two weeks, but none was ever issued and its work was eventually absorbed in the parliamentary enquiry. The latter's findings were published in January 1991 and coincided with another report into the even more serious violence that occurred in Bucharest in June 1990 about which government and opposition failed to agree. It was common knowledge that the timing of both reports was bound up with Romania's application to join the Council of Europe, whose parliamentary assembly aims to protect human rights and freedom in its member states. Serious concern had been expressed in the Council about the NSF's human rights record and, in November 1990, a delegation visiting Romania stated that it would only be in a position to consider Romania's application for membership after parliamentary commissions investigating the Tirgu Mureş violence and the disturbances in Bucharest on 13–15 June 1990 released their findings.[74] Professor Ion Minzatu, chairman of the commission of enquiry, admitted that the report's findings were incomplete and it could be more accurately described as 'an essay' or as 'a theoretical study'; nevertheless, the report drew fierce criticism from Vatra Româneaşca, which felt that not only it but also 'all Romanians in Transylvania' had been gravely insulted by its findings.[75]

Long before the Romanian parliament delivered its own overdue assessment of the Tirgu Mureş violence, the importance of the events that had taken place there was already apparent. The depth of hatred that was revealed showed that the nationalist rivalry licensed under Ceauşescu and feeding on conflicts from the recent and more distant past had not abated with the collapse of his regime. Indeed, the potential for a collision had increased owing to the replacement of a totalitarian state which monopolised expressions of chauvinism by a relatively weak state prepared to exploit nationalism in order to boost its credibility but unable or unwilling to prevent others going to even more extreme lengths to exploit nationalism for their own ends. The eruption of the fighting initiated by Romanian ultra-nationalists left the state with the choice of confronting hate-laden nationalism or appeasing it. The direction taken by the NSF since December 1989 and its attitude to the first wave of relatively minor inter-ethnic disputes probably meant that its unwillingness to condemn the violence unequivocally or seek to pursue its chief culprits, irrespective of ethnic background or political affiliation, was almost inevitable. Leaders of the NSF were prepared to overlook the role that Vatra Româneaşca had played in Tirgu Mureş before and during the violence and treat its leaders as respectable negotiating partners. Thus, ultra-nationalists were able to remain in the political foreground and be regarded as legitimate political actors.

Bucharest was probably in little doubt that the friendly relations which it had enjoyed with the Hungarian government were unlikely to survive owing to the way that the events in Tirgu Mureş had been handled. A message to Petre Roman from his Hungarian counterpart, Miklos Nemeth, on 20 March showed the extent to which these relations had deteriorated:

> I am sorry to say that in the wake of the December turning-point, the relationship of the Romanian majority with the Hungarian minority has not moved in the direction of reconciliation but in that of confrontation in some quarters of Romania. It is depressing that the assertion of the individual and collective rights of minorities brings more and more often into the resistance of the Romanians [sic] incited by aggressive and chauvinistic forces.
>
> We have tried on several occasions to draw the Romanian leadership's attention to the growing threat of nationalism, with a request to do their utmost to prevent these extremely bad signs unfolding. To our deepest regret, the Romanian leadership seems – despite official statements – to subordinate the Hungarian issue to the internal power-struggle, making unacceptable concessions to forces of explicit racial discrimination . . .
>
> Hungary is greatly concerned over the rise of national ungenerosity, gradually removing Romanian society from the chance of democratic advance and incurring great damage not only for the minority but the Romanians themselves.[76]

Petre Roman riposted with the claim that Hungarian nationalism had been revived in Transylvania by the actions of parties competing in the Hungarian general election which took place shortly after the Tirgu Mureş

events. But despite the concern and anger expressed during the final
stages of campaigning, none of the contenders took radical positions and
Transylvania was soon pushed into the background by domestic problems
as Hungary's transition from a communist state to a multi-party one
entered its critical stages.

Hopeful signs from the Tirgu Mureş explosion were not easy to find.
But at least the city avoided sporadic long-term violence which examples
from ethnic conflict zones as far apart as Northern Ireland and the Indian
subcontinent show is often the result of an inter-communal collision. The
fact that the peace held in Tirgu Mureş in the years immediately after 1990
(even though the process of mending community relations is probably one
that will need decades) strengthens the argument that the violence was
artificially manufactured rather than being a spontaneous phenomenon.
In the days after the Tirgu Mureş riots, rallies were held across Romania,
including the cities of Bucharest and Iási, around the common theme that
it was in the interests of both Romanians and Hungarians to promote inter-
ethnic harmony.[77] In Tirgu Mureş, the Pro-Europe League was founded
which for several years performed useful work trying to break down
existing community barriers and prevent new ones from being erected,
especially among the young. It sought to keep channels of communication
open with western Europe but, undoubtedly, it was fellow east Europeans
who had most to learn from the collapse of human tolerance and restraint in
Tirgu Mureş. The conflict in Tirgu Mureş possessed features which would
recur, often with far more devastating intensity, in later ethnic disputes
that tore apart not just cities but whole regions as in the case of the former
Yugoslavia.

The role of the media in sharpening ethnic resentments in an atmosphere
of personal and group uncertainty was highlighted by the Tirgu Mureş
events. So was the power of rumour in breeding suspicion and confusion
among groups long used to relying upon informal means of communication. Dozens of newssheets emerged whose chief product was rumour or
opinions masquerading as news, some of which succeeded in placing citizen against citizen on ethnic grounds. Rival national communities proved
relatively easy to manipulate by forces intent on promoting ethnic antagonism. Perhaps this was due to the isolation that they found themselves in,
to the powerful hold that local elites had over them, and to the fact that
some community members retained sharp memories of historical wrongs
committed against their ancestors by people whom they were now ready
to view as ethnic adversaries.

The government's reaction to the Tirgu Mureş events revealed a great
deal about the character of the new political order. The rhetoric about
Iliescu and Roman standing for technocratic efficiency was shown to be a

sham when they could not preserve order in a city located in the very centre of the country where reports of trouble had been filtering out before the violence of 19 March; similarly, the difficulties in producing a report about what happened and why was a telling reflection on the inadequacy of the state. Secondly, the regime's claim to embody the spirit of consensus was tested in Tirgu Mureş and found wanting. Opposition groups and minority interests were to be included in governing bodies and representative fora only as decorative elements, not as forces that had a legitimate point of view that would help to shape policy. The long tradition, that in the case of Romania preceded communist times, whereby groups outside the ruling circle might be given honorific positions devoid of power to convey an image of benevolent and responsive authority, was swiftly restored under Iliescu.

A useful comparison might be made with Spain, whose prospects of peacefully democratising its institutions were seen as almost as difficult to realise as in Romania before the death of the dictator Franco; its shift towards pluralism would be overseen by members of the authoritarian political elite who had distanced themselves from an intransigent and increasingly isolated ruling circle. But in Spain, the democracy-builders were prepared to share power with the opposition and allow the mechanisms of the transition to be worked out via negotiations and pacts. Reformers dismantling the Franco dictatorship were also intent on marginalising hardliners who were clearly opposed to genuine liberalisation. But Iliescu soon showed that, far from purging officials who endorsed all or part of Ceauşescu's hardline approach on questions like democracy and minority rights, he was prepared to make strategic compromises with them. The Romanian equivalents of the Spanish ultras, who drifted into obscurity as a democratic Spain took shape, never really came under pressure except in the first weeks of 1990. Hardline nationalists were able to return to the limelight as soon as the NSF showed a readiness to exploit anti-democratic elements in political culture rather than encourage voters to become familiar with the expression of differences and the arrangement of compromises to minimise their impact. Iliescu showed a preference for restoring an ethnic state that combined symbols and values from the two political systems that had existed in post-1918 Romania rather than building afresh by seeking a genuine accommodation between different ethnic, political and regional interests that might have enabled Romania to move towards being a polity shaped by civic and representative values. The political decisions taken in the first months of 1990 were made in a rushed and ad-hoc manner, but they showed a clear preference for continuity as much as change; Iliescu's Romania was to be a hybrid system which contained elements of both democracy and authoritarianism but, as John Sislin has commented, 'the authoritarian attitudes won out ... because with each aspect of the political system it is the face of it that is democratic, while the soul remains tied to the old ways of doing things'.[78]

NOTES

1. Aleksander Solzhenitsyn, *Rebuilding Russia: Reflections and Tentative Proposals*, Farrar, Strauss, and Giroux, New York 1991, p. 6. Solzhenitsyn is referring to his native Russia, but his comments apply with particular force to most other ethnically-mixed societies where communism was installed.

2. J. F. Brown, *Surge To Freedom: The End of Communist Rule in Eastern Europe*, Duke University Press, Durham NC and London 1991, p. 199.

3. The best early assessment exploring the nature of the December 1989 events is Matei Calinescu and Vladimir Tismaneanu, 'The 1989 Revolution and Romania's Future', in Daniel Nelson (ed.), *Romania After Tyranny*, Westview Press, London and San Francisco CA 1992. Another account which is more impressionistic is Edward Behr, *'Kiss the Hand You Cannot Bite': The Rise and Fall of the Ceauşescus*, Hamish Hamilton, London 1991. The Munich-based *Report on Eastern Europe*, published weekly by Radio Free Europe, published acute and comprehensive assessments about the nature of the anti-Ceauşescu uprising throughout 1990 as more information became known and fresh theories were advanced.

4. This view is advanced in the thoughtful survey of the post-Ceauşescu political landscape produced by Mary Ellen Fischer. See her 'The New Leaders and the Opposition', in Daniel Nelson (ed.), *Romania After Tyranny*, Westview Press, London and San Francisco CA 1992.

5. Peter Sani Davis, 'Political Legitimisation and the Romanian Revolution', paper presented at the University of London's School of Slavonic and East European Studies one-day conference on Romania, May 1994.

6. Ibid.

7. For biographical details of Iliescu, see Vladimir Tismaneanu, *Reinventing Politics*, p. 225; Bogdan Szajkowski, *Romania: New Political Parties of Eastern Europe and the Soviet Union*, Longman, London 1991, p. 221; and Vladimir Socor, 'The New President', *Report on Eastern Europe* (8 June 1990).

8. Vladimir Tismaneanu, 'The Quasi-Revolution and Its Discontents: Emerging Political Pluralism in Post-Ceauşescu Romania', *East European Politics and Societies*, Vol. 7, No. 2 (Summer 1993).

9. Szajkowski, op. cit., p. 220.

10. Judith Pataki, 'Free Hungarians in a Free Romania: Dream or Reality', *Report on Eastern Europe* (23 February 1990), p. 19.

11. Rompres, 6 January 1990, BBC World Service, Survey of World Broadcasts (hereafter SWB) EE/0657 B/11 (9 January 1990).

12. Ibid.

13. Martin Rady, *Romania in Turmoil*, IB Tauris, London and New York 1992, p. 149; Dennis Deletant, 'The Role of Vatra Romaneasca in Transylvania', *Report on Eastern Europe*, Vol. 2, No. 5, (1 February 1991).

14. Bucharest home service, 4 January 1990, SWB EE/0657 B/10 (9 January 1990).

15. Rompres, 11 January 1990, SWB EE/066 B/13 (19 January 1990).

16. Rady, op. cit., p. 149, SWB (23 February 1990), p. 18.

17. Budapest home service, 19 January 1990, SWB EE/0688 B/12 (22 January 1990).
18. Patacki, *Report on Eastern Europe* (23 February 1990), p. 22.
19. Paul Hockenos, 'Bloodletting in Transylvania', *In These Times* (4–10 April 1990), p. 13.
20. Rady, op. cit., p. 149.
21. Rompres, 27 January 1990, SWB EE/0676 B/11 (31 January 1990).
22. Szajkowski, *New Political Parties . . .*, p. 222; R. R. King, 'Romania', in R. Staar (ed.), *1991 Yearbook of International Communist Affairs*, Hoover Press, Stanford CA 1991, p. 333.
23. Szajkowski, op. cit., p. 222.
24. Ibid.
25. Michael Shafir, 'The Provisional Council of National Unity: Is History Repeating Itself?', *Report on Eastern Europe*, Vol. 1, No. 9 (2 March 1990), p. 21.
26. Szajkowski, op. cit., pp. 222–3.
27. Dan Ionescu, 'Countdown for Romania's Germans', *Report on Eastern Europe* (13 September 1991), p. 32.
28. Richard Bassett, *The Times* (1 March 1990).
29. Rompres, 27 January 1990, SWB EE/ 0676 B/11 (31 January 1990).
30. Ljubomir Madzar, 'The Roots of Nationalism', *Balkan Forum*, Vol. 2, No. 1 (March 1994), p. 82.
31. Radio Budapest, 29 January 1990, quoted by Patacki, *Report on Eastern Europe* (23 February 1990), p. 23.
32. Rompres, 22 February 1990, SWB EE/0701 B/7 (1 March 1990).
33. Rompres, 10 March 1990, SWB EE/0712 B/5 (14 March 1990).
34. Rompres, 6 February 1990, SWB EE/0683 B/9 (8 February 1990).
35. Rompres, 31 January 1990, SWB EE/0678 B/9 (2 February 1990).
36. Patacki, *Report on Eastern Europe* (23 February 1990), p. 23.
37. Rompres, 13 February 1990, SWB EE/0690 B/6 (16 February 1990).
38. SWB EE/0707 B/5 (8 March 1990).
39. Michael Shafir, 'The Romanian Authorities' Reactions to the Violence in Tirgu Mureş', *Report on Eastern Europe*, Vol. 1, No. 15 (13 April 1990). In the spring of 1990 Motiu gave an interview in which he claimed that the Hungarian community wished to introduce separatism in factories, hospitals and commercial premises, as well as in schools, in order to be in a position to detach Transylvania completely from the rest of Romania. See *Vatra Româneasca*, Vol. 1, No. 1 (June–July 1990).
40. Budapest home service, 19 February 1990, SWB EE/0695 B/5 (22 February 1990).
41. Rompres, 17 March 1990, SWB EE/0717 B/5 (20 March 1990).
42. Patacki, *Report on Eastern Europe* (23 February 1990), p. 24.
43. Budapest home service, 19 February 1990, SWB EE/0695 B/5 (22 February 1990).
44. Budapest home service, 20 March 1990, SWB EE/0720 B/3 (23 March 1990).
45. Vladimir Socor, 'Forces of Old Resurface in Romania: The Ethnic Clashes in Tirgu Mureş', *Report on Eastern Europe*, Vol. 1, No. 15 (13 April 1990), p. 42, n. 6.
46. Rompres, 23 March 1990, SWB EE/0722 B/7 (26 March 1990).
47. E. Illyés, *National Minorities in Romania: Change in Transylvania*, Columbia University Press, Boulder CO and New York 1982, p. 65.

48. Illyés, op. cit., pp. 56–7.
49. I interviewed a range of people in Tirgu Mureş and Cluj in order to obtain a cross-section of views about the state of inter-ethnic relations before and after March 1990 and was able to view conditions for myself on fieldwork trips starting in May 1990.
50. Rompres, 23 January 1991, SWB EE/0980 B/6 (26 January 1991).
51. Socor, *Report on Eastern Europe* (13 April 1990), p. 39; Andras Süto interviewed on Hungarian television, 30 March 1990, SWB EE/0731 B/9 (5 April 1990).
52. Deletant, *Report on Eastern Europe* (1 February 1991), p. 32.
53. Socor, *Report on Eastern Europe*, (13 April 1990), p. 39.
54. Bucharest home service, 21 March 1990, SWB EE/0720 A2/3 (23 March 1990).
55. Ibid.
56. Rompres, 21 March 1990, SWB EE/A20 A2/2 (23 March 1990).
57. Hungarian television, 28 March 1990, interview with Petre Roman, SWB EE/0727 B/1 (31 March 1990).
58. Hungarian television, 30 March 1990, SWB EE/0731 B/9 (5 April 1990).
59. For details of the parliamentary report on the Tirgu Mureş events, see Rompres, 23 January 1991, SWB EE/0980 B/6 (26 January 1991).
60. Bucharest home service, 20 March 1990, SWB EE/0719 B/5 (22 March 1990).
61. Budapest home service, 22 March 1990, SWB EE/0723 B/4 (27 March 1990).
62. Rompres, 23 March 1990, SWB EE/0722 B/7 (26 March 1990).
63. Bucharest home service, 24 March 1990, SWB EE/0723 B/4 (27 March 1990).
64. *Human Rights in Romania since the Revolution*, Helsinki Watch Report, New York 1991, p. 16.
65. Ibid., pp. 15–16.
66. SWB EE/07190 (22 March 1990).
67. Radio Bucharest, 22 March 1990, quoted in Socor, *Report on Eastern Europe* (13 April 1990), p. 41.
68. Rompres, 24 March 1990, SWB EE/0722 B/9 (26 March 1990).
69. Rompres, 2 April 1990, SWB EE/0731 B/8 (5 April 1990).
70. Shafir, *Report on Eastern Europe* (13 April 1990), p. 46.
71. Bucharest home service, 25 March 1990, SWB EE/0724 B/3 (28 March 1990).
72. Bucharest home service, 22 March 1990, SWB EE/0722 B/5 (26 March 1990).
73. Rompres, 24 March 1990, SWB EE/0723 B/5 (27 March 1990); Bucharest home service, 10 April 1990, SWB EE/0735 B/7 (10 April 1990).
74. Rompres, 15 November 1990, SWB EE/0926 A1/3 (20 November 1990).
75. Rompres, 30 January 1991, SWB EE/0988 B/2 (5 February 1991).
76. SWB EE/0720 A2/1 (23 March 1990).
77. Socor, *Report on Eastern Europe* (13 April 1990), p. 42.
78. John Sislin, 'Revolution Betrayed? Romania and the National Salvation Front', *Studies in Comparative Communism*, Vol. 24, No. 4 (1991), p. 408.

Chapter 4

From Salvation to Social Democracy: Reluctant Pluralists Bury Communism, 1990–1994

The sharply contrasting reactions to the Tirgu Mureş violence of March 1990 opened up a gulf between ethnic Romanians and Hungarians and between the Romanian and Hungarian states. Perceptions about what had happened and who was responsible were totally at variance. What many, perhaps most, Transylvanian Hungarians saw as a pogrom was described by Ion Iliescu as 'regrettable events caused by *their* insistence and haste . . . deepening suspicion and mistrust'[1] (my emphasis). Even without the benefit of an official report into the disturbances, he was prepared to single out Hungarian pressure for educational change as a prime detonating factor, a line to which he adhered long afterwards.

The manner in which the emergent NSF elite closed ranks behind Iliescu by endorsing his euphemistic and incomplete summary of the Tirgu Mureş events was also striking. None of the former communist officials who were grooming themselves for forthcoming elections chose to dissent from his analysis. Indeed, feelings of injured patriotism were so fiercely held among pro-government members of the Provisional Council of National Unity that a session to discuss the Tirgu Mureş events early in April 1990 had to be cut short as it became clear that it would be impossible to hold a debate in a calm and measured atmosphere.

ROMANIA'S STORMY ELECTORAL DEBUT

But inter-ethnic recriminations were soon eclipsed by bitter controversies among Romanians as campaigning got under way for elections due on 20 May 1990. Opponents of the NSF accused it of seeking to impose a neo-communist solution on the country by pressing ahead with elections before its competitors had a chance to organise themselves. The report of the international delegation of observers who monitored the electoral process in its final stages confirmed many, though not all, criticisms about the state conduct of the elections.[2]

From the outset, the NSF enjoyed massive advantages over a weak and fragmented opposition. Its position as the dominant force in government gave it control over state assets, from access to printing presses and to transportation, to control over radio and television. The last advantage was a crucial one in a society where television had shaped the outlook of millions of people, particularly poorly-educated ones living in small towns and villages in remoter areas which received few other sources of information about the world beyond their immediate localities. The totalitarian state had found it easier to manipulate rural dwellers than other sections of the population, and television was a key weapon in moulding loyal and uncritical citizens. Anger about the manipulative role of television had led thousands to demonstrate outside the studios of 'Free Romanian Television' on 4 February 1990 even before events in Tirgu Mureş, and the acrimonious election campaign that followed, underscored the state media's capacity for bias, distortion and character assassination.[3] Starting on 22 April, the centre of Bucharest had also become a rallying-point for a peaceful sit-in by students, intellectuals and others making up the informal opposition, who claimed that former communists were trying to create a democratic Romania in their own distorted image. They demanded that RCP leaders, members of the Securitate, and leading nomenklatura officials should be barred from competing in the first three elections for any public office, including the presidency; this was Article 8 of the proclamation drawn up by democrats in Timişoara and released on 11 March.[4]

The conviction of anti-government protesters that cosmetic changes were leaving old power structures intact was strengthened when, on 24 April, it was announced that a new 'information service' was being formed to replace Ceauşescu's secret police, the Securitate. The Romanian Information Service (RIS) was to employ 6,000 out of the 15,000 personnel who had belonged to the Securitate up to December 1989.[5] The need to protect Romania from external threats to its security was cited as the reason for creating this successor intelligence service.[6] But to vocal critics, statements that the Securitate of old was no more were as bogus as the claim that the NSF had no connection with the party that had been the dominant force in Romanian society until the previous December. Many, far beyond their ranks, wondered what had happened to the RCP and why Romania was exceptional among post-communist states in that none of the eighty-two parties competing in its elections admitted to having had any connection with the previous ruling party.

But those Romanians whose reference-point in measuring change in their country was how elections were conducted in western Europe, or in recently liberated neighbours, proved only to be a minority. Most Romanians, due to the isolation which they had endured for forty-five years, had much narrower horizons. They compared Iliescu's performance not with Havel's or Gorbachev's but with Ceauşescu's, whose rule had become increasingly oppressive *in material terms* for them in the 1970s and 1980s. For Romanians unconcerned with party manifestoes, Ceauşescu 'the bad father' had been replaced by Iliescu 'the good father'.

Writing in 1988, Vládimir Tismaneanu had predicted that:

> anybody who would succeed Ceauşescu, even an ardent, seasoned apparatchik, would be the most popular leader in the whole of Romanian history . . . because such a person will benefit from comparisons with the worst period in Romanian history. It would, of course, be an undeserved and passing popularity. But it would be enough for Ceauşescu's successor to renounce some unpopular laws to achieve an extraordinary upsurge in popularity.[7]

This turned out to be highly prescient forecasting; probably it was far too much to expect that a people with traditionally low expectations, for whom a benevolent ruler was a rarity, would replace a ruler who, in his first months in office, had undoubtedly lightened the burdens of daily life: supplies of heat and light had been restored, peasants were being promised land, rationing was being scaled down despite continuing food shortages, and a full television service was being provided which offered entertainment as well as coverage of the exploits of those in power.

The close identification between one party and the state, abhorrent to many urbanised Romanians who wished to see a complete break with the past, was not necessarily viewed in this light by less sophisticated Romanians in the villages and provincial towns, among whom Iliescu was well received. Romanians had long been used to being ruled by an authority figure in charge of a powerful set of centralised institutions. Before, as well as during, the communist era, political legitimacy had been sought by rulers who promoted themselves as defenders of national security against traditional foes like Russia or Hungary. This was a tradition that the NSF showed every sign of wishing to uphold during the election period and beyond.

The NSF's readiness to play the nationalist card was shown by the respectability which it bestowed upon Vatra Româneaşca. Ion Iliescu never criticised Vatra leaders by name for the organisation's role in the Tirgu Mureş disturbances. (The National Peasant Party was the only Romanian organisation which he criticised by name in connection with these events, even though all evidence points to its role having been insignificant.[8]) Well-publicised meetings with Iliescu and Roman helped transform Vatra from a marginal provincial group into a national political player. Its nominees were included in the new administrative bodies set up in Tirgu Mureş and Mureş county.[9] A Vatra member was even included as part of the official Romanian delegation attending the Conference on Security and Co-operation in Europe meeting in Copenhagen in June 1990 examining ways of standardising treatment of minorities among the member states.

The NSF showed itself ready to deal on favourable terms with any group that did not threaten it and which posed problems for its opponents. Top-level statements about foreign interference being behind the Tirgu Mureş violence helped legitimise the Vatra Românescã viewpoint. An opinion poll carried out in the spring of 1990 showed that public opinion reflected the government's position: half of those interviewed laid the blame for the clashes on 'foreign instigators of extremist groups', while only 11.4 per cent thought that the clashes had been triggered off by the low tolerance shown by Romanians.[10]

In its bid to mobilise the language and symbols of nationalism when appealing to the public, the NSF struck up an informal alliance with the Romanian Orthodox Church, an important repository of national consciousness for many Romanians. The Orthodox Church had been tarnished by its close links with the communist regime. Teoctist, the Orthodox Patriarch, had sent a telegram to Ceauşescu on 19 December 1989 (two days after protesters had been shot in front of the Orthodox cathedral in Timisoara), praising him for his 'brilliant activity', 'wise guidance' and 'daring thinking'.[11] The patriarch's re-emergence in the spring after rescinding an earlier decision to retire, paralleled the new-found assertiveness of traditional forces in Romanian political life whose eclipse proved equally brief. Leading elements in a revamped state and church who had a questionable past to live down or an interest in avoiding drastic change struck up an informal alliance. Iliescu was seen on television attending church services even though he admitted that he was and remained a free-thinker, while several priests ran as NSF candidates. Church support may even have assisted the NSF as it sought to acquire massive electoral majorities in provinces like Moldavia, where religious observance is high in parts of the countryside.

But perhaps the most effective means that the NSF had of boosting its patriotic credentials was to deny that its opponents had any. Early in the election campaign, the NSF and its allies claimed that the opposition parties were willing to permit the dismemberment of Romania and to return Transylvania to Hungary.[12] The NSF's own daily, *Azi* (Today), launched on 11 April 1990, published articles that evoked the chauvinist invective that had been commonplace up to six months earlier. It gave several of Ceauşescu's most energetic propagandists the opportunity to revive their skills in disinformation and character assassination so that, before long, articles were appearing alleging that leading opposition figures had non-Romanian (usually Hungarian) ancestry.[13] The first edition of *Azi* included an article by prominent Vatra spokesman, Ion Coja, in which readers were reminded that certain Hungarians had obtained a wide range of advantages in the early years of communist rule.[14] But Hungarians were not the principal targets of NSF media attacks perhaps because of the unfavourable reaction which this might have generated among the correspondents and election observers present in Romania still mindful of the events in Tirgu Mureş. The strongest attacks were, instead, directed against Iliescu's two presidential challengers, Ion Raţiu of the National Peasant Party (NPP-CD) and Radu Campeanu of the National Liberal Party (NLP), who had both plunged into active politics after years (five decades in Raţiu's case) spent living abroad. They were regularly criticised for having lost touch with the country – for eating caviare in Paris instead of salami and soya at home – and, in Raţiu's case, for forgetting part of the language he had been born with. Both men were physically attacked while campaigning by mobs of people who had been inflamed by media invective in a not dissimilar fashion to what had happened in Tirgu Mureş.[15]

Revived after a long interruption, multi-party politics in Romania brought to mind Henry Adams's definition of politics as 'the systematic organisation of hatreds'. The NSF slogan 'we shall never sell the country' was countered by the 'Down with Communism' of Iliescu's most dogged opponents in the 'Communist-Free Zones' set up in central Bucharest and several other Romanian cities.

The result of the 20 May elections showed that the NSF was the overwhelming choice of the great majority of voters. On a turnout of eighty-six per cent, Ion Iliescu received 85.1 per cent of the vote and was thus elected President of Romania on the first round (a second ballot being required if no candidate had got more than fifty per cent).

Meanwhile, the NSF obtained 66.31 per cent of the vote in the parliamentary elections which would enable it to devise a new constitution largely according to its own tastes, the chief task of the two-chamber legislature. Numerous irregularities in the electoral process were pointed to by election observers and others, but it was clear that the NSF was the preferred choice of a substantial majority of the electorate. Iliescu's message of social and economic paternalism and unabashed nationalism was appealing to millions of people who regarded it as a genuine advance over anything that they had been offered by Romanian rulers for a long time. But others chose Iliescu because he was simply the least risky of the alternatives on offer.

In second place to the NSF was the HDFR on 7.2 per cent of the vote. Hungarian areas were among the few where the election campaign proceeded normally and where no significant irregularities were reported. The ability of Transylvanian Hungarians to maintain a united front enabled the party to put in a strong performance. Arguably, the two main Romanian parties challenging the NSF, the NPP-CD and the NLP would have performed much more effectively if they had sunk their differences and formed an opposition alliance. As for the scattered forces of dissent, they failed to produce a political party capable of mounting a successful electoral challenge. Whereas Vatra intellectuals had entered parliament, their liberal counterparts who had played a prominent role in the events of December 1989, such as Ion Caramitru and Mircea Dinescu, failed to obtain enough backing in Bucharest where they stood as candidates.

THE STATE AND POST-ELECTORAL VIOLENCE

However, the limelight remained focused on the informal opposition which defied the authorities by remaining encamped in Bucharest's University Square for a further three weeks after the elections. They were finally removed on 13 June 1990 following a broadcast by Ion Iliescu on that day, calling on loyal citizens to come to the aid of the government. Some 10,000 miners arrived in the capital and, for the next two days, went on the rampage, attacking opposition party headquarters and the offices of civic groups, as well as gypsies.[16] Iliescu had warned that the country was facing a 'legionary rebellion', a reference to the extreme-right movement of the 1930s. No evidence was produced by Ion Iliescu for linking opponents with a group which Romanians had been taught to regard as hostile to their interests. But the *golani* (the Romanian word for 'hoodlum' which was adopted by the University Square protesters after Iliescu had used it to describe them) had certain features in common with Legionary members, being alienated from the state, radical in intent, believers in a revolution created by youth, and motivated by a spirit of sacrifice.

There were several striking parallels between the June 1990 violence and what had occurred in Tirgu Mureş three months earlier. Evidence of the involvement of state officials in bringing large groups of people to the locations where they carried out violence exists.[17] As with Tirgu Mureş, President Iliescu preferred to condemn not those who carried it out but others whose allegedly irresponsible behaviour had led to people taking the law into their own hands. At a rally in Bucharest on 15 June, he thanked the miners for displaying workers solidarity in the face of a plot by forces inside and outside the country who believed that 'right-wing forces should come to power in all East European countries'.[18] Thus the claim that violence involving Romanian citizens had been part of a conspiracy hatched by unidentified forces outside the country was made for the second time by the President.[19]

Iliescu publicly congratulated the miners on their 'civic awareness', declaring that 'we know that we can rely upon you. When necessary we will
call upon you.'[20] Not surprisingly, this group of workers was left with the
impression that it had the right to intervene in politics, which it would do
in spectacular manner a year later.

A final parallel is offered by the way in which the authorities took
advantage of the uproar surrounding both sets of violent acts to carry out
controversial security decisions. The Committee for Action to Democratise the Army (CADA) was banned on 14 June, the security services having
been revived under a new name in April following the Tirgu Mureş events.

The international condemnation resulting from the government's role
in the June 1990 violence was virtually unanimous. Romania's leaders
increased their discomfiture by giving explanations for the events and
attaching blame for them which differed sharply from earlier statements.[21]
Economic assistance from the EU was frozen immediately after the miners'
violence. In October 1990, Iliescu was the only east European leader not
received by President Bush when he attended the UN General Assembly
meeting in New York.[22] Later, Prime Minister Roman's request that
Romania be included in the Visegrad group of former Warsaw Pact
countries that were pooling their energies in order to speed up the process
of integrating with west European institutions was met with a rebuff.
President Havel of Czechoslovakia felt that the Visegrad partners' agenda
would be hampered if they were associated with a country whose level of
democracy was regarded with disfavour in the west;[23] in June it had been
Havel who had written a sharply-worded letter to his Romanian counterpart expressing his 'consternation at the wave of arrests and violence in
Romania' and asking for 'full respect for fundamental human rights'.[24]

The Bucharest authorities quickly took steps to repair their public image,
which suggested that a return to isolationism was not an option felt to be
open to them. The scale of the economic damage inflicted on the country
during Ceauşescu's relentless attempt to impose economic self-sufficiency
did not make autarky an attractive option even for those public figures
clearly ill-at-ease with having to operate in a democratic environment. The
reappointment of a government headed by Petre Roman demonstrated
that Iliescu wished to develop beneficial economic and political links with
the west that would enable the country to emerge from isolation, albeit
on its own terms. The important economic portfolios were filled by men
who gradually convinced western visitors in contact with them of their
seriousness in wishing to discard past economic models and press ahead
with a rapid liberalisation of the economy. Indeed, the Roman government borrowed much of its economic rhetoric from the opposition whose
pro-capitalist proposals it had denounced as an economic sell-out of the

country in the spring. Privatisation measures were announced in August just as radical as the ones the opposition had promised earlier. These made an impression in west European capitals and financial centres among experts unfamiliar with the fact that government programmes and rhetoric often bore even less relation to intentions than in other east European countries.

Silviu Brucan, who had decided that the role of political commentator was more fulfilling than that of activist in the NSF where he had played a critical early role, argued in a Romanian television interview on 31 May that political openness needed to accompany economic renewal for Romania's attempt to break free of the authoritarian past to succeed. He urged the NSF to provide autonomy for local organisations and to allow a democratic internal party life which would include the acceptance of groups and factions. He worried about the many 'yes-men' and opportunists surrounding the new President, people who would never dare to contradict him and, despite expressing his great admiration for Ion Iliescu, he stated that he no longer believed in people only in institutions as a defence line against the abuse of power.[25]

THE AUTHORITARIAN SPIRIT PERSISTS

The key test about whether the government was interested in pursuing a policy of political *glasnost* would be provided by decisions which it took in the area of local government. In July 1990, Petre Roman began replacing mayors who had been appointed at the beginning of the year with appointees who were clearly loyal to the NSF. The office of prefect was also re-established, the holder being the highest authority in each Romanian county and directly answerable to the Prime Minister in Bucharest.

In areas of the country where the NSF had failed to score more than fifty per cent of the vote, there was fierce resentment when Roman not only imposed pro-government prefects but also replaced those city mayors who had reflected local opinion. The appointment of an ethnic Romanian prefect in the overwhelmingly Hungarian county of Covasna produced large protests. After a government delegation of ministers, deputies and journalists visited the area, a compromise was reached whereby, in the counties of Harghita and Covasna, mixed pairs of ethnic Romanians and Hungarians were appointed as joint prefects.[26] However, this propensity to compromise was an isolated occurrence. The government ignored protests in the village of Sapinţa, in the Maramureş area of northern Romania, over the removal and arrest of its anti-communist mayor appointed by a majority of peasants who had abolished the collective and state farms in the area, dividing the land and livestock among themselves. This example of rural self-reliance was unusual, and it was not one that a governing party dependent on a sea of compliant rural voters was ready to encourage. The pro-government press alleged that there was an anti-national and anti-Romanian goal behind the Sapinţa events and, eventually, Mayor Toader Steţca felt obliged to seek exile abroad.[27]

The newly-elected government showed itself particularly unresponsive to regional groups which had a grievance arising from the communist period. For instance, a National League of Counties Abusively Abolished by the Communist Dictatorship appealed in vain for the government to return to the pre-communist form of territorial organisation. Pressure groups in areas which had been swallowed up in other counties emerged which expressed a defiant form of local patriotism whose independence was not to the liking of the government. Nor did it feel inclined to support the demands of the Uniate Church (also known as the Greek Catholic or Eastern Rite Church) for the restitution of between 1,800 and 2,000 places of worship confiscated by the state in 1948 and handed over to the Romanian Orthodox Church. The Uniates, who had played a prominent role in the struggle for Romanian unification, also expressed the local patriotism of Transylvania, the region where they were most numerous. Although the Uniate church was legalised in 1990, after long years of persecution, the new law obliged the Orthodox Church, not the state, to restore church property voluntarily even though it had been seized by the latter.[28]

Another test of the Romanian authorities' readiness to make amends for past injustice towards its own citizens concerned its attitude to King Michael I of Romania, whose Romanian citizenship had been revoked by the communist authorities in 1948, one year after he had been forced to abdicate and go into exile. King Michael was expelled again from the country on 26 December 1990 less than twelve hours after he had been processed through customs and passport control at Bucharest airport without incident.[29] The attitude of the government to a figure who lacked widespread support in the country revealed an insecurity that was at variance with the large electoral mandate which it had received in May 1990.

RENEWED MANIPULATION OF THE PAST

Although the government was concerned to minimise the influence of forces ranging from the National Peasant Party to the former monarchy which possessed a record of service to the nation, it was far from neglectful of the past. It quickly seems to have grasped that if it proved able to redefine the past in ways that suited its own political agenda, this could strengthen its legitimacy. Starting in 1990, the government thus began to use historical commemorations to identify with the episodes and individuals from Romania's past best felt to exemplify the country's greatness.

Of course, the Ceauşescu regime had made use of such symbols to clinch its authority and to forge a band of identity between rulers and ruled at a time of mounting privation resulting from failed economic policies. The context in which the Iliescu regime was re-evaluating the past on its own terms was also one of economic hardship. The disputed circumstances in which it came to power, as well as the bleak economic prospects facing perhaps millions of citizens as the wreckage of the Ceauşescu era was cleared away, meant that it was worth fixing the attention of citizens onto a longer time-frame.

The Romanian government turned the inter-war period into a major reference-point. Political glories were lacking and the 1930s had been marred by political misrule as well as by severe internal conflict along ideological, regional and even generational lines. Nevertheless, the years between 1918 and 1940 were ones in which the borders of the state had expanded to include nearly all Romanian speakers and there were anniversaries of illustrious figures from these years which were commemorated after 1989 as state occasions.

The fiftieth anniversary of the assassination of Nicolae Iorga was treated as a solemn event, as was the fiftieth anniversary in February 1991 of the death of Nicolae Titulescu, Romania's most successful foreign policy practitioner. Weeks rarely went by in the second half of 1990 without the president being filmed at a graveside or historic monument flanked by Orthodox priests and army officers, the event often being the main item on the evening television news irrespective of what was happening elsewhere in the world. Not a few of President Iliescu's visits to Transylvania were ostensibly to commemorate historic events in the struggle to unite all the Romanian-speaking territories. In March 1991, a visit by the President to Cluj coincided with the 200th anniversary of the *Supplex Libellus Vallochorum*, an important eighteenth-century treatise setting out Romanian national aims. It was also the eighty-ninth birthday of David Prodan, the chief historical specialist of the period. Iliescu declared that his chief reason for visiting Cluj was to offer his good wishes to this illustrious historian.[30] He also made sure that he returned to Cluj in June 1992 for the ceremony marking the centenary of the Memorandum trial in which Transylvanian nationalists were put on trial by the Hungarian authorities after unsuccessfully appealing to the Emperor Franz Josef for a redress of some of their grievances.[31]

Undoubtedly, the most controversial excursion into the past made by Romania's post-1989 rulers came when they decided to commemorate the fiftieth anniversary of the Vienna Accord or Diktat signed on 30 August 1940 at German and Italian insistence, under which northern Transylvania was ceded to Hungary. The event had been downplayed in Ceauşescu's time perhaps out of reluctance to dwell on past national disasters or because of a desire not to break too publicly with one of the cherished myths of Soviet-led east European communism that it had opened up an era of genuine friendship among peoples.

As early as 31 March 1990, Petre Roman had referred to the events following the Vienna Accord when he declared at a press conference that, from 1940 to 1944 when Hungarian rule collapsed, many Romanians had been subject to inhumane treatment.[32] The government decided to mark the occasion with a special meeting of parliament, a television address by the President, visits by government leaders to sites in Transylvania associated with Hungarian oppression, as well as encouraging many local events. Whatever hesitation may have existed about implanting memories of past ethnic oppression in Romanian minds so recently after the Tirgu Mureş clashes was brushed aside in favour of marking an anniversary which ultra-nationalists certainly had no intention of allowing to slip by unnoticed.

In a radio interview some weeks before the anniversary date, President Iliescu had noted that 'it is in the interest of us all not to play into the hands of those who want to use this opportunity to poison the relationship between the citizens of our country'. He went on to urge that 'we should be guided . . . by the best examples in our long-standing common history of co-existence and co-operation among the simple people in this country who always found a common language to understand, help and respect each other'.[33] But at no time did he explain how the revival of interest in such a bloodstained event could assist a healing process. Indeed, part of his own television address on the day of the anniversary could have been seen as frustrating that process, when he referred to the Vienna Diktat as 'one of the most abominable acts carried out in the modern history of mankind'. Such language was not designed to encourage a detached view among ordinary Romanians, who were already being persuaded by nation-alist extremists that guilt for the occupation of northern Transylvania not only lay with the Horthyite dictatorship in wartime Budapest but was also hereditary and collective and could thus be assigned to Hungarians who may not even have been alive in 1940.

In the same address, Iliescu stressed the contemporary relevance of the 1940 loss of territory and the need for continuing vigilance to prevent something similar happening in the future: 'we recall those events not to sow hostility or hatred among the successors of those who lived in those times but because we do not want such events ever to happen again'.[34]

Alexandru Bîrladeanu, President of the senate, also referred to a contemporary dimension in his parliamentary address, stating that an award which allowed Romania to become 'one of the first victims of the fascist policy of aggression ... [had] deeply damaged the relationship between the Romanians and Hungarians in Transylvania. The poisoned root of that state of affairs still exists ...'

Meanwhile, the President of the Chamber of Deputies, Dan Marţian, moved beyond the Vienna Diktat to claim that 'in the 1980s, the whole of the Romanian nation, as well as the ethnic minorities, were subjected to a systematic programme of wiping out the moral and historical values that define their national identity'. In other words, the claim that Hungarians had been treated worse than other Romanian citizens in the last phase of Ceauşescu's rule was unfounded. Having established this point, Marţian went on to argue that there were no grounds for special minority rights which could prove dangerous for the unity of the country:

> Parliament ... reaffirms the desire to build a pluralist society as soon as possible with the same rights, freedoms and responsibility for all citizens of our country be they Romanians or other ethnic minorities [sic] ... democracy ... does not mean the creation of autonomies, of extra-territorial enclaves which would finally lead to the creation of a multi-national territory and to the country's dismemberment.[35]

This is perhaps the first time that a key argument of Vatra Românească, concerning the likelihood that national disintegration would result from granting concessions to minorities not possessed by other citizens, had been endorsed so openly by a leading state official. The 30 August anniversary enabled the government to devote more attention to minority issues than it had done on any occasion since the series of pronouncements issued in January 1990 about future policy goals in which plans were outlined to protect minority rights which it later retreated from. The fact that the present status of the Hungarian minority was being referred to in events marking previous unjust Hungarian behaviour towards Romania, was hardly likely to foster reconciliation despite Iliescu's call for inter-ethnic peace. None of the government spokesmen sought to dissociate the present-day Transylvanian Hungarians from the events of 1940–4 or to emphasise that, among them, irredentist aspirations were conspicuous by their absence. The ambiguity of much of the oratory stemming from leading state officials and the government's reluctance to dissociate itself from the interpretations of 1940 provided by ultra-nationalists (who played a prominent role in official celebrations) were unsettling portents. The government's failure to prevent the 1940 anniversary from being used for such divisive political ends showed an insensitivity towards the Hungarian minority which, in turn would deepen the sense of isolation felt by the latter.[36]

The NSF's concern to divert public attention away from controversial episodes in the communist period may also have been a factor behind the government's readiness to commemorate the Vienna Accord in a manner similar to that preferred by ultra-nationalists. In choosing a new national day for Romania, the authorities also chose a date strongly favoured by ultra-nationalists, 1 December, the day Transylvania had united with Romania in 1918. It replaced 23 August, the date in 1944 when Romania broke free of the Axis alliance and which marked the start of the rise to power of the communists. However, on 24 July 1990 the Senate voted unanimously for 1 December, and a special sitting of parliament was convened on 1 December 1990 in Alba Iulia, the site of the declaration of unity between Romania and Transylvania in 1918.

Over 100,000 people attended the first celebration of the new national holiday, many of whom were ultra-nationalist supporters. Opposition deputies who spoke were booed and controversy ensued when Prime Minister Roman was seen to act as cheer-leader when part of the crowd booed, the veteran NPP-CD leader, Corneliu Coposu, in the course of his address.[37] On the same day, Roman claimed that he was the offspring of a family with an ancient tradition of struggle for Romanian rights in Transylvania. This was only the best-known example of an attempt by Roman to appeal to the nationalist gallery and to play down the fact that his father, the son of a Hungarian-speaking rabbi in Oradea, had been a member of the RCP central committee until his death in 1983.[38] Roman even published his own birth certificate in the NSF daily newspaper, *Azi*, on 13 September 1990 to refute critics in anti-Semitic publications who questioned his Romanian credentials.

The President and government leaders played a prominent role in celebrations marking the first anniversary of the popular revolt against Ceauşescu. However, Iliescu, in his television address on 24 December 1990, stressed the need for national unity and opposed the drive for blind revenge against officials in the former regime. 'The fact', he told listeners, 'that the repressive apparatus abandoned the dictator and that the army and personnel of the ministry of the interior sided with the revolution, constituted a key element in the predestined progress of the events that followed'. He went on to say that 'we have to appreciate the decisive contribution made by the army . . . and by some elements who understood . . . where their place was in this confrontation'.[39]

In December 1991 on the second anniversary of the revolution, President Iliescu chose the occasion of an address to parliament to suggest that the communist era itself deserved more measured treatment than it had got: 'one cannot disregard the constructive work and efforts of the people over the past forty-five years'.[40]

The President was probably more in touch with public opinion than the opposition was when he called for an end to recriminations about the immediate past. However, Hungarians reacted with bitterness at the way in which the state chose to revive memories of past inter-ethnic collisions, as in 1940, while preferring to draw a veil over the communist period with its mountain of human rights violations, so as not to endanger national unity. Disgruntlement increased in May 1991 when Hungarian teenagers who had pulled down a Romanian flag in Tirgu Mureş were given prison sentences as long as the majority meted out to those accused of 'genocide' in December 1989.[41]

In March 1991, the Romanian authorities banned public gatherings from 14 to 22 March in Mureş county which prevented public com-memorations of the anniversary of 1848 in Tirgu Mureş. Elsewhere, joint Romanian-Hungarian celebrations were held to emphasise a common historical heritage and interdependence, but these were less in evidence than in 1990. An HDFR deputy, Béla Markó, appealed to Romanians to understand that 'those who speak a different language are also enti-tled to have their own customs, songs, and holidays'.[42] But there was an unavailing response from leading NSF Senator, Vasile Vacaru who spoke in parliament on 7 March 1991 about events on 15 March 1848 when Romanians were alleged to have been attacked by Hungarians.[43] Senator Vacaru chose to dwell on events of 143 years previously the day after the foreign minister, Adrian Năstase, had pointed out one way in which the perspectives of the Romanian and Hungarian states were at variance concerning disputed issues: 'the Romanian side chooses to approach . . . issues not looking back but setting its eyes on the future'.[44]

BUDAPEST AND BUCHAREST REMAIN ESTRANGED

In the twelve months following the Tirgu Mureş violence, the tension in relations between the Hungarian community and the Romanian authorities had been reflected at inter-state level between Bucharest and Budapest. Hopes that the two countries were about to mark a historic turning-point in the wake of their disengagement from communism were dashed when Hungary played a leading role in condemning the bloodshed of March 1990. Thereafter, the NSF showed that it was prepared to sacrifice good relations with Hungary for its own domestic political requirements. Deep resentment was shown when Geza Jeszenszky, the Hungarian foreign minister, said in August 1990 that the Romanian government should admit that Romania is a multi-national state. The Romanian foreign minister had described this assertion as 'something that does not correspond to reality but might serve revisionist objectives pursued by the current Hungarian foreign policy vis-à-vis Hungary'.[45] This broadside was delivered in the same month that Hungarian prime minister Antall issued his controversial statement that 'in spirit' he was the prime minister of 15,000,000 Hungarians throughout the world.[46]

Hungarian leaders were quick to point out on numerous occasions that Hungary had no territorial claims over any other country. The seventieth anniversary of the 1920 Trianon peace treaty, which saw two-thirds of what had been Hungarian territory pass to its neighbours, was used as an opportunity to show that Hungary had come to terms with its past by rejecting irredentism. On this occasion, all six parties represented in parliament issued a statement that expressed support for the 1975 Helsinki Final Act's ban on unilaterally changing frontiers by force and declared that the present borders were a component of European stability 'irrespective of this being just or unjust'.[47] However, Romania was unimpressed with such declarations as long as Hungary insisted on the right to speak out on behalf of its co-nationals in Transylvania. The firmly-held Romanian view has been that the situation of the Hungarian minority in Romania is a purely internal matter and cannot be subject to discussion between Romanians and Hungarians.[48]

Talks between Romanian and Hungarian state officials in 1990–1 never got beyond deputy foreign minister level. Adrian Nastase, Romanian foreign minister from July 1990 until November 1992, was perhaps not the best person to faciliate a bilateral meeting. He came from a nomenklatura background, members of his family having held important positions in the diplomatic service during the Ceauşescu era. The foreign ministry under Ceauşescu had been a strong-hold of doctrinaire views, and there was no more evidence that a change of personnel had taken place here than in other branches of state. The extent to which official suspicion about Hungarian intentions could be openly taken was shown by a statement about Romania's foreign policy role written in 1991 by Ioan Mircea Paşcu, who in 1993 was appointed head of the defence ministry's military policy and international relations bureau.

Paşcu expressed the view that 'one of our former allies Hungary has transformed herself openly into a potential enemy', citing as evidence 'statements and actions that interfere in Romania's domestic politics'.[49] He displayed concern at the prospect that co-operation between Hungary, Czechoslovakia and Poland might contain security aspects, and he cited as grounds for Romanian insecurity the emergence of a bloc of Catholic states emerging on her western borders (in conjunction with a Slav bloc to the north and east, with Islamic Turkey becoming more and more active in the south).[50]

President Iliescu's comments on bilateral relations with Hungary were usually far less contentious, but there were occasions when he took the

opportunity to contrast minority rights in Romania favourably with those
in Hungary. Thus, when interviewed on Austrian television in October
1990, he argued that minorities in Romania enjoyed 'infinitely better' rights
than in Hungary because they are represented in parliament whereas this is
not the case in Hungary. However, he failed to show what tangible benefits
minorities had obtained from symbolic representation in parliament and
how Hungary's 15–20,000 Romanian speakers were at a disadvantage
through not having a seat in the Budapest parliament.[51] In the following
autumn he made reference to the security services in order to contrast
Romania's recent record with that of Hungary, the claim being made by
the president that the Hungarian intelligence services carried on as normal
after the change of regime unlike in his own country, where the Securitate
had been dismantled and an information service organised in its place.[52]

Amid the diplomatic skirmishing and point-scoring, some gains were
made in Romanian–Hungarian relations in the 1990–1 period. When
reviewing the Romanian army's links with other European armies, defence minister Nicolae Spiroiu declared in October 1991 that 'our best
relations . . . are with the Hungarian army'.[53] Speaking of his links with
his Hungarian counterpart, he declared that 'we intend military relations
to represent a model for political relations'; in August 1991, Janos Für,
the Hungarian defence minister (known for his own nationalist views),
had stated that 'good military relations can counterbalance political
differences'.[54]

Romanian and Hungarian citizens were also starting to enjoy greater
contact with one another than for many years; the abolition of visa requirements meant that they were able to travel to each other's countries
relatively freely. The breaching of the mutual isolation that was a feature
of most of the Ceauşescu era helped to reduce the ignorance upon which
national enmity was able to breed. But diplomatic ties failed to keep pace
with greater human contact and one expert even claimed that by the end
of 1990 bilateral relations had moved to a point where, if anything, they
were worse than under Ceauşescu.[55]

THE NSF: SEARCHING FOR A POST-COMMUNIST IDENTITY

As long as the NSF felt the need to go before the electorate as the champion of Romanian national interests, relations with Hungary were bound
to be problematic. The failure of the party to acquire a secure political
identity based on a programme or a set of philosophical ideas meant that
its legislators and chief spokesmen often took a nationalist high profile.
But the NSF had presided (however warily) over a democratic opening in
Romania, and, unlike the RCP, it was unable to monopolise expressions
of nationalism. It found itself in competition with other forces intent on

playing the national card, but in 1991 the growing nationalist trajectory of the NSF halted. Previously harmonious relations between the NSF and Vatra Românească grew cooler as Vatra's political counterpart, the PRNU, viewed itself as an active competitor of the NSF in Transylvania. A public breach occurred in January 1991 when the NSF approved the parliamentary report into the Tirgu Mureş violence which was at variance with the blameless role that Vatra claimed to have played.[56]

Irritation with ultra-nationalist pretensions led Petre Roman to declare in July 1991 that it should not be said 'that some are more Romanian than others. We are all Romanians . . . except that some, by their deeds, prove it more'.[57]

President Iliescu also felt obliged to speak out against the anti-Semitic tones of the ultra-nationalist press: 'I disavow all anti-Semitic positions . . . The article in *România Mâre* terrified me. It had everything short of the attitude that we should go and kill the Jews.'[58] This statement was made shortly before President Iliescu embarked upon a state visit to Israel in September 1991 and followed an appeal from the ministry of culture asking the government to condemn two weeklies, *România Mâre* and *Europa*, 'because they are causing serious damage to the reputation of the country'.[59]

The growing clamour to rehabilitate Marshal Ion Antonescu, Romania's wartime head of government, threatened to have international repercussions, since large numbers of Jews had been killed by forces answerable to him. For Romanians seeking a strong ruler who would sweep away internal malcontents, put an end to foreign meddling and make the country great again, Antonescu was an inspiring figure. However, Iliescu defied a tide of opinion in Antonescu's favour, that extended beyond the ultra-right, by declaring openly in July 1991 that he 'did not share the opinion of those who wished to rehabilitate him, keeping silent on the negative aspects of his activity'. The President did not question Antonescu's qualities as an army man, but he refused to overlook the fact that 'he took power with an Iron Guard government, that he was Hitler's ally, that he pushed the country into war . . . I can't see the merit Ion Antonescu had as a political man and that is why I do not agree with those who praise him so much today'.[60]

THE SEPTEMBER 1991 CRISIS AND THE FALL OF ROMAN

It is probably no coincidence that the more balanced evocation of the country's past coincided with a period of domestic calm in which the need by office-holders to make bold nationalist pronouncements may have seemed less pressing. However, at the end of September 1991, this calm was shattered by a renewed onslaught on the capital by coal-miners from the Jiu valley who forced Prime Minister Roman from office. By now, a new word, *mineriada*, had entered the Romanian language to describe the action of coal-miners who, in 1990, had acted as pro-government shock-troops on no less than three occasions. But finally the government became their target as they found that their conspicuous loyalty was not shielding them from the tightening economic squeeze being imposed on the general population.

Sky-rocketing prices and accelerating unemployment had been unwelcome by-products of Romania's uncertain lurch towards the semblance of a market economy. The Roman government's stated aim of transforming a deeply-entrenched socialist economy into a competitive one had improved the country's battered image abroad; however, it had also divided the NSF, and President Iliescu's public endorsement for his Prime Minister's strategy became increasingly lukewarm. At what turned out to be the NSF's first and only national conference in April 1991, a majority of delegates backed Roman, who was also the president of the party. But the backing for the man who could hinder or advance their careers in the party was essentially opportunistic and would later be withheld when Roman had the greatest need of it.[61] The western-orientated technocrats with whom Roman had surrounded himself remained a minority in the party. Conservative, party-educated deputies with a background in the state bureaucracy had already proven their strength in the autumn of 1990 by blocking proposals that civil-service staff should be appointed on the basis of proven competence.

Later, Eugen Dijmarescu, Roman's economy minister, was to complain about 'an unseen but operational establishment' formed after the revolution by 'a conservative stratum of the former nomenklatura' intent on retaining the main levers of control in Romanian society.[62] Attempts to shed light on the degree of political continuity with the pre-1989 system proved unavailing even when the initiative came from an NSF deputy such as Claudio Iordache, one of the few government deputies who had never been an RCP member. In May 1991, Iordache introduced a bill that would have required the secret police files of officials in the three branches of government to be checked to determine how many had been compromised by collaboration with the Securitate. The bill was supported by 146 deputies, but it 'mysteriously' got lost when it was forwarded to the Senate.[63] Iordache was later jeered by other NSF deputies, and he resigned from parliament in June 1991, accusing Romania's leaders of being puppets of the former Securitate which, he said, had 'penetrated almost the entire national administration'.[64]

Out of office, Roman spoke on 29 October 1991 of the dangers facing Romania as a result of the survival of 'the mentality and methods of the Ceauşescu Securitate'.[65] Like Ceauşescu, Roman had fallen in little over twenty-four hours, being unable to mobilise popular support against his extra-parliamentary foes in the way that Boris Yeltsin had managed to do in August 1991 against Soviet pro-communist conspirators. The security forces had melted away before the marauders who had occupied the parliament building on 26 September 1991. Roman then handed in his mandate to facilitate a political solution to the crisis, saying afterwards that he had had no intention of resigning. Police and soldiers were then able to restore order. But President Iliescu refused to annul the resignation, which fuelled speculation about an internal power struggle. A new caretaker government was then appointed under Teodor Stolojan, finance minister in the first nine months of the Roman government, which parliament duly swore in on 16 October 1991. 'Under circumstances of violence,' Roman affirmed, 'there can be no resignation' and he criticised Iliescu's willingness to negotiate under the threat of force as 'an act of cowardice' bound to prove disastrous for democracy.[66]

This public breach was the beginning of a power struggle to gain control of the NSF which would split it asunder within six months. Roman presented himself as the true defender of democracy and depicted the President in the role of 'the nostalgic communist'.[67] However, he had failed to create an accessible democracy based on trust or popular confidence in his governing record, which meant that he was deserted by the people in his hour of need.

The verdict of the well-known dissident Doina Cornea was even more damning on Petre Roman. To her mind, 'the name Petre Roman was closely associated with the concept[s] of lie[s] and violence . . .While abroad he pretended to be a Prime Minister who was in favour of reform and a friend of the west . . . here at home many innocent people were beaten up with his consent'.[68]

THE IMPERATIVE OF UNITY AND THE ENEMY WITHIN

One of Petre Roman's last acts as Prime Minister revealed his capacity for manipulating public opinion rather than channelling it in a responsible direction. On 25 September 1991, while debating the miners' strike that would shortly lead to his removal, Roman suddenly changed the subject and announced that news had just been received that a Transylvanian government-in-exile had been set up in Budapest. A parliamentary debate was immediately called over what Roman described as 'a stupefying action'.[69] But it soon emerged that it was the work of a handful of insignificant people, and, after being speedily condemned by the HDFR and the Budapest government, no more was heard of what appeared to be a phantom Transylvanian government.

The existence of a Hungarian threat posing a danger to the well-being of Romania was revived with much greater emphasis in October 1991 with the publication of a parliamentary report into the situation in the predominantly Hungarian-speaking counties of Harghita and Covasna (known as the Szekler counties)in the weeks following the overthrow of Ceauşescu. The report found that Romanians had been subjected to a systematic campaign of intimidation which resulted in large numbers abandoning their homes and fleeing the area. Also falling into the category of Hungarian persecution were the deaths of four Romanian members of the Securitate and the militia in the last days of 1989.[70]

HDFR deputies, defying the nationalist clamour, pointed out that members of the security forces killed in the Szekler counties lost their lives not because they were Romanians but because, rightly or wrongly, they were associated with state repression; indeed, three sub-officers who were ethnic Hungarians, were among the dead, the object of popular fury towards a system that repressed everyone. But what were revolutionary acts of justice in other places where Securitate personnel were killed became anti-Romanian acts in Harghita and Covasna.[71]

The commission appointed by parliament in October 1990 to investigate the situation in Harghita and Covasna produced a report which claimed that 4,000 Romanians had hurriedly left the Szekler counties due to an outbreak of intimidation in early 1990. However, Ioan Oancea, the NSF's sole deputy in Harghita, while acknowledging the existence of an anti-Romanian mood in the area at the start of 1990, claimed that many young people who had been sent to the Szekler towns as part of the scheme of compulsory labour direction for recent graduates had left voluntarily because they preferred to return to their homes in Wallachia and Moldavia.[72]

Such moderate voices were, however, drowned out in the two-day debate on the report which was broadcast live from parliament, in which NSF deputies competed with PRNU ones in the expression of anti-Hungarian remarks. One senator alleged that real terrorism occurred when Szekler children were forced to learn a language that was spoken by only 13,000,000 people worldwide. Several others claimed that the HDFR was no political party but a faction whose behaviour was unpatriotic and deeply damaging to the country.[73] Ex-Premier Roman also expressed his indignation upon learning of the 'persecution' to which Romanian citizens had been exposed. But the government's main press critic, *România Liberă*, put his indignation in perspective by asking who had been Premier during the period with which the report dealt. Who had the means to intervene to prevent such human rights abuses? Why had no legal proceedings been taken against those supposedly guilty of crimes of violence? How many times had the former Premier been to the Szekler counties to interest himself in the situation there?[74]

Geza Domokos, the HDFR leader, ruefully observed that 'Transylvania was again being used to distract the attention of the public from the true problems of Romania'.[75] In August 1990, he had complained that a high-level delegation of ministers, deputies and journalists which had just returned from the area had declined to issue a statement which might have cut through the swirl of rumours about the reasons behind the exodus of Romanians and what the situation was really like in the Szekler counties.[76]

The impression that Hungarians in Romania were being made scapegoats by a political establishment in deep disarray which needed to cover up its own divisions by seeking out an internal enemy was strongly felt in Budapest in the wake of the parliamentary report and the storm arising from it. Gyula Horn, chairman of the foreign affairs committee of the Budapest parliament, complained on 21 October 1991 that the Romanian parliament was responsible for stirring up new inter-ethnic tensions.[77] State secretary Geza Entz declared two months later that a substantial part of the statements made in the Romanian parliament about Hungarians fell into the category of racial incitement against an ethnic group.[78]

Entz, a Transylvanian Hungarian by origin, headed a Secretariat of Hungarians Abroad which was attached to the Prime Minister's office. It had been set up in 1990 at the initiative of Prime Minister Antall, and it had the task of maintaining contact with Hungarian organisations in neighbouring countries as well as in the rest of the world.[79] This initiative was the most concrete example of the Hungarian government's belief that it was entitled to defend the interests of its co-nationals in other states. It collided with Romania's view that the situation of its Hungarian minority was purely an internal matter. However, it is worth noting that Romania was prepared to relax this stipulation in its protracted negotiations with the Council of Europe, a body it was keen to join as a full member in order to fulfil its goal of being reintegrated into mainstream European life. Between 1991 and 1994, several delegations despatched by the Council of Europe to assess the progress that Romania was making in safeguarding human rights had specifically raised minority issues in submissions accepted by the Bucharest government.

The freeze in Romanian–Hungarian relations led to some internal criticism in Hungary that disagreements over minority issues were being allowed to block progress in other bilateral relations.[80] Antall, while denying that minority questions were the only factors in inter-state relations, stated in April 1991 that 'we find it impossible to have good relations with a country that mistreats its Hungarian minority'.[81] The UN Commission of Human Rights in Geneva was told by Hungary that its co-nationals in Romania remained the frequent object of 'harassment, intimidation, and interference'. The Romanian authorities were also accused of discriminating against minorities in the administration of justice by singling out Hungarians and gypsies for punishment in the courts of Tirgu Mureş after March 1990.[82]

Hungary has been foremost among European states pressing for a code of minority rights applying to all member-states in the Council of Europe to be drawn up with machinery in place to ensure that such rights are properly adhered to. Its own mission to safeguard the rights of co-nationals in neighbouring states through bilateral initiatives met with an isolated breakthrough in May 1992 when newly independent Ukraine signed an agreement with Hungary on the basic principles of guaranteeing the rights of national minorities. Both parties agreed that members of ethnic minorities should have guaranteed rights both as individuals and 'together with other members of their groups'. This was the first time that a neighbouring country with a Hungarian minority had formally recognised the concept of collective rights.[83]

The Hungarian government and the HDFR were at one in believing that individual rights were not enough to preserve the ethnic identity of minorities. Collective rights would entitle minorities to the free use of the mother tongue in the administrative and judicial systems in minority-inhabited areas, to education in the mother tongue up to university level, and to proportional minority representation at all levels of the administration.[84] But for such rights to be included in the new constitutions being drawn up for east European states in their post-communist guise would have required a revolution in political attitudes in which highly centralised administrative systems were replaced by a much more autonomous form of government. Given the insecurity over borders and the degree of internal disunity which led to the collapse of several long-established east European states in 1991–2, the climate was not propitious for the adoption of a system of government which would break up the concentration of power in the capital city and allow minorities control over their own affairs which had previously been denied to them.

The Romanian constitution drawn up by parliament and placed before the electorate for approval on 9 December 1991 embodied the centralising ethos that had been at the heart of state formation in eastern Europe for over a century. Unmistakeably a liberal democratic document, the constitution defined Romania as a unitary state. The HDFR deputies had raised no objection to this designation in parliament, but they had opposed the definition of the country as a 'national state'. This was regarded as a contradiction in terms in a state with fourteen recognised national minorities.[85] However, Romanian national ideology had always insisted on the Romanian state being the state of the Romanians only. The existence of

Hungarians could not be denied, but they were regarded as members of the sole political nation. The claim expressed by the HDFR that the Hungarians of Transylvania were a co-inhabiting nation living in the Romanian state who deserved special laws that would safeguard their national personality could not be accepted, otherwise it dissolved the idea that Romania was a single national state. The state's uni-national character was reinforced by Article 13 which stipulated that the country's official language is Romanian. Members of national minorities are unable to use their mother tongue in a court of law, but Article 6 of the Constitution (Section 1) 'recognises and guarantees the rights of conservation, development, and expression of ethnic, cultural, linguistic and religious identity for persons belonging to national minorities' without setting out how such rights will be guaranteed. To the HDFR and other critics of the provisions set aside for minorities in the 1991 constitution, such protection is a dead letter in the absence of laws denying minorities collective rights.[86]

The HDFR voted en bloc to oppose the new constitution, and one member, Karoly Király boycotted the vote in parliament where it received endorsement from eighty-one per cent of deputies. In the subsequent referendum on 9 December 1991, 78.5 per cent of voters approved the document, 14.1 per cent disapproving on a 69.7 per cent turnout. Only fourteen per cent voted yes in Harghita and twenty-one per cent in Covasna, the main Hungarian-speaking counties being the only ones where a 'no' vote was returned.[87]

THE 1992 LOCAL ELECTIONS AND INTER-ETHNIC RIVALRY

The NSF had received a convincing endorsement for the constitution despite its own widening splits and the collapse of governmental authority that had occurred ten weeks earlier. But the extent to which voters still saw the ruling party as a guarantor of stability would be tested by fresh parliamentary and presidential elections which were required to be held within a year of parliament approving the new constitution.

But before this important test of political credibility, local elections were due to be held to elect mayors, local councils and county councils on 9 February 1992. For the first time in over fifty years, Romanians would also be able to elect, from among their own numbers, citizens entrusted with the task of providing effective and accessible local government. The mainstream opposition parties, which had formed an electoral alliance known as the Democratic Convention, seemed poised to make a strong showing, especially in the cities. By contrast, the NSF was in mounting difficulties. The austerity measures which the Roman government had introduced, and which its successor led by Teodor Stolojan was pressing ahead with, had reduced the appeal of the party among many voters who had rallied to it in May 1990. Besides, the divisions within the NSF had resulted in an open breach between Roman and Iliescu, the President intervening openly in the party's factional struggles to rally his own supporters, despite the constitution forbidding the head of state to be a member of any political party.

At each stage of the escalating power struggle within the NSF, ex-Premier Roman presented himself as the genuine partisan of democracy while casting his chief adversary in the role of the 'nostalgic communist'.[88] Local activists, who had in many cases enrolled in the NSF not for ideological reasons but in order to obtain the benefits associated with belonging to a ruling party, were confused about which side to support. Their preference was for an uncomplicated chain of command in which they knew their place and whom to defer to. Given the personality-driven character of Romanian politics and the preference for one-man rule, the Iliescu-Roman alliance may have had as little prospect of success as that between Gheorghiu-Dej and Ana Pauker or between Antonescu and Horia Sima of the Iron Guard. The nature of the personalities involved was probably immaterial since such power-sharing arrangements ran counter to deep-seated trends in Romanian political behaviour.

Since losing the premiership, Petre Roman had been deprived of the powers of patronage which had brought him the support of activists sceptical about his economic reforms, while at the same time President Iliescu's re-election prospects in 1992 looked distinctly uncertain. In what at the top level was also a battle for political influence and even survival, the ideological distinctions between Iliescu and Roman still seemed more apparent than real.

In Cluj on 29 November 1991, Roman made the promise that 'no former Communist Party activist or employee of the Securitate will be a candidate on the NSF list in the next election.[89] But, weeks earlier, many of his own supporters in the NSF had failed to back an opposition amendment to the local government law which would have prevented RCP activists from being named prefect or sub-prefect of a county.

At the same Cluj press conference, Roman proclaimed himself to be a 'moderate nationalist committed to peace'.[90] However, the NSF produced an inflammatory election newspaper in Cluj, *In faţa alegatorilor*, impugning the patriotic credentials of its Democratic Convention opponents, and, when a second round was held to elect a mayor, it supported the PRNU candidate, Gheorghe Funar, thus giving a vital boost to the career of someone soon to become Romania's best-known ultra-nationalist.

Cluj was the only large populated centre in Transylvania which opponents of the government had failed to capture in local elections. The NSF's national percentage of seats fell from sixty-five per cent in 1990 to thirty-three per cent by the 1992 local elections. The party's ability to keep control of rural areas prevented further erosion; the influence that local power-holders such as the local police chief, the doctor and sometimes the village priest had over voters often counted in its favour.[91]

After the local elections, the NSF formally split into two rival parties. Petre Roman's control of local NSF branches was sufficient to enable his faction to retain the name and emblem of the 'National Salvation Front'. However, the majority of the parliamentary party went over to the Democratic National Salvation Front (DNSF), which was less of a political party and more of a platform designed to secure the re-election of President Iliescu. Almost a dozen deputies would also defect to the most extreme of the nationalist parties, the Greater Romania Party (GRP), during the period of political realignment that stretched between the local election and the parliamentary and presidential contests due on 27 September 1992. This was a period when ultra-nationalists first emerged in Romania as a distinctive force in their own right rather than as a group which operated in the shadow of the ruling party. Gheorghe Funar, Cluj's newly-elected mayor, quickly emerged as a figure of national prominence thanks to a series of controversial decisions, some of doubtful constitutional legality, designed (in his own words) to allow the Romanians to be 'masters in their own house'.[92]

Iliescu reacted with prudence towards a headline-grabbing populist who was the first Romanian politician to take full advantage of the nationalist political climate which the NSF had played no small measure in creating. The nearest he came to criticising Funar was a statement issued on 19 June 1992 in which he appreciated that some of the decisions he had taken were excessive while others had 'real motivation'.[93] After referring to dissension being sown by foreign circles, he invited the PRNU to enter into dialogue with the HDFR. But the likelihood of such talks taking place or leading anywhere was dashed when Funar accused the HDFR's leaders of fomenting inter-ethnic tension and of trying to create a situation in Romania similar to that in the former Yugoslavia.[94] When an HDFR delegation went to see the President in June 1992 with a list of anti-Hungarian measures which it claimed that the Cluj mayor had been responsible for, Iliescu responded that he had no personal control over local authorities but, owing to the importance of the situation, he was prepared to ask the government to take measures to improve the situation.

It is not clear what steps, if any, were taken by the government, but the situation in Cluj eased over the summer and autumn of 1992, perhaps in connection with the fact that its mayor was preoccupied with gaining control of the PRNU, whose presidential candidate he became in July.

Iliescu's cautious stance towards the deterioration of inter-ethnic relations in Cluj can be contrasted with the more interventionist approach of Prime Minister Stolojan towards the question of government-appointed prefects in Harghita and Covasna. In July, two Romanian prefects were appointed to these mainly Hungarian-speaking counties. This led to mass protests in the main populated centres of Szeklerland. Critics pointed out that, even in Ceauşescu's time, there had always been Hungarians at the head of these two counties. Geza Domokos, the HDFR leader, argued that here was an action by the government itself, not a hardline mayor or a party leader, or an extremist newspaper which was harming community relations.[95] Stolojan, having at first declared that the matter was non-negotiable, paid a fact-finding visit to the region. Upon his return, he announced that a pair of Romanians and Hungarians would act as joint prefects until after the autumn elections, thus restoring the formula that had existed after 1990. His willingness to take local feelings into account and reverse a government decision on the strength of these was an unusual response from a Romanian chief executive in a country where the incentive to maintain the prerogative of central government has nearly always overridden other considerations. Stolojan's willingness to compromise in the face of local feelings was publicly appreciated by the HDFR. Smaranda Enache of the CAP found his decision to be 'absolutely unusual [for] here': 'he listened to people and tried to form his own opinion. He recognised he had made a mistake . . .'[96] There was also little outcry from ethnic Romanian opinion; Stolojan probably felt able to hold out against the predictable cries of betrayal from ultra-nationalists because he was planning to withdraw from Romanian political life in a matter of months in order to take up a post with the World Bank.

THE SEPTEMBER 1992 ELECTIONS AND A NEW POLITICAL BALANCE

The one month of electioneering which got under way for parliamentary and presidential elections being held on 27 September 1992 revealed a political landscape greatly altered from that of May 1990. Ultra-nationalists had emerged as a force in their own right, with Gheorghe Funar fighting a high-profile battle for the Romanian presidency as the candidate of the PRNU. Mainstream democratic opposition parties (including the HDFR) had rallied around a single candidate for the presidency, Professor Emil Constantinescu. He had spent all his life in Romania and he was more in touch with political realities than the émigrés who had been opposition standard-bearers in 1990. Iliescu was the last of the front-runners to declare his candidacy. His campaign was in the hands of old-guard members of the NSF whose successor party, the DNSF, lacked a clear ideology and contained few people who seemed capable of guiding the country through difficult economic times. Much of the press was hostile to the President, whose image as a guarantor of stability had been impaired by the turbulence of 1990–1. However, he had certain advantages whose overall importance would emerge as the campaign unfolded. Television remained in the hands of government supporters. The local elections had shown that government officials were able to sway votes in rural areas by making it clear that political loyalty was the sole criterion for state resources being granted to them.

Considering the tightness of the race, it is surprising that inter-ethnic factors did not play more of a role. The DNSF may have been dissuaded from playing the nationalist card in case it only strengthened the visibility of the avowed nationalist challenging Iliescu for the presidency.

Romania's second set of elections were also taking place after a year of unaccustomed calm which had been in marked contrast to the May 1990 contest, which preceded and succeeded acts of political violence. The calm was momentarily disturbed in the first official week of campaigning, when Lászlo Tökés (now a Hungarian Reformed Church Bishop) embarked upon a hunger strike in Timisoara in protest at what he saw as the betrayal of those who had laid down their lives for freedom in 1989 by a government which he claimed was prepared to use violence to retain power. An exchange of letters took place between Bishop Tökés and President Iliescu at this time; in an open letter to the Bishop, on 3 September 1992, the President showed that, if anything, his explanation for the Tirgu Mureş events had moved closer to that of ultra-nationalists:

> We have different ways of looking at what happened in Tirgu Mureş. To me, it is clear that the respective events were fomented from abroad and started when massive groups of thousands of citizens of Hungary, who behaved in a manner that is unqualified in Romania, had arrived . . . I cannot agree to your calling these events 'an anti-Hungarian pogrom'.

In the letter, the President denied that the state was giving the Hungarian minority an 'enemy image' and he expressed his worries about the risk of moving political debate back on to the streets again.[97] However, Bishop Tokes was prevailed upon to call off his hunger strike before the issue came to dominate the election campaign. Generally, DNSF statements on minority questions were relatively uncontroversial. The statement by the Bucharest leader of the DNSF on 21 August 1992 backed all actions aimed at favouring the conservation of the minorities' cultural identity while opposing the granting of rights which the Romanian people itself did not enjoy. Opposition was expressed to 'chauvinism' and 'exaggerated nationalism', and an excerpt from a letter sent in 1848 by Romanian nationalist hero Avram Iancu to a Hungarian military leader was quoted in order to underline its contemporary relevance:

Why don't you want to understand that weapons can never decide between you and us? Fate put us in a homeland so that together we can wish
to improve it and enjoy its results.[98]

Towards the end of the campaign, when fears were being expressed that
a strong showing by Funar might jeopardise Iliescu's chances of victory,
a shriller nationalist note crept into DNSF campaigning. In one television
election spot, Emil Constantinescu was accused of being willing to sell out
Transylvania to the Hungarians, but the main thrust of DNSF propaganda
concerned his alleged lack of personal fitness to be president rather than
his patriotic credentials, or lack of them.[99]

The intervention of a nationalist challenger was probably the main
factor resulting in the presidential election going to a second round. Iliescu
obtained 47.34 per cent of the vote, thus falling short of the fifty per
cent that would have enabled him to be elected on the first round; Emil
Constantinescu was second on 31.24 per cent and Gheorghe Funar came
third with 10.87 per cent, three other candidates receiving percentages
below five per cent. As in 1990, the President had received resounding
mandates in Moldavia and much of the south. His results had reflected
those of his party, the DNSF which had gained only nineteen per cent in
large towns, thirty per cent in small towns and thirty-five per cent in the
villages.[100] Sharp contrasts also emerged in voting patterns on the basis
of ethnic factors. Ion Iliescu did worst of all in ethnically-mixed areas or
ones where Hungarians were in a majority. In Transylvania, he was nearly
twenty percentage points behind Emil Constantinescu, who had received
42.70 per cent of the vote compared to Iliescu's twenty-three per cent.[101]

In the parliamentary election, the DNSF emerged as the largest party on
27.71 per cent of the vote, but this was not enough to enable it to govern
in its own right. The pro-reform forces grouped in the Romanian Democratic Convention (RDC)[102] were greatly strengthened when this coalition
of avowedly democratic parties came in second with 20.16 per cent (although this was lower than many had expected), with Petre Roman's NSF
a distant third on 10.18 per cent. The DNSF proved to be the largest party
in Bucharest, the south and Moldavia, the challenge of its NSF rival being
repulsed nearly everywhere (with the exception of the southern district of
Constanta). But in Transylvania, there had been a three-way split in the
distribution of votes, the HDFR emerging first on 20.5 per cent, the RDC next
on nineteen per cent and the PRNU close behind on 18 per cent. The DNSF
could only manage twelve per cent in those counties making up historic
Transylvania (with the NSF on eleven per cent). In Mureş county, the DNSF
and NSF got only four per cent each in 1992 compared with 14.2 per cent
for the united NSF in 1990. The position was even worse in the city of
Cluj, where the NSF vote in 1990 of twenty-eight per cent collapsed to just

7.36 per cent for its two segments. The weakness of the Cluj NSF had been revealed as early as 1991 by the decision of one of its Senators, Vasile Aileni not to return from a trip to the United States. The omens were not good for a party that could not retain its own elected members.

The Cluj result of September 1992 showed, in sharp relief, the vulnerability of the DNSF in large populated centres where nationalist rivalries made it difficult to carve out an appeal based on trust in the president as a symbol of national unity or gradual change. The 28.42 per cent fall in the NSF vote registered between 1990 and 1992 occurred in the most urbanised parts of Romania; in the second round, President Iliescu forsook the cities and concentrated on remoter agricultural and industrial settlements where his most loyal supporters were to be found. The failure of any party to gain a parliamentary majority enabled him to stress his unifying role in a fluid political situation; this may have ensured a high turnout of 73.20 per cent in the second round, especially from middle-aged and elderly Romanians influenced by a lifetime of state paternalism who feared any uncertainty or interruption of established routines.

On 11 October 1992, Ion Iliescu was elected for a second term, this time of four years. He got 61.43 per cent of the vote as against 38.57 per cent for Emil Constantinescu. His rival won in six of the eleven districts comprising historic Transylvania, but he made little dent on traditionally pro-Iliescu areas in the east and south of Romania. The political deadlock resulting from the inconclusive parliamentary result created a situation in which the President wielded considerable power entrusted to him by the constitution. He called RDC leaders in for talks about a coalition government but without offering them terms that made their agreement to participate in government with previously bitter rivals a serious possibility. The DNSF (in which former members of the communist nomenklatura were far more prominent than in the time of Petre Roman) was reluctant to attempt to govern alone and take responsibility for difficult economic portfolios which the parliamentary party had few suitable people able to fill. Finally, in November 1992, a non-party government was sworn in under Nicolae Văcăroiu, a senior civil servant close to Iliescu. It was sustained in parliament by the ultra-nationalists as well as by the DNSF, whose combined votes gave it a narrow working majority.

ILIESCU VICTORY IMPAIRS TIES WITH HUNGARIANS

As the Vacaroiu government was being formed, the Romanian foreign ministry issued a directive instructing the postal authorities to return immediately to the sender any official letter coming from abroad which carried the Hungarian name for Transylvania, *Erdely*.[103] A statement issued on 30 October 1992 noted a growing tendency on the part of Hungary to 'accredit the idea that Transylvania has a special identity, apart from Romania'. The foreign ministry felt that an attempt was being made to persuade international opinion that 'Transylvania and Romania are two special entities', something which required the Romanian government to 'protect the country's territorial integrity'.[104]

Further grounds for Romanian suspicion were provided in February 1993 when an economic co-operation agreement signed between Hungary, Poland and the Ukraine was given the title of the 'Euro-Carpathian project'. President Iliescu noted that Hungary was a non-Carpathian country with the bulk of the mountains lying in Romania and only fragments existing in the other two countries.[105]

On 25 October,the HDFR had issued a declaration backing 'internal self-government along community lines'.[106] What was interpreted as HDFR backing for a system of autonomy amounting to segregation along ethnic lines brought condemnation from nearly all Romanian parties, President Iliescu adding his voice to the critical chorus.

The HDFR congress in January 1993 would decide whether the radical statement known as 'the Declaration of Cluj' was to become party policy. Meanwhile, in December 1992, inter-ethnic tension in that city revived when Mayor Funar introduced measures designed to counter-act 'anti-national forces' which, in turn, led to demonstrations by Hungarians.[107]

Asked on 6 December 1992 about the situation in Cluj, Premier Vacaroiu replied by saying: 'let us not speak about it now because we still have to co-ordinate views'.[108] Such a response suggested that the prime minister was unsure about what to do in the face of an inter-ethnic flare-up, or else that, being a non-party technocrat dependent upon President Iliescu for continued support, the matter was perhaps out of his hands altogether. Văcăroiu's confused response made a contrast with the decisive way that his predecessor, Stolojan, had intervened to defuse the crisis over the choice of prefects for the Szekler counties nearly six months earlier.

Calm returned in January 1993 when there were no further incidents in Cluj and the HDFR backed away from its radical stance on territorial autonomy at its congress in Braşov. In a message to the new HDFR leader, Béla Markó, President Iliescu expressed his 'satisfaction over the note of balance and reason that prevailed at the HDFR conference'. He also promised that 'the presidency will show complete openness and give the necessary support to everything connected with the intellectual life and preservation of the Hungarian ethnic minority in Romania'.[109]

By making such a statement, Iliescu was distancing himself from ultra-nationalists who believe that the ethnic character of the HDFR makes it an illegitimate and dangerous presence in Romanian political life regardless of what it says or does. It was a continuation of the balancing act between Romanian nationalists and minority interests without any sign that President Iliescu was ready to take the initiative to resolve any of the outstanding difficulties that continued to make inter-ethnic relations in Romania so problematic.

A three-hour meeting duly took place between the President and HDFR parliamentarians on 24 February 1993. Ion Iliescu acknowledged the HDFR to be the legitimate organisation of the Hungarians in Romania and said that it was important to meet with it regularly.[110]

However, in his role as the point of balance between conflicting party and ethnic interests, Iliescu was also making overtures to ultra-nationalists in the first part of 1993. The main one involved the appointment, as head of Romanian television, of Paul Everac, a writer known for his anti-Semitic and anti-western views. He also sent a cordial message to the leader of the Greater Romania Party, the most extreme and uninhibited of the nationalist parties, on the occasion of its first congress in March 1993.[111] *România Mâre*, the influential weekly attached to the GRP, had earlier urged its readers to support Iliescu in the presidential elections while persisting with its customary mixture of praise for Ceauşescu and anti-western diatribes.[112] It felt that Iliescu was a politician trying to defend the national interest even if there were mistakes in his record. Despite being pressed, Iliescu refused to disavow GRP support, and there had even been active speculation that, in the February 1992 local elections, he had cast his vote for a GRP candidate rather than vote for any of those which his rival, Petre Roman, had chosen for the NSF list in Bucharest.[113]

The GRP supported the government when it faced a parliamentary vote of no confidence in March 1993. But there was speculation that one of the conditions it had laid down for such backing was that Romanian prefects would be appointed in Harghita and Covasna to end the anomalous situation whereby each of the posts was split between a Romanian and a Hungarian.[114] The dual authority formula was terminated on 26 March 1993 when two Romanian prefects were appointed. According to one HDFR deputy, the government had responded to requests that justice suggested these prefects should be Hungarian by saying 'find us two Hungarians prepared to sign their applications for DNSF membership', a revealing indication of how little standing the DNSF enjoyed within the Hungarian minority.[115]

Two days before the controversial decision on the prefects for the Szekler counties, the government had announced that it was setting up a Council of National Minorities. This was seen as an attempt to reduce the impact of Hungarian protests over the decision that followed and to show the government in a reasonable light.[116] The initiative was also connected with Romania's long-running attempt to join the Council of Europe, where progress had been stalled over the country's patchy record on minority rights.[117] The text of the government communiqué setting up the CNM was ambiguous and there had been no prior consultation with representatives of the HDFR, which, like other minority organisations, had read about the formation of the council in the press. The response of minority leaders to an initiative whose structure was to be decided by the government was not favourable. Varujan Vosganian, a parliamentary deputy for the Union of Armenians, deplored the lack of consultation: 'I don't know how the council will function, what will be the system of voting, what is our role on it and what is the role of the government . . . Our fear is that we are being used in a propaganda exercise, something we are not disposed to accept.'[118]

The HDFR's response was the key one, and it said that its participation was dependent on the CNM's procedures and mode of activity being clarified. On 11 May 1993, the government announced measures which seemed to respond to minority concerns about becoming involved in what might be little more than a rubber-stamp body. Decisions adopted by the CNM were to be adopted by a two-thirds majority; every minority was to have the right of veto on questions affecting its immediate interest; the government and national minorities were to be on an equal footing in the body, which would be able to work out proposals and submit them for action by the executive.[119] The HDFR initially decided on 'conditional participation' in light of these assurances, but by the autumn of 1993 it had quit the CNM.

On one issue, integration with the political and economic institutions of western Europe, there was a surprising degree of consistency in the government's attitude. The 'return to Europe' remained a major foreign policy goal even after the removal of Petre Roman, who had been most closely associated with the drive to end Romania's self-imposed isolation. Admission to European institutions, generous economic aid, official visits and cordial inter-state relations were regarded as goals which would max-imise political stability and undermine opposition charges that Romania remained a pariah state under the successors of Ceauşescu.[120]

Romania was given associate status with the European Community in November 1992. This facilitated trading links and enabled Romania to gain more immediate access to the aid programmes being administered by the European Commission.

Full membership of the European Community was not an option for Romania due to its economic backwardness compared with countries like Poland and the Czech Republic, which entertained hopes that they might be accepted as full members by the end of the century. However, Romania put particular effort into gaining entry to the Council of Europe. The

Parliamentary Assembly of the Council of Europe, set up in 1949, is the most widely-based European political forum. Admission is an important badge of respectability for post-dictatorial states like Romania, given that the Council aims to protect human-rights and democratic freedoms. In the past, members like Greece have had their membership discontinued if their behaviour is seen to violate accepted standards in these areas. Romania's own uncertain human rights record after 1989 slowed up its admission for membership. Romania was given special guest status in February 1991 after countries like Hungary, Poland and Czechoslovakia had been granted full membership.[121] Progress towards full membership was conditional on there being no reversion to totalitarian practices. Romania's human-rights record was also to be made subject to periodic review by visiting Council of Europe officials. Romania was thus prepared to relax its insistence that the treatment of minorities by the state was purely an internal matter.

Romania's desire to join the Council of Europe was a factor which influenced the final shape of Romania's constitution.[122] But although there were no recurrences of human rights violations on the scale of those in 1990, officials monitoring the Romanian record remained unconvinced that the country fulfilled the criteria to justify entry. The ability of Cluj's Mayor Funar to disregard the constitution in the treatment of the city's Hungarian population was noted by the Council of Europe. The creation of the CNM in 1993 was regarded as a positive development by Friedrich König, Council rapporteur with responsibility for Romania, but his colleague, Gunnar Janssen, criticised the decision taken in March 1993 over the appointment of ethnic Romanian prefects in largely Hungarian-speaking counties and expressed his backing for the restoration of the Hungarian university in Cluj and Hungarian-language secondary schools.[123]

The HDFR argued in 1992–3 that Romanian membership of the Council of Europe should be conditional on further improvements in its record on minority rights.[124] As for the Hungarian government, it stated that the way in which a country treats its minorities should be regarded as a measure of how democratic it is and should serve as a criterion for admitting it to European institutions.[125] Hungary has raised the issue of minority rights in Romania at various international fora; the UN Commission on Human Rights in Geneva was told in 1991 that Hungarians in Romania remained the frequent object of 'harassment, intimidation and interference'.[126] Such a move by Hungary may have been behind the complaint by Ioan Mircea Paşcu, Romanian foreign policy adviser that the sharp decline in Romania's international standing was attributable to the 'intense activism of foreign circles unfavourable to the government elected in May 1990'.[127]

Hungary was aware that undue emphasis on the poor state of its relations in Romania might only raise doubts about the stability of the Danubian area, ones that might adversely affect its plans to be a target of inward investment. Instead, it sought to improve the position of its co-nationals in Romania by seeking international support for the adoption of an institutional framework for the protection of minority rights. It supports a stringent, legally binding protocol to the European Convention on Human Rights which would lay down basic rights for minorities. The Council of Europe acts as an important guardian of human rights by upholding this Convention, which is already enforced by a European Court of Human Rights with supra-national powers. But Britain, France, Greece and Turkey, have been opposed to a new international framework for minority rights because it may contain troublesome domestic implications.[128]

Another important forum for safeguarding minority rights has been the Conference on Security and Co-operation in Europe which emerged from the process of east-west detente culminating in the Helsinki Accords of 1975 but which only acquired its first institutions after the end of East–West confrontation in 1989–90. The CSCE held conferences at Copenhagen in 1990, Geneva in 1991 and Helsinki in 1992 examining the human rights dimension of European security. The declaration agreed in Copenhagen asserted the right of 'persons belonging to national minorities to exercise and enjoy their rights individually as well as in community with other members'. What was known as the Geneva Expert Meeting on National Minorities stressed that issues concerning national minorities 'are matters of legitimate international concern and consequently do not constitute exclusively an internal affair of the respective state'. A High Commissioner on National Minorities was established after the Helsinki meeting with the aim of preventing conflict in disputed areas, the CSCE until then having rarely intervened in minority and ethnic trouble-spots until violence had broken out; the commissioner's mandate is to provide 'early warning' and, where appropriate, 'early action' in regard to tensions involving national minority issues.[129] Max van der Stoel, former Dutch foreign minister, became the first holder of the post in 1993, and one of the first countries he visited in eastern Europe was Romania.

Hungary welcomed the establishment of a High Commissioner on National Minorities given the number of actual or potential ethnic disputes to be found in states adjacent to it and often involving its co-nationals. However, CSCE decisions are reached by consensus, its organisation is minimal, and it showed its limitations in conflict-prevention by its ineffectiveness in halting the slide to war in Yugoslavia.[130]

Hungary failed in its attempt to obtain agreement that the concept of collective rights should be codified in international documents and that there should be a means of monitoring government's compliance with international agreements on minority rights.[131] Such a regulatory approach to minority protection may have too many awkward implications for west European states with minorities which are too jealous of their own state sovereignty to allow it to be adopted in the foreseeable future. Within the CSCE and the Council of Europe, there is a continuing struggle among participating states to find an appropriate and sustainable balance between minority freedom and internal self-determination, and state power and authority.[132] Adrian Nastase, the Romanian foreign minister, felt moved to complain at the March 1992 CSCE conference in Helsinki that the CSCE process was one-sided in its approach to minority issues because it seemed to his government only concerned with emphasising the rights of minorities and the obligations of states in which they lived.[133] The Romanian position, as advanced at CSCE meetings and other international gatherings, was to emphasise the responsibility of minorities towards the state in which they lived rather than the state's obligation towards minorities. Romanian delegates pointed out the need for minorities to respect the territorial unity of the states in which they lived and to offer loyalty, while insisting that minority rights were enshrined in its own constitution as well as in international agreements.[134]

ROMANIA AND THE YUGOSLAV CONFLICT

Bucharest's emphasis on territorial integrity rather than minority rights may have contained uncomfortable throwbacks to the Ceauşescu era. But, with the rapid break-up of the Soviet Union, Yugoslavia and Czechoslovakia in 1991–2, two of which had long borders with Romania, it seemed an increasingly understandable concern. It had been to Yugoslavia that President Iliescu had made his first official visit abroad in September 1990. When internal conflict broke out in June 1991, the Romanian foreign ministry issued a statement expressing the hope that 'a country which is a neighbour and friend' would maintain 'its territorial integrity and stability'. The 'responsibility and duty of Yugoslavia's neighbours . . . to keep themselves from taking any acts that . . . endanger Yugoslavia's unity and territorial integrity' were also stressed.[135] Romania was no different from west European countries in allocating more importance to the territorial status quo than to the fate of the inhabitants trapped in the crumbling federation. However, unlike the states of the EC, it was reluctant to make its views public about the massive human-rights violations that the United Nations and other agencies were laying at the door of the Belgrade regime of Slobodan Milosevic as it sought to carve out a Greater Serbia from the ruins of Yugoslavia. Foreign minister Năstase, in his March 1991 visit to Belgrade, had described it in terms of 'showing our friends that we will remain at their side during hard times'.[136] There is no evidence that

Romania used its traditionally close ties with Serbia to urge moderation on the hardline Belgrade leadership regarding the way that it was conducting warfare in Croatia and later Bosnia-Herzegovina.

Inevitably, there was government concern that a complete disintegration of Yugoslavia could affect Romanian unity and serve as a beacon for Transylvanian secessionists.[137] But it was rarely expressed publicly, President Iliescu criticising Bishop Lászlo Tökés in November 1991 for saying that a conflict situation similar to that in Yugoslavia could develop in Romania. Iliescu ruled out such a scenario in the light of the fact that Romania was not a federal state and thus would be spared the prospect of republics engaging in internecine disputes.[138] However, other pro-government spokesmen were not as sanguine, as the conflict in the western Balkans intensified. In November 1992, Senator Gheorghe Dumitrascu called for a revival of the pre-war Little Entente to block Hungarian 'revanchism', the DNSF parliamentarian envisaging a diplomatic partnership comprising Romania, Slovakia and Serbia.[139] However, by now Romania was being pressed to participate in sanctions against Serbia by an international community which increasingly viewed it as a dangerous aggressor.

In December 1991, when diplomatic sanctions against the state claiming to be the Federal Republic of Yugoslavia (FRY) were first imposed by the EC, President Iliescu stated that Romania would not join in because of the harm that would be caused to the Romanian economy.[140] But Romania later joined an economic embargo on the FRY imposed by the United Nations without severing political and diplomatic ties with Belgrade, a step taken by many other European countries.[141] Romania had, however, been unhappy at the exclusion of the FRY from the CSCE in 1992 and, in June of that year, Premier Stolojan declared that Romania would never participate in any international military intervention against the former Yugoslavia.[142]

Romania was prepared to go along with action by the international community to punish Serbian aggression without severing its long-standing contacts with Belgrade. In 1992, *Dréptatea*, the outspoken Bucharest opposition paper, accused President Iliescu of trying to bring Romania into a union of 'disgrace, failure and misery' with an economically-ruined Yugoslavia, abhorred by the entire civilised world.[143] This was criticism that the government could afford to brush aside, but Bucharest could not so easily discount criticism from leading western countries about its weakness in enforcing sanctions against the FRY. At the economic summit of the Group of Seven (G-7) leading industrialised nations in July 1992, participants, including Canadian foreign minister Barbara McDougall, accused Romania of violating the trade embargo against Serbia.[144] Pressure on Bucharest to ensure its compliance with sanctions was stepped up and met with the desired response: the British Foreign Secretary, Douglas Hurd, on a visit to Romania in June 1993, was able to praise the government for what he saw as its co-operative attitude.

The Yugoslav conflict has not polarised public opinion in Romania. In a small way, it has enabled Iliescu to revive the role which he played in 1990, that of a reliable bulwark against forces of disintegration. But Iliescu's own sympathies were perhaps most clearly exposed when Serbia's Slobodan Milosevic paid an official visit to Bucharest on 5 April 1994. Iliescu said on that occasion:

> We have hailed the presence of President Milosevic in the context of the good and traditional relations that prevail between our countries . . . Our relations . . . are positive from every point of view . . . These relations continued to develop after the December 1989 revolution and the economic relations between our countries also registered an upward course until the establishment of the embargo . . .
>
> The way of force, of military conflict, or of taking measures such as the embargo – which is also a measure of force- are not meant to ease actions of finding solutions to the problem. On the contrary.[145]

Iliescu's criticism of the sanctions imposed upon the Belgrade regime in 1992 after Milosevic had been clearly linked with massive human-rights violations carried out by surrogates in Croatia (ones that would be eclipsed by what happened in Bosnia after April 1992) is bound to raise questions about how faithfully Romania sealed its own borders with what much of the rest of the international community regarded as a pariah state.[146] His claim that good relations with Belgrade have been undisturbed appears incongruous in the light of the hijacking of oil-laden ships that were taken through Romanian territorial waters to Serbia during 1993. Ioan Mircea Paşcu, a key presidential aide, shed light on official thinking in a paper delivered at a 1993 conference on European security: he delivered veiled criticism of the nature of western involvement, deprecated 'forcible action to compel the Bosnian Serbs to accept a detailed [peace] plan which does not respond to either their major interests or the reality on the ground', and expressed concern about 'fundamentalist Muslim involvement'.[147] He also showed some irritation at the consequences of the western media's preoccupation with wartime atrocities while displaying a marked reluctance to criticise Serbia's President Milosevic for his role in the conflict.

It would be unnatural if there was not an affinity between President's Milosevic and Iliescu. Both of them have built a power-base upon the support of apolitical citizens whose livelihood was bound up with the command economy and who were responsive to paternalistic appeals often couched in nationalist terms. Milosevic, in his defiance of accepted norms of political behaviour in post-1945 Europe, may even have been encouraged by the way that Iliescu had brushed aside criticism of his own conduct in 1990 as he consolidated his hold on power.

In May 1994, Iliescu secured an important victory when the International Monetary Fund agreed to loan Romania one billion dollars, the first such loan in two years.[148] Historical precedent suggests that her rulers will not be tied to western norms and conventions about the way in which this money ought to be used. Unless the donor agency imposes stringent conditions, there is every likelihood that the sections of the pre-1989 nomenklatura who have enriched themselves by the conversion of power and connections into wealth will find further scope for entrenching themselves as a new oligarchy. The manner in which people not unlike those running Iliescu's regime manipulated both the capitalist west and Moscow on their own nativist terms in the 1960s and 1970s suggests that it will not be difficult to carry on like this in the 1990s.

CONCLUSION

The institutional advantages that the NSF possessed enabled a dominant party system to emerge after the May 1990 elections. After 1989, the NSF acquired the most sweeping plurality of any post-communist ruling party in eastern Europe. The triumph of a party largely composed of holdovers who received their political education and administrative experience in the communist years showed how the emphasis was on continuity as much as change. A political transition punctuated by savage government-opposition clashes in 1990 and the removal in 1991 of the prime minister from office by a mob, with the president playing an ambiguous role in the background, were incidents which tarnished the prestige of representative government at a crucial moment for Romania. Suspicions were inevitably raised that the liquidators of the communist dictatorship had only a limited commitment to democracy and preferred a hybrid system in which power could be exercised sometimes arbitrarily but without too much international hostility. John Sislin was by no means the only commentator to glimpse the continuity of 'Ceauşescuism . . . the political, economic and social system which the NSF has inherited'. Writing in 1991, he forecast that 'the system will define much of what the NSF can do: not only is it the last step Romania took prior to the revolution, but it is the path Romania has been on for many years . . . its political, economic and social structures condition what is possible in the future'.[149]

The departure of reformists from the ruling party by 1992 reduced the disparity in electoral strength between government and opposition. But Iliescu's supporters were still able to shape the constitutional order according to their preference, which was for a semi-presidential republic in which the head of state is elected by universal suffrage, the holder having important discretionary powers. In the autumn of 1992 when the pro-Iliescu party (then known as the Democratic National Salvation Front) lost its parliamentary majority, his supporters entered into an informal alliance with various ultra-nationalist parties which removed any possibility of mainstream democrats achieving office. This was the culmination of a trend whereby the government has used or tolerated nationalist dema-gogues who offer simple and immediate solutions to complex problems by focusing attention on a range of internal enemies. The Iliescu regime looks less tainted before international opinion if it can point to extremist forces beside whom it looks moderate, even if their strength stems partly from its patronage. Although it is doubtful if Iliescu shares the chauvinism and anti-Semitism of the ultra-nationalists, like them he has no interest in replacing a passive political culture in which a low value is placed on participation with an active one in which voters acquire the information and confidence to assess demagogic appeals sceptically. His regime has placed nationalists in top jobs in order to block attempts to create the autonomous space necessary for genuine pluralism to flourish. His critics allege that he is also ready to mobilise one social group against another (like the miners against students and intellectuals in 1990) in order to reinforce his own power-base and prevent serious alternatives to his rule from emerging.

Unfortunately, parliament has not been able to integrate the country's diverse political forces and provide a counterweight against the unrestrained use of personal power. Since October 1992, the Vacaroiu government has shown a disinclination to co-operate with parliament on major issues. It has been very reluctant to allow parliament a supervisory role over the state media or the security services, two areas which are regarded as crucial for the maintenance of political authority.[150]

In a 1993 poll, twenty-seven per cent of Romanian respondents when asked what sort of government they would like, expressed a preference for 'an authoritarian, iron-fisted leadership'.[151] Later in the same year, a different poll found that 58.8 per cent of respondents had no confidence in the ability of the government to solve outstanding national problems, while 66.8 per cent felt that a government reshuffle would make no difference. To make matters worse, thirty-nine per cent of respondents in a further 1993 poll doubted the ability of the reformist opposition to rescue the country, fifty per cent of respondents had no confidence in any party, and sixty per cent were disenchanted with the performance of both parliament and government.[152]

The strength of populist nationalism, the ability of the president to exercise major influence over the daily political process extending beyond his normal constitutional prerogatives, and the failure of political institutions to acquire widespread respect, gives Romanian democracy a provisional character even after the constitutional machinery of the new state has large-ly been put in place. In the event of a major crisis, Iliescu's semi-presidential regime would appear to have as much chance of being removed by force as through the ballot-box, and there is the danger that if the ballot-box proved decisive, power might still pass to anti-democratic forces.

The questionable commitment of the ruling party to liberal democratic values is one of the greatest perils that Romanian democracy faces in the years ahead. The following chapter will examine what kind of counter-weight the opposition has provided and whether there is much chance that it can acquire greater influence over the political process in the remainder of the 1990s.

NOTES

1. Budapest radio, 23 March 1990, BBC Survey of World Broadcasts (hereafter SWB) EE/0722 (26 March 1990).
2. *The May 1990 Election in Romania*, International Delegation Report, NDIIA/NRIIA, Washington DC 1991, passim.
3. Crisula Stefanescu, '"Free Romanian Television" Loses Its Credibility', *Report on Eastern Europe*, Vol. 1, No. 8, (23 March 1990), p. 26.
4. The full text of the Timişoara Proclamation was carried in *Report on Eastern Europe*, Vol. 1, No. 14 (6 April 1990).
5. Walter Bacon, 'Security as Seen from Bucharest', in Daniel Nelson (ed.), *Romania After Tyranny*, Westview Press, London and San Francisco CA 1992, p. 199.
6. Mihai Sturdza, 'The Files of the State Security Police', *Report on Eastern Europe*, Vol. 2, No. 35 (13 September 1991), p. 22.
7. *Romania, A Case of Dynastic Communism*, p. 61.
8. Rompres, 24 March 1990, SWB EE/0722 i (26 March 1990).
9. Socor, *Report on Eastern Europe* (13 April 1990), p. 41.
10. Michael Shafir, 'Schopflinian Optimism and Romanian Reality', *Report on Eastern Europe* (15 February 1991), p. 38.
11. Tom Gallagher, 'Time to Build Bridges in Romania', *Studies* (Autumn 1992), p. 271.
12. *Romania Libera* (Bucharest), 11 April 1990.
13. Dan Ionescu, 'The NSF's Anti-Opposition Campaign Escalates Following Elections', *Report on Eastern Europe*, Vol. 1, No. 30 (10 August 1990), p. 31.
14. Ibid.
15. Vladimir Socor, 'Foreign Policy in 1990', *Report on Eastern Europe*, Vol. 1, No. 50 (28 December 1990), p. 29.
16. *Human Rights in Romania since the Revolution*, Helsinki Watch Report, New York 1991, pp. 26–30. Only one trial resulted from the June 1990 events: three officials attached to the ministry of the interior were accused of wrecking the house of opposition leader Ion Ratiu: ARPRESS, No. 688 (14 June 1993).
17. For a searching appraisal of the 13–15 June 1990 violence in Bucharest, see Michael Shafir, 'Government Encourages Vigilante Violence in Bucharest', *Report on Eastern Europe*, Vol. 1, No. 26 (6 July 1990).

18. R. R. King, 'Romania', in R. Staar (ed.), *1991 Yearbook of International Communist Affairs*, Hoover Press, Stanford CA 1991, p. 341.
19. Later, it would be an explanation given an additional twist by the NSF group leader in the Senate, Vasile Vacaru, who speculated that American foundations, funded by the US Congress, whose goal was to strengthen democracy, had chosen to interpret this goal in the Romanian context by funding extra-parliamentary demonstrators who had threatened the country's stability until they were stopped on 13 June: Rompres, 13 June 1991, SWB EE/1102 B/12 (19 June 1991).
20. *The Independent*, 21 June 1990.
21. Mihai Sturdza, 'The President and the Miners: The End of a Privileged Relationship', *Report on Eastern Europe*, Vol. 1, No. 37 (28 September 1990), p. 35.
22. King, 'Romania', p. 359.
23. Mihai Sturdza, 'The Politics of Ambiguity: Romania's Foreign Relations', *Report on Eastern Europe*, Vol. 2, No. 13 (5 April 1991), p. 16.
24. Mihai Sturdza, 'Worldwide Indignation at the Miners' Rampage in Bucharest', *Report on Eastern Europe*, Vol. 1, No. 25 (6 July 1990), p. 40.
25. Romanian television interview, 31 May 1990, SWB EE/0799 B.7 (26 May 1990).
26. Budapest home service, 4 August 1990, SWB EE/0836 B/14 (7 August 1990).
27. Dan Ionescu, 'Government Moves to Recentralize Local Administration', *Report on Eastern Europe*, Vol. 1, No. 33 (7 September 1990), p. 23, n. 21; *Cuvîntul* (Bucharest), 9 March 1993.
28. Details in Gallagher, 'Building Bridges . . .'. The Bucharest weekly *Baricada* of 23 July 1991 carried a detailed investigation of the conflict between the Orthodox and Greek Catholic churches in Transylvania; the bi-monthly religious newspaper *Viaţa Creştina*, published in Cluj since 1990, contains much information on the conflict from the Greek Catholic point of view. The Orthodox Church is less forthcoming in its view, though hardline attitudes are occasionally expressed by the Metropolitan of Transylvania, Antonie Plamadeala. See for instance the text of a sermon which he delivered at Easter 1994 which was carried by *Telegraful Roman*, No. 17–18, 1994; and the response in *Viaţa Creştina*, No. 12–13, June–July 1994.
29. *Human Rights in Romania since the Revolution*, p. 54.
30. *Adevârul de Cluj*, 16 March 1991.
31. *Mesagerul Transilvan*, 6–8 June 1992.
32. Rompres, 2 April 1990, SWB EE/0731 B/8 (3 April 1990).
33. Bucharest home service, 10 August 1990, SWB EE/0841 B/4 (13 August 1990).
34. Bucharest home service, 30 August 1990, SWB EE/0858 B/14 (1 September 1990).
35. Rompres, 29 August 1990, SWB EE/0857 B/6 (31 August 1990).
36. The manner in which the fiftieth anniversary of the Vienna Accord was commemorated by the Romanian authorities and political parties is explored in detail in Tom Gallagher, 'Vatra Româneascã and Resurgent Nationalism', *Ethnic and Racial Studies*, Vol. 15, No. 4 (1992).
37. *Dreptátea* (Bucharest newspaper), 4 December 1990.
38. A Government spokesman on 4 December 1990 criticised the BBC World Service for claiming that Petre Roman had whipped up the crowd: SWB EE/0940i

(6 December 1990). For Roman's attempt to play down his father's active role in the RCP see V. Tismaneanu in *22* (Bucharest weekly), 23 June 1993.

39. Bucharest home service, 21 December 1989, SWB EE/0985 B/11 (24 December 1990).

40. Romanian radio, 21 December 1991, SWB EE/1264, B/7 (28 December 1991).

41. Budapest home service, 7 May 1991, SWB EE/1067 B/7 (9 May 1991).

42. Edith Oltay, 'Anniversary of 1848 Revolution celebrated', *Report on Eastern Europe*, Vol. 2, No. 13 (5 April 1991), p. 6.

43. Rompres, 7 March 1991, SWB EE/1018 B/7 (12 March 1991).

44. Rompres, 6 March 1991, SWB EE/1018 B/7 (12 March 1991).

45. Ionescu, 'Government Moves to Recentralize Local Administration', p. 24.

46. Edith Oltay, 'Minorities as Stumbling Block in Relations with Neighbours', *RFE-RL Research Report*, Vol. 1, No. 19 (8 May 1992), p. 28.

47. Edith Oltay, 'Minority Rights Still an Issue in Hungarian–Romanian Relations', *RFE-RL Research Report*, Vol. 1, No. 12 (20 March 1992), pp. 16–17.

48. Socor, *Report on Eastern Europe* (28 December 1990).

49. Ioan Mircea Paşcu, 'Romania's Response to a Structured World', in Daniel Nelson (ed.), *Romania After Tyranny*, pp. 278–9.

50. Ibid., p. 284.

51. Interview with Ion Iliescu on Austrian television, 31 October 1990, SWB EE/0912 B/6 (3 November 1990).

52. Romanian radio, 15 November 1991, SWB EE/1236 B/14 (22 November 1991).

53. Rompres, 23 October 1991, SWB EE/1213 B/4 (26 October 1991).

54. Daniel Nelson, 'Post-Communist Insecurity: The Romanian Case', in idem (ed.), *Romania After Tyranny*, p. 183.

55. Ronald Linden, 'After the Revolution: A Foreign Policy of Bounded Change', in Nelson (ed.), *Romania After Tyranny*, p. 215.

56. Rompres, 30 January 1991, SWB EE/0988 B/2 (5 February 1991).

57. Rompres, 12 July 1991, SWB EE/1126 B/9 (16 July 1991). However, in February 1991, Roman had stated that he was not a member of the foundation recently set up by the România Mâre group but that he failed to see what would be wrong if he eventually became a member. Geron Pilon, op. cit., p. 68.

58. Rompres, 15 August 1991, SWB EE/1158 B/2 (23 August 1991).

59. Budapest home service 25 July 1991, SWB EE/1158 B/2 (23 August 1991). President Iliescu's willingness to receive those at the head of România Mâre in future years and even to vote for the party in the 1992 local elections suggests this to have been an isolated gesture made with international opinion in mind. See *Eastern Europe Newsletter*, Vol. 6, No. 4 (17 February 1992).

60. Rompres, 7 June 1991, SWB EE/1095 B/12 (11 June 1991).

61. Ion Cristoiu, *Expres Magazin* (17 December 1991).

62. Rompres, 17 December 1991, SWB EE/1413 B/12.

63. Gabriel Topor, 'The National Salvation Front in a Crisis', *Report on Eastern Europe*, Vol. 2, No. 35 (16 August 1991), p. 27

64. Sturdza, *Report on Eastern Europe* (13 September 1991), p. 29.

65. Michael Shafir, '"War of the Roses" in Romania's National Salvation Front', *RFE-RL Research Report*, Vol. 1, No. 3 (24 January 1992), p. 19.

66. Report on Eastern Europe, *Digest of Weekly Events* (20 October 1991).
67. Michael Shafir, *RFE-RL Research Report*, Vol. 1, No. 3 (24 January 1992).
68. Hungarian radio, 4 October 1991, SWB EE/1197 B/17 (8 October 1991).
69. SWB EE/1188i (27 September 1991).
70. 'The Report of The Parliamentary Commission which Interviewed People who, after 22 December 1989, had to Leave their Places of Work and Homes in the Counties of Harghita and Covasna', Editura Scripta, Bucharest 1991.
71. *NU* (Cluj political magazine), 28 October 1991; *Baricada* (12 November 1991).
72. Hungarian radio, 20 October 1991, SWB EE/1213 B/6 (28 October 1991); see also Rady, op. cit., p. 147.
73. SWB EE/1217 B/4 (31 October 1991).
74. *Romania Libera* (25 October 1991).
75. Dan Ionescu, 'Riots Topple Petre Roman's Cabinet', *Report on Eastern Europe*, Vol. 2, No. 41 (18 October 1991), p. 21.
76. Rompres, 9 August 1990, SWB EE/0841 B/6 (13 August 1990).
77. Hungarian radio, 21 October 1991, SWB EE/1211 A/2 (24 October 1991).
78. Oltay, *RFE-RL Research Report* (8 May 1992), p. 29.
79. See Oltay, *RFE-RL Research Report* (20 March 1992).
80. Alfred Reisch, 'Hungary's Foreign Policy Reorientation A Success', *Report on Eastern Europe*, Vol. 2, No. 51 (20 December 1991), p. 19.
81. Oltay, *RFE-RL Research Report* (20 March 1992), p. 16.
82. Ibid. (8 May 1992), p. 30.
83. Ibid., p. 31.
84. Ibid. (20 March 1992), p. 19.
85. Michael Shafir, 'Romania's New Institutions: The Draft Constitution', *Report on Eastern Europe*, Vol. 2, No. 37 (20 September 1991), p. 23.
86. Ibid.
87. Michael Shafir, 'Romania: Constitution Approved in Referendum', *RFE-RL Research Report*, Vol. 1, No. 2 (10 January 1992), pp. 53, 55.
88. Shafir, *RFE-RL Research Report* (24 January 1992).
89. *NU* (2 December 1991).
90. *Adevârul de Cluj* (3 December 1991).
91. Tom Gallagher, 'Ultra-Nationalists Take Charge of Transylvania's Capital', *RFE-RL Research Report*, Vol. 1, No. 13 (27 March 1992), p. 28.
92. Tom Gallagher, 'Ethnic Tension in Cluj', *RFE-RL Research Report*, Vol. 2, No. 9 (26 February 1993), p. 28.
93. Rompres, 19 June 1992, SWB EE/1414 B/11 (25 June 1992).
94. Hungarian radio, 24 June 1992, SWB EE/1419 B/8 (29 June 1992).
95. Hungarian radio, 27 July 1992, SWB EE/1443 B/16 (27 July 1992).
96. *The Free Romanian* (September 1992).
97. Rompres, 3 September 1992, SWB EE/1480 (8 September 1992).
98. Rompres, 21 August 1992, SWB EE/1471 B/4 (28 August 1992).
99. Michael Shafir, 'Romania's Elections: Why the Democratic Convention Lost', *RFE-RL Research Report*, Vol. 2, No. 43 (30 October 1992), p. 5.
100. Shafir, *RFE-RL Research Report* (30 October 1992), p. 5, n. 20.
101. *Pro-Minoritate* (journal of the Hungarian political party Fidesz), October–November 1992, p. 25.
102. The Democratic Convention was obliged to change its name to the Romanian Democratic Convention owing to a provision in the electoral law that forbade

political coalitions to use the name under which they had run in previous elections unless all former members of the coalition agreed to it.

103. Hungarian radio, 23 October 1992, SWB EE/1521 B/13 (26 October 1992).

104. Rompres, 30 October 1992, SWB EE/1530 B/11 (5 November 1992).

105. SWB EE/1623 A2/1 (26 February 1993).

106. Rompres, 27 October 1992, SWB EE/1542 B/18 (29 October 1992).

107. See Tom Gallagher, 'Ethnic Tension in Cluj', *RFE-RL Research Report*, Vol. 2, No. 9 (26 February 1993).

108. Hungarian radio, 6 December 1992, SWB EE/1559 B/10 (9 December 1992).

109. Radio Bucharest, 22 January 1993, SWB EE/1598, B/12 (27 January 1993).

110. Rompres, 24 February 1993, SWB EE/1626 B/6 (2 March 1993).

111. *Politica* (Bucharest), (13 March 1993).

112. *România Mâre* (Bucharest), 4 September 1992.

113. *Expres Magasin*, 22 January 1992.

114. ARPRESS, 627 (29 March 1993).

115. ARPRESS, 631 (2 April 1993).

116. Michael Shafir, 'Minorities Council Raises Questions', *RFE-RL Research Report*, Vol. 2, No. 24 (11 June 1993), p. 37.

117. *22*, 6 May 1993.

118. Ibid.

119. Shafir, *RFE-RL Research Report*, Vol. 2, No. 24 (11 June 1993), p. 40.

120. Socor, *Report on Eastern Europe* (28 December 1990), p. 28.

121. Socor, *RFE-RL Correspondents' Reports* (5 April 1991).

122. Aurel Zidaru-Barbulescu, 'Romania Seeks Admission to the Council of Europe', *RFE-RL Research Report*, Vol. 2, No. 2 (8 January 1993), p. 13.

123. Shafir, *RFE-RL Research Report* (11 June 1993), p. 38.

124. Zidaru-Barbulescu, *RFE-RL Research Report* (8 January 1993), p. 14.

125. Oltay, *RFE-RL Research Report* (20 March 1992), p. 19.

126. Oltay, *RFE-RL Research Report* (8 May 1992), p. 30.

127. Pascu, 'Romania's Response to a Structured World', in Nelson (ed.), *Romania After Tyranny*, p. 277.

128. Andrew Marshall, 'Britain obstructs action on minority rights', *The Independent* (13 July 1993).

129. Rachel Brett, *The Challenges of Change*, Human Rights Centre, University of Essex 1992, p. 29.

130. Rachel Brett, *The Development of the Human Dimension Mechanism of the Conference for Security and Co-operation in Europe*, Human Rights Centre, University of Essex 1992, p. 1.

131. Oltay, *RFE-RL Research Report* (8 May 1992), p. 32.

132. Elaine Eddison, *The Protection of Minorities at the Conference on Security and Co-operation in Europe*, Human Rights Centre, University of Essex, 1993, p. 19.

133. Oltay, *RFE-RL Research Report* (8 May 1992), p. 33.

134. Ibid., pp. 27, 33.

135. Rompres, 27 June 1991, SWB EE/1114 A2/4 3 July 1991.

136. Dan Ionescu, 'Concern over the Yugoslav Crisis', *Report on Eastern Europe*, Vol. 1, No. 29 (19 July 1991), p. 24.

137. Ibid.

138. Hungarian radio, 26 November 1991, SWB EE/1246 (4 December 1991).

139. Hungarian radio, 4 November 1992, SWB EE/1533 (9 November 1992).

140. Dan Ionescu, 'Striving for a Better Image', *Report on Eastern Europe*, Vol. 2, No. 49 (20 December 1991), p. 30. One official Romanian source claims that by the end of 1992, 'direct and indirect losses and damages to the Romanian economy were . . . approximately 7 billion US dollars'. See Ioan Mircea Pascu, 'Romania and the Yugoslav Conflict', in Charles L. Barry (ed.), *The Search for Peace in Europe; Perspectives from NATO and Eastern Europe*, National Defense University Press, Fort Lesley J. McNair, USA 1994, p. 238.

141. Dan Ionescu, 'Romania Straddles the Fence on the Yugoslav Conflict', *RFE-RL Research Report*, Vol. 1, No. 35 (4 September 1992), p. 27.

142. Brett, *The Challenges of Change . . .*, p. 17.

143. *Dreptáteă* (5–6 August 1992). Occasional commentaries in *Dimineátă*, the Bucharest daily that has regularly been used as a news outlet by President Iliescu, suggest that the anti-western views endorsed by Milosevic have their adherents in Iliescu's circles. For example, an article by Viorel Cacoveanu in the 23 September 1992 edition of *Dimineátă* in which he writes: 'Under the leadership of Ion Iliescu, Romania has avoided a civil war – one that has been prepared from outside and which many countries would permit in a period when the West has encouraged the weakening and disintegration of the East'.

144. Ionescu, *RFE-RL Research Report* (4 September 1992), pp. 27–8.

145. Romanian radio, 5 April 1994 in SWB EE/1965 B/3 (7 April 1994). Croatia's President Tudjman also paid an official visit to Romania in 1994, but the welcoming statement made by Iliescu on that occasion was far less effusive than the one received by Milosevic.

146. Evidence of Romanian sanctions-busting is provided by Chris Stephen, 'Letter from Romania', *New Statesman and Society* (21 October 1994).

147. Pascu, 'Romania and the Yugoslav Conflict', pp. 233, 236, 239.

148. *The Economist* (9 July 1994).

149. John Sislin, 'Revolution Betrayed? Romania and the National Salvation Front', *Studies in Comparative Communism*, Vol. 24, No. 4 (1991), p. 396.

150. In 1993, the opposition parties won a rare victory in parliament by obtaining a majority for the setting-up of a commission that would control the intelligence services, but the deputy later appointed as its head turned out to be the President's closest parliamentary ally, Senator Vasile Vacaru. ARPRESS, Selective Daily Bulletin, No. 693 (18 June 1993); No. 698 (24 June 1993).

151. Michael Shafir, 'Romanians and the Transition to Democracy', *RFE-RL Research Report*, Vol. 2, No. 18 (30 April 1993), p. 47.

152. The findings from the various opinion surveys cited here were taken from the Bucharest political magazine *Sfera Politicii*, No. 10 (October 1993).

Chapter 5

The Democratic Parties and Nationalism

The dictatorship had smashed life into a thousand pieces, but what were we to do with our freedom which had come to us, as it were, from the skies? Yes, hundreds of people had died for it, their sacrifice a wonderful gift, but we still felt very confused. It seemed that we had to learn everything all over again: thinking, speaking, trading, printing, papers and books, re-establishing connections with the rest of the world, and a great many other things.

Nicolae Manolescu[1]

THE HISTORIC PARTIES

The December 1989 revolt was initiated by non-conformists, students and anonymous citizens who sensed that a rare moment had come in which to direct their rage at an oppressive system which finally seemed to be shedding its invulnerability. But, except in Timişoara, the birthplace of the uprising, no durable organisation sprang from the ranks of the protesters which might have enabled them to play a role in shaping the new political order. It had taken a great effort of will for citizens to defy a regime which, in its final moments, still proved capable of tremendous brutality. Those protesters were soon reduced to being bystanders as the political vacuum was filled by the National Salvation Front as it rapidly moved from being a caretaker government to a political movement which wished to dominate in its own right within a semi-pluralist context. The cries of betrayal from protesters who rushed back onto the streets in January and February 1990 were easily stifled by the acting government.

Opposition was increasingly expressed by the remnants of parties which had last played a role in politics before the implantation of communism. Two parties, the National Peasant Party (NPP-CD) and the National Liberal Party (NLP), were hastily reconstituted, the former adding the suffix 'Christian Democratic' in 1991. But they proved to be pale shadows of their former selves. For over forty years, the activities of what were known as 'the historic parties' had been suspended. The severity of the communist regime meant that it had been impossible to carry on even an underground existence or to enrol members of the new generation into these parties. Young Romanians did join the NPP-CD and the NLP in 1990 but these parties found that they no longer possessed the social and economic bases which had sustained them between the two world wars. The worlds of private agriculture, urban business and commerce and independent religious organisations from which these parties had derived values, material support and a steady flow of recruits had been shattered in the communist era.

The National Peasant Party's task in reconstituting itself, was especially arduous. The victorious communists had dealt ruthlessly with the NPP, which was widely felt to have won the general election held in 1946 just before the RCP took complete control.[2] Corneliu Coposu, who had taken the initiative in reviving the NPP-CD in late December 1989, was one of the few leading figures to survive the repression which virtually wiped out a whole generation of party activists, including Iuliu Maniu, the party's greatest leader. Coposu had been Maniu's secretary and had been acting general secretary of the NPP-CD before embarking upon seventeen years in prison, to be followed by another twenty-five years of tight restrictions upon his movements and activities. His links with Maniu, a political figure respected for his high ethical standards and for having played a key role in uniting Transylvania with the Romanian state, lent stature to Coposu, whose dignity, simplicity of manner and clarity of expression also proved appealing to younger people searching for a moral lead in what were confused political times. But Coposu was one of the few assets the party possessed in the task of reconstruction. Its links with the countryside, its main reservoir of electoral support until 1947, had been severed. The *chiaburi*, or medium-sized rural proprietors, who had strongly identified with the NPP-CD, had been swept away during the first years of communism. In Transylvania, the Uniate Church, which had been a close ally, had gone under in 1948 when the state had handed over its churches and rural congregations to the more pliable Orthodox Church. The ruthlessness which the RCP displayed in the countryside derived from its own weak hold there and from the need to eliminate a rival that had remained in better moral and organisational shape than other parties much discredited by the misrule and scandals of the inter-war period.

Once campaigning started for the election which the NSF had called for 20 May 1990, the historic parties found that little advantage was to be gained from stressing their involvement in politics in the years before 1947. Under the influence of state indoctrination, many poorly-educated people (however dissatisfied they may have been in the final Ceauşescu years) associated the inter-war years with exploitation by rural landlords and urban capitalists, and were disinclined to vote for any parties which might restore such conditions.

Gradually, it dawned on the more perceptive opposition officials that, although the dictator had perished, the world that had sustained him – along with its structures, mentalities and customs – lived on; it was especially painful for parties that prided themselves on the role that they had played in creating the Greater Romania which emerged after 1918 that the ex-communists still in charge of Romania in 1990 were able to exploit nationalism for their own ends, even though the communist system had been installed by a foreign power. The historic parties failed to realise the extent to which much of the population had come to link the successful assertion of Romanian national interests with the communist regime of the 1960s. Romania's limited declaration of independence from Moscow at that time had also been accompanied by a relaxation of social control and a distinct improvement in the availability of consumer goods. Those 'good times' were still remembered in the 1990s as a welcome respite from austerity and shortages, and it is not surprising that the NSF and overt nationalists campaigning in the 1990 and 1992 elections sought to exploit the popularity that the communists had managed to acquire in the 1960s through their foreign policy successes and attention to the consumer.

The recovery of the historic parties was also blocked by the fact that large elements of the population seemed to have a vested interest in the reconstruction of a modified version of communist Romanian society. Opinion polls after 1989 found that Romanian citizens continued to possess a strongly egalitarian outlook. Between seventy and seventy-four per cent believed that income levels should be almost equal for all while in a poll simultaneously carried out by the Gallup agency into attitudes to the market economy, there was more opposition in Romania to reducing sharply the role of the state in the economy than in any of the other countries polled (which included Albania, Bulgaria and the former Soviet Union).[3]

Such disconcerting poll findings revealed how successful the communist state had been in transmitting its values across Romanian society to a population which may have questioned particular policies or leadership styles but which never showed any sign of challenging the core beliefs underpinning the communist system. Understandably, the historic parties found it hard to obtain a hearing from social groups that remained strongly attached to egalitarianism and to state control of the economy. The negligible support which the NPP-CD enjoyed in the countryside showed how collectivisation had turned much of rural Romania into an alien world for that party. In the cities, all of the opposition forces found it difficult to establish any common ground with the ex-peasants who formed a numerically large social grouping in huge housing estates. The successive efforts to expand Romanian heavy industry from the 1950s to the 1980s had created a group variously described as 'worker-peasants' or 'neo-urbanites' who looked to the state for direction and who reacted with puzzlement or hostility to parties which urged them to stand on their own two feet and look for salvation outside large redundant industrial enterprises.

The historic parties responded in different ways to their lack of popularity in post-Ceauşescu Romania. A returned émigré like Ion Raţiu, the NPP-CD's 1990 presidential candidate, insisted upon invoking a romantic past; in a parliamentary speech on 21 December 1990, he declared that 'our country used to be a happy country. Communism destroyed it. Communism destroyed the person and destroyed his internal integrity, his self-respect, honesty, correctness – that is what I have found in this country.'[4]

Others actively looked for scapegoats for the communist dystopia that had so transformed the land. In the pages of *Dreptátea* (Justice), the NPP-CD's official daily paper, the Jews were a target in the early months of 1990.[5] In one edition, it was argued that 'the Jewish holocaust, with its loss of six million lives, paled against the "Holocaust of the Romanian people" with its twenty million "psychological victims of communism" . . . "all the victims of a doctrine brought to Romania by Jews"'.[6] The view that it had been the 'traditional enemies' of the Romanian people who were responsible for inflicting communism on the country, and that 'true' Romanians had been innocent victims, was one that ultra-nationalists would energetically promote in order to absolve those who had served the Ceauşescus of responsibility for the damage done to the country. Fortunately, Coposu, the NPP-CD general secretary, opposed anti-Semitism within the party, which he branded as 'false patriotism'. Drawing upon his own prison experiences, he testified that he had met many Jews who had been the victims of communism, and he recalled that there had been a time under Stalin when imprisoned Jews had been treated more harshly than anyone else.

Anti-Semitic outbursts from NPP-CD veterans diminished in intensity once it was clear that these could be exploited by well-placed elements who wished to restore the full-blown chauvinism of the Ceauşescu era. However, the party revealed its social isolation when senior officials referred to 'that great manipulable mass of working-class people created by Ceauşescu' and deplored the egalitarian mentality which, 'after 45 years of communism, has considerably eroded the moral foundation of the Romanian people'.[7] Each of the historic parties compounded their isolation by failing to make a distinction between crying 'Down with Communism' and 'Down with the Communists'. The first slogan had to do with the destruction of a system, while the second one implied a clear threat to the welfare of millions of Romanians who had joined the RCP more out of convenience than out of any conviction.[8]

Given the handicaps that the historic parties faced in trying to reintegrate themselves with national life, it is hardly surprising that they turned in on themselves, being worn down by internal rivalries and suspicions. Returned émigrés found it difficult to work with activists who had endured the communist period at home, and younger recruits found that prospects of advancement were blocked by veterans determined to pick up the threads of political careers interrupted in 1940.

EARLY REACTIONS TO NATIONALISM

The historic parties' hopes of playing a leading role in national affairs were retarded by the rise of Romanian–Hungarian tension in parts of Transylvania. Vatra Românească quickly acquired a great deal of support by insisting that Hungarian pressure for the restoration of cultural and educational rights would place at risk Romanian sovereignty in Transylvania. The rapid rise of a self-proclaimed cultural movement which quickly displayed vaulting political ambitions showed how the barrage of chauvinist propaganda directed at the population in the 1980s had kindled a sense of 'collective psychosis' about Transylvania. These words appeared in the 30 April 1990 issue of *Dreptátea*. But, for a long time, the NPP-CD was unsure of how to react as inter-ethnic relations deteriorated in parts of Transylvania.

The NPP-CD had nursed harsh memories of the wartime occupation of north-western Transylvania by Hungary in which many of its leading officials had suffered harsh treatment. In 1989–90, there was bound to be some resentment at the speed with which Hungarians had formed a national political organisation; it was one which, initially, seemed ready to ignore the doubtful pedigree of the NSF government provided that the latter was prepared to make the restitution of minority rights an early priority.

The patriotic slogans and songs which Vatra used to mobilise Romanians struck a chord with elements of the NPP-CD. In the past, it had made similar appeals to Romanian solidarity whenever Hungarian assertiveness was felt to be a danger. But the party kept its distance from Vatra as it emerged that some of its leading members in Tirgu Mureş, its birthplace, had been figures closely associated with the Ceauşescu regime, ones who had benefited personally from its nationality policies.[9]

Nevertheless, the NPP-CD was slow to realise that a nationalist movement promoted by communist officials who wished to minimise political change in their districts posed a very real threat to its own prospects of recovery.

Once the origins and character of Vatra Românească became more widely understood, NPP-CD officials were prepared to state openly that it was part of a strategy to prolong neo-communist influence in Transylvania at the price of wrecking inter-ethnic relations. Coposu declared in 1991 that the Party of Romanian National Unity which had quickly emerged from Vatra had been part of a diversion by the NSF regime to distract people from its own shortcomings.[10] But it was not until the Tirgu Mureş clashes of March 1990, followed by an informal alliance between Vatra and the ruling NSF alliance, that the NPP-CD began to realise that neo-communist manipulation lay behind ethnic polarisation.

The issues of *Dreptátea* that appeared between 17 and 29 March, when the tension in Tirgu Mureş was most acute, made references to ill-treatment that Romanians had received in the past from Hungarians, and depicted Romanians as innocent parties in the latest outbreak of hostilities. Many in the party seemed ready to equate the group rights requested by Hungarians with unacceptable privileges and insisted that members of the minority were entitled only to individual rights accorded to them as citizens of Romania;[11] Liviu Petrinu, vice-president of the NPP-CD, even criticised President Iliescu for implying that Romanians might share some of the blame for Tirgu Mureş violence.[12] But once it had become apparent that strife in the city had been choreographed by persons with an RCP and a Securitate background, well versed in the arts of manipulation, the NPP-CD began to retreat from positions which it had shared with Vatra; and, by August 1990, the National Peasants were ready to abandon dabbling in ethnic politics and make common cause with the Hungarian HDFR in initiatives like the Democratic Anti-Totalitarian Forum.

The National Liberals (hitherto always overshadowed by the NPP-CD in Transylvania) had begun co-operating with the chief Hungarian party as early as 22 March 1990, when both organisations issued a joint statement on inter-ethnic relations. Any attempt to make political capital out of inter-ethnic tensions was condemned, and a parallel was drawn between the events of Tirgu Mureş and earlier confrontations in Bucharest (of a non-ethnic character) in which the hand of state forces had been detected. The need was stressed for 'our common history to be written again in the spirit of truth by eliminating all distortions caused by totalitarianism in Romania and Hungary'. Administrative decentralisation, enabling 'ethnic minorities to enjoy their own cultural and religious institutions and the use of their own mother tongue', was described as an important objective of Romania's liberal restoration. Finally, both parties repudiated any expression of Hungarian irredentism or Romanian extremist nationalism.[13]

TIMIŞOARA AND THE OTHER ROMANIA

The NLP-HDFR joint statement showed that Romanian and Hungarian political forces were not fated to be on a collision course and that they shared
several important common objectives. It had been preceded by a far more
eloquent and forceful statement, known as the Timişoara Declaration,
which had been released on 11 March 1990 by the Timişoara Society,
formed in January 1990 by young writers and journalists in that city keen
to promote human rights and fight for the implementation of democracy.

Organisations committed to equivalent aims were to be found in several
other Romanian cities, but Timişoara was the only place where a local
democracy movement acquired a significant following. This was because,
as the 11 March document pointed out, 'citizens of Timişoara had initiated
the revolution by waging a fierce war alone for five days against one of the
world's strongest and most hatefully repressive systems'. A revolution 'had
been initiated in Timişoara against the communist regime and its entire
nomenklatura, and by no means in order to create the opportunity for a
group of anti-Ceauşescu dissidents from within the RCP to gain power'.[14]
Unlike Bucharest, Cluj and other cities which had been the scene of fighting
in 1989, the embryo citizens' movement of Timişoara was able to prevent
the NSF from monopolising positions of authority. A situation of dual power
existed after January, when the leaders of the democracy movement held
local elections and formed a city council which had substantial local support as it set out to improve social and economic conditions.[15] Government
displeasure at finding that its own hand-picked nominees installed in the
mayor's office were being defied in this way resulted in the flow of food
and raw materials to Timişoara being reduced. It was a lesson to politically-
aware citizens that their city faced penalties if it decided to become a centre
of opposition.

In due course, the challenge of the Timişoara movement to the government would be blunted as the city found itself isolated in the absence of
comparable popular movements elsewhere in the country. But Timişoara
and (to a lesser degree) the Banat region were places in which the
opposition possessed the social bases that were lacking in the rest of the
country.

The key factor in enabling the opposition to acquire an enduring power-
base in the Timişoara region was probably the absence of inter-ethnic
tension in an area where many different ethnic groups were found. Not
only Romanians, Germans and Hungarians, but also smaller communities
of Serbs, Czechs, Croats and Bulgarians inhabited the Banat, making it the
most ethnically mixed part of Romania. The degree of inter marriage in
Timişoara and the fact that Romanians and Hungarians were bolstered by

other ethnic communities able to act as buffers between them reinforced harmonious links. The Banat had been relatively unaffected by the wartime occupation of Transylvania and, throughout the worst years of the communist dictatorship, when attempts were being made to indoctrinate the population along nationalist lines, the region was able to receive Yugoslav and Hungarian television broadcasts. Traditionally, economic prospects had been better than elsewhere in Romania owing to the fertility of the soil, and the resultant level of economic development meant that both political awareness and expectations tended to be higher than elsewhere.[16] All these factors may help to explain why thousands of Timişoara's citizens were prepared openly to confront the Ceauşescu regime on the streets in December 1989 and – three months later – give their backing to a declaration whose second clause affirmed that all sections of the community had taken part in the Timişoara uprising: blue-collar workers, white-collar workers, intellectuals, university students, secondary school pupils, children and village-dwellers.

This clause had been inserted so as to combat 'the typical communist technique of dominating the people by provoking feuds among the social classes and groups'; this concern also lay behind the affirmation that citizens from all Timişoara's ethnic groups 'sacrificed their lives for the victory of the revolution'. To the framers of the declaration, this revealed Timişoara to be 'a European city whose people have refused and are still refusing to accept nationalism'. In a bold departure, they invited 'all the country's chauvinists – whether Romanian, Hungarian or German – to come to Timişoara to take a course in tolerance and mutual respect, the only principle that will rule in the future European house'. A call was made for the 're-Europeanisation' of Romania based on the concept of private initiative but without copying wholesale 'western capitalist systems, which have their own deficiencies . . .'.

Beyond Timişoara itself, the opposition was galvanised by Clause 8, which insisted that 'the President of the Republic should be one of the symbols of our parting from communism'. But, in the state media, it was clause 11 which received most attention; it proclaimed that 'Timişoara has decided to take seriously and put into action the principle of economic and administrative decentralisation' with the ultimate aim being 'to establish an experiment in Timiş county, a model of a market economy because of the area's strong economic capacity and the skill of available specialists.

Romanian television interpreted clause 11 as a desire that the Banat be given full-blown autonomy.[17] The Timişoara Society's outspoken defence of decentralisation was bound to have infuriated many nationalists since it was breaking a taboo which insisted that if power was removed from the heart of the national state in Bucharest, the country faced the risk of dismemberment.

This exaggerated response highlighted the validity of Clause 6, which drew attention to the survival of prejudices symptomatic of communist ideology persisting in the consciousness of all Romanians for which it was not the people, but groups keen on manipulating them in order to reinstate communist power, that were to blame.

No document of equivalent weight or clarity emerged from the democratic opposition in a year which was to see a torrent of rhetorical and sometimes downright incoherent press statements and speeches. The declaration put the interests of the people of Timişoara above the wider national interests which Ceauşescu's ex-communist successors were still able to interpret on their own behalf.

The movement which gave rise to the Timişoara declaration was a collective and impersonal one which lacked a commanding personality to whom everyone was expected to defer. Its character made it difficult for the pro-government media to harm it by spreading rumours based on real or invented personality disputes, which would prove to be an effective way of discrediting other opposition movements. In April 1990, the Timişoara Association suggested that Ion Iliescu and his two opposition challengers should withdraw from the presidential race so that the country could be ruled for two years without a president in the period that a new constitution was being drawn up. According to Nicolae Harsanyi, a leading democracy activist from Timişoara, 'it would have been a chance for Romanians to learn to think for themselves and to become less dependent upon powerful personalities who might treat them better than Ceauşescu had done but who were unwilling to offer them significantly greater opportunities to determine their own futures'.[18]

EMIGRÉS AND THE 1990 ELECTORAL DEFEAT

But by being asked to vote for a president entrusted with strong executive powers, millions of Romanians were encouraged to see politics in terms of strong leaders rather than competing programmes.[19] The NSF was promoted as 'Iliescu's party' while the opposition, in its turn, reflected the importance of personality by directing much of its campaigning against the person of Iliescu and by pushing forward its own would-be saviours.

Protestations about the communist character of the NSF lacked conviction when neither of the historic parties proved willing to put aside their factional spirit and close ranks against this danger. Radu Campeanu, general secretary of the National Liberals, and Ion Raţiu of the NPP-CD were two elderly presidential challengers who failed to convince many of the undecided voters that they could offer Romania stable and responsible government. Neither man had lived through the final decades of communist rule and both lacked the insider knowledge and the moral stature to convincingly challenge ex-communists seeking to build a democracy in their own image. NSF criticisms that they had completely lost touch with the country – 'they ate caviare in Paris instead of salami and soya at home' – hit their mark.

Ion Raţiu, the returned millionaire shipowner, with his bow-tie and jovial air, indeed resembled an archetypal pre-war tycoon. Until weeks before entering the presidential race, he had not set foot in Romania since 1940 when he had been in his early twenties. His lack of familiarity with current realities showed on the campaign trail and in television appearances. Upon singling out privatisation as a cornerstone of his economic programme, he made it very easy for the NSF to depict him as a ruthless money-grabber intent on restoring the bad old times of exploitation and misery. He failed to understand that the Romania of his youth, which the perspective of exile made him depict in elegiac terms,, had become for millions of Romanians dependent upon the state for their knowledge of the past an era of grim class oppression. Most Romanian cities had streets named after Lupeni and Grivita, the locations of bitter coal-mining and railway disputes in 1929 and 1933 which were forcibly suppressed by governments controlled by both of the historic parties seeking a mandate in 1990. The NSF insisted that these parties, in their new guise, were just as contemptuous of workers' rights as they had been in the 1930s and that their commitment to privatisation showed their readiness to inflict a fresh round of social misery on them. Neither Campeanu nor Raţiu had a suitable reply to this charge, and it is understandable that a people with traditionally low expectations, for whom a benevolent ruler was a rarity, were drawn in their millions to a figure like Iliescu who not only promised social protection but also during his first months in office, seemed to lighten the burdens of daily life for many of them.

If elections had not been held so soon after 1989, the opposition might have become more familiar with Romanian social realities and taken steps to fight a better campaign with more credible presidential candidates. But the democratic parties would still have had to face the barrage of disinformation which the NSF waged through its control of the state media. Romanian voters were informed in 1990 that opposition leaders were playing politics for personal gain, that their pasts were dubious, and that they were ready to be the tools of external interests hostile to Romania.[20] Given the great faith that ordinary Romanians, especially from the countryside and small towns, had in official news sources, these proved to be damning accusations however groundless they may have been.[21] When the official election results were published nearly a week after the polls had closed on

20 May, it was only the scale of Ion Iliescu's victory that generated surprise. Campeanu and Rațiu managed to obtain only 10.2 and 4.3 per cent of the vote respectively. In parliamentary elections, the National Liberals acquired 6.4 per cent of the vote, with the NPP trailing badly on 2.6 per cent. Even Coposu failed to gain a seat in his native rural district, claiming electoral irregularities.[22]

The scale of the historic parties' problems in Transylvania was shown by the unexpected success of a party spawned by Vatra Românească known as the Party of Romanian National Unity. Although it had registered with the electoral commission on the very last day that parties could apply to be contestants (suggesting a degree of improvisation), the PRNU won 12 seats in Transylvania . In Cluj county it gained 13.5 per cent of the vote as against only 3.6 per cent for the NPP-CD in what had been one of the latter's strongholds. Radu Ceontea had shown the radical nationalist body's close links with the NSF by urging Transylvanians to spurn candidates newly returned from exile and to vote instead for Ion Iliescu.[23]

LIMITATIONS OF DEMOCRATIC INITIATIVES

The fact that the democratic opposition in Transylvania had been squeezed both by former communists and ultra-nationalists helps to explain why the first successful initiative to form a united front took place there. On 9 August 1990, the Democratic Anti-Totalitarian Front (DAF), an umbrella organisation of the main opposition parties, was formed in Cluj. Its manifesto emphasised the danger of a communist restoration which it was felt required the unification of all anti-totalitarian forces, irrespective of profession, faith or ethnicity. In its ten-point programme, the DAF called for the collective rights of national minorities to be respected which was a sign that it was prepared to defy the line adopted by the NSF and fast becoming a prevailing orthodoxy – that minorities should not possess rights denied to other Romanian citizens. Some 1,000 delegates attended the DAF's first national conference in Cluj in October 1990, and Doina Cornea was elected president of the forum.[24]

The impetus that lay behind the formation of the DAF in Cluj was the decision of Petre Roman's newly-installed government to appoint a pro-NSF mayor in a city where the ruling party had received only twenty-nine per cent of the vote. Throughout the country, independent mayors were being supplanted by appointees chosen in Bucharest, but the strength of the Cluj reaction stemmed from the character of the new appointee; Mihai Talpeanu had been director-general of Cluj's leading heavy-industry plant, and he had been a member of the RCP leadership in Cluj county. Local democrats condemned him as 'one of the most flagrant opportunists of the party who, in the revolutionary days of 1989, opposed the workers coming out onto the streets and then subsequently informed the Securitate when his attempts proved to be of no avail'.[25] Grigore Zanc was chosen as county prefect; he was another former local RCP leader who, in his role as censor, had impeded much literary work, according to a petition requesting that both men be replaced by individuals with less tarnished pasts.[26]

But, despite a promising start, the DAF failed to provide an effective rallying-point for opposition parties, and it soon fell from view. The historic parties succumbed to in-fighting and, in the case of the NLP, serious splits. Younger deputies broke away from the NLP in the summer of 1990, disillusioned by Campeanu's autocratic ways. Ever since he had been elected president of the party 'through acclamation' in March 1990, without a vote being taken, he had sought to promote officials whose first loyalties were to him.[27] This was not an unusual occurrence in Romanian politics, but Campeanu's failure to obtain a significant breakthrough for his party meant that dissidents were likely to challenge his authority; further defections in 1991–2 weakened the NLP's claim to be the most vigorous branch of the opposition. Meanwhile, the NPP-CD was faced by recurring tensions between those who had gathered around wealthy former émigré, Ion Raţiu, and others who had sat out the communist era at home. For long periods, the NPP-CD in Cluj, where Raţiu had been narrowly elected a deputy, was paralysed by such dissensions, and in 1992 Coposu was compelled to suspend the local party for a cooling-off period. He also made attempts to bring more young people into the party leadership, notably at the September 1991 conference, but accusations that it remained a gerontocracy continued to be levelled.[28] None of the democratic parties (including new ones founded after 1990) proved appealing to young people, who generally preferred to remain aloof from politics.[29] Even the Movement For Romania (MFR), a party deliberately aimed at young people, set up in 1991 by Marian Munteanu, a student leader who became a symbol of the democratic opposition after being beaten up and imprisoned in June 1990, remained small and was prone to splits. Its main claim to fame was that it looked to the pre-war radical right for inspiration, to the extent that Munteanu was prepared to praise the Iron Guard and excuse some of the crimes associated with it. Munteanu and his youthful followers dismissed Ceauşescu's nationalism as a false variety, believing that genuine nationalism could not be associated with communism owing to Marxism's international character;[30] his drift towards the far right caused dismay among observers who described, as the ultimate triumph of communist brainwashing, the tendency of some of those who had taken to the streets to overthrow a dictator to 'now indulge in the glorification of his no less ignominious predecessors'.[31]

The danger of Munteanu's movement lay less in its electoral potential and more in the fact that it might ease the passage of young people into the more professional ultra-nationalist movements spawned by former communists. In March 1992, Munteanu anticipated the formation of a 'national bloc' when he declared that a future alliance between elements of the Greater Romania Party and the PRNU, based on defence of the 'national interest', could not be ruled out.[32]

One new movement determined to prevent the memory of the 1989 revolution from being hi jacked for nationalist ends, and which sought to appeal to young people unimpressed by the parties' emphasis on the electoral struggle, was the Civic Alliance. Formed in the autumn of 1990, it reflected a belief that there was space for a broad front which drew in groups whose existence did not revolve around contesting elections. This umbrella organisation of the non-party opposition was promoted by local civic groups and by the Bucharest-based Group for Social Dialogue, an intellectual forum set up in December 1989 which published the weekly *22*. The Civic Alliance's advocacy of a self-limiting state, based on the rule of law, proved appealing for those Romanians who had concluded that (without exception) the parties were primarily driven by the ambition of exercising power on their own behalf.

But the Civic Alliance suffered dissension in its turn. In 1991, an important segment argued that its goals could only stand a chance of being realised if the defenders of civil society cast aside their inhibitions and set up their own electoral organisation. A Civic Alliance Party (CAP) was created in July 1991. Its leader, the literary critic, Nicolae Manolescu, described it as 'a party that wishes the reconstruction of the state of law and of civil society in Romania in the conditions of a market economy and of democratic legislation'.[33] Members of the creative intelligentsia based in Bucharest were disproportionately to be found at the upper echelons of the party. Although Manolescu had recognised the gravity of the ultra-nationalist challenge much earlier than any other senior politician and would choose to fight a Transylvanian constituency in the 1992 election, the Bucharest emphasis of the party meant that it was ill-equipped to resist the nationalist juggernaut.[34] It is significant that someone like Smaranda Enache who, in the difficult testing-ground of Tirgu Mureş, had worked consistently to bring young Romanians and Hungarians together, failed to obtain a place in the leadership of the CAP even though, in a secret ballot of 400 founding members, she was placed third in the election for a twenty-five-member national council. These twenty-five then chose nine from among themselves to occupy key positions, Enache being sidelined by a phalanx of Bucharest-based literary politicians and academics who divided the major portfolios among themselves.[35]

The CAP split in 1993, shortly after it had returned sixteen deputies to parliament. A faction opposed to Manolescu's leadership broke away to explore the possibility of creating a new liberal party; meanwhile the Civic Alliance remained in existence, working on numerous projects to strengthen human rights in Romania and diminish the prospect of some kind of restoration of authoritarian rule.

Nearly all Romanian parties have been prone to splits, including the ultra-nationalist ones despite their fetish regarding unity at all levels of Romanian reality. Against such a background, a party system based more on slogans than concrete ideas and issues has taken shape. One negative outcome has been the inability of parties to interact effectively with sections of the electorate whose welfare they claim to be defending. But internal fragmentation was less easy to explain away in a party like the CAP, which encouraged voters to have high expectations and also claimed to eschew the personality factor.

DEMOCRATS AND NATIONALISTS, 1990-1

When it came to responding to ultra-nationalists, the historic parties proved to be more cautious than the informal democratic opposition (the Timişoara Society, Civic Alliance), perhaps because they felt they had more to lose. The NPP-CD derived no comfort from the way that Vatra and the PRNU took a leading part in the official ceremonies commemorating the fiftieth anniversary of the Vienna Award (allowing the Hungarian state to seize north-western Transylvania) which fell on 30 August 1990. But the NPP-CD seemed to have concluded from earlier experiences that it was futile to compete with Vatra in making nationalist declarations. Instead, the party sought to prevent the emotionally-charged anniversary from being used to strain inter-ethnic relations further. *Dreptátea* on 30 August 1990 carried an article which insisted that no guilt was attached to the Hungarian minority, or even to the Hungarian state of today, for the atrocities that flowed from the wartime occupation of Romanian territory. The party's statement released on 30 August was more restrained and thoughtful than that of any other Romanian political organisation:

> We humbly pay homage to the hundreds of peaceful citizens who were killed by the Horthyite military and paramilitary operations, to the Romanians forcibly enrolled in work battalions inside Hungary, to those sent to the Vorenzh eastern front, to the over 300,000 refugees . . . and, especially, to the scores of thousands of Romanian soldiers who sacrificed their lives for the liberation of northern Transylvania and Hungary in 1944 and 1945 . . .
>
> The NPP-CD refuses to remain anchored in the past and acknowledges that Hungary has dissociated itself from Horthy's crimes and abuses . . .
>
> The imperatives of our times are to bring peace and peoples closer to one another by gradually eliminating frontiers . . .[36]

In November 1990, Matei Boilă, a Uniate priest in Cluj and later to be a NPP-CD deputy, warned in *Dreptátea* of 'a violent campaign designed to promote bloody incidents' having disfigured recent months, its perpetrators being 'neo-communists promoting nationalism through a so-called cultural organisation'. He did not refer to Vatra Românească by name, even though the implication was an obvious one (indeed, the NPP-CD would instruct its members to have no dealings with Vatra). He described the objectives of the nationalist offensive as being to 'distract people's attention from socio-economic problems created by the NSF government . . . to gain a portion of the NPP-CD electorate . . . and to create disorders designed to offer an excuse for re-activating the Securitate'.[37] Boilă's statement represented a turning-point in the NPP-CD's attitude to ultra-nationalism, and soon afterwards he was prepared to enlarge upon his comments, describing the ultra-nationalists as posing a greater threat to democracy in Transylvania than the NSF.[38] But at public meetings in Cluj 1990–1, it was still rare to hear local opposition figures denouncing Vatra or the PRNU as agents of neo-communism despite mounting evidence that they were perpetrating a strategy, dating from the Ceauşescu era, of dividing people according to ethnic criteria. Hesitation about condemning Vatra-PRNU outright stemmed from an understandable fear of being branded 'anti-national' by a movement which was swiftly acquiring a popular audience not possessed by Cluj democrats.

There was no systematic effort to confront Vatra and the NSF as they formed an informal alliance in the city, the mayor allowing ultra-nationalists to profit from the selling of state assets while denying Romanian citizens of Hungarian origin opportunities to take part in the privatisation process.[39] Doina Cornea was the only prominent Romanian dissident in Cluj ready to make common cause with Hungarians in condemning nationalist excesses. In July 1991 she spoke at a public rally called by the HDFR to protest over restrictions on Hungarian-language teaching in Cluj schools. She condemned the head of the schools inspectorate for claiming that there had been 'separatist tendencies' in the Hungarian schools re-established in Cluj. 'It is absurd', she said, 'that at a time when Bessarabia is occupied and we do nothing to liberate it, we say instead that the Magyars want to take Transylvania. We are the ones in control of Transylvania and it is the duty of a landlord to be generous.'[40]

The vilification which Doina Cornea received in the daily papers published by the prefecture and the mayor's office may well have proved a disincentive to others who contemplated standing up to ultra-nationalists. Dr Petru Forna, president of Vatra Românească in Cluj (until he was appointed Romania's ambassador to Vienna in 1993), dismissed Doina Cornea in terms that were customary for those nationalists outraged that she continued to make regular criticisms of Romania's human rights record to a western audience. He denied that she was an intellectual and could not see any reason why she should be reinstated in the city's university where she had lost her teaching job for criticising the regime; he believed that the extent of her opposition to the Ceauşescu regime had been greatly exaggerated and that the unwarranted reputation that she enjoyed in the west stemmed from misperceptions about the realities of life in his country that were commonplace there.[41]

In Bucharest, the popular impact of *România Mâre* (Greater Romania), the chauvinist weekly, generated concern among liberals in the capital as it became clear that populist chauvinism stemmed not merely from internecine disputes in Transylvania.[42] On 29 June 1991, a round-table on the 'Danger of Extremism' held by mainstream opposition parties issued a warning about an alarming growth of 'leftist and rightist extremism', especially journals that 'tolerate and encourage xenophobia, chauvinism [and] anti-Semitism . . .'.[43] Nicolae Manolescu warned in 1991 that 'the "nationalists" are no less hostile to liberalism than the communists . . . The nationalists speak not of my rights as an individual to liberty and justice, but only of my rights as a Romanian to have a state able to protect me against external aggression.'[44]

Although the democratic opposition became increasingly aware of the readiness of the NSF and several of its satellites to use nationalism to deflect criticism of its economic policies and to cast doubts on the patriotic credentials of its opponents, no counter-strategy was elaborated. The vulnerability of the government was perhaps at its greatest in the weeks following the enforced removal from office of Petre Roman in September 1991. Nevertheless, the NSF succeeded in diverting attention from its own internal disarray and its inability to maintain order in Bucharest, by releasing a parliamentary report which alleged that Romanians had been subjected to persecution at the hands of Hungarians in the counties of Harghita and Covasna at the very end of 1989.

A two-day debate on the report was broadcast live from parliament in which Romanian democrats conspicuously refrained from joining their Hungarian colleagues in defying the nationalist clamour. Deputy Ion Raţiu of the NPP-CD offered an account of the Hungarian role in recent Romanian history, which would not have disgraced an ultra-nationalist deputy: he claimed that, after 1956, Hungarians in the RCP had 'demonstrated they were Hungarians first and communists second', after which they were removed from positions of authority.[45] Simultaneously, 'a violent and sustained campaign of Magyar chauvinism started up in the west so that nowadays the moment one speaks of Transylvania, the western mind immediately thinks of the destruction of the Hungarian minority at the hands of Romanians. This has to be halted and it is we who have to do it.' Later, in another speech on 11 November 1991, Raţiu said that Hungarians and Szeklers had an obligation to 'prove what they are loudly saying: that they are loyal citizens of the Romanian state'.[46]

A statement like Raţiu's, endorsing the nationalist view that Romania was threatened by the action of Hungarians abroad, added weight to the highly-charged communiqués of Vatra Românească. Cluj's opposition paper, *NU*, condemned the historic parties for voting in parliament in favour of the Harghita-Covasna report, behaviour described as peddling to nationalism so as not to lose more votes to the PRNU.[47] The paper also had harsh words for the NLP, which joined a caretaker government under Teodor Stolojan, approved by parliament on 16 October 1991. Campeanu, the NLP leader, had argued that, by entering government, the NLP would be able to insert democratic safeguards before the new cycle of local, parliamentary and presidential elections fell due in 1992. But there was little evidence of this. One of the most pressing needs was the removal of prefects appointed by Roman, many with an active communist past, who would be helping to prepare for elections in their counties. But this demand was never publicly made by the NLP, whose ministers proved ineffectual as democratic counterweights in a government still dominated by the NSF.

I. V. Sandulescu, the NLP deputy who became deputy foreign minister, justified being part of an NSF-controlled government by arguing that, with a history stretching back 150 years, the NLP had been present at all decisive moments in Romanian history.[48] However, critics of the move argued that by entering a 'so-called government of national unity, the NLP had saved the face of the NSF at the gravest moment for it since the 1989 revolution'.[49]

What was more perplexing was that the NLP soon afterwards was persuaded to join the Democratic Convention, a coalition of opposition parties, including the NPP-CD, the HDFR, the CAP and several minor ones, to enable the opposition to present a united front in local elections. The press was quick to make the point that to be at the same time in government and in opposition placed the NLP in a rather unique situation and was 'a performance which showed an enormous aptitude for political compromise'.[50]

The Democratic Convention's intention to offer a powerful moral contrast to the NSF was further eroded in the parliamentary vote for the proposed new constitution in November 1991; some deputies belonging to the DC parties cast their votes in favour, others against. The final choice was given to the electorate in the 9 December 1991 referendum. Once again, the opposition parties gave contrasting signals to the electorate. The HDFR and the NLP offered their supporters 'the possibility of voting according to their consciences', while the NPP-CD asked voters to boycott the referendum because it imposed a republican form of government and contained clauses which helped to perpetuate communist influence in Romania.

Ion Cristoiu, the influential press columnist, reckoned that the NPP-CD's call for a boycott saddled the party with an extremist image at a time when citizens reeling from economic hardship and two years of political crises yearned for a period of normality.[51] But the NPP-CD's call for an abstention should not just be put down to a lack of political judgment. After its headquarters had been wrecked in the second *mineriada*, of June 1990, the NPP-CD had lost most of its equipment, which left it with few means to make propaganda.[52] The millionaire Ion Raţiu belonged to the party, but he was a detached member who funded his own personal initiatives, such as the Bucharest daily *Cotidianul* launched in the spring of 1991.

The successful passage of the constitution into law restored to the NSF some of the credibility lost in the autumn of 1991. According to Ion Cristoiu, 'the authorities installed in December 1989 had once again shown themselves to be more politically adept than the opposition which continues to be divided, lacks coherence, and often takes illusion for reality'.[53]

The next major challenge for the democratic camp was the set of local elections due to be held in February 1992. From Cluj, Doina Cornea issued a statement in which she claimed that the country's future was bound up with the decision people made at this poll:'elections make it possible for the simple citizen to contribute either to the salvation of, or to the irreversible condemnation of our country'. She appealed to her fellow citizens to 'vote for candidates who have never been party activists or Securitate agents . . . people who are not attracted by power, ones who remain brave even when confronting the powerful, and for those who are not tempted by money or corruption'.[54]

THE CRUCIAL BATTLE: CLUJ 1992

Probably unbeknownst even to Doina Cornea, the local elections in Cluj, her own city, would give rise to a major confrontation between the forces of liberal democracy and those of hardline nationalism whose echoes would reverberate far beyond Transylvania's principal city. Owing to the crucial nature of the Cluj contest, much of the rest of this chapter will focus on the nature of the electoral struggle there both in the local and parliamentary elections.

The Democratic Convention (DC) in Cluj made a promising start to the campaign when the constituent elements agreed to throw their weight behind a candidate for mayor who appeared capable of halting the nationalist bandwagon in the city. Petru Liţiu was a former air-force officer who had been a founder member of CADA (the Committee for Action to Democratise the Army). Reform-minded officers who wished for a decisive rather than a cosmetic break with the past had formed CADA in February 1990. They pressed for elements in the military, implicated in the repression of 1989, to be brought to justice. The government dissolved CADA in June 1990, and, along with other officers who failed to sever their links with it, Liţiu was expelled from the army. Having swapped a Romanian colonel's salary for an uncertain future, it was hoped that Liţiu's devotion to his principles would make an impression on sectors of the electorate which, hitherto, had not found the opposition to be morally inspiring, particularly the young.

Despite being a university town in which over 20,000 students swelled the population for six to eight months of the year, Cluj had not been a growth point for the democratic opposition. There was palpable disappointment with politicians and political programmes. The CAP, to which Liţiu belonged, had failed to recruit widely among students despite being unburdened by the gerontocratic image of the historic parties. Nor did the local elections prove to be a turning-point, since a clause in the electoral law prevented students from voting in the towns where they studied if they lived elsewhere, as was the case with a large proportion of those in Cluj. Since the elections coincided with a busy examination period, relatively few students shared much enthusiasm for voting, and an important opportunity which might have enabled some of them to obtain political experience and acquire party affiliations was lost.[55]

The effective disqualification of thousands of student residents was a grievous blow to Liţiu's chances, and this part of the electoral law perhaps had greater effect on the result in Cluj than anywhere else in the country. (Soldiers garrisoned in towns far from their own localities were, by contrast, able to vote in their temporary place of abode.)

The absence of its own media outlets which could reach large sections of the electorate was another handicap faced by the Cluj opposition. An opposition daily was finally launched in the city on 1 February 1992, but by then the election campaign was nearly over and the pro-government press had enjoyed an unchallenged run in defaming the main opposition candidate; *Tribuna Ardealului* (Tribune of Transylvania) aimed to be a daily paper of record. But it was not as professional in its layout or as incisive in its political comments as its two local rivals, *Adevărul de Cluj* (Truth of Cluj) and *Mesagerul Transilvan* (Transylvanian Messenger), although it carried information and opinions which would never have got into either.

Mesagerul Transilvan was the newspaper of the prefecture and, throughout the election campaign, its coverage was marked by verbal extremism; the front page of the issue on 17 January carried an image of a skeletal face wrapped in a pointed hood, next to which was a key in the shape of an axe, the key being the symbol of the DC which appeared on its electoral literature as well as the ballot paper. Underneath this spectral figure was written the message: 'For the Future of Your Children, VOTE FOR THE KEY!' There were also skilfully-drawn cartoons of Doina Cornea which showed the pre-1989 dissident in various ridiculous poses.

On 23 February, *Mesagerul* carried an article entitled 'It is still not too late' in which its readers were warned that the DC was 'a monstrous coalition against the national interest of Romanians . . . It is too much to contemplate what will happen in our country . . . if this Convention gains the local and national elections'. It then listed five likely scenarios which included the annulment of the constitution and Romania's emergence as a multi-national state; the restoration of the monarchy under 'five heirs who do not know Romanian but are ready to stroll in their finery into each of the castles and palaces of Romania'; the introduction of passport controls between Cluj and Bucharest; Hungarian becoming an official language alongside Romanian; and perhaps even an attempt at 'general genocide against those who were part of the defunct RCP'.

The article ended by asking 'how, good people, is it possible to elect as mayor Petru Liţiu, someone who was expelled from the army for placing himself in the service of the enemy and who is ready at any moment to weaken and disable it?'.[56] This kind of article appealed to the subliminal fears and ignorance of large sections of the electorate who because of their lack of exposure to different newspapers, treated such stories very seriously and did not question the veracity of the information and views contained within them.

An additional handicap under which the DC laboured was a lack of resources with which to wage an effective campaign. Under the law, the DC received a subvention of 500,000 lei but a ton of paper cost 400,000 lei and virtually the only other source to which the alliance could turn for backing was its own members. Very few, if any, of the private businesses that had sprung up in Cluj made contributions to the DC. Very few of its members seem to have been involved in business, unlike the NSF, whose control of the city's daily affairs had enabled profitable ties to be developed with many budding capitalists. Indeed, the profits of one of the companies identified with the NSF were used to bring out five issues of a professionally-produced newspaper, *In faţa alegatorilor* (In Front of the Voters), whose tone and content made a mockery of the public promise made earlier by the NSF leadership in Transylvania that 'it was going to work for a decent and honest election campaign without unrealistic promises couched in demagogic and populist terms'.[57] As well as attacking Liţiu's personal character, this newspaper questioned his democratic credentials, claiming that CADA had been ready in 1990 to act in a manner reminiscent of recent events in Georgia where dissident soldiers had overturned an elected president, installing a military dictatorship that they regarded as 'the highest form of democracy' in its place.[58] It also claimed that, on ւe basis of previous pacts, 'it was not difficult to guess the concessions concerning Transylvanian integrity that the Democratic Convention had made to the HDFR'.

It was not only the newspaper's job to prevent Liţiu winning in the first round but also to prevent the NSF's more nationalist rival from pushing it into third place, which would have meant its elimination from the race. But the swipes at the PRNU were low-key compared with the unrelenting onslaught on the DC: despite Petre Roman's recent announcement at a conference in Strasbourg that the NSF would never ally itself with extremist groups, it became clear as the election progressed that the NSF could tolerate a PRNU victory and would indeed help to engineer one to foil their common opponents in the DC.

Copies of *In faţa alegatorilor* were freely available inthe lobby of the town hall to which hundreds of ordinary residents came each day in search of forms and signatures that would enable them to enlist the help or neutrality of the state in any one of hundreds of petty transactions that citizens were required to undertake through the good offices of local officialdom. The DC enjoyed no such preferential access in the town hall or any other Cluj public building.

With his meagre resources, Liţiu resolved to fight a clean campaign based on upholding the rule of law, ensuring that an honest form of privatisation was carried out in the city, and upgrading services that would improve its neglected infrastructure. The need to introduce honesty and transparency in the local government world was a concern that he constantly stressed, no doubt in order to convince citizens that it was not just through *bakshish* that a favour or a routine service could be obtained; on being asked what he would do to those businessmen who had obtained space to set up a business without buying a licence and largely at the whim of the mayor, Liţiu promised that those who had proved their commercial skills without exploiting the community would not be touched, but that those who had abused the opportunities provided to them by the former mayor would have to withdraw.[59]

The DC stressed its commitment towards clean government at indoor meetings in schools and community centres in different parts of the city. Nearly all electoral activity took place indoors. The DC candidates were largely middle-aged or elderly men. There were no women on the list and relatively few young people. Calin Nemes, the young actor who had rallied opposition to the dictatorship in Cluj on 21 December 1989 and had been badly wounded by the army, was placed eighteenth on the list of candidates, an indication that in Cluj public identification with the anti-totalitarian views embodied by Nemes was weak.

The DC election campaign had even less resonance in the sixty-two villages of Cluj county where contests were being held to elect a local mayor and a representative to a newly-formed county council. The historic parties possessed a tenuous existence there, and the CAP was largely an urban phenomenon. As well as the NSF and the PRNU, the DC had to contend with a specifically rural party called the Democratic Party of Romanian Farmers (DPRF), which was a satellite of the NSF.

The DPRF had been set up in early 1990 by officials in the state co-operatives, its leader Victor Surdu having been head of the board of agriculture in the Moldavian district of Iaşi when Iliescu had been party secretary there in the early 1970s. The DPRF was described by *NU* as 'the party of those which made collectivisation and are now preparing privatisation'.[60] Thanks to the intervention of Iliescu, who sensed correctly that his political future was bound up with his ability to keep the Romanian peasantry insulated from alternative political ideas, what was an artificial top-down party obtained plenty of television air-time in the pre-election period.[61]

One opposition candidate described (in an interview with this author) the villages in places like Cluj county as 'confined worlds at the mercy of television, rumours and the local nomenklatura'. Democratic Convention activists from the city who tested the voting intentions of adjoining villages found that local power-holders such as the village priest, the local police chief and the doctor had a considerable influence on people's voting intentions. Indeed, several DC members claimed that this local trinity could effectively decide how a village voted and that it rarely worked in their favour.

Doctors, whose occupation brought them into daily contact with a large number of people, obtained their influence by being able to dispense free or cheap services. The fact that they were one of the few professional groups able to exercise some control over their own working lives in the communist system often gave them self-confidence as well as standing in the communities where they operated; therefore, it is hardly surprising that in countries like Croatia, Serbia and Bulgaria, doctors have been returned to parliament in large numbers in the elections held after 1989.

The DC badly missed the support of the Uniate Church, which was trying to re-establish its presence in what often proved to be a hostile rural milieu. The Uniate Church had been the dominant religious force in the Romanian villages of northern Transylvania for over two centuries until 1948. Upon emerging from clandestineness in 1989, the Uniates faced enormous difficulties in trying to regain a rural foothold. In early 1992,

Virgil Lazar, the Cluj correspondent of *România Liberă* (and a member of the Orthodox Church), related how a Uniate missionary and theology professor had been held under siege in one village to which he had been invited to preach to a small group of Uniate families. (The assailants in all probability were the descendants of Uniates.) The incident made Lazar wonder 'how peasants, generally wise, industrious and God-fearing people, could suddenly become so violent against their fellow countrymen and that for "religious reasons"'. The answer he got from one elderly villager suggested that they were not acting on their own volition: 'We are again and again told at various meetings that the Uniates are in the Hungarian's pay. And they don't stop threatening us about it. That's the trouble, Sir!'[62]

The accusation of being the tool of unspecified Hungarian interests dogged the DC campaign in Cluj. Owing to the prevailing climate of nationalism, Cluj was one of the Transylvanian districts where the common list of candidates excluded the HDFR. It was felt that including the Hungarian party would simply reduce the DC's chances; however, while running its own separate electoral list, the HDFR supported Lițiu's candidacy for mayor.

MILITARY INTERVENTION IN LOCAL ELECTIONS

In the last days of campaigning before voting on 9 February, it was apparent that Lițiu would be comfortably ahead of all other challengers due to the NSF and PRNU splitting the vote of those citizens committed to a slow pace of change. Optimists in the DC camp even hoped that he would get fifty per cent or more of the vote which would rule out the need for a second ballot. This prospect prompted a dramatic last-minute intervention by General Paul Cheler, commander of the Romanian Third Army, based in Transylvania.

On 7 February, the last day of full campaigning, Cheler issued a long statement that many felt infringed Article 40 of the Romanian Constitution, preventing the armed forces from intervening in politics.[63] According to Pro-Democracy (a civic body monitoring the conduct of the election that had been given formal observer status by the National Electoral Commission), 'General Cheler made base accusations about the character of the Democratic Convention candidate, attempting to discredit him publicly in two articles in three local dailies, including the propaganda newssheet of the NSF'.[64]

Cheler was an officer in his early seventies who had been the protégé of General Nicolae Militaru, briefly minister of defence in the period after December 1989. Militaru restored Cheler to active service, along with other officers, in order to 'defend the revolution'. Following several years of training in Moscow, Cheler had scaled the military hierarchy until his career came to a complete halt in 1984 and he was placed in reserve with the right to wear a general's uniform and collect a full pension. At least two explanations for his temporary demise were current in Cluj during 1992. The most common one, which Cheler's nationalist supporters did not discourage, was that he had fallen victim to Ceauşescu's growing suspicion of any leading figures who had possessed close ties with the Soviet Union. The alternative one alleged that Cheler, who in 1984 had been in charge of the military celebrations in Bucharest for Romania's national day under communism, 23 August, was punished for bungling this set-piece occasion.

Cheler's return to active service in 1990 just as a reform-minded officer like Liţiu was being banished from the air-force was an eloquent comment on the nature of the Romanian revolution and who stood to benefit from it. Instead of quietly interpreting his duties, Cheler carved out a high profile and revealed himself to be a hardline nationalist. He first came to national attention following a speech he made at Alba Iulia in 1990 for Romania's new national day of 1 December in which he warned that the armed forces under his command would not flinch from using whatever force was necessary to prevent the first anniversary celebrations of the 1989 revolution from being marred by untoward scenes.[65] Later, he warned that paramilitary units of Hungarians had been discovered drilling in the mountains, contributing to the fears that in 1991 were giving increased legitimacy for those, like the editors of *România Mâre* calling for an authoritarian military government.[66] The weekly newspaper of the Transylvanian army, *Scutul patriei* (Shield of the Nation), was a vehicle for his nationalist statements; moreover, under Cheler, officers engaged in political education work before 1989 were promoted to leading positions, causing NU to express fears that it was not a depoliticised army that was emerging, but one poised to take part in 'the nationalist offensive that was becoming a prevalent feature of Romanian life'.[67]

The nub of Cheler's attack on Liţiu concerned the allegedly flawed character of the DC's candidate, whom he described as 'a man who has shown that he has little ... contact with honesty, honour or truth'; he accused Liţiu of 'organisational incompetence', of carrying out 'amorous adventures' and neglecting the affairs of his unit, and of being an informer to counter-intelligence.[68]

It is difficult to know what impact the Cheler intervention had on voting behaviour;it probably stands to reason that its instigators were seeking to influence those voters who in opinion surveys ranked national institutions which bolstered populist, ethnocentric or nationalist values, such as the Orthodox Church and the military, higher than those associated with democratic pluralist values.[69]

The report issued by Pro-Democracy claimed that 'the electoral process in Cluj was managed correctly from a technical point of view, in flagrant contrast to the atmosphere of verbal violence that had marred the last stages of the one in May 1990. Those irregularities that did occur were mainly owing to negligence or insufficient knowledge of the electoral law on the part of those appointed by the electoral commission'.[70] Liţiu won 44.7 per cent of the votes cast in the mayoral race, Gheorghe Funar of the PRNU was second with 27.54 per cent while Mihai Groza of the NSF was a distant third with 18.1 per cent, voter turnout having been seventy per cent. As no candidate gained over fifty per cent of the vote, preparations for a second round between the two front-runners on 23 February soon got underway.

Liţiu was well ahead of his opponents in the mayoral race in Cluj city, but the results for the city council were much less encouraging. The DC and the HDFR between them obtained 42.72 per cent of the votes, whereas the NSF, the PRNU and smaller parties with a similar outlook got 46.41 per cent. The PRNU received ten of the thirty-one council seats, followed by the DC with seven, the HDFR also with seven, the NSF with four, and one each for three smaller parties, one of which was the Româniâ Mâre Party.[71]

The arithmetic left the Romanian democratic parties and the Hungarians in a minority position; the DC's vote had risen seven per cent over that obtained by the historic parties in May 1990 and the NSF had crashed by twenty-five per cent, but the PRNU had been the greatest beneficiary its vote rising by thirteen per cent to give it 28.4 per cent of the city's votes.

In the villages and towns of Cluj county, the democratic opposition was much further behind its rivals – by 35.01 to 55.22 per cent. The towns of Dej, Gherla and Turda voted predominantly for the NSF or the PRNU, and it was only in Hungarian settlements that their opponents made a strong showing.

FUNAR VERSUS THE DEMOCRATIC CONVENTION

In the deciding round, Liţiu confronted the PRNU candidate, Gheorghe Funar, a forty-year-old university expert in Romania's collective agricultural system. The DC hoped to snatch victory by persuading a large enough percentage of NSF voters either to abstain or to come over to Liţiu. In the final manifesto, he tried to widen people's horizons by urging them to aspire to a lifestyle and political standards felt to be commonplace in western Europe. Thus, in his message to pensioners, he asked: 'how many old people have to wait in queues in Germany or Italy? Vote for your grandchildren but also on your own behalf.' Romanians and Hungarians were reminded that they had managed to live together for a long time:

This land is ours in common in which our grandfathers and great-grandfathers have co-existed. Not a single one of you ought to have any cause to leave. There is only one solution: to reach a permanent understanding. Show me any part of the world where unrestrained nationalist extremism has brought good (Yugoslavia? Ireland?). Only a deranged society can stand by and allow the spread of inter-ethnic conflict.

While the DC appealed to a sense of relative deprivation and wished to break down the isolation which prevented the citizens who had emerged from Ceauşescu's Romania from comparing their lot with people in the west, the PRNU appealed to a threatened sense of Romanian identity. Their stickers and posters, couched in terms of 'Brother Romanians', and 'Wake Up Romanians' struck an undoubted emotional chord, as even DC members ruefully admitted. In the second round, ultra-nationalists repeated with greater insistence the themes coined by the NSF that voting for the symbol of the key would install a mayor who had sold out to Hungarian interests and that the corollary would be a Hungarian deputy mayor, a Hungarian consulate in Cluj, and an escalation of demands that could lead to the detachment of Transylvania from the rest of Romania.[72] The tenor of its campaign suggested that it was committed to a relationship between Romanians and the Hungarians making up around one-quarter of Cluj's population, based upon subordination and antagonism rather than on mutual respect and co-operation.

During the campaign, NU, the Cluj opposition paper, criticised the DC for having paid insufficient attention to 'that great manipulable mass of working-class people created by Ceauşescu'. It predicted that on the basis of what had been observed in Cluj,

> the battle for Romania would in reality be the battle for the lumpen-proletariat. Whoever wins it will rule this country. If the Democratic Convention fails to win, voters will go to the 'nationalists' and then we will all remember with pleasure the era when Iliescu was president and when it was possible to criticise him every day.[73]

NU described a disorientated mass of 'semi-urbanites', living on the perimeters of the city, who, woefully under-educated, had not adapted to the urban existence: 'they use transport in common and have no job prospects as the giant industries which employ them will shortly cease to exist. For them the past no longer exists but the future is full of uncertainty.'

The DC found it difficult to establish a discourse with Cluj's newest residents located in blocs which surrounded the city on three sides. Older residents living in the inner city, in districts where Liţiu won outright, were known to criticise the rural immigrants for their lack of civic culture and for having helped to turn Cluj into a grim industrial city over previous decades.[74] The newcomers were sometimes referred to derogatively as 'Moldavians', as migrants from a province which had historically lagged behind Transylvania. But although some were Moldavian (and a smaller number came from Wallachia), the great majority of new Clujans were Transylvanians originating from nearby counties as well as rural parts of Cluj county itself. They were Transylvanians, often from unrewarding mountainous terrain, whose poverty and rustic ways might have made them appear to be Moldavian in a country where the absence of distinctive regional accents often makes it hard to discover someone's geographical origins. But, unlike Moldavians, it proved possible to appeal to large numbers of them on anti-Hungarian grounds owing to the fact that in areas where many of them hailed from, folk memory about Hungarian oppression had been part of the popular culture.[75] Gheorghe Funar, the PRNU candidate, was able to appeal to peasants from the Apuseni mountains (or western Carpathians) whose poverty had made Cluj a welcome magnet, by invoking memories of wartime massacres and other brutalities carried out by Hungarian troops occupying the region; they were also reminded that their region had been the home of the nineteenth-century Transylvanian patriot, Avram Iancu, who had defied the Hungarians in 1848.[76]

The PRNU appealed to a sense of threatened Romanian identity and to Romanian cultural and political assertiveness, both of which were often expressed simultaneously in its electoral propaganda. In Latin America, urban populists had successfully used not dissimilar techniques for controlling uprooted individuals from the countryside. Migrants to the cities were often enrolled into movements which promised economic wealth distribution and identified 'imperialism' or 'Uncle Sam' as a source of their poverty and hardship.[77] The PRNU offered similar categories of explanation which could enable migrants to make sense of their marginal situation and dream of improvements. In the process, the Hungarians replaced the Americans as the external enemy ready to buy up their factories, use them as cheap labour, throw them into destitution and, in the final analysis, seize back all of Transylvania.

It was only in the middle of February 1992 that leading opposition figures in Cluj publicly acknowledged that the PRNU had grown to be their chief opponent.What marked the shift was the appearance in *Tribuna Ardealului* of a series of articles from Dr I. Z. Boilă, chairman of the NPP-CD in Cluj. Although all indications suggest that their influence on the outcome of the election was very slight, they are worth quoting at some length since they reveal a viewpoint which had rarely if ever been publicly expressed by a Romanian source in Cluj:

among the Transylvanian population, there does not exist a desire to break away from Romania. Romanians making up seventy per cent of the population of Transylvania, are practically unanimous in wishing to live in a Romanian unitary state. Analysing their situation realistically, the majority of Romanian Magyars have, in their turn, renounced autonomy in any shape or form. Romanians must realise this . . . and not be influenced by those who invent or exaggerate separatist actions which, thankfully, have no place in the minds of a majority of Transylvanian Magyars . . .

Primitive nationalism is being manifested which creates a false image of Romanians unable to respect the rights of national minorities. The principal guilt for this lies not with Magyar extremists but with Romanian parties which want to maintain communist structures through embracing extreme nationalism; it is necessary to demolish these structures and to remove the communist and egalitarian mentality which, after forty-five years of communism, has considerably eroded the moral foundations of the Romanian people.[78]

The critique was stepped up three days before the poll in an article in *Tribuna Ardealului* entitled 'An appeal to good sense'. In it, Dr Boilă claimed that:

In the leadership of the PRNU, there is not a single authentic representative of the Romanian resistance from 1945 to 1989. By contrast, many former RCP activists have been discovered along with others whose connections with unnamed compromised organisations makes them the object of suspicion.

The PRNU has not condemned the crimes and abuses of the communist epoch . . .From the beginning until now, directly or indirectly, the PRNU has attacked, calumnied and denigrated with absolute priority the NPP-CD . . .[79]

In a remaining article, Dr Boilă acknowledged that 'very many of those who have inscribed as members of Vatra Românească and even the PRNU are true patriots of good sense. Our appeal addressed to them is . . . to be aware of how you are being manipulated'.[80]

It cannot have been easy to admit so publicly that Romanians of good standing, whose place by right was in the NPP-CD which since the 1880s had stood for a tradition of enlightened nationalism in Transylvania, had been enticed into a movement whose nationalism was of the counterfeit and communist variety. The timing of the articles may have been influenced by mounting evidence that the PRNU bandwagon was in danger of becoming unstoppable, so that painful truths would need to be uttered in a desperate hope that some people might be persuaded to come to their senses.

Members of the DC acknowledged that the PRNU had fought a professional campaign with ample resources. One activist knew personally of several private companies which had made donations to their campaign fund, small factories which had been set up as a result of siphoning goods and materials from ailing state concerns.He also alleged that 4,000,000 lei had been given to the PRNU by RENL, the state electrical company, through a recently-created private bank controlled by Vatra Românească. If true, this is a vivid example of the way that the state is being used as a milch cow by well-placed contestants for power, and it reveals an attitude to seizing control of state assets no different from that discovered by the foremost foreign scholar of pre-communist Romania, Henry L. Roberts, in his book *Rumania: Political Problems of an Agrarian State* (1947). The claim that any small firm known to be oppositional was likely to have difficulties if their electricity bills were not paid promptly, while others who had not paid for months could get away with it, was another indication of the way that political partisanship intruded deep into the workings of the state.

The Cluj periodical, *NU*, had warned on 28 October 1991 that parts of the state media were prepared to exploit anti-Hungarian feelings in order to influence the outcome of forthcoming elections. In the aftermath of the second round of voting in Cluj, it referred on 3 March 1992 to 'the most enormous anti-Magyar campaign of recent times' promoted in the media during the last week of campaigning. This culminated in a lengthy broadcast on Radio Cluj on the evening before polling of a report that a party of Romanian tourists had been prevented from entering Hungary and that some had actually been beaten up. An interview with a hysterical, crying woman, who alleged that she had been assaulted by border guards, made a strong impression.

A journalist with contacts among radio personnel learned shortly afterwards that special preparations had been made in the radio station to intervene in the election campaign: any staff who were suspected of not being sympathetic to the PRNU were given the Friday and Saturday of the campaign off. The hysterical woman interviewed in the studio turned out to be a businesswoman who regularly made trips back and forth across the border. A statement quickly issued on Radio Budapest which denied that the Romanians had been maltreated but had been sent home because they had nothing to live on in Hungary was ignored.[81]

Perhaps more significant still was a statement of the Romanian Foreign Minister, which was carried on Romanian television on the same evening as the Cluj radio broadcast. It was a response to an unguarded statement made by the Hungarian defence minister, Janos Für, in which he said that safeguarding Hungarians everywhere was an 'inseparable facet' of the security of his nation, adding that the Hungarian government and parliament 'should do everything in their power, using all legal and diplomatic means, to end the threat to the minorities and to guarantee their survival'.[82] Für was regarded as a major contender for the Hungarian premiership in any change of leadership and it is likely that his comments were made with domestic opinion in mind. His statement had been made on 14 February, but the usually very prompt foreign ministry in Bucharest did not issue a rejoinder until the eve of the election, unlike the Slovaks, whose rebuttal was made earlier. Both the PRNU and *Mesagerul* also held back from issuing critical statements until the last Friday of the campaign which convinced those familiar with the tactics of manipulation employed by those schooled in communist methods that there had been co-ordination involving the Romanian foreign ministry and those determined to prevent an opposition victory in Cluj.

Nicolae Manolescu, the CAP leader, reckoned that the 'declaration by Für fell like a bombshell between the two voting rounds, profoundly altering the voting intentions of Clujans'.[83] When the results of the second-round voting were declared on 21 March 1992, it emerged that the PRNU had taken nearly all of the NSF's votes as well as those of smaller parties. Its vote was pushed up from 27–52.5 per cent, making Funar the winner. Handicapped by a hostile media, an under-financed campaign, and poor co-ordination among the different parties in the DC, Lițiu's vote rose slightly from 44–47.5 per cent; on a 70 per cent turnout, he was 10,000 votes behind Funar.

România Liberă which had heavily backed Lițiu's campaign, declared 'Clujans have said "yes" to the Nationalists'.[84] Virgil Lazar, the Bucharest daily's Cluj correspondent, reckoned that 'the citizens of Cluj had said No to democracy for four years'. He predicted that a sense of isolation would envelop the city because of the PRNU success in popularising the slogan 'we will not sell the land'.

1992 ELECTION RESULTS: A COMPARISON

The Cluj result proved to be untypical of the rest of Transylvania and of Romania as a whole. In Tirgu Mureş, Vatra's birthplace, the party fell short of a majority. In south Transylvania, it made little impact: its candidates were defeated by the DC in Sibiu and Braşov and, in the region as a whole, it did not receive more than twenty per cent of the vote.

PRNU strength was highly localised. Outside Transylvania it had no impact at all. It was the DC which won the mayoral election in Iaşi, the Moldavian capital where, in 1990, the NSF had captured over eighty per cent of the vote in the Iaşi electoral district. In Timişoara, the DC had swept to victory in the first round; its mayoral candidate, Viorel Oancea, was like Lițiu, a former army officer with a CADA background.

Evidence points to the PRNU's best results coming from areas in northern Transylvania where memories of the wartime Hungarian occupation could be stoked up. In such areas, according to Cluj NPP-CD member

Adrian Marino, 'history gives legitimacy to the idea of voting along ethnic lines . . . Old humiliations and resentments, injustices and painful memories are rekindled by frenzied propaganda'.[85]

A brief comparison of the cities of Braşov and Cluj might highlight some of the factors which helped to produce contrasting electoral outcomes in both cities. Braşov had grown at a much faster rate than Cluj, or indeed most other Romanian cities, and had absorbed large numbers of rural migrants. Many came from Moldavia, which caused one Cluj observer to express surprise that the DC candidate, Adrian Moruzi, had been elected so convincingly in Braşov. However, another Cluj democrat, who did not see the Moldavians in such stereotypical terms believed that in order to be a nationalist, an individual needed a little culture, however distorted it might have become, and that the Moldavians, many of whom arrived footloose and itinerant in the big city, were simply too marginal and helpless to be good material for nationalist recruiters.[86] Besides, as they settled down in a city like Braşov, they became familiar with its past, particularly the fact that it had had a revolutionary experience, in the form of the 1987 workers' revolt which had shaken the dictatorship, many of the participants probably being first-generation peasants. Besides, Braşov was much closer than Cluj to Bucharest, which was the chief beacon of radical ideas challenging the NSF government, and it was able to obtain the second television channel which was much less biased than the main one, something Cluj could not receive.

Despite the city's outward calm, the February election had shown that two props of totalitarianism – ignorance and fear – were still very much visible in Cluj. A candidate whose reputation for probity and courage would have been a commanding asset in most places had tried to rally people behind a vision of the future which did not rely on ethnic stereotypes. But his attempt to generate open discussion about what were the practical problems that needed to be overcome in order for Cluj to become a well-run city failed to evoke a strong enough response. The majority of Clujans were in no hurry to endorse someone ready to dismantle the apparatus of the party-state; incidents like the unfounded allegations made by General Cheler and the insensitive comments of the Hungarian defence minister helped to determine the result. A majority of Clujans chose instead to vote for a candidate whose appetite for confrontation became evident in his first weeks of office and who polarised opinions in ways that elsewhere in eastern Europe were leading to much tragedy and bloodshed.

Some time would need to elapse before the ability of an ultra-nationalist (enjoying connections with the former regime) to defeat a strong liberal opponent in Transylvania's principal city began to alarm the wider Democratic Convention. After two years of recurring political disappointments, the democratic camp was at last winning significant victories. The Civic Alliance Party's candidates for mayor achieved victory in Timişoara, Ploiesti, Iaşi, Sibiu, Braşov, Arad and Sinaia; in Bucharest, Crin Halaicu of the NLP was elected, an advance which raised expectations that the DC was poised to drive the divided NSF from office in forthcoming national elections.

DEMOCRATS QUARREL AS NATIONALISTS ADVANCE

However, the fragility of opposition unity was illustrated when the NLP quit the Convention in the spring of 1992; Campeanu had argued that the opposition alliance had only been set up to fight the local elections, and he set stiff terms for extending it which included the removal of the HDFR; having co-operated with the Hungarian party in 1990 (and received the backing of many Hungarians in the presidential election), Campeanu seemed ready to exploit, for electoral purposes, the hostility of the Hungarian minority that had become evident among parts of the electorate. The NLP leader attacked the HDFR for failing to react to 'irresponsible declarations by members of the Budapest government';[87] and by May 1992 he was asserting that the main reason for the NLP's separation from the DC was the insistence of other parties in the alliance of running joint lists with the HDFR.[88]

If the rest of the Romanian democratic opposition had accepted the NLP's terms for preserving the alliance, it would have accomplished the political isolation of the Hungarian minority and been a milestone in the creation of a political culture polarised along ethnic lines. However, the other parties had grown increasingly distrustful of Campeanu, whose political ambitions had caused him to behave in increasingly high-handed ways that finally snapped the unity of his party which began to disintegrate in 1992.

As the opposition made its preparations for the national election, a series of anti-democratic decisions by the mayor of Cluj, Gheorghe Funar, revealed how conditions were once more ripe for the promotion of authoritarian nationalism by a senior public official. One of Funar's moves that affected the DC directly was the banning, on 24 April 1992, of a symposium on the relevance of the Dutch local government experience for Romania. Newly-elected councillors from ten western Romanian counties arrived in Cluj, along with local councillors from the Netherlands as well as officers of the moderate Fidesz Party in Hungary, to find that the event had been banned. Funar declared in a statement that the title of the symposium, 'The Self-Government of Localities', was contrary to the Romanian Constitution since it proclaimed Romania to be a 'unitary state' and that it posed a threat to the integrity of the country.[89]

On 7 July 1992, a new proclamation from the Timişoara Society gave more space to the nationalist danger than the earlier one of 1990, an indication of how pressing the issue was becoming. It observed that 'the noisy and aggressive actions' of chauvinist parties had 'succeeded in discrediting the Romanians in the eyes of international public opinion and at the same time in encouraging [Hungarian] irredentist groups . . . These false defenders of our homeland have only succeeded in damaging the interests of the Romanians. We do not need them to defend our interests in a country where we form a large majority of the population'.[90] Meanwhile, in May 1992, Nicolae Manolescu expressed the fear that 'the forthcoming elections could be delayed or rendered void, by the provocation of social, inter-ethnic, inter-religious and other tensions'.[91]

The democratic opposition was presented with increasing evidence that it needed to offer a vision of Romanian nationalism different from the one being successfully marketed by chauvinists if it was to hope to make a decisive impact in the parliamentary and presidential elections which, after much delay, were to take place on 27 September 1992. Two events being held in Hungary, coinciding with the opening of the election campaign, raised potentially serious problems for Romanian democrats while enabling ultra-nationalists to trumpet the Hungarian danger.

The first one was the World Congress of Hungarians in Budapest from 19 to 21 August 1992. Moderate Romanians feared that unguarded statements, particularly at the first event, which was attended by political leaders and personalities from Hungary and the diaspora communities, might give Romanian nationalists powerful ammunition. However, controversy was avoided and the event soon slipped from view in the Romanian media. Chauvinist press organs like *România Mâre* were reduced to demanding that Romanian citizens attending the conference (leaders of the HDFR attended in a private capacity) should have their passports revoked and they should face criminal charges. A second World Conference on Transylvania, held in Budapest on 22 August, also had potential to engender controversy even though it was a much smaller affair organised by Brazilian-based émigrés. However, the HDFR shunned it and the party's honorary president, Bishop Lászlo Tökés, defused the impact of its attacks on Romanian minority policies by insisting that 'on the question of Transylvania, final decisions can only be taken with the Romanians. Transylvania is the common land of all those who live there. So I think it is extremely absurd that they announce such a World Conference.'[92]

The NPP-CD was the dominant element in the renamed Romanian Democratic Convention (RDC), and its calm reaction to both Hungarian events revealed a determination not to be unnerved by Romanian ultra-nationalists. A statement released by the NPP-CD on 21 August declared:

It is certain there will be extremist voices [in] Budapest from people still living in the past, torn from real facts of international life. We express our belief that such people will get the reply they deserve from such Hungarian officials, the HDFR and the public opinion which knows that both peoples have only one way out towards democracy and prosperity: Peaceful Co-Existence. The same duty is incumbent on us: to isolate Romanian extremists who use every newspaper article or statement of some backward Hungarian politicians to exaggerate the size of the danger . . . to Romania.

We assure all Romanians that, in the case of proven danger, the NPP-CD will be prompt, as in the past.[93]

Lászlo Tökés has shown himself to be an unpredictable spokesman for Transylvanian Hungarians in the years since he rocketed to fame for his role in triggering off the revolt against Ceauşescu. On 2 September 1992, he ensured that Romanian-Hungarian relations revived as a campaign issue by launching a hunger strike in Transylvania to demand that steps be taken by the Bucharest government to clear up a list of human-rights abuses. The comment in the *Cuvîntul* newspaper that this action 'will reactivate the nationalist instincts of the electorate and boost the cause of Gheorghe Funar' reflected widespread dismay in the opposition camp and, after a week, Tökés heeded advice to call off the protest.[94]

NATIONALISM REDEFINED BY DEMOCRATS

The campaigning strategy of the parties in the RDC pinpointed the failure of the NSF, particularly in the socio-economic realm, while trying to convince the electorate that an RDC government had the ability to place Romania on the road to economic recovery and social peace. However, there were also well-choreographed displays of moderate nationalism which culminated in a rally in Cluj on 12 September 1992. Before a crowd of 15,000 people, a 'Proclamation of Cluj' was issued which rejected 'primitive national-ism, chauvinism and extremism', described as damaging to Romania's future prospects and to its standing in the world. However, the content of the proclamation was not without stirring nationalist language: 'all we Romanians in the Carpatho-Danubian region form, through blood, language, thought, religion, tradition and aspirations, a single nation'. The proclamation's most interesting feature according to one Romanian source, was that 'it gave equal weight to Romanian and Hungarian extremism both at home and abroad', an approach hitherto avoided 'in order to maintain correct relations with the HDFR'.[95] The speeches delivered at what was the Democratic Convention's main Transylvanian rally had strong nationalist overtones which sprang from the need to squash the PRNU claim that the Convention was anti-national and even controlled by Hungarian interests. There were no Hungarian speakers on the platform.

Corneliu Coposu, leader of the National Peasant Party, declared in Cluj that 'Transylvania has been and always will be a Romanian land', but the proclamation also quoted his mentor, Iuliu Maniu, the party's founder, that 'having been oppressed it is not our job to become the oppressors'.[96]

Lacking in the RDC's election manifesto were any concrete policies for dealing with inter-ethnic relations; if included, they might only have provided an inviting target for its opponents. However, reunification of Bessarabia with Romania received a prominent place in the manifesto which promised a reformed state based on the rule of law, a President who acted as a 'moderator between social and political forces', a free-market economy based on 'large-scale privatisation', a 'social contract' between employer and employee, increased foreign investment, and greater responsibilities for traditional institutions like the church, the army and the schools.[97]

The pro-government forces which had rallied around the Democratic National Salvation Front (DNSF), formed in April 1992, ignored the RDC's campaigning promises. Instead, they revived the charges made against the opposition in May 1990 that it intended to turn the clock back to an era of harsh economic exploitation and that it could not be trusted to safeguard Romania's national interest. Emil Constantinescu, the RDC presidential candidate, declared afterwards that he and his supporters had been accused of five fundamental sins: bringing back the king, restoring landlords, reviving capitalism, selling Transylvania to the Hungarians, and persecuting former communists.[98] Although the RDC campaign was attuned far more to the social realities of Romania than the one in 1990 had been, there were some features which the DNSF was able to exploit. According to the pro-Convention journalist, Andrei Cornea, the opposition overestimated royalist sentiments among the electorate: 'for many opposition figures, the king appeared as a messianic figure capable, by a single gesture, of re-establishing not only a normal political life in Romania, but also a new morality . . .'.[99]

Too much emphasis was still given to the past abuses of communism and not enough to the main concerns of voters – rising prices, declining living standards and growing unemployment, according to Manolescu, the leader of the CAP who did not play a significant role in the election campaign, despite heading what was widely felt to be the most moderate and realistic of the opposition parties with the greatest chance of appealing to floating voters. The reasons why Manolescu was not picked as an RDC presidential candidate remain unclear. His party's excellent showing in the local elections boosted his prospects, but personality disputes, the dominant role of the NPP-CD in the Convention and the fact that he had taken such a strong line against chauvinism that it was likely to make him an ultra-nationalist target in the election, are factors that cannot be discounted.[100]

The opposition's campaign was centred around Emil Constantinescu, a geologist and rector of Bucharest University chosen by the RDC to challenge Iliescu for the Romanian presidency. His advantages were that he had spent all his life in Romania and that he was more in touch with popular feeling than the émigrés who had been opposition standard-bearers in 1990. But he was a relative unknown who belonged to no party and was chosen as the RDC candidate only in the summer of 1992, largely at the behest of the NPP-CD, which had no suitable candidate of its own to push forward.

Corneliu Coposu, the leader of the NPP-CD, had been the architect of the opposition alliance and had successfully revived it on each occasion it faltered. But the extent to which the NPP-CD dominated the candidate list suggested that the alliance was a most unequal one. Forty-six per cent of RDC candidates were NPP-CD members compared with 18.5 per cent for the CAP, the rest being divided up among smaller parties.[101] The NPP-CD's phalanx of elderly candidates made it easier for the DNSF to claim that it wished to take its revenge on the country and its blameless citizens for the persecutions which its members had suffered in the past.[102]

The result revealed that the familiar values of security and state protection represented by Iliescu, still exercised a powerful appeal, despite the fact that his first term had seen declining living standards for the bulk of those who had supported him in 1990. On twenty per cent of the vote, the RDC fell far short of the parliamentary majority it had hoped for. It now had eighty-two of the 341 seats in the chamber of deputies, but even in alliance with the breakaway NSF (as well as the HDFR) it was far short of the majority needed to sustain a government.

In 1990, the parties making up the RDC had obtained only 4.65 per cent of the vote, so the 1992 result was a great advance, the best result being in the Banat, where the RDC captured 37 per cent of the vote. At last there was evidence that the RDC parties were starting to acquire a social base among certain groups of urban workers as well as among middle-class professionals. But the RDC was gravely hampered by the absence of social forces which represented private ownership. New capitalists were, in many instances, drawn from the ranks of old communists; they relied on the state for protection, and quite often their ventures were launched by diverting resources from state companies.[103] An emergent group of private capitalists, engaged in speculative ventures, was hardly likely to be drawn to a coalition committed to a public administration based on a firm code of ethics. Unless the economic changes began to produce a new middle class committed to political pluralism and defending the right of the individual, the RDC parties were likely to find the quest for a parliamentary majority a long and tiring one likely to generate strife within their own ranks.

TROUBLED RELATIONS WITH THE HUNGARIANS

The first major split in the RDC, involving the National Liberals, led to the NLP running separately in the 1992 election. However, the NLP failed to pass the three-per-cent threshold needed to enter parliament and was thus effectively sidelined. It was good for the health of a fragile democracy that the NLP's appeal to nationalism among anti-communist voters proved unavailing. However, the RDC was unable to avoid the corrosive effects of inter-ethnic tensions within its own ranks as relations between the HDFR and other Convention parties underwent great strain at several moments in 1992–3.

The first one came in October 1992 at a meeting of the HDFR that committed the organisation to support 'internal self-government along community lines'. Divisions within the HDFR meant that the wording was vague, but expressions of concern and outright condemnation from virtually all Romanian parties left no doubt that most believed that the HDFR was preparing the ground for advocating a system of autonomy along ethnic lines.[104]

Coposu, the chairman of the RDC, urged Hungarians to show less concern with acquiring their own group rights and instead to pay more attention to the need to obtain reforms meant to safeguard democracy by working with like-minded Romanians.[105] Constantinescu urged the Hungarians to explain what their policies were in a way that left no room for dangerous confusion.[106] Before the HDFR statement, he had challenged ultra-nationalists who insisted that the Hungarian party was Romania's greatest enemy, arguing instead that 'Romania's greatest enemy is the communist mentality'.[107]

The RDC was anxious to dissuade the HDFR from adopting a programme which committed it to political autonomy along ethnic lines. Instead, spokesmen like Coposu and Constantinescu argued that the concept of 'administrative decentralisation' contained 'ideal solutions for [the] self-administration of all communities in Romania, including those in the regions inhabited by minorities'.[108] Both men then took their message to the HDFR congress at Braşov in January 1993, where many other RDC members attended as guests. There was relief when the HDFR decided to shelve its radical proposals and refrained from electing its most radical spokesman, Bishop Lászlo Tökés, as the new party leader.

The attendance of much of the RDC leadership at the Braşov conference and its ability to influence the outcome made the ultra-nationalist charge that the HDFR stood for Hungarian separatism appear less convincing. The experience of Horia Rusu, an RDC deputy from Timişoara, even prompted him to declare that 'many Hungarians in Romania are better Romanians than many Romanians', such as those belonging to the Greater Romania Party 'who are a shame for us and whom we have to fight with'.[109]

However, the Braşov conference failed to bring Romanians and Hungarians in the RDC much closer together. The lack of contact has only been broken by occasional symbolic gatherings, or else colloquia of anti-communist intellectuals in which no real dialogue gets going after the reading of prearranged statements. Mrs Eva Gyimesi, a Cluj philology lecturer who had smuggled out letters for Doina Cornea in the 1980s, was in the minority when she tried to persuade fellow Hungarians that their problems could not be solved without engaging positively with Romanians. This approach even brought a rebuke from Andras Süto, the well-known writer, who insisted that building ties of friendship would have to wait since the priority was for Transylvanian Hungarians to reclaim their rights.[110]

Probably the public figure who had the best opportunity to mix on a regular basis with influential Romanians was Geza Szöcs, general secretary of the HDFR from 1990 to 1992. As a deputy and a distinguished poet, he rarely availed of opportunities to mix with Romanian public figures, preferring instead to spend much of his time in western Europe, building alliances with proponents of minority cultures. Accordingly, it is not surprising that the HDFR has taken stands and pursued policies that damage the credibility of the RDC. In 1993, the party tried unsuccessfully to block Romania's admission to the Council of Europe. In the same year, the party drew up a bill for Hungarians to be 'co-nationals of the Romanian state', the more realistic HDFR deputies knowing that this would antagonise Romanians even of a liberal persuasion who were aware that the Romanian movement for national separation had begun with similar demands two centuries before. Even more disappointingly, the HDFR proved reluctant to co-operate with a Council of National Minorities created in 1993 by the government to consider legislation for minorities. The Romanian state had a history of pursuing cosmetic measures in this field but, arguably, the HDFR, was not even prepared to give it a preliminary chance, the party pulling out in September 1993, accusing the government of being unwilling to carry out Council recommendations.[111]

Bishop Lászlo Tökés was the main public hardliner in the HDFR. He justified playing a political role by referring to the biblical prophets who 'lived in the present and criticised society, those in power, and the everyday life of the people'.[112] Among Hungarians, Tökés was a figure beyond public questioning because of his pivotal role in the events of 1989. But in informal conversation, there were more than a few who wished him to confine his public role to religious duties and who feared that his headstrong and insensitive public statements might unwittingly create fresh dangers for the community he sought to champion. But, after failing to become leader of the HDFR in 1993, Tökés refused to retire to the sidelines. Later that year, he publicly slammed moderate HDFR deputies who had been involved in a Carnegie Foundation-sponsored mediation project involving talks with senior government officials that held out the possibility of improvements in the provision of minority languages in the education system as well as multi-lingual street-signs.[113] Evidently, the bishop preferred megaphone diplomacy rather than the patient behind-the-scenes confidence-building encounters which, as the experience of Palestine, South Africa and Northern Ireland showed in 1993–4, can lead to dramatic improvements in the position of subordinate communities. Tökés mixed calls for unity in the HDFR with demands that certain deputies involved in the Carnegie mediation should be punished.[114] His insistence on Hungarian uniformity may unwittingly have reinforced Gheorghe Funar when he insisted that it was pointless to group Hungarians into moderate or radical camps given their allegedly separatist aims in Transylvania.[115]

In fact, there are different political tendencies in the HDFR which have co-existed, often uneasily, but without an open split. Liberal, Christian, radical democrat, independent and moderate factions have been officially recognised as well as the Gabor Bethlen faction advocating Transylvanianism, and a social democratic one formed in 1994 shortly before the left's victory in the Hungarian state election. The dominant element are probably ex-state officials, removed quite early in the Ceauşescu period, who in 1990 had the expertise to put together a party which possessed some of the professionalism not always to be found in the Romanian opposition parties. They provided a support base for Geza Domokos, HDFR president until his retirement in 1993; before 1989, Domokos had sought to defend Hungarian interests as best he could from within the system, and he enjoyed genuine popularity in the Szekler areas of eastern Transylvania where the strength of numbers of the Hungarians enabled moderate views to predominate. A radical youth movement called Miszsz had grown spontaneously in the larger towns threatened with Romanisation in 1990 which had a more militant agenda. But the threat to Hungarian interests from influential Romanian nationalists and an unsypathetic government allowed very dissimilar persons to co-operate inside the HDFR. Becase it is a coalition of different interest groups rather than a party, it bases its appeal around a programme rather than a high-profile leader, which makes it unusual in the current Romanian context. Indeed, the HDFR initially had advantages lacking to the Romanian opposition. It had the support of the different church denominations which lent their prestige to the HDFR and whose leaders presided over public meetings, a link which Romanian parties emphasising a Christian formation could not duplicate. Because most Hungarians had been frozen out of politics before 1989, the HDFR was spared the allegations of collusion with the Ceaușescu state that retarded the historic parties; attempts to set up splinter parties to confuse Hungarian voters also proved far less successful.

The relative political unity of Hungarians, set against the relative disunity of the Romanian opposition, encourages some Romanians to view the Hungarians as a well-organised group towards whom they need to show vigilance. It also strengthens the tendency to relate to Hungarians not on the basis of the job they do or their character or hobbies but as members of an ethnic category who have never reconciled themselves completely to living in Romania under the same rules as everyone else. This image might not have sprung up so easily if Hungarians had been elected for other opposition parties or if more than one Hungarian party had emerged (as was the case in Slovakia). But the testimony of Hungarians suggests that the HDFR is increasingly facing much the same problems that have held back its Romanian allies. The lack of options available to the Hungarian minority means that politics is not a vocation that attracts the most capable members of the community. No talented new faces appeared among the crop of HDFR deputies elected in 1992, and young people were conspicuous by their absence. Frank and profound internal party discussions are rare, perhaps so as to avoid painful divisions among the various factions being exposed. In the Hungarian press of Transylvania, there is little factual reporting about the problems of the community or about fresh developments in specific localities that are worthy of emulation. Within this self-imposed isolation, intellectuals talking in generalities and reducing the complex reality of the Hungarian Transylvanian existence to the national question dominate the press columns which, in a surprising way, means that the Hungarian press is a mirror image of its Romanian counterpart.[116] This sterile cultural background produces a sense of introspection in which apocalyptic statements from Bishop Tökés can be made without pondering their impact on the Romanian majority.

In one such statement, which emerged from an interview on 3 April 1993, he argued that the Hungarian minority over the previous seventy years had been subject to a long-drawn-out campaign of 'ethnic cleansing' by different rulers united in the aim of homogenising the country.[117] In a long open letter to the Bishop, deputies from each of the main Romanian branches of the RDC then took issue with his assertion.[118] The claim from Tökés that Hungarians had been systematically removed from the public services was denied and he was reminded that, upon the installation of communism, 'the control of very many institutions, (especially the Securitate and administrative and economic ones) was held by members of the minority communities'. Normally the role of the minorities in the communist seizure of power was only alluded to by ultra-nationalists; the anger at Tökés shown by the signatories of the open letter suggests that they were not afraid of reinforcing a key chauvinist argument. However, if extremists were to benefit from such a row, Tökés's critics insisted that the fault lay with him on account of 'many declarations that create a sense of panic and enmity . . . thus boosting the size of the audience that extremists could appeal to'. Tökés was accused of delivering 'a stab in the back' to the RDC, 'prejudicing its electoral prospects and aiding nationalists seeking to divert people from grave moral, economic and political problems towards a false danger' regarding Transylvania.

To refute Tökés's claim that the Hungarians had encountered persistent state oppression, his critics, in the teeth of much contrary evidence, insisted that pre-war Romanians had been 'true European pioneers in their attitude towards minorities, applying with rigour the highest democratic principles'.

This romantic interpretation of majority–minority relations in Greater Romania was reinforced by reference to a 1939 statement from the leaders of the non-Hungarian minorities attesting to the favourable behaviour of Romanian governments towards them. In 1939 Romania was already a dictatorship, and, during the last years of shaky parliamentary rule, the Transylvanian Saxons had lost their remaining group rights while the Jews were subject to increasingly punitive legislation.

The outburst of a sizeable portion of the RDC parliamentary party against the man whose defiance had helped to ignite Romanian opposition to Ceauşescu showed the brittleness of relations between Romanians and Hungarians within the democratic camp. The severity of the language used suggests that relations between Romanians and Hungarians within the RDC were formal and distant;[119] relatively few Hungarians belonged to any of the RDC historic parties or even to the Civic Alliance Party, individuals who by their membership of Romanian parties could have helped to erode suspicion and promote dialogue. The available evidence also suggests that the HDFR and the Romanian parties did not have a great deal to do with one another within the loose umbrella of the Convention, which was essentially an electoral mechanism that fell into inactivity outside election periods. Splits within Romanian parties suggested that the RDC lacked mechanisms whereby it could resolve internal problems or keep in touch with its supporters. Lacking a clear sense of direction, it is not surprising to find deputies making declarations about the role of minorities in the communist takeover, more often to be heard from ultra-nationalists. However exceptional such outbursts may have been, they reflected a willingness on the part of opposition elements to use nationalism in order to sharpen a weak profile.

DEMOCRATS MISCALCULATE OVER MOLDAVIA

Nationalism from the anti-communist opposition was at its most un-inhibited over the question of Bessarabia, a mainly Romanian-speaking territory between the rivers Prut and Dniester. Most of the present territory was part of the Principality of Moldavia from the fourteenth century until 1812 (under Ottoman suzerainty for much of this time); part of the Russian empire from 1812 to 1917 as the province of Bessarabia; under Romanian rule from 1918–40 and 1941–4; and then controlled by the USSR from 1940–1 and 1944–91.[120]

After 1859, the emergent Romanian state had wished to add Bessarabia to its territory, which it succeeded in doing after 1918. But Romanian control was short-lived. Stalin forcibly annexed Bessarabia and the northern portion of the Bukovina (never previously under Russian rule) in 1940. These territories were divided up between the Soviet Ukraine and the newly-created Moldavian Soviet Socialist Republic.

Fifty years of Soviet power wrought great changes and Russification advanced steadily, especially in the cities. However, Moldavia was caught up in the nationalist upsurge which shook the Soviet state after Gorbachev's accession to office. The adoption of 'Moldavian' as the state language on 1 September 1989, along with the reinstatement of the Latin alphabet in place of Cyrillic, were signs of waning Russian influence. On 23 June 1990, Moldavia declared its sovereignty, the official name of the Republic of Moldova was adopted on 23 May 1991 and, three months later when the failed communist coup in Moscow led to the unravelling of the Soviet Union, formal independence was declared on 27 August 1991.

Once opposition parties had become legitimised in Romania in 1990, the most radical positions on the Bessarabian question were quickly taken by the NPP-CD and eventually by the CAP. Statements like the one issued by the Cluj NPP-CD in February 1992 summarised the depth of opposition commitment to unification:

> Recovering Bessarabia has to be the cause of each Romanian and each party. Anyone who opposes this position or leaves it suspended on the pretext that Transylvania is in danger cannot call himself a patriot.[121]

When an independent Moldova was formed in 1991, numerous opposition statements were issued which condemned the absurdity of two sovereign and independent Romanian states. This particular opposition approach towards Moldova was based on a number of premises. The historic parties saw themselves as the architects of inter-war Greater Romania and responsible, in large measure, for whatever achievements could be associated with that period. Unification would, it was hoped, enable that period to be seen in a more positive light and strengthen the legitimacy of the parties with pre-communist roots in the eyes of the public. At the same time, there was little desire to examine the record of Romanian rule in Bessarabia between 1918 and 1940, an exercise which might have produced a more circumspect attitude on the part of the opposition. The democratic parties were choosing to act as the heirs of pre-war Romanian centralism, believing that there was no right higher than that of the Romanian state to recover one of its former provinces.[122]

'Moldova' was seen as an integral part of the ideal homeland by most Bucharest democrats; they criticised President Iliescu for his more cautious approach to the question, and they frequently accused him of being deficient in patriotism. By adopting this cause, the opposition was helping to legitimise the tactic, first tried out by the NSF and ultra-nationalists, of boosting one's own nationalist credentials at the expense of one's political rivals. But any benefits expected to flow from promoting unification in this way have largely eluded the opposition.

The Moldovan public has rejected the Popular Front and other pro-unification groups while rewarding President Mircea Snegur and other proponents of independent statehood.[123] There is no sign that Romanian nostalgia for pre-war times has any echoes in what was Bessarabia. Bucharest rule proved economically crippling for Bessarabian peasants who lost their chief markets for their agricultural produce and could not find new ones in Romania owing to its large agricultural surpluses and to the fact that appalling communications hampered the flow of trade.[124] Grim memories of purges, executions and mass deportations in the first years of Soviet rule made the corrupt and overbearing nature of Romanian rule seem mild by comparison.[125] But Moldova was arguably in better economic shape than Romania was upon emerging from communist rule. It lacked Romania's disastrous legacy of obsolete heavy industry, Moldova's industry being mainly based on processing its agricultural products. Unlike Romania, Moldova enjoyed 'Most Favoured Nation' status with the USA, while fifty years of Soviet rule meant that it was closely linked with the trade, communications and energy systems of the Soviet successor states.[126] According to at least one area specialist, strong perceptions of Moldovan identity were to be found among both young Romanian and Russian speakers alike, especially young urban dwellers who are often the product of mixed marriages.[127] There was little prospect of growing trade links with Romania that might offset the continued isolation of the two

states on each side of the river Prut from one another: none of the
100 joint economic ventures anticipated by both governments in 1990–1
had materialised by mid-1992.[128] Just as preoccupation with unification
seemed to be confined to certain intellectual circles in Moldova, survey
evidence suggests that enthusiasm for the issue in Romania itself did not
extend far beyond the political class. Polls revealed that Romanian support
for early unification stood at only twenty-two per cent in June 1991 and
seventeen per cent in May 1992 'which suggests an attitude of quasi-
indifference to the issue among the public'.[129] The escalation of Russian
insurgency in parts of Moldova failed to generate noticeable public protest
in Romania despite its highly emotional treatment by the media. In September 1992, Mircea Druc, a Moldovan politician who had lost influence
at home as a result of promoting unification, was last of six candidates when
he stood for the Romanian Presidency.

There were problems associated with Moldova which were bound to
make Romanians oppressed by a range of worries, wary of closer involvement. The status of its non-Romanian ethnic minorities and the role of
Russian Federation troops stationed along the Dniester river were particularly serious ones. The democratic opposition's statements also failed to
appreciate the complexity of the Moldovan question; its language reflected
'the absence of professional advice and a profound information gap'.[130] A
serious miscalculation occurred when the NPP-CD placed Leonida Lari, a
Bessarabian poetess and one of the loudest advocates of unity, on one of its
constituency lists in the 1992 parliamentary election. Upon being elected,
she quickly drifted towards the ultra-right, the NPP-CD admitting that she
had abandoned the party when it refused to provide her with an apartment
in Bucharest out of party funds, an indication that intellectuals in Bessarabia who were Romanian in outlook were prepared to use nationalism often
for reasons of self-advancement.[131]

The amateurish quality of the democratic opposition's stance on
Moldova reflected badly upon it. President Iliescu behaved more cautious-
ly. He seemed prepared to accept a relationship akin to that of Germany
and Austria, of two states bonded by a common culture, rather than
one between two parts of Germany on the fast track towards unification,
the opposition's preferred model. On an official visit to Romania in
February 1991, President Snegur enunciated the doctrine of 'one people,
two states', or two independent Romanian states co-operating with each
other, which Bucharest later endorsed. Iliescu would have been aware
that a Romania restored to its 1940 frontiers would have brought in
large ethnic minorities. There would be every prospect that Russia and
Ukraine might join with Hungary in wishing to monitor the treatment
of its minorities in an enlarged Romanian state. In 1992, Moldova fell

out of step with Romania by offering its most recalcitrant minorities, the Transnistrians and Gagauzi, the most wide-ranging political and cultural rights afforded to any minorities in eastern Europe or the former Soviet Union.[132] In Bucharest, there were fears that any changes to the boundaries agreed at the Paris peace conference of 1947, might provide a precedent for Hungary to press for adjustments in its frontiers with Romanian Transylvania.[133]

Overall, the Romanian opposition emerged empty-handed from its excursion into irredentist nationalism over Moldova. Having based emotive appeals to nationalism around real or imaginary threats to Transylvania, Iliescu's followers and his nationalist allies were, in their turn, largely undamaged by their low-key approach to the Bessarabian question upon its revival in the 1990s.

CONCLUSION

This chapter has examined the record of those parties lacking compromising links with the pre-1989 state to which the label 'democrat' can be attached without stretching the meaning of that term. Since 1990, they have struggled against huge odds to offer themselves as a credible alternative to the ruling NSF and its successors. The formation of an electoral pact known as the Democratic Convention was no small achievement given the rivalry between parties and the in-fighting that has overtaken all but the NPP-CD. The inclusion of the ethnic Hungarian party in the DC umbrella was even more of an advance given the existence of powerful foes ready to denounce this action as treasonable.

The opposition polled best in the winter 1992 local elections. But they turned out to be a Pyrrhic victory rather than a springboard for national office. Reforming mayors have been unable to win control of the local bureaucracy or to fend off state pressure. This means that it has been hard to deliver on their electoral promises, something that nationalists are keen to exploit.

Local experience suggests that if the opposition had formed a government after the autumn 1992 general election, it might well have found itself a prisoner of the state bureaucracy. The state in Romania shows an undiminished ability to incorporate new political forces and drain them of any reformist potential. It is certain that nationalists would have created a storm over any minority policies introduced by a DC administration that differed from those of the previous government. State agencies like the RIS (successor to the Securitate) would have been able to demonstrate a knack for promoting ultra-nationalist scares if their interests had been encroached upon in any way.

Without autonomous power-bases, the opposition is poorly placed to implement a reformist agenda if it ever acquires the parliamentary votes to form a government. Its lack of strong social bases is a formidable handicap: without a coherent and active social constituency to sustain them, opposition parties have shown that they are prone to behave in a short-term and inconsistent manner.

Perhaps owing to its social isolation, the DC has been unable to sketch convincingly a vision of a better society which can raise Romanians from their political torpor. The endorsement of a free-market economic philosophy in 1990 simply drove many workers towards neo-communist or ultra-nationalist positions. It was not matched by any consistent emphasis on the need for the rights of individuals to precede those of the state. The anti-communist, pro-monarchist and anti-Iliescu rhetoric of the opposition all too often acted as a substitute for the need to put together a citizen-centred manifesto. The failure of new ideas based on strengthening the individual in relation to the collective and the state was shown by the failure of the Civic Alliance Party to make its mark in politics.

There is widespread support for the opposition view that state institutions are the monopoly of a privileged elite and their clients from the old nomenklatura. But the opposition has been unable to puncture the widespread cynicism about the possibility of replacing a corrupt order with anything better.

But it is the absence of a strategy for dealing with ultra-nationalists that has dogged opposition footsteps since 1990. A form of civic patriotism was promoted in the 1992 general election, but it did not mark a turning-point. In the face of a nationalist offensive in parliament during 1992–3, the opposition was cowed and defensive. In the two years after Iliescu's re-election, the opposition has concentrated on futile votes of no confidence and – in mid-1994 – a bid to impeach President Iliescu after failing to exercise any sway over government legislation. The radicalisation of the Hungarian party – in response to the ultra-nationalists – has also provoked strains in the DC. Meanwhile, the NPP-CD, the lynch pin of the Convention, insists on demonstrating its patriotism by taking a hard line over Moldova, a state which in 1994 dashed any lingering hopes that it would allow itself to be reincorporated into Romania.

Opinion polls in 1994 suggested that voters unhappy with the government were undecided about switching to the DC or to the ultra-nationalists. Lacking resources, proper access to the media or an influx of new blood, the opposition is poorly placed to go on the offensive or to renew itself. The next set of elections due in 1996, will show if it can stave off the ultra-nationalist challenge. There is every likelihood that the formula for taking power that nationalists perfected in Cluj during 1992 can be applied elsewhere. Lessons from that city's experience need to be learnt if the opposition is not to be marginalised by nationalists who are even more reluctant democrats than Iliescu and his supporters.

NOTES

1. Nicolae Manolescu, *East European Reporter*, (Spring-Summer 1991), p. 79.
2. D. Chirot, *Social Change in a Peripheral Society*, Academic Press, New York 1976, p. 463.
3. Ioan Mihailescu, 'Mental Stereotypes in Post-Totalitarian Romania', *Government and Opposition*, Vol. 28, No. 3 (1993), p. 318; details of the second poll were in the Romanian daily, *Adevărul de Cluj* (14 February 1992).
4. Rompres, 21 December 1990, SWB EE/0955 B/17 (24 December 1990).
5. *Dreptátea* (16 February 1990).
6. *Report on Eastern Europe* (28 June 1991), p. 28.
7. I. Z. Boilă, *Tribuna Ardealului* (18 February 1992).
8. *România Liberă* (weekly English-language edition), 21 May 1992.
9. See Deletant, 'The Role of Vatra . . .'; Gallagher, 'Vatra Românească . . .'; and Socor, 'Forces of Old . . .'.
10. V. Arachelian, *Corneliu Coposu, Dialoguri*, Editura Anastasia, Bucharest 1992, p. 139.
11. *Report on Eastern Europe* (13 April 1990).
12. *The Independent* (London), 31 March 1990.
13. Bucharest home service, 22 March 1990, SWB EE/0722 B/6 (26 March 1990); see also *Report on Eastern Europe* (13 April 1990).
14. The complete text of the Timişoara declaration was published in *Report on Eastern Europe* (6 April 1990).
15. Information about Timişoara democracy movement and government response from Nicolae and Doina Harsanyi.
16. Seton-Watson, *Eastern Europe, 1918–41*, p. 94
17. Nicolae and Doina Harsanyi.
18. Nicolae Harsanyi.
19. The strength of the personality factor in political culture was shown by the reaction of a fifty-two-year-old rural resident on the eve of poll: 'Now Mr Iliescu is the president. When somebody else takes his place, I will vote for that one'. See *România Liberă* (25 September 1992).
20. See Dan Ionescu, 'Violence and Calumny in the Election Campaign', *Report on Eastern Europe* (25 May 1990).
21. See Mihailescu, 'Mental Stereotypes . . .'.
22. Arachelian, *Corneliu Coposu*, p. 134.
23. *NU* (Cluj newspaper), No. 41 (11 February 1991).
24. M. Shafir, 'Oppositional Regrouping: The Democratic Antitotalitarian Front and the Civic Alliance', *Report on Eastern Europe*, Vol. 1, No. 50 (14 December 1990).
25. *Zig Zag* (6 February 1992).
26. *România Liberă* (2–3 November 1991).
27. Dan Ionescu, 'Romania's Liberals', *RFE-RL Research Report*, Vol. 2, No. 22 (28 May 1993).
28. *România Liberă* (31 October 1991).
29. *NU*, a paper directed at young people and produced from Cluj regularly expressed the frustrations of young people with conventional opposition politics.

30. M. Shafir, 'The Movement for Romania: A Party of "Radical Return"', *RFE-RL Research Report*, Vol. 1, No. 29 (17 July 1992), p. 20.
31. V. Tismaneanu and M. Mihaies, *East European Reporter* (January–February 1992).
32. Michael Shafir, 'Growing Political Extremism in Romania', *RFE-RL Research Report*, Vol. 2, No. 14 (2 April 1993), p. 25.
33. *România Liberă*, Weekly International edition (14 May 1992).
34. His writings, many of which concern the escalating nationalist threat, were collected in *Dreptul la Normalitate: Discursul politic și realitate*, Editura Litera, Bucharest 1991.
35. Private information from a non-party member who has observed closely the evolution of the CAP.
36. Rompres, 30 August 1990, SWB EE/0858 B/16 (1 September 1990).
37. *Dreptátea* (2 November 1990).
38. Interview with Matei Boilă, September 1991.
39. *România Liberă* (26 November 1991); for details in English, see Tom Gallagher, 'Ultra-Nationalists . . .', p. 26.
40. *Expres* (26 July 1991).
41. These views were expressed in a taped interview given by Dr Forna in August 1992.
42. See Manolescu, *Dreptul la Normalitate*, pp. 94–100, 212–16, 245–50, 261–7.
43. Nelson, in idem (ed.), op. cit., pp. 174–5.
44. Juliana Geron Pilon, *The Bloody Flag*, pp. 31–2; see also *Romania Literara* (7 November 1991).
45. Raţiu's speech was published in full by the chauvinist paper *Adevârul de Cluj* on 31 October 1991. He further elaborated his views on the minority question in an interview with *22* (2 March 1994).
46. Rompres, 11 November 1991, SWB EE/1230 13/17 (15 November 1991).
47. *NU* (28 October 1991).
48. *România Liberă* (30 October 1991).
49. *Baricada* (21 April 1992).
51. *Expres Magasin* (12 December 1991).
52. *România Liberă*.
53. *Expres Magasin*.
54. *România Liberă*, Weekly International edition (6 February 1992).
55. Personal observation in Cluj during the election campaign and its aftermath.
56. *Mesagerul Transilvan* (23 January 1992).
57. This promise carried in *România Liberă* (13 September 1991).
58. *In faţa alegatorilor*, No. 1, no date.
59. *Puntea* (Cluj newspaper), February 1992 interview with Liţiu.
60. *NU* (3 March 1992).
61. *Expres Magasin* (11 February 1992).
62. *România Liberă*, (international edition), 30 January 1992.
63. See *Zig Zag*, 5 (97), February 1992.
64. *Report asupra alegerilor locale din Cluj*, February 1992 (Report on the Cluj local elections), Pro-Democracy, Cluj 1992.
65. See Larry L. Watts, 'The Romanian Army in the December Revolution and Beyond', in D. Nelson (ed.), *Romania After Tyranny*, p. 110
66. *Dreptátea*.

67. *NU* (19 August 1991).
68. *Mesagerul Transilvan* (13 February 1991).
69. M. Shafir, 'Public Opinion One Year After the Elections', *Report on Eastern Europe* (14 June 1991), p. 27.
70. *Report asupra . . .* (see n. 64 above).
71. *Mesagerul Transilvan* (13 February 1992).
72. *Zig Zag* (6 February 1992).
73. *NU* (18 February 1992).
74. See Schopflin, 'Transylvania . . .'.
75. This view was confirmed by a wide number of people I talked to while in Cluj, one that was based also on my own impressions.
76. Funar launched his campaign for the Romanian presidency in the Apuseni mountains during the summer of 1992, and the main priority of his mayorship has been to erect a huge statue to Iancu in one of Cluj's main squares.
77. See A. Hennessy, 'Latin America', in G. Ionescu and E. Gellner (eds), *Populism: Its Meaning and National Characteristics*, Weidenfeld & Nicholson, London 1969.
78. *Tribuna Ardealului* (18 February 1992).
79. *Tribuna Ardealului* (20 February 1992).
80. *Tribuna Ardealului* (21 February 1992).
81. *Tribuna Ardealului* (3 March 1992).
82. M. Shafir, 'Transylvanian Shadows, Transylvanian Light', *RFE-RL Research Report* (26 June 1992), p. 29.
83. *Tribuna Ardealului* (21 March 1992).
84. *România Liberă* (25 February 1992).
85. *Tribuna Ardealului* (27 February 1992).
86. Conversations with Cluj DC members in February 1992.
87. Michael Shafir, 'Romania: National Liberal Party Quits Democratic Convention', *RFE-RL Research Report*, Vol. 2, No. 24 (12 June 1992), p. 27.
88. Ibid.
89. *Tribuna Ardealului* (5 May 1992).
90. *România Liberă*, Weekly international edition (24 July 1992).
91. *Romania Libera*, Weekly international edition (14 May 1992).
92. Hungarian Radio, 21 August 1992, SWB EE/1468 C/3 (25 August 1992).
93. Rompres, 21 August 1992, SWB EE/1468 C2/5 (25 August 1992).
94. *Cuvîntul* (15 September 1992).
95. *NU* (21 September 1992).
96. *Tribuna Ardealului* (15 September 1992).
97. Michael Shafir, 'Romania: Main Candidates in the Presidential Elections', *RFE-RL Research Report*, Vol. 1, No. 35 (4 September 1992), p. 16.
98. *22* (18 March 1993).
99. *22* (7 January 1993).
100. See letter of Ioan Oprea in *22* (22 July 1993) for the controversy that Manolescu's rejection still engendered one year later.
101. Michael Shafir, 'Romania's New Electoral Laws', *RFE-RL Research Report*, Vol. 2, No. 36 (11 September 1992), p. 28.
102. See *Dimineata* (23 September 1992).
103. This accusation was aired by the columnist Andrei Cornea in *22* (5 August 1993).
104. See Tom Gallagher, 'Ethnic Tension in Cluj', *RFE-RL Research Report*, Vol. 2,

No. 9 (26 February 1993), p. 31; Shafir, 'Transylvanian Shadows', pp. 35–6.
105. Rompres, 27 October 1992, SWB EE/1524 B/18 (29 October 1992).
106. Ibid.
107. Hungarian television, 4 October 1992, SWB EE/1504 B/11.
108. SWB EE/1524 B/18 (29 October 1992).
109. Rompres, 17 January 1993, SWB EE/1592 B/12 (21 January 1993).
110. Private information from a well-connected Hungarian source.
111. *RFE-RL Correspondents' Reports* (3 September 1993).
112. N. Thorpe, 'Bishop of revolution in shadow of death', *The Observer* (London), 1 March 1992.
113. For details of the mediation, see David Binder, 'Romania Widens Hungarian Minority Rights', *International Herald Tribune* (21 July 1993).
114. Hungarian radio, SWB EE/17779 B/1–2 (28 August 1993).
115. Hungarian radio, Budapest, 30 January 1993, SWB EE/1603 B/13 (3 February 1993).
116. This assessment of the Hungarian press in Romania is derived from Eva Cs. Gyimesi, 'The Ethnic Excuse', *New Hungarian Quarterly*, Vol. 34 (Summer 1993).
117. *Tribuna Ardealului* (3 April 1993).
118. The letter was drawn up on 15 April 1993 and an edited version was published in *România Liberă* on 30 April 1993.
119. See Peter Banyai, writing in *22* during 1992.
120. Vladimir Socor, 'Moldova', *RFE-RL Research Report*, Vol. 3, No. 16 (22 April 1994), p. 17.
121. *Tribuna Ardealului* (18 February 1992).
122. See Vladimir Socor, 'Moldovan-Romanian Relations are Slow to Develop', *RFE-RL Research Report*, Vol. 1, No. 26 (June 1992).
123. Ibid.
124. Bernard Newman, *Danger Spots of Europe*, The Right Book Club, London 1939, p. 225.
125. For the nature of Romanian rule in Bessarabia, see Henry L. Roberts, *Rumania: Political Problems of an Agrarian State*, Yale University Press, New Haven CT 1951, pp. 35, 118.
126. Charles King, 'Moldova and the Bessarabian Question', *The World Today* (July 1993), p. 136.
127. See articles by Vladimir Socor carried by the *RFE-RL Research Report* in 1994 cited in the bibliography for an elaboration of this view.
128. Socor, 'Moldovan-Romanian Relations are Slow to Develop', p. 41.
129. Ibid., p. 40.
130. Ibid., p. 41.
131. *Evenimentul Zilei* (22 March 1993).
132. King, 'Moldova . . .', p. 137.
133. Jacques Rupnik, 'Europe's New Frontiers: Remapping Europe', *Daedalus*, Vol. 123, No. 3 (Summer 1994), p. 103.

Chapter 6

The Ultra-Nationalists

If we do have an identity, it is absurd for us to find it only in the Middle Ages or at the dawn of modernity, or in the purest figures the Romanian people could create . . .We [thought] the nationalist lie had died with the one who had forced [the Romanian] people to love itself through idiotic hymns and a gun at its head. But lo and behold, this lie continues to live on in a manner that makes us doubt ourselves once again.

Vasile Popovici[1]

CULTURAL POLITICS AND NATIONALIST RECOVERY

The Vatra Românească Union was the first ultra-nationalist organisation to come to prominence in eastern Europe after the collapse of communist rule. Less than six weeks after its formation in February 1990, its birthplace, the city of Tirgu Mureş, witnessed the first inter-ethnic collision in the region that resulted in casualties. The estimates of the dead and injured have varied widely.[2] The Transylvanian question which, ever since attracting west European attention in the 1890s, had been the paradigm example of an ethnically-based territorial dispute in eastern Europe, appeared once more to be back on the agenda as an intractable problem. Suspicion of Hungarian motives, and refusal to acknowledge any basis for laws safeguarding Hungarian minority rights, coloured the early statements of Vatra leaders. Interviewed on Hungarian state radio on 24 March 1990, Radu Ceontea, Vatra's chairman, revealed the gulf that existed between his supporters and a co-inhabiting community in Transylvania which some nationalists would soon brand as 'the enemy within':

Fifty days have passed since the formation of Vatra Românească. One week after it was created, we held a large-scale people's meeting in the sports stadium in Tirgu Mureş, in which around 15,000 people took part. A few hours later we learnt with astonishment that in Budapest they had reported that a nationalist, fascist-type organisation had been formed in Romania at Tirgu Mureş . . . They said it was a question of an anti-Magyar Ceauşescuite organisation . . . This is how they slandered us . . . The Magyars . . . forget that the Ceauşescu system had repressed the

Romanians with just as much harshness as it had the Magyars and they also forget that they perhaps had more rights than the Romanians for, through contacts with relatives and friends, they were able to travel more than the Romanians.[3]

Ceontea's tendentious and emotion-laden statement was typical of many others that would follow. The same ignorance and hostility would be echoed by Hungarian commentators, especially in Hungary itself, where the consequences of making unguarded remarks about Transylvania were often wantonly disregarded. The general Hungarian view was that Vatra represented a logical outcome of the chauvinistic indoctrination that had marked Ceauşescu's rule after 1980. In the last years of the dictatorship, Hungarian refugees from Romania often claimed that the repression of the Hungarian minority was no longer perpetrated merely by administrative measures but also by the acts of ordinary Romanians. In 1988, László Hamas of the New York-based Hungarian Human Rights Foundation wrote, after speaking with those refugees, that 'the anti-Hungarian campaign has trickled down. The effort to provoke hostile sentiments of Romanians against Hungarians is unfortunately becoming more and more successful. A lot of people who came out of Romania recently came out for this specific reason'.[4]

Even if the Transylvanian Hungarians had been more circumspect in their political behaviour and had not called for rapid educational changes (which to many insecure citizens were tantamount to separatism), a nationalist reaction would have been difficult to avert; even if the Hungarians had proven as politically fickle or as disorganised as the Roma (gypsy) population who surpassed them in numbers, it is likely that members of the communist establishment would have attempted to exploit the nationalist conditioning of the population, in order to manage political change on their own terms.

After all, the Ceauşescu era – one largely devoid of any useful experiences for building a democratic society – had repeatedly shown how nationalism could be a source of power to whoever was capable of tapping its emotional energy. Chapters 1 and 2 showed the close connection between appeals to nationalism and efforts to utilise it for personal or group advancement from the nineteenth century onwards. It generated political legitimacy in a system of governance where the gulf between largely peasant households and the oligarchy was immense owing to the absence of intermediate institutions that played an integrative role in society.

Intellectuals have always played a vital role as guardians of nationalism, one that Ceauşescu later recognised. Vatra, a self-styled cultural organisation with a clear-cut political agenda, used high-minded language about completing the cultural mission of Romanian unification just like its pre-cursors. But, upon stripping away the rhetoric, evidence quickly emerged that Vatra was also being pushed forward by bureaucrats and other state officials with a record of manipulating the state to serve their own caste interests.Some of its leading early office-holders were professional people from the worlds of medicine, administration and education, several of whom had been under pressure to quit on the grounds of incompetence or misconduct before a nationalist backlash got under-way in Tirgu Mureş.[5]

The spectacle of party officials in Transylvania collaborating with local intellectuals to minimise political change ran counter to the predictions made by scholars in the late 1980s. Writing in the last months of Ceauşescu's life, Trond Gilberg declared that:

> The alienation among Romanian intellectuals of all kinds is much more fundamental. . .The chauvinist statements and falsification of history and contemporary reality produced by alleged 'scholars' engenders nothing but cynical contempt among the real intellectuals of the country . . . It is quite clear now, at the end of the 1980s, that nationalism and chauvinism cannot possibly restore the support that Communism may once have had in this social stratum.[6]

But by 1992 Gilberg was far less sanguine; then he felt able to write that 'Ceauşescuism as a political philosophy, a programme of socio-economic development, and a system of rule, represented an element of continuity in Romanian history, rather than an aberration or deviation from it'.[7] By now, attempts to rehabilitate Ceauşescu were in full swing. Ion Coja, Vatra's first vice-president, declared in 1991 that 'history will evaluate Ceauşescu much differently from how many do today . . . I think we are much too harsh in our judgment of him'.[8]

Vatra's initial statements contained vague, all-purpose sentiments of the kind often put out by populist movements as they seek to build up a following. It proclaimed itself to be a cultural body entrusted with the aim of protecting the Romanian national interest which it based around the defence of the Romanian language. Ever since the nineteenth century, the Romanian language had been a primary factor of identification for a people who, until 1918, had been dispersed among different states.[9] By claiming that Hungarian demands for cultural and educational concessions placed the language in peril, Vatra leaders were able to strike an emotional chord during a period of widespread uncertainty. Radu Ceontea, its first chairman, was soon boasting that, in its first forty days, Vatra had enrolled more genuine members than the Romanian Communist Party had in forty years.[10] Ceontea proved to be an indifferent politician without the leadership skills needed to establish Vatra as a movement of the first rank beyond Transylvania. The fact that someone like this dreamy and often incoherent artist controlled the movement in its first two years suggests that Vatra enjoyed a spontaneous birth, at least in Tirgu Mureş. During this formative period, it was difficult to single out any nationalist visionary able to mount an effective critique of materialism and western liberalism and to invoke powerful images of faith and land so that Romania could rediscover her roots. Rather, Vatra managed to benefit from the depleted political and social psychological state of a section of the population that, largely through no fault of its own, lacked the perspective with which to appraise coolly the message of nationalist populism and its usefulness to them.

In earlier phases of history, mediocrity had not prevented an indifferent politician like Alexandru Cuza from making a successful career out of nationalist intolerance. Ceontea, like Cuza, reduced everything to an ethnic threat, believing that the danger which Hungary posed to Transylvania even superseded the country's economic crisis in its gravity.[11] Just as Cuza excused anti-Semitic violence by describing it as a healthy expression of the popular will, Ceontea seemed ready to minimise the violent actions of Romanians in his city on 19 March 1990:

> The demonstration in Tirgu Mureş on 19 March 1990 was a spontaneous popular revolt, as the patience of the Romanians in the Mureş valley and Tara Giurgiului was stretched to its limit. The outburst of yesterday originated in numerous and painful events that started on 26 December 1989 ... That does not mean that we approve of what happened yesterday.[12]

According to Ceontea, the violence of 19 March 1990 needed to be placed in the context of allegedly provocative actions by Hungarians, starting with the lynching of members of the security forces on 26 December 1989.[13] The bloody events in Tirgu Mureş catapulted Vatra to national prominence. Favourable exposure in the state media and meetings with top officials boosted its visibility and prestige during the spring of 1990, as Vatra insisted upon its apolitical character. A statement was issued in May 1991 declaring it to be 'a socio-cultural and civic organisation whose programme and activities serve no political party', exactly a year after a Vatra-sponsored electoral alliance had participated in post-communist Romania's first competitive election.[14]

The Party of Romanian National Unity in Transylvania (PRNUT) had been formed on 15 March 1990 as a political adjunct of Vatra.[15] It formed an electoral alliance with the Republican Party known as the Alliance For Romanian Unity (the acronym resulting from this produces the Romanian word for 'gold': AUR). It won 2.12 per cent of the national vote, making no impression outside Transylvania. But in Mureş county it won 34.36 per cent of the vote and in Cluj 13.5 per cent. Its strong showing in these ethnically-mixed Transylvanian counties secured it nine seats in the lower house of parliament and two in the senate. In November 1990, the PRNUT would amalgamate with a much smaller party in Moldavia to become the Party of Romanian National Unity (PRNU). In May 1991, Ceontea, by now a PRNU senator, was elected chairman of the party, having relinquished the leadership of Vatra some months earlier. This switch was an indication that for ultra-nationalists the new centre of gravity was switching from the 'cultural' to the political sphere.

But insistence on the apolitical character of Vatra enabled it to function in areas like the church, the armed forces and government ministries, where activity of a political character is normally banned. In 1991, Dr Zeno Opris, Ceontea's successor as Vatra chairman, made it clear that these were target areas for the future:

> For the future we are thinking of . . . making contact with those whose professions or statutes bar them from making politics (army activists from the interior ministry, journalists, priests) . . . people who constitute an element of stability and national equilibrium.[16]

This drive to extend Vatra's influence made headway in some quarters even as its cultural activities declined. There were persistent reports in Cluj after 1990 of certain senior academics using authoritative persuasion to get their postgraduate students to enrol. Meanwhile, a foreign analyst of the Romanian army reported that General Cioflina, the chief of the general staff, was setting up affiliates of Vatra in military units in 1990–1.[17]

UNITY IS THE WATCHWORD

Vatra spokesmen have often described the movement as being 'equidistant with respect to all political parties'.[18] Being in such a position makes it easy for Vatra (and the PRNU) to promote themselves as unifying forces able to exercise a brokerage role in a fractured political landscape. The unity of all national forces which have a true appreciation of the national interest is one of the most consistent themes in the Vatra-PRNU repertoire. It is calculated to appeal to citizens who have no enthusiasm for the party warfare or the media denunciations that to them appear as unnecessary and disturbing features of life after Ceauşescu.

The emphasis on unity dominated Radu Ceontea's speech at the first conference of Vatra Românească in 1990:

> We have just finished the demolition of the dictatorship and here are dissension and enmity. The spirit of solidarity, of unity among the citizens of the country, has weakened . . . The political pluralism established by the December revolution . . . has not yielded the expected fruits . . . offering us a saddening image of disunity, of misunderstanding among brethren. Only united will we be able to preserve our national identity.[19]

A question mark must hang over the strength and resilience of Romanian national identity if it can only be secured by a dropping of normal party differences. But it is clear that Vatra and the PRNU do not regard as appropriate for Romania the expression of conflicts of interest regarded as everyday occurrences in established democracies. It is possibly no exaggeration to describe the stress on unity as a legacy of the process of homogenisation that occurred under communism. The nature of Romanian communism made the task of ultra-nationalists easier by greatly reducing social diversity and by constantly seeking to promote a single unified stance on many issues, both large and insignificant. Thus Romanian social reality, after four decades of rigorous attempts at totalitarian control, gives the unity discourse of nationalists a resonance which it lacks even in other communist countries.

The insistence on a compulsory consensus, which is one of the hallmarks of totalitarianism, often came across in Ceontea's speeches in the early 1990s. Speaking in 1990, he expressed a desire to merge the people with his movement in order to recreate the purified Romanian nation:

> We should all unite; let there not be a single Transylvanian Romanian who is not a member of Vatra Românească, so that when we have more than six million members there will be no need to declare ourselves a party because then we shall be the Romanian nation itself, dignified and free, upright and tolerant.[20]

Ceontea frequently suggested that his movement was uniquely placed to determine what the greater national good might be. If it was open to misrepresentation and attack, it was because its capacity to defend the national interest excited the ill-will and the enmity of others who had much baser motives for being in public life. In 1990 and 1991, Ceontea claimed that Vatra was the most slandered organisation in Romania and that attempts were being made to sabotage its work.[21] Attacks on Vatra were depicted as part of a wider scenario to cause internal dissension that would enable Transylvania to be detached from the rest of Romania.

Vatra's insistence that the national interest must take precedence over group or individual identity or minority allegiances was designed to be a soothing message for many people profoundly influenced by the Ceauşescu era who found it difficult to imagine a state that was not centrally directed in an authoritative way. Such people tend to have little interest in politics, and polls revealed that the apolitical citizen comprises a large swathe of the population. Sixty-eight per cent of people surveyed in one poll of March 1992 claimed that they either had 'little interest' or were 'not at all interested' in politics.[22] On occasion, Vatra has felt the need to urge traditionally apolitical groups not to be seduced by politics. In May 1990,

Ceontea called on all peasants 'not to mix agriculture with politics, to till the land with the faith that they do it for the country and for God.[23] Those who seek to assert group or individual rights independent of the state have not infrequently found themselves criticised by ultra-nationalists for infringing the national interest. Thus, young people in Bucharest protesting about the domination of Romania by neo-communists received no sympathy from Vatra when they were driven from the streets in 1990. Shortly afterwards, Vatra issued a statement expressing support for government efforts to 'dam the flood in the face of the violence in Bucharest as well as demonstrations of a destabilising and anti-Romanian character in other towns'.[24] Strikes have been a regular target of Vatra criticism. In May 1993, when industrial action coincided with a massive rise in prices for basic foodstuffs and eating supplies, Vatra issued a statement claiming that 'a good part of the responsibility for the country's difficult situation goes to the trade-union movement after December 1989'.[25]

The press, an important island of genuine pluralism in Romania, has also been a nationalist target. In November 1993, Senator Valer Suian of the Cluj PRNU tried to persuade parliament to adopt a law that allowed for any-one 'receiving or communicating false, exaggerated or tendentious views, and information that disturbed the Romanian state, to be punished by up to five years' imprisonment'. Defamation by any means, of parliament, the head of state, the government or the armed forces, was to be punished by a prison sentence of between six months and three years.[26] The press was the obvious target of such restrictions: it most clearly embodied the cosmopolitan and free-thinking tendencies entering Romanian public life after the iron conformity of the Ceauşescu years, which the PRNU most disliked.

Whereas Vatra has been hostile to institutions associated with pluralist values, it is impossible to find criticism of institutions like the Orthodox Church or the military. This is hardly surprising, since leading churchmen and military officers have embraced the ethnocentric values promoted by Vatra.

The army officer who aligned himself most closely with Vatra was General Paul Cheler, head of the army in Transylvania.[27] In 1990, he made several calls for unity that were backed up by a coercive threat. On the eve of Romania's national day, 1 December, Cheler warned that the army would 'ensure an atmosphere of security and order' and, if necessary, 'open fire against anyone who attempts to disturb the celebration'. He also maintained that the army should be ready to use deadly force to quell socio-economic disturbances, a view rejected by the then defence minister, General Victor Stanculescu. He also echoed Ceontea by berating the opposition for misdirecting the population towards 'non-essential issues' and away from the situation in Transylvania.[28] By the first anniversary of the 1989 events, Ceontea was calling for a military government, believing that 'no other form of government is good for Romania now'.[29]

THE HUNGARIAN DANGER

It was the presence of an all-consuming Hungarian danger that ultra-nationalists used as an excuse to demand vigilance, discipline, unity and, if necessary, the suspension of normal political activity. The one consistent note in the PRNU discourse is the existence of an alleged threat to Romanian sovereignty over Transylvania by Hungarian groups both within the province and across the border in Hungary. It draws no comfort from the recognition of the Romanian state by the HDFR, whose efforts to obtain collective rights for the Hungarian minority, particularly in the spheres of education and local government, are seen as attempts to undermine the Romanian character of Transylvania prior to detaching it completely from Romania.

Ceontea claimed that Vatra was formed as a direct response to the creation of the HDFR.[30] Initially he rejected Hungarian requests for instruction in their own language within the state educational system on the grounds that it was virtually without precedent anywhere else in Europe. But when evidence from countries as diverse as Spain, Denmark, Finland and Britain was presented, conditions specific to Romania were cited as a reason for promoting the monolingual educational system that Ceaușescu was introducing; in Ceontea's words, 'all the comparisons are misplaced since we are talking about different historical situations. Perhaps if we too had the neighbours that Switzerland has, we could discuss matters in another way'.[31]

Occasionally, the assertion that provisions for minorities to be found elsewhere were unsuitable in Romanian conditions was replaced by the claim that Hungarians enjoy more rights than any other European minority thanks to the benevolence of the Romanian authorities. In 1991, the Hunendoara branch of Vatra claimed that 'the Romanian state has granted great rights to minorities unparalleled anywhere else in the world, not even in the most advanced democracies'.[32] Earlier, when cuts had been made in Hungarian-language television, the Cluj branch of Vatra released a statement claiming that the Hungarian minority enjoyed more privileges in broadcasting than minorities 'anywhere else in the world'; it went on to insist that the HDFR ought to ensure that television broadcasts in Hungarian promote 'respect towards their unique homeland and towards the Romanian people'.[33] Later still, a call was made by the Cluj and Tirgu Mureş branches of Vatra for Romanian subtitles to be included in all Hungarian programmes.[34] However, the concept of bilingualism is abhorrent to ultra-nationalists in all other spheres: in the summer of 1993, the PRNU threatened to table a vote of no confidence in the government and to suspend President Iliescu, if a proposal to introduce bilingual signs in areas where minorities made up more than ten per cent of the population passed into law.[35]

Ultra-nationalists often deny the validity of specific group rights for the Hungarians by arguing that the latter (in Ceontea's words) constitute a part of the Romanian nation 'whether they like it or not'.[36] Under this definition of nationalism, the state is the organising principle for the nation. But when it is necessary to single out Hungarians for special condemnation, ultra-nationalists are quite ready to concede them their Hungarian nationality, as when the Cluj Vatra leader, Dr Petru Forna, pointed out during a radio debate that in 1945 ninety per cent of the members of the RCP in Cluj were of Hungarian nationality, the numbers involved being hardly more than 100 or 200 people.[37]

Whatever variations there may be in the way in which Romanian nationalists choose to define 'the Romanian nation', it is clear that there is little room for a 'co-inhabiting nationality' like the Hungarians. Gheorghe Funar, the PRNU's leader since 1992, has frequently called for the banning of the HDFR and the dismissal of all elected mayors who belong to it.[38] Accordingly, ultra-nationalists rarely bother to distinguish between moderates and radicals within the HDFR, since their shared ultimate aim is to take control of Transylvania and they only differ over timing and tactics.

Given the Hungarian party's illegitimate character, ultra-nationalists have no hesitation about using the most provocative language to describe it. Ioan Gavra, the PRNU's deputy leader, described the HDFR as 'the disease of AIDS that is working in the organism of the Romanian state'.[39] A fellow deputy, Senator Valer Suian, described the HDFR as 'a political monstrosity, the unique party of communist inspiration'.[40] A lesson of the destruction of Yugoslavia is that the distance between verbal violence and physical violence need not be a vast one in the Balkans.

Highly emotive language is also used by ultra-nationalists when commemorating past events, especially ones which brought Romanians into conflict with neighbouring peoples. Much of Vatra's influence stems from its ability to revive the past in a suitably heroic manner for a people denied proper access to their own history for half a century. Whoever can redefine the past in ways that suit a pre-determined political agenda is bound to acquire considerable influence in a country as disorientated and as unsure of its future direction as Romania was in the early 1990s.

Vatra's reinterpretation of the past for contemporary political purposes was not particularly original in terms of either Romania or the region it was in. Since the creation of independent east European states over a century ago, the state has often encouraged nationalist intellectuals to redefine the past – creating achievements and continuity out of random and often distant historical events – in order to speed up the process of nation-building. In Romania, much emphasis has been placed upon the role played by Transylvania in ensuring the survival of the Romanian nation into the modern period. Ultra-nationalists in Transylvania have also exploited its role as a touchstone of the nation to argue that they are the true gatekeepers of national identity. Gheorghe Funar has even argued that the Romanian capital ought to be located in Transylvania, Bucharest, having, in his eyes, forfeited the right due to becoming 'a city of corruption and filth'.[41] After becoming mayor of Cluj, Funar did his best to put a Romanian stamp on Transylvania's capital, whose historical centre is still replete with buildings and monuments dating from the period when the city was known by its Hungarian name, Kolozsvar. A decision at the end of 1992 to alter the inscription on the statue of Hungary's King Matthias revealed how sensitive Hungarians as well as Romanians were to attempts to interfere with their place in Transylvanian history. Public protests took place, resulting in troops being rushed from Bucharest to patrol the centre of the town.[42]

The controversial inscription ordered by Funar was a quote from the historian Iorga, pointing out that Matthias had suffered a defeat at the hands of King Stephen the Great, prince of Moldavia and one of Romania's national heroes. Matthias, by contrast, was an anomalous figure, born in Cluj the son of a Romanian nobleman, who went on to become the most popular king the Hungarians ever had, being known as 'Matthias the Just' (he reigned from 1458 to 1490).[43]

Dinu C. Giurescu, a well-known historian, argued that history was being manipulated for political purposes in a bid to erect barriers between peoples.[44] Funar had ignored the National Commission for Historical Monuments which had jurisdiction over the statue, a sign that no Transylvanian patriot need look to Bucharest for advice about how best to defend the historical patrimony.

Both the main communities in Transylvania are highly sensitive to each other's symbols and anniversaries. Funar's decision to erect a huge statue to the nineteenth-century Romanian hero Avram Iancu (paid for from state funds as well as private subscriptions) is bound to deepen the Hungarian sense of isolation in Cluj. His threat to melt down the statue of King Matthias and use the bronze for this new project could well push feelings to breaking point if it was ever to be carried out.[45]

MANIPULATING HISTORY TO ALTER CONTEMPORARY REALITY

Community relations have been impaired by Vatra's efforts to revive memories of the Hungarian occupation of north-west Transylvania between 1940 and 1944. Vatra sponsored a variety of organisations with names like 'the League of Victims in North-West Transylvania', 'the Association of Refugees from North-West Transylvania' and 'the Tirgu Mureş Alliance of Magyarised Romanians', which reinforces the image of Romanians as a 'victim nation'.

Vatra was seeking to highlight an event in which Romanians in a large part of the state had been victims of collective aggression just when other Romanians preferred to emphasise the iniquities of the communist period, for most of which it had been Romanians who had maltreated and suppressed fellow Romanians.

An outspoken group of nationalist intellectuals who launched the weekly *România Mâre* (hereafter *RM*) in 1990 have shown considerable energy and boldness in seeking to alter popular perceptions of the communist period. In *RM*'s eyes, it is Romania's ethnic minorities who were responsible for the worst excesses of communism; times were hardest for the Romanian people when Jews, Hungarians, and others who slavishly executed Moscow's orders, exercised disproportionate influence in the upper reaches of the RCP. The sufferings of the people were only eased when native Romanians came to the fore within the party from the mid-1950s onwards. Gheorghiu-Dej and his successor Ceauşescu, may have been communists, but they showed their fidelity to national values by doing their utmost to make the country autonomous from the Soviet Union.

The division of the communist period into an anti-national phase and a national phase has enormous contemporary relevance. Not least, it enables a defence to be made of ethnic Romanian members of the communist establishment still holding important positions in the 1990s; this is done by arguingthat they had embarked upon their careers after the worst excesses of communism were over and at a time when the party was willing to recognise the specificity of the Romanian nation and its right to enjoy a separate historical development from other nations which might possess the same social system.

To bathe the Romanian communists responsible for consolidating party control in the purifying light of patriotism, it was necessary to depict the initial years of communism in lurid terms. *RM* did not flinch from this task, as an article entitled 'Who has brought Bolshevism, Terror and Crime to Romania?' would go on to show when it appeared in the autumn of 1991.[46] The unequivocal answer of the paper's chief editor and author of the article was that it was the Jews. Several quotes from the article will serve to show how far Tudor's indictment of the Jews extends:

It was the Jews who arrived on the tanks of the Red Army, who brought bolshevism to Romania, who contributed decisively to the massacre of Romanian patriots, and who smothered any popular resistance . . .

I have heard some excuses such as: the Jews having suffered too much at the hands of European Fascism, embraced the communist ideology and it was a natural reaction. Nonsense!

The Jews did not embrace the communist ideology, they created it. The proof lies in the fact that long before fascism and nazism, they led the Bolshevik Revolution in Russia along with those in Germany and Hungary . . .

Of course it can be said that it wasn't only the Jews who ran the party, the Securitate and the jails. Of course there were Romanians, but very few of them. More numerous were the Jews followed by the Hungarians, gypsies and Russians. But even among those Romanians, there were many who had contracted mixed marriages with Jews . . .

Corneliu Vadim Tudor had enjoyed mutually advantageous relations with the security services before 1989. Along with his long-time ally Eugen Barbu, he used the weekly *Saptamina*, which they both edited, to smear Romanian intellectuals suspected of liberalism; they worked in tandem with a Securitate colonel who passed on dossiers, this privileged access to state information continuing into the 1990s thanks to ongoing links with unreconstructed elements of the state bureaucracy.[47]

RM's access to the files of early communist activists, and to photographs and other materials not in the public domain, gave it an important advantage when seeking to persuade its target audience that its assessment of the recent past was based on first-hand evidence. The paper, with its irreverent and hard-hitting style of journalism, became a best-seller in 1990–1. Its political influence was shown in 1993 when Mihai Ungheanu, a regular columnist specialising in articles alleging that Jews had been to the fore in carrying out a 'Holocaust of Romanian Culture', became state secretary of culture.[48] By now, *RM* had spawned the Greater Romania Party (GRP), which in 1992 returned sixteen deputies and twenty-two senators to parliament.

In nearly every issue of *RM*, several pages are devoted to 'The Struggle Against Hungarian Fascism and Irredentism'. Readers are frequently reminded that the demands for cultural autonomy made by the HDFR are along the lines of those granted to Hungarians in the pre-nationalist phase of communist rule from 1947 to circa 1958. Bilingualism and the restoration of a Hungarian university are viewed as wrong not only because they run counter to the state-building process of integrating the entire population behind an identical set of Romanian values, but also because they were last tried out during what is seen as one of the darkest moments in the history of the Romanian people. Advocates of minority group rights might reply that it was during the initial brutal phase of communism that women were enfranchised for the first time, a right that has not subsequently been thrown into question. However, many Romanians (uncomfortable with much of the ultra-nationalist agenda) are ready to agree with Ceontea and Tudor that Hungarians are being insensitive and even provocative in reclaiming rights that were given to them just as the whole country was falling under alien control and which may even have contributed to the success of the Soviet takeover.

The emphasis upon the wartime Hungarian seizure of Romanian territory and the early stages of communism, when minorities were felt to be in the ascendant, is meant to reduce the sense of hurt about more recent episodes when ethnic Romanians maltreated one another (as well as minorities). The political utility of Tudor and others helps to explain why they have been rehabilitated so quickly. The RM group have made resounding comebacks as elected politicians and newspaper commentators when their public careers seemed to be entering permanent eclipse in 1989.

Ultra-nationalists have even created new nationalist symbols in post-communist times. It was Vatra that was most energetic in lobbying for 1 December, the day in which Transylvania became united with the rest of Romania in 1918, to be the country's new national day. It is likely that they will enjoy further influence in minting new national symbols in which the heroism of those who rose against Ceauşescu is unlikely to be included, except in the most sanitised of ways. One new hero in the making is Mihaila Cofariu, a Romanian who was shown on television being ill-treated by Hungarians in Tirgu Mureş on 20 March 1990. The fact that he was part of a detachment of villagers, at least some of whom had played a role in violence the previous day, is generally glossed over even in the mainstream press, which has followed Cofariu's slow recovery from serious injuries. Vatra is campaigning for Cofariu to be declared a national hero by the state, while the GRP placed him in a seat of honour at its first conference, Cofariu agreeing to become an honorary member of Tudor's party.[49]

XENOPHOBIA AND THE ART OF FOSTERING INSECURITY

Foreign interest in Romania has often been viewed with distrust, and ulterior motives for foreign visits to Romania have sometimes been suspected. Less than four months after onerous restrictions had been lifted that had curtailed the chances of visitors easily meeting with, or staying with, ordinary Romanians, the Bucharest branch of Vatra was angrily condemning 'distorted' foreign coverage of Romania and urging that the movements of foreigners be controlled.[50] Later, in 1991, it condemned Moses Rosen and the Nobel Peace Prize winner Ilie Wiesel for claiming that the Romanian army had played a prominent role in the 1941 pogrom in which thousands of Jews in the city of Iasi were slaughtered.[51] By 1992, Tudor, the GRP leader, was expressing concern over 'the ever more violent interference of foreign diplomats accredited to Bucharest in the state affairs of Romania'.[52]

Vatra statements have often alleged that 'both at home and abroad, there are scenarios meant to destabilise and disunite the country'.[53] By 1992, the leadership was in no doubt that Romania was 'the target of a conspiracy of domestic and external forces that pursue the dismemberment of its being [and] the degrading of human values that have characterised us all along our history'.[54] One perennial concern has been the possibility that extensive tracts of land might fall into foreign hands. In 1993, Cluj Vatra addressed a letter to government leaders protesting against proposals to allow foreigners to buy land in Romania. The issue, it argued, went to the basis of the Romanian state's existence, and it felt confident enough to demand a referendum on the issue.[55] Despite the fact that Romania's poor crop yields stood to be boosted by the introduction of new farming methods and technology, the Văcăroiu government bowed to the nationalist clamour. It also faced criticism from the PRNU for giving in to the 'diktat' of the International Monetary Fund and allegedly selling out the country to foreign interests.[56] However, afterwards the government slightly relaxed its stance by allowing firms whose capital was mainly foreign in origin to buy property in places where their investments were located. The PRNU declared that Transylvania was now in danger of being bought up piece by piece by Hungarians in the manner that the Jews had bought up Palestine.[57] Understandably, it was less forthcoming about opposition charges that, in Cluj, the rules designed to regulate land sales had been flouted to enable PRNU officials to receive plots of land for building purposes.[58] Meanwhile, Tudor, the GRP leader, had assisted his comeback in the early 1990s by becoming a considerable landowner in the strategically located district of Butimanu north of Bucharest.[59]

Vatra members in different parts of Romania took to the streets in January 1991 when the Romanian parliament's report on the March 1990 Tirgu Mureş violence referred to the provocative role played beforehand by Vatra members. The report was seen as a concession to western sentiment meant to hasten Romania's accession to the Council of Europe. Placards carried by Transylvanians who travelled to Bucharest read 'Better Dignity at Home than Humiliation in Europe'. It was reported that a special train bringing several thousand Vatra demonstrators to the capital was prevented from reaching its destination on government orders.[60] Nationalist intellectuals have frequently asserted that Romania has no need to court western Europe since its own European credentials are unimpeachable ones that were visible when other countries ready to give lessons to Romania were sunk in backwardness.

The Bucharest government has usually sidestepped or ignored outright xenophobic demands from ultra-nationalists. But after February 1992 the PRNU had the opportunity to give free expression to its animus against certain foreign interests with the election of Gheorghe Funar as mayor of Cluj. In April 1992, he sabotaged the visit to his city of a delegation of elected representatives from the Netherlands who had come to Romania to talk to councillors from parties making up the Democratic Convention about ways in which democracy was practised at the Dutch local level. Funar suspended the event, having taken exception to the title of the conference, 'The Self-Government of Localities'. He declared that this was contrary to the constitution which proclaimed Romania to be a unitary state, and he contended that if the event had gone ahead, it would have posed a threat to the integrity of the country.[61]

Mayor Funar used this incident as a pretext to issue a decree on 29 April 1992 requiring 'all conferences, symposia and other meetings of a public character' to be registered at his office at least three days in advance. Before approval could be given, 'appropriate details about the organisation, the aim, the location, the duration, and the participants attending the event were required.[62] It was in contravention of clauses in the Romanian constitution allowing freedom of speech, the Cluj opposition daily remarking that 'our lack of consideration towards personalities from democratic countries in Europe shows that we are not interested in refurbishing the image of Romania in the eyes of the outside world'.[63]

THE ELECTORAL CHALLENGE OF NATIONALISM

In 1992, the PRNU enjoyed a real political breakthrough with Gheorghe Funar's election as mayor of Cluj. Without the assistance which it received from the NSF in Cluj, it is likely that the party would have made much less impact in the election year of 1992 and beyond. Nationally, the PRNU received no more than five per cent of the vote in local elections, and it is quite possible that Funar's bid to force his way to the top of the PRNU – without an electoral power-base of his own – might have created a split in the party. In Chapter 5, it was shown how the local and central state authorities helped to clinch victory for him against a strong reformist challenge.[64] But, once in office, Funar showed that he was more than capable of constructing his own power-base which gave him important freedom of action from central government. He represented the interests of important segments of an ethnic Romanian bureaucratic elite which Ceauşescu had fostered in Transylvania. It is clear that this elite had its own particular agenda based on asserting Romanian ethnic interests and that it did not automatically look to Bucharest for guidance or instruction. Indeed there was a sense that Bucharest, and the south generally, did not sufficiently appreciate the special needs of the administrative and economic elite in Transylvanian cities which had only acquired Romanian majorities in the last twenty to thirty years, sentiments which Funar was prepared openly to voice.

The Cluj mayor's preoccupation with the danger posed by 'anti-national' forces invites comparison with Nicolae Ceauşescu in the later stages of his rule, as does his much-vaunted desire to make Romanians 'masters in their own house'. Like Ceauşescu, Funar was a believer in one-man leadership who had risen from an obscure background (he had been an academic expert in state farming) by exploiting or manufacturing destructive and irrational feelings in order to construct an enduring power-base. His methods and discourse reveal the extent to which the Ceauşescu era had left its mark on the behaviour and outlook of many middle-aged Romanians who may have obtained career fulfilment and security by working for the state before 1989. Funar was the first elected Romanian politician of the 1990s prepared to praise Ceauşescu. He described him as 'a good Romanian' on account of having safeguarded Romanian independence.[65] Elsewhere, he was prepared to criticise Ceauşescu for erring on the side of generosity by 'granting privileges to the Magyar minority'.[66] (But when asked to give examples, he was only able to mention 'the occupation of leadership roles in professional and public activity on the basis of ethnic criteria', a reference to the small number of Hungarians who were placed in honorific positions by Ceauşescu in a bid to convince the rest of the world that they enjoyed full rights in his country.)

Corneliu Vadim Tudor, leader of the Greater Romania Party, went much further than Funar in attempting a positive re-evaluation of Ceauşescu. Unlike the Cluj mayor, he had already been a well-known figure before 1989 owing to the way in which he had serviced the dictator's personality cult with a stream of odes and eulogies. He also had a proven record of collaboration with the secret police, who relied on certain ultra-nationalists to monitor the activities of mainstream and dissident intellectuals.[67] Three years after Ceauşescu's overthrow, Tudor was well aware that the rehabilitation of the dictator could enhance his own already blossoming political career. The positive reassessment of Ceauşescu had been stepped up in 1992 as memories of the privations associated with his rule started to fade owing to the economic hardship which large sections of the population were experiencing.

At the first congress of the GRP in March 1993, Tudor, the party chairman, felt able to praise Ceauşescu for a long list of policy achievements which included the creation of a skilled workforce, the abolition of illiteracy, and a vast programme of economic modernisation. He was praised for defending Romania's national integrity and winning the respect of 'Soviet

imperialism when it was at its most expansionist'. Finally, praise was extended for his success in keeping under control wrongdoers, among whom
minorities such as gypsies and Hungarians were felt to be predominant.

Ceauşescu's policy of economic nationalism, by which Romania sought
to industrialise through its own efforts, has been regularly applauded.
Tudor views the emphasis on self-sufficiency as having pre-communist
roots, parallels being drawn between Ceauşescu and the National Liberal
governments of the 1920s which sought to develop industries based on
mineral resources without making Romania dependent on foreign interests. When arguing that Ceauşescu was attempting to build upon past
achievements by his policies of economic nationalism, ultra-nationalists
insist that his rule should be judged by Romanian national criteria, not
by standards imposed by outsiders ready to dwell upon his final years
of power.

RM asserts that Ceauşescu's success in maintaining Romania's national
sovereignty against a powerful and expansionist neighbour is an achievement which dwarfs all other aspects of his rule. Its editor-in-chief refuses
to express regret for anything that he wrote while in the service of
Ceauşescu, 'because I had the guts to recognise publicly that the man had
great merits seen in terms of the history of this country'.[68] Elsewhere, it
has been argued that the campaign launched against Ceauşescu and his
policies is merely a pretext for an attack on Romania itself, the nation
as well as the state. The same writer claims that the disturbances in
Timişoara which marked the beginning of the end for Ceauşescu in 1989
were far from being a spontaneous explosion of popular anger and had
all the hallmarks of Hungarian involvement.[69] He was also critical of the
way in which Ceauşescu was killed on 25 December 1989, and suggested
that Ceauşescu's remains deserved to be in a national mausoleum just like
Franco's in Spain:

> Nicolae Ceauşescu was head of state for a quarter of a century, a period
> in which Romania registered so much progress! Why has Franco in Spain
> the right to a mausoleum and why do the Spanish people, including King
> Juan Carlos reckon that, leaving aside the conduct of the Franco dictator-
> ship, Franco never betrayed his country, just as Nicolae Ceauşescu never
> betrayed his?[70]

By contrast, politicians like Ceontea, and Gheorghe Dumitrascu of the
government party, were prepared to deny their opponents any legitimacy
on account of branding them as 'anti-national'. In 1992–3, fierce statements
were delivered, especially by the GRP, denouncing the opposition for being
a nest of traitors ready to sell the country to rapacious foreign interests.
A typical one appeared in *RM* of 7 May 1993 in which Corneliu Coposu,

president of the Democratic Convention was, along with colleagues, branded 'a traitor to the nation':

> We know only too well that foreign forces are behind them and that they allow themselves to be shamelessly used in order to Yugoslavise Romania. We invite theRomanian Information Service [successor to the Securitate] to bring to the public attention at an appropriate moment all their dossiers on what is a theme of national concern.

As for the Magyar HDFR, no accusation from Romanian chauvinists was too fantastic if it further damaged its reputation in the eyes of citizens lacking the information to make their own assessments. While the PRNU was seeking to rehabilitate aspects of the pre-1989 era, it did not hesitate to accuse the HDFR of promoting 'retrograde and bolshevik ideas . . . and the policy of the narrow-minded and paranoid proletarian internationalism'.[71] The idea of bargaining and compromise among different interest groups was alien to the PRNU when it denied the HDFR (between 1990 and 1992 the second largest party in parliament) basic legitimacy and demanded its unconditional surrender. When electoral challengers are seen as permanent enemies rather than as competitors with whom dialogue and even compromise are permissible, then the democratic arena becomes a battleground in which checks and balances have no meaning.

In Tirgu Mureş, the behaviour of both PRNU and NSF councillors after the 1992 local elections, showed a contemptuous attitude towards the democratic process. Outraged that the HDFR had won a narrow victory, they boycotted the town council, a move which effectively prevented it from functioning, since two-thirds of elected members needed to attend its first session for it to commence its activities. After elections for the post of mayor of Tirgu Mureş had to be refought on 24 May 1992, owing to the disqualification of the Hungarian victor, ultra-nationalists tried to use their presence on bodies overseeing the electoral process, to prevent another Hungarian challenger standing.[72] Eventually, the Stolojan government had to intervene to ensure that a proper contest was held; on a high 77.6 per cent turnout, the new HDFR candidate, Victor Nagy, received 56.6 per cent of the vote while the PRNU-led alliance fell below 40 per cent, a sign that many Romanians had spurned the nationalist appeal to vote along ethnic lines.

The failure of the PRNU to turn Tirgu Mureş into an electoral stronghold, despite its influence in the administration and the growing economic power which Vatra officials enjoyed as state assets were being sold off to local nationalists, showed the limits of chauvinist strength in the city of Vatra's birth. At the national level, this did not stop the PRNU from manipulating electoral laws in a bid to emasculate its reform-minded opponents; in May 1992 it opposed a law designed to allow state financing of parties, on the grounds that the state had more urgent spending requirements; the resultant blocking of funds to the insolvent Democratic Convention was a serious blow, but it hardly affected the PRNU, which had access to funds from banks and private companies established by sympathisers in Transylvania. The PRNU made one more pre-election bid to harm reformist prospects by pushing up the threshold by which an electoral alliance could enter parliament to an artificially high level, but here it was frustrated by other parties.[73]

Perhaps the incident which illustrated most clearly ultra-nationalist contempt for opposing viewpoints took place in the Romanian parliament on 27 May 1993. It involved Corneliu Vadim Tudor, by far the most uninhibited of ultra-nationalist deputies, who had delivered a speech in which he contrasted his own patriotism with that of Petre Roman who had passed over to the reformist opposition after twenty-one months as prime minister. Uproar ensued when Tudor argued that Roman was the son of a secret agent who had been a Soviet NKVD general whereas he, Tudor, had been the son of a worker who had been a wartime 'hero'.[74] Afterwards in the parliamentary corridor, when Aristide Dragomir, a member of Roman's party, remonstrated angrily with Tudor, the GRP leader called for the assistance of a member of the state security services who was acting as his unpaid bodyguard. Deputy Dragomir was then beaten unconscious in the lobby of parliament.[75]

This incident contained disturbing implications for Romanian democracy. It revealed collusion between members of the security services and extremist parties. Moreover, no disciplinary action was taken against the state employee seen assaulting a deputy in parliament; nor were opposition deputies able to persuade the parliamentary speaker to suspend Tudor or condemn his actions. Indeed, Vasile Vacaru, leader of the ruling party's parliamentary group, defended Tudor and demanded that the parliamentary immunity of the injured deputy and of Petre Roman should be lifted. He had described Roman as 'the moral author' of the whole incident since he had tried to interrupt Tudor's speech.[76]

The feeble reaction of office-holders charged with upholding correct standards of behaviour suggests that neither the guiding principles nor the specific procedures of democracy are understood by certain well-placed members of the Romanian political elite. Unfortunately, the opposition could not entirely exempt itself from responsibility for lowering standards of political behaviour, as was shown by the only serious breach of public order in the election campaign of September 1992.

On 12 September 1992, Gheorghe Funar was besieged inside Timişoara's Orthodox Cathedral by a crowd protesting against his presence in the city. Timişoara had frequently been denounced as a nest of anti-Romanian sentiment in the chauvinist press. Funar's visit occurred at a sensitive moment, days after an attack on Bishop Tökés in which Funar had declared: 'I hope that God will find a suitable punishment for the bishop, or else we will send him to jail after the election in order to give him a chance to reflect upon his deeds'.[77] After several hours of captivity, Funar was able to leave without mishap, but sympathisers claimed that he had narrowly escaped an attempt on his life and that the incident demonstrated the dangers facing anyone ready to defend Romania's national integrity. One of the ringleaders named by the Timişoara police chief was Francisc Baranyi, the local HDFR deputy.[78] The comment in *România Liberă* that 'the fact that the people of Timişoara utterly abhor the political discourse of Gheorghe Funar is no excuse for the aggression committed against him' indicated the opposition's dismay that Funar's standing had been boosted by such a crass incident.[79]

The attack on Funar increased the validity of his claim (for which no hard evidence was ever provided) that a paramilitary organisation existed among Hungarians and that several thousand had left Transylvania for camps to be trained in 'diversionary activities'.[80] It also enabled him to call for a severe law-and-order crackdown in the aftermath of the 27 September election and for the imposition of martial law in Hungarian areas.

The statements of PRNU spokesmen frequently offer an image of democracy in which those who can plausibly claim to interpret the will of a nominal majority deserve absolute power. Its conception of post-communist politics has little time for alternative points of view, competing power centres, or the devolution of power from the centre to self-governing localities. It is not the first time, either in Romania or in the wider east European context, that aspiring elites have been content to import the shell of pluralist forms while rejecting the values and conventions that made them practical propositions in the countries where they had earlier taken shape.

The strength of values from the communist period is shown by the PRNU's deep-seated reluctance to proceed towards a market economy unless the influence of existing power structures is safeguarded. In 1991, party spokesman Coriolan Bucur argued that only thirty per cent of state assets should be privatised in order not to endanger the strength of the state.[81] Cluj and Tirgu Mureş, the party's two main strongholds, had already shown that selective privatisation was possible which enabled favoured elements of the old party-state establishment to recycle themselves as aspiring entrepreneurs. Reports of Hungarians being dismissed from state concerns in both cities were frequently heard in 1992–3. A well-informed Romanian source who had worked in the Cluj mining research and design institute reported in 1992 that, of the 1,200 workers, 300 had been dismissed, seventy per cent of whom were Hungarians. Those who were particularly compliant to authority were retained by the director, who carried out this action shortly after being elected to Cluj city council for the PRNU.[82]

Funar also struck at Hungarian property-holders by declaring on 16 June 1992 that it was his intention to persuade parliament to transfer to the state all buildings whose owners lived in Hungary and who received rents from such properties. Since much of this kind of property was located in the city centre, the press referred to an attempt to 'nationalise' it.[83]

Ethnic Romanians have not been exempt from the ultra-nationalist drive to make political criteria the basis of holding state jobs in areas where they enjoy influence. Those who take practical steps to reduce ethnic polarisation are especially vulnerable, for they contradict the view that the gulf between Romanians and Hungarians with different cultural backgrounds is a natural and permanent one.

Mrs Smaranda Enache was one of the first Romanians to fall foul of ultra-nationalists as they strengthened their grip on public affairs. An advocate of good relations between the two main communities in Tirgu Mureş, she had enjoyed success in bringing young people closer together and had turned the Pro-Europe League into a forum where people concerned with the future welfare of the city could discuss practical problems. In March 1991, she lost her job as director of the Ariel puppet theatre after she had been summoned to the city's cultural centre to face an examination board consisting of three persons closely identified with Vatra. They ruled that Mrs Enache lacked the qualifications to remain in her post; at no time did they visit the theatre to talk to the staff or the management board, forty-one of whom signed a petition appealing against her dismissal (a gesture of defiance that involved no small risk for them). Nor was it felt necessary to take into account the overseas awards won by the theatre.[84]

An even better-known figure who fell foul of ascendant ultra-nationalists was Octavian Buracu, a geologist who had been president of Cluj county council in 1990. In 1993, not long after setting up the Association for Inter-Ethnic Dialogue in Romania, Buracu lost his job. Leading Vatra members were in charge of the newly-privatised institute where he worked, and Buracu was in no doubt that his public activities had resulted in his dismissal.[85]

By contrast, the nationalist Cluj historian, Stefan Paşcu, who had been a public defender of the Ceauşescu regime until its final moments, was swiftly rehabilitated after Funar took charge of Cluj. A man who had publicly endorsed the repressive measures used to repress demonstrations in Timişoara on the very day that Ceauşescu's security forces shot down thirty people in Cluj was given the freedom of the city in October 1992.[86] Funar has consistently downplayed the 21 December 1989 events in Cluj presumably because he does not regard them as helpful for the nationalist identity that he wishes to bestow on the city. He banned a 1992 rally organised by the democratic opposition due to be held on the anniversary of the shootings (this was one week after the military prosecutor's office had announced that criminal charges were being dropped against civic leaders and army officers stationed in Cluj at that time).[87]

In July 1993, after Calin Nemes, the leader of the anti-Ceauşescu demonstration in Cluj's Liberty Square, hanged himself, the city authorities even refused permission for him to be buried in the cemetery plot reserved for heroes of the revolution. These events reveal how marginalised the forces of civil society had become in a city where members of the former communist establishment had successfully regrouped to defend their own power and privileges.[88]

INTERNAL NATIONALIST RIVALRIES

Ultra-nationalists were capable of turning on each other and behaving in the vengeful way that was normally reserved for enemies of the true nationalist faith. Radu Ceontea and the editor of *România Mâre* fell out badly after a decision had been taken in June 1991 by Tudor to form the Greater Romania Party (GRP). Ceontea insisted that the place for Tudor and his supporters was inside the PRNU, otherwise the voters would be baffled by two competing parties. Tudor declared that 'we have not stolen any electors. Anyone who wanted to identify with the PRNU already had time enough to do so'.[89] Soon the level of invective between the two men rivalled that which Romanian nationalists normally reserved for their Hungarian foes. Tudor branded Ceontea 'the Hamlet from across the Carpathians' who was burdened with various complexes that made him unfit for leadership.[90] Meanwhile, a pro-PRNU daily in Tirgu Mureş chose to repeat the well-known claim that Tudor had been a Securitate agent, operating in the Romanian Union of Writers.[91] It was in vain that an *RM* reader wrote in appealing for reconciliation: 'just as we cannot have two flags with different colours, so we cannot have two different leaders in conflict with each other . . . Do not give the Hungarians the opportunity to rejoice at our weakness.'[92]

In 1992, Ceontea got into trouble within his own party. The Hungarian electoral success in Tirgu Mureş was a massive blow to his prestige. He soon faced a challenge from the Cluj wing which had steered the party to victory there. The Cluj leadership was dominated by hard-nosed professionals who had been adept at bargaining for resources and preferment in the Ceauşescu era. Proof that Ceontea was on the way out came in July 1992 when the Cluj wing drafted their mayor as the PRNU candidate for the presidential election. This manoeuvre violated the party's constitution, which had laid down that only the PRNU national council could take such a decision through a secret vote.[93]

Ceontea was replaced as party chairman by Funar in a hastily-convened conference held in Cluj in October 1992. Ioan Gavra, the new leader of the parliamentary party, issued a vicious personal attack on Ceontea that was fully in accord with the way in which hero-worshipped party chiefs of the communist period could suddenly become non-persons for whom no abusive epithet was too inadequate.[94] The wild charges directed at the founder of the PRNU by a former disciple like Gavra devalue the charges which ultra-nationalists level against Hungarians and reformist Romanians because the language is so uncannily similar. It suggests that those hurling the invective do not believe in the substance of their charges but are making them to advance whatever happens to be the goal of the moment.

The intellectuals who had formed the GRP enjoyed more success in retaining control of their creation. Tudor and the novelist Eugen Barbu had enjoyed a fruitful collaboration in the last decade of Ceauşescu's rule. The survival skills learnt then, and useful contacts with the most hardline elements of the state bureaucracy, ensured that their disgrace was short-lived. Members of the political establishment had reason to be grateful to Tudor: he expertly set out to discredit the anti-communist dissidents who were seeking their removal from public life. *România Mâre* ran a campaign against 'False Dissidents' who it argued had done nothing to merit special consideration. It drew on personal files which, could only have been pro-vided by well-connected state officials to argue that dissidents had made shabby compromises like everyone else in order to survive the rigours of life before 1989. Tudor eventually promoted himself as one of the few genuine dissidents in existence before 1989; he claimed to have resigned from the party in June 1989 disgusted at the decision to knock down a building associated with the national poet Eminescu.[95]

But Tudor's cult of personality inside the GRP led to high-level defections in 1992–4.[96] It is no coincidence that these upheavals occurred as the PRNU and GRP were sensing the possibility of gaining access to government itself following elections which left Iliescu loyalists dependent on the 'nationalist bloc' for their parliamentary survival. Clearly, the drive for power had proven too intoxicating for unity to be preserved within the ranks of ambitious nationalists.

THE SEPTEMBER 1992 ELECTIONS

The outcome of the first election fought under the 1991 constitution, while far from being a triumph for the PRNU, allowed it to enter the first division of Romanian politics. Funar's actions in Cluj had already turned him into a national celebrity. With some success, the PRNU overcame the image of being a single-issue movement concerned with the Hungarian danger. Funar was packaged as a serious contender who lost no opportunity to assert that he was out to win in the first round. He proposed a series of economic targets that could be met in his presidency. Agriculture would be revived in two years, industry relaunched in a maximum of three, and jobs would be found for all those prepared to work.[97] He was short on the specifics of implementing what would be a turnover of the Romanian economy as dramatic as that seen in Germany after 1945, but he refuted the widely-held view that Ceaușescu had saddled Romania within efficient industries, arguing instead that the country still had the opportunity to recapture markets it had once had in Third World countries.[98]

Funar was the only one of the presidential candidates who made categoric promises of short-term material benefits. In the classic populist mode, he argued that the formula whereby he had risen from village origins to acquire a university post and become mayor of a large city through hard work and belief in his own ability could be applied to a whole country if he was entrusted with its leadership for four years.

Funar polarised Romanians. For every one of those who saw him as a charlatan ready to destroy the country to satisfy his own ego, there were possibly as many again who regarded him as an honest and straightforward man who had not forgotten his origins.[99] In Transylvania, Funar was able to appeal to regional feeling in ways which might have been denounced as encouraging autonomy if taken up by any of his opponents. Despite insisting that Transylvania was an integral part of Romania, a sub-theme in Funar's campaign emphasised certain characteristics which distinguished it from the rest of the country, particularly the south.[100]

The presence of the GRP was far less obvious on the campaign trail in 1992. Its lack of a strong regional base became apparent in the winter 1992 local elections, where its best result had been in Bucharest with around seven per cent of the vote compared with 1.6 per cent nationally. Tudor had no chance of winning the presidential contest and was likely to run behind Funar, which would have been a blow to his vaulting ego. Accordingly, the GRP decided to support Ion Iliescu's bid for a second term on the grounds that he was to be trusted to defend Romania's national interest;[101] Iliescu, upon being asked to repudiate support from such an apparently tainted source, refused to disavow Tudor.

In the presidential election, Funar received 10.87 per cent of the vote, far behind the reformist challenger, Emil Constantinescu, on 31.24 per cent and Iliescu (the winner in the second round) on 47.34 per cent. Not even in Cluj county had Funar emerged on top, Constantinescu obtaining 40.53 per cent to Funar's 32.08 per cent. His candidacy had, however, boosted his own personal influence within the PRNU as well as establishing the party as an independent force ready to challenge the government party for power.

The PRNU's national vote rose from 2.12 per cent to 7.7 per cent. For the first time, it received seats (seven in all) in Moldavia and the south where before it had none. In Transylvania, it won seats in all but one of the region's electoral districts. The PRNU vote was fairly equally distributed between town and country: in Cluj city, the party got 30.6 per cent of the parliamentary vote compared with 29.5 per cent in the county as a whole. Overall, Transylvania was left with a party system markedly different from the rest of the country: two parties, the HDFR and the PRNU, got over half the votes (the Hungarian party being slightly ahead). As for the GRP, it got 3.89 per cent of the vote, which earned it twenty-two seats, thirteen of which were in Bucharest and the south. So, paradoxically, the party that had been the most vitriolic in its attacks on the Hungarians did best where there was no identifiable Hungarian presence. In the capital, its success was partly accountable for by the concentration there of groups drawn from the former Communist Party.

Joining the GRP in parliament was the Socialist Labour Party, which regarded the communist period as having been largely beneficial despite irregularities in the final years. It also argued that in the realm of culture the Romanian state had been more supportive of the Hungarian heritage than the Budapest government in Janos Kádár's time.[102] But its eighteen-member parliamentary group included nationalists who had actively promoted the most extreme forms of ethnocentrism. Adrian Păunescu, a leading promoter of the dictator's personality cult, was returned as the SLP Senator for Dolj in the province of Oltenia. Nostalgia for the Ceauşescu regime had been noted in the dictator's home province, where he had located much industry. In the Gorj electoral district, better known as the location of the Jiu Valley mining industry, the SLP picked up more seats. This was an indication, if any were necessary, of the sympathies of many of the miners who had stormed Bucharest at intervals in 1990–1 to seek revenge against those whom they perceived as threatening their own and the national welfare.

POST-ELECTORAL ADVANCES

Ultra-nationalist parties may only have won twelve per cent of the seats, but they held the initiative owing to the importance of these seats. The government party (still known by the acronym DNSF) held 117 out of 341 seats, which was far short of a secure majority. Lacklustre attempts were made to entice the reform parties into a coalition, but Iliescu refused to make any real concessions, which suggested that he was not interested in sharing power with his main rival. Instead, the new government, under

Nicolae Văcăroiu, a senior bureaucrat whose career had been in state planning, was dependent upon the ultra-nationalists for its survival. They had already paved the way for co-operation by endorsing Iliescu in the second round of the presidential election which he won on 11 October 1992 with 61.43 per cent of the vote. The government retained the backing of its allies even when it was assailed in June 1993 for planning to sell off a majority interest in the Romanian merchant fleet to a Greek businessman for a price that was seen as being disadvantageous to the Romanian state; nationalists, usually hyper-sensitive about anything that could be perceived as reducing economic independence, remained silent, but they swung behind the government after the head of a special anti-corruption unit had accused leading government officials of influence-peddling.[103] The GRP sought to blur the issue by mounting furious allegations of wholesale corruption against Petre Roman and his team of ministers when they had passed radical economic legislation in 1990–1. Iliescu did not conceal his complete estrangement from his former close ally, and there was no-one who could assail Petre Roman with the fiery rhetoric that Tudor brought to the task of political character assassination. However, Tudor may have overdone it by accusing the Democratic Party of being 'the first Jewish party in contemporary Romania' and its leader, Roman, of being a tool of the chief rabbi, Moses Rosen.[104] The anti-Semitism of the RM circle was embarrassing to a government looking for western respectability but the political usefulness of the chauvinists outweighed whatever disadvantages their unsavoury views provided for Iliescu and his team.

Ultra-nationalists were cheered by the neo-communist character of the ruling Party of Social Democracy in Romania (PSDR) which, despite its July 1993 name-change, was more than ever a party of patronage dominated by ex-communist officials. Appointments down to the most junior level were made on the basis of loyalty rather than ability (long gone being the days in 1990 when liberals with technical skills could be appointed to important public posts).[105] Not expecting to offer their services for free, nationalists expected a share of the spoils and got it. The PRNU acquired increasing control over government appointments in Transylvania, and Funar enjoyed an increasingly free hand in Cluj. The Bucharest-appointed Cluj county prefect was reduced to a cipher, the primacy of local over central power being most unusual in the Balkan context. Until Funar's emergence, the determination of the centre to regulate local government down to a very minute level had been one of the constants of Romanian political life irrespective of what kind of regime was in charge. The PRNU had turned this convention on its head due to holding the balance of power: a local luminary like the Cluj Vatra chief, Petru Forna claimed, and was given, the Romanian embassy in Vienna; in January 1993, Paul Everac, a dramatist 'whose literary output served the decision-makers of the RCP in the time of Ceauşescu', was appointed head of Romanian television.[106]

Everac soon became famous for regular weekend broadcasts in which he assailed western influences in Romania from blue jeans to computers and applauded Ceauşescu's mammoth 'House of the Republic'.[107] Soon, he restricted the frequency with which a television series called 'Sorrowful Memories' was broadcast, one which had carried out in-depth interviews with survivors of communist repression, offering a very different account from the sanitised version to be found in *RM*. Not only did the parliamentary speeches of Corneliu Vadim Tudor receive considerable television exposure in 1993, but also the émigré businessman, Iosif Constantin Dragan, who had Iron Guard links and access to Ceauşescu, was the subject of a flattering television interview in June 1993.[108]

Iliescu's need to control the state electronic media had grown as his political base shrunk as a result of an inconclusive election result and worsening economic news. The state's need to monitor the cultural world was not as urgent but, presumably as a result of pressure from nationalist intellectuals, the ministry of culture swung from being one of the most refreshingly open government departments during the ministerial tenure of philosopher Andrei Plesu in 1990–1 to one where nationalist hardliners enjoyed mounting influence.

THE CARITAS AFFAIR

The GRP had good cause to be satisfied with having evolved from being intellectual pariahs to intellectual power-brokers. Unmistakeable signs that the PRNU was shedding its subsidiary role came in 1993 when it energetically promoted a pyramid-savings operation called Caritas, which enabled investors to obtain an eightfold return on their money within three months. An estimated 3–4,000,000 Romanians – a fifth of the adult population – enrolled in the scheme, parting with around one billion dollars which was equivalent to half of all state spending in 1993.[109] The lack of attractive investment rates from the banks and the ravages of inflation, which had reached 314 per cent for the first nine months of 1993, meant that there was a huge amount of personal capital looking for a quick return.

The political importance of Caritas stemmed from the decision to base it in Funar's stronghold of Cluj. Ioan Stoica, the mastermind behind the scheme, was offered premises at a nominal rate by Funar, who welcomed the publicity which it brought him during a period with no elections in prospect. The influx of people and investment to Cluj, attracted by Caritas, made it the chief news-making centre for Romania during much of 1993. Funar also inevitably capitalised upon the fact that his city was bidding to become the most prosperous in the country with a growing number of

'Caritas millionaires' and outward signs of wealth reflected by rising car sales, a steep rise in house prices, and the sudden popularity of holidays to exotic destinations.[110] These signs of the good life in a depression-ridden country were a boon to any politician who planned in the future to convince a sceptical electorate that he was better able than his rivals to promote good economic times. Meanwhile, the amount of revenue flowing into the city's coffers as a result of Caritas's success gave Funar access to funds which counterparts in other cities lacked.[111]

The response of the state authorities to the Caritas affair was confused. Still in the throes of institutional rebuilding and reforming its laws, Romania had no legislation to protect consumers, or indeed the state itself, from a scheme into which hopeful investors had channelled a large part of the country's liquid assets before Caritas started to default on repayments in October 1993. Government inaction reinforced the image of Romania as 'a soft state' whose leading officials had only the shakiest grasp of long-term planning or crisis management. When Adrian Năstase, one of the few heavyweights in the ruling party, visited Cluj in October 1993, he urged the PRNU to distance itself from Caritas. However, the PRNU's Ioan Gavra warned of social turbulence in which several million people could descend on the streets if the state moved against Caritas.[112]

The ability of the PRNU to benefit electorally from Caritas was shown in July 1993 when it swept to victory in a by-election held in the mining centre of Petrosani after its candidate had promised to see what could be done about setting up a branch of Caritas among the 60,000 miners of the politically influential Jiu valley. In August, Mayor Funar offered to act as a mediator between the government and the miners, who wanted a huge pay increase on top of earlier ones. Any alliance between the miners' leader Miron Cosma and Funar was bound to generate unease in government circles, since both men had succeeded in creating autonomous power centres where Bucharest's reach did not extend.

Appeals to ethnic loyalties or threats directed against national foes were conspicious by their absence in the midst of the Caritas affair. Its proponents had an interest in shielding the game from too much controversy. It needed to appeal to the lowest common denominator of the most people, a route often undertaken by populist movements with politically vague programmes. With Hungarians joining Romanians in the search for prosperity via Caritas, it was noticeable that the heat went out of inter-ethnic tension. The number of provocative statements made by Funar fell in 1993 as he admitted that inter-ethnic relations were going though a calm phase.[113] This was to his advantage, since it is doubtful if the PRNU will prevail by emphasising nationalist values and threats to them largely to the exclusion of everything else. It needs to appeal to voters who are unlikely to make their electoral choices on ethnic grounds alone by relying on other criteria, and Caritas enabled it to do this up until near the end of 1993.

Caritas received the most enthusiastic response from city-and town-dwellers of rural origins. The benevolent, fatherly image projected by Stoica, its proprietor, was reassuring to people in a still unfamiliar urban environment, some of whom found the image of a traditional patron appealing. The appeal to material interest was combined with a rhetoric of social justice and evocative religious rhetoric meant to influence simple, God-fearing people. The religious motif has often been exploited by Vatra and the PRNU, giving its nationalism an emotional depth which that of Ceauşescu could not match.

In a land of low expectation, the failure of many small investors to recoup their winnings when Caritas ran out of funds did not result in widely-predicted violence. Some investors had a protective attitude towards Caritas even when it had left them insolvent, and there were far more people ready to blame the government, the central bank or the media rather than 'Papa Stoica'. Here was evidence of popular goodwill towards a populist movement even where it had resulted in personal economic loss. It was a reassuring sign for Funar that there were many citizens prepared to judge him not on his record as an economic housekeeper whether in Cluj or on a wider stage, but on his ability to satisfy the collective emotional needs of a large swathe of the population susceptible to nationalist appeals.

The Romanian press criticised Caritas for offering poorly-educated citizens the prospect of wealth without working for it, reinforcing a sense of personal dependence and sapping individual initiative. Those press outlets which saw Caritas as an irrational phenomenon soon became scapegoats blamed for the shortcomings of a scheme which needed to attract investors at a rate unable to be sustained by the adult Romanian population in order to remain feasible.

Perhaps the most surprising critic of Caritas was the GRP leader, Tudor. He denounced it as 'a vicious and unhealthy game' and criticised Funar for promoting it (no member of the PSDR daring to be as forthright).[114] As an expert in the art of manipulating people's emotions, he was in the frustrating role of being a mere spectator as the Caritas phenomenon took off. It brought to the fore PRNU-GRP differences, the GRP preferring to rely on the protection of the most hardline elements of the state bureaucracy rather than make a bid for power in its own right. Given its close ties with the former Securitate, it would not be an exaggeration to compare it with 'the police parties' which the Czarist authorities in Russia promoted in order to prevent a genuine popular challenge to absolutist rule from

emerging. Meanwhile, the PRNU and Vatra comprised a much broader segment of the pre-1989 elite at provincial level and were less compromised
politically than Tudor and his clique.

CONCLUSION

To expunge the malign effects of Ceauşescuism from the Romanian body
politic would probably have required something akin to the process of
de-Nazification seen in post-war West Germany. Even then, it is unlikely
that it would have been completely successful. Ceauşescuism was far from
being a complete aberration: its emphasis upon one-man rule, xenophobia
and corrupt authoritarian practices had roots deep in the Romanian past.

Since 1990, the new Romanian leadership has included leaders who
held high office in the Ceauşescu era. But the most authentic heirs of
the national communist era are the ultra-nationalist parties which allege
numerous conspiracies against the country and which insist that multiple
threats to Romania's national integrity can only be repulsed by suspending
normal political rules and forming a united front behind individuals and
social forces with a proven record of standing up for national values.

Ultra-nationalists emerged as important players in Romania's qualified
democracy first at regional level and then nationally. Much attention has
been paid to the circumstances in which Vatra Românească and the PRNU
first emerged and to the contributory role of the government, the Securitate
and the state media. But there has perhaps been too much emphasis upon
the manipulative role of the post-Ceauşescu state, which overlooks the
fact that some sort of nationalist restoration was probably unavoidable. In
Transylvania, there was an administrative and technocratic elite which in
order to hold on to its privileges was likely to argue that any threat to its core
interests was also a threat to the Romanian nation as a whole. Secondly,
Ceauşescu's policy of breakneck industrialisation had created a large social
constituency receptive to a nationalist appeal. Many, though by no means
all, peasant migrants to the city could be persuaded that the assertiveness
of the Hungarian minority posed an economic threat to them and that they
would be the ones to fare worst of all if there was an attempt to detach
Transylvania from Romania.

Post-1989 Romania is a clear example of how nationalism can play
an important role in fostering a sense of solidarity even where consensus
around a specific political agenda and set of goals is lacking. Ultra-
nationalists were recruited to fashion new symbols of national legitimacy as
the 1989 revolution was quickly discarded as an event which could enable
the new leadership to demonstrate its fitness to rule.

The Ceauşescu years had shown the importance of symbols and
carefully-choreographed political rites for rulers who wished to provide

a regime deficient in economic success with an aura of legitimacy and permanence. The emphasis upon nationalist commemorations was a sign that Iliescu and those around him had taken to heart Machiavelli's advice to rulers 'to keep the people occupied with festivals and shows'.[115] But the pride of place given to nationalism in the state-dominated political culture that was springing up may have been an unconscious admission by the new political establishment that the nation entrusted to their care was a weak and troubled one; otherwise, less attention would have been paid to bolstering it in symbolic ways when there were more pressing political tasks waiting to be accomplished.

While nationalist intellectuals found a comfortable niche in Romania's new nationalist democracy, care was also taken to satisfy the economic aspirations of the technocrats and administrators who had promoted the Romanian nationalist upsurge in Transylvania. Many office-holders benefited from the way in which the sale of state assets was carried out on a discretionary basis in the cities of Cluj and Tirgu Mureş. But if President Iliescu had hoped that ultra-nationalists would be content with auxiliary roles as cultural or economic power-brokers in Transylvania, he was to be disappointed.

Those belonging to the nationalist bloc have shown mounting political ambitions as the government party has signally failed to extricate the country from a deep economic depression or to show that it is anything other than a personal platform for the president. The rise to power of ultra-nationalist counterparts in Serbia, Croatia and Slovakia, and the tendency of leaders like Walesa in Poland and Klaus in the Czech Republic to strike increasingly nationalistic poses, made Romanian ultra-nationalists seem less anachronistic and probably reduced any reticence among them about promoting their own nationalist agenda. Pro-Ceauşescu sentiments (which were described as slanderous attacks when ascribed to Vatra in 1990) have been aired with growing pride by some prominent figures like Gheorghe Funar. There have been growing calls that Romania should reject foreign models of political and economic change and pursue a culturally-specific path based on indigenous Romanian traditions and values.

Twelve to fifteen per cent of the electorate endorsed ultra-nationalists in the 1992 election. The figure would have been higher if Iliescu had not shielded ordinary citizens from some of the effects of market-led economic changes, not least by retaining significant elements of economic state control. In 1992–3, boundaries between the ruling party and ultra-nationalist ones became increasingly fluid as well-known chauvinists were given high-profile jobs in sensitive areas. Iliescu was still careful about playing a balancing role by distancing himself from the nationalist right on some issues, such as anti-Semitism. But, in his absence, there would be little to stop significant elements of the governing party from coalescing with ultra-nationalists and creating a new ethnocentric (and anti-democratic) majority.

Given the choice of western-style reformers or nationalist xenophobes as his successors, all available evidence suggests that Ion Iliescu would prefer the latter, as he would have less to fear from investigations into controversial aspects of his acquisition and consolidation of power in 1989–90. He has shown his preferences by allowing ultra-nationalists important leverage within the media, certain government ministries, and parts of the education system and the armed forces. The Caritas phenomenon of 1992–3 showed just how far nationalists were capable of generating a political momentum of their own. It revealed strong support for populist nationalism among former peasants whose massive influx into the towns (spurred by ill-planned industrialisation schemes) has led to their partial 'ruralisation' with the values and norms of traditional rural culture influencing city life.

In its chief power centre, Cluj, the PRNU has been hard at work devising nationalist rituals and identifying threats to national security in the actions of the Hungarian party in the hope that this will boost popular enthusiasm for it. If Mayor Funar is successful in creating a set of values and an image of the nation able to make those peasants feeling uneasy with city life aware of where they belong, he will have accomplished one of the key tasks of any nationalist movement wanting to acquire political relevance.

Funar has left himself little time to deal with the appalling infrastructural problems faced by Cluj; his political manifesto in the 1992 election revealed that his economic programme consisted largely of platitudes. But success in the material sphere is not crucial for the well-being of a nationalist leader who has achieved power by mobilising ancestral loyalties or contemporary ethnic rivalries.

The discourse of the local nationalists who took charge of Cluj in 1992 was often absorbed in a world of fantasy populated by mythic native heroes as well as alien dragons that needed to be driven out; the latter assume unlikely forms such as Hungarian educators, Dutch local government officials, and philanthropists from the Open Society Fund. The rise of nationalism in Cluj shows how ordinary citizens who were not preoccupied in their daily lives with the themes on the nationalist agenda can still become pawns of individuals alienated from the values of democracy. Currently, Romania, along with eastern Europe in general is going through economic and political upheavals resulting in plunging living standards and even personal ruin for millions of people. The crisis is a generalised one, being felt in the economic sphere as well as in politics, and in society. When western and central Europe experienced a crisis of values and material well-being on a similar scale at the end of the First World War, it enabled movements with a fundamentalist view of the world to prosper mightily.

These ideologies have had more influence on people's consciousness in the eastern half of the continent than democracy or liberalism. Combined with an often virulent nationalism arising from group rivalries or the manipulation of past ethnic disputes, the result has been to make post-communist eastern Europe vulnerable to fresh authoritarian power-grabs. The nature and extent of the authoritarian experience also means that a sizeable proportion of the population has become accustomed to the conformity of an authoritarian state. An exclusive ideology like ultra-nationalism can provide an escape from the risks and complicated rules of inhabiting a free society. The fact that Cluj was the first east European city outside the Yugoslav war zone to elect a civic leader who argued openly that too much freedom was a dangerous thing reveals the extent to which its inhabitants had been subject to totalitarian indoctrination and the hold that it had acquired on susceptible minds.

In Romania, the race between those committed to a democratic, liberal and neighbourly path and those wedded to nationalist, centralist and authoritarian precepts is well on its way. Chauvinists have benefited from the nationalist conditioning to which much of the population was subjected before 1989 and from the backing of important sections of the Iliescu state. Newspapers like *România Mâre* and *Europa*, which in 1991–2 enjoyed a combined print-run approaching 1,000,000 copies, have propagated national-communist views with more verbal extremism than was permitted before 1989.[116] Their capacity for poisoning the atmosphere by creating nationalist panics in parliament or in ethnically-mixed areas generates confusion that may make anti-democratic solutions increasingly tempting for weary citizens.

In 1994–5 ultra-nationalists made striking political gains, starting with the hounding from office of the defence minister, General Nicolae Spiroiu, in March 1994. His political liberalism and desire to maintain inter-ethnic peace made him anathema to Vadim Tudor who launched a press campaign against him. Spiroiu was demoted to being Romania's representative at NATO headquarters in Brussels, his old job going to a civilian. The government made much play of the defence ministry being in civilian hands, claiming that it amounted to a strengthening of the democratic process. However, it was not an untypical exercise in simulation in which a cosmetic measure of liberalisation in fact concealed a victory for authoritarian forces.

Worse was to follow. A government reshuffle in August 1994 saw two cabinet posts allocated to the PRNU. Then, on 20 January 1995, the ultra-nationalist parties signed a pact of co-operation with the government. The ruling party chairman, Oliviu Gherman, made the nonsensical statement that the pact with parties that had openly praised the dictatorship was 'an expression of the democratic nature of Romania's political life and it meets the increasing demands of contemporary European life for . . . an approach consistent with the highest international standards'. In fact, it was precisely owing to the West's declining concern with what political standards existed in Romania that such a pact was possible. Western disinterest also enabled President Iliescu to lavish praise on Vatra as it celebrated its fifth anniversary in February 1995. The President saw the movement that was the first to rehabilitate chauvinism as 'an element of balance . . . acquiring an important place in the public conscience owing to the force of its civic and social message.' The language of politics has become thoroughly debased when such praise can be lavished on a movement so destructive, not least to genuine Romanian patriotism. One thing is clear, as nervous Hungarians responded by delaring the 'self-determination of local communities': ultra-nationalists are unlikely to rest content with the political gains which they have made in the early 1990s. If political power can be transferred to them via the ballot-box or by other means, then they will not be slow in seizing their advantage.

NOTES

1. Geron Pilon, *The Bloody Flag*, p. 73.
2. Paul Hockenos reckons that several dozen may have been killed. See his *Free to Hate: The Rise of the Right in Post-Communist Eastern Europe*, Routledge, London 1993, p. 179.
3. Budapest home service, 24 March 1990, SWB EE/0723 B/6 (27 March 1990).
4. *Romania: A Case of Dynastic Communism*, p. 77.
5. Biographical details of the 1990–1 Vatra leadership were contained in NU, No. 41 (11 February 1991), where these allegations were raised. Serious allegations of professional misconduct against Dr Zeno Opris, a gynaecologist who succeeded Radu Ceontea as Vatra's president in June 1991, were contained in the independent weekly *Gazeta de Mureş*, Vol. 1, No. 25 (25 November 1991), which published correspondence sent by a senior medical colleague to the Prefect of Mureş County concerning Dr Opris's medical conduct. There is no record of these allegations being taken up, nor of any action being taken against the newspaper for airing them.
6. Gilberg, *Nationalism and Communism*, p. 180.
7. Trond Gilberg, 'Romanians and Democratic Values: Socialization After Communism', in Nelson (ed.), *Romania . . .*p. 86.
8. Quoted by Hockenos, *In These Times* (24 July 1991).
9. Schöpflin, 'Rumanian Nationalism', p. 84.
10. NU, No. 41 (11 February 1991).
11. *Adevârul de Cluj* (27 December 1990).
12. Rompres, 20 March 1990, SWB EE/0720 B/3 (23 March 1990).
13. Hungarian militia members were also killed, but they are rarely mentioned. The parliamentary commission investigating the Tirgu Mureş events found that both ethnic Romanians and Hungarians from the Interior Ministry police

had been killed on or after 26 December. See Rompres, 23 January 1990, SWB EE/0980 B/17 (26 January 1990).

14. Rompres, 12 May 1991, SWB EE/1075 B/9 (18 May 1991).
15. *NU* (11–18 February 1991).
16. *Natiunea*, No. 26 (1991).
17. Watts, 'The Romanian Army . . .', in Nelson (ed.), *Romania After Tyranny*, p. 117.
18. *Desteapta-Te Romane* (1991).
19. Rompres, 7 May 1990, SWB EE/0759 B/8 (9 May 1990).
20. Deletant, 'Vatra . . .', p. 30.
21. Budapest home service, 3 June 1991, SWB EE/1093 B/7 (8 June 1991); Budapest home service, 29 August 1990, SWB EE/0857 B/8 (31 August 1990).
22. *IRSOP* poll quoted in Michael Shafir, 'Growing Political Extremism in Romania', *RFE-RL Research Report*, Vol. 2, No. 14 (2 April 1993), p. 18.
23. Rompres, 7 May 1990, SWB EE/0759 B/8 (9 May 1990).
24. *NU* (11–18 February 1991).
25. Rompres, 4 May 1993, SWB EE/1681 B/7 (6 May 1993).
26. *22* (10 November 1993) published Senator Suian's proposals under the title 'The Road to Dictatorship'.
27. Information about Cheler's background is contained in *NU*, No. 82 (8 July 1992).
28. Watts in Nelson, op. cit., pp. 110, 114.
29. *Baricada* (8 January 1991).
30. Rompres, 19 March 1990, SWB EE/0719 B/6 (22 March 1990).
31. Deletant, op. cit., p. 33.
32. Rompres, 21 October 1991, SWB EE/121 B/6 (26 October 1991).
33. Rompres, 6 February 1991, SWB EE/0994, B/12 (12 February 1991).
34. Rompres, 11 April 1991, SWB EE/1047 B/12 (16 April 1991).
35. Rompres, 25 August 1993, SWB EE/1775 B/5 (24 August 1993).
36. Budapest home service, 3 June 1991, SWB EE/1093 B/7 (8 June 1991).
37. *Puntea*, 45 (April-May 1992).
38. Rompres, 27 October 1992, SWB EE/15424 B/17 (29 October 1992); and Hungarian radio, 26 February 1993, SWB EE/1627 B/6 (3 March 1993).
39. Hungarian radio SWB EE/1591 B/9 (20 January 1993).
40. Rompres, 29 March 1993, SWB EE/1651 B/7 (31 March 1993).
41. Hungarian radio, 3 May 1993, SWB EE/ 1680 B/11 (5 May 1993).
42. See Gallagher, 'Ethnic Tension in Cluj', *RFE-RL Research Report*, Vol. 2, No. 9 (26 February 1993), p. 28.
43. For the historical background to the controversy, see *Gazeta de Mureş* (7 December 1992).
44. *Expres* (14 December 1990).
45. Budapest radio, 1 February 1993, SWB EE/1603 B/13 (3 February 1993).
46. *România Mâre* (25 October 1991).
47. Details provided in *Evenimentul Zilei* (16 March 1993).
48. *România Mâre* (25 October 1991).
49. Romanian radio, 7 March 1993, SWB EE/1633 B/13 (10 March 1993).
50. Rompres, 31 March 1990, SWB EE/0731 B/12 (5 April 1990).
51. *Adevârul de Cluj* (19 July 1991).
52. Rompres, 7 August 1992, SWB EE/1458 B/12 (13 August 1992).
53. Rompres, 12 October, 1991, SWB EE/1204 B/8 (16 October 1991).

54. Hungarian radio, 10 May 1992, SWB EE/1379 B/17 (13 May 19 92).
55. Rompres, 31 May 1993, SWB EE/1709 B/12 (8 June 1993).
56. Shafir, 'Romanian Prime Minister . . .', p. 19.
57. *22* (4 March 1993).
58. *GM Transilvan* (4 May 1993).
59. *Evenimentul Zilei* (16 March 1993).
60. *NU*, No. 41 (11 February 1991).
61. Shafir, 'Transylvanian Lights . . .', p. 30.
62. *Tribuna Ardealului* (1 May 1992).
63. *Tribuna Ardealului* (5 May 1992).
64. Adrian Marino, a well-known Cluj intellectual and one of the founders of the Democratic Anti-Totalitarian Forum, outlined the role of the Foreign Ministry and the local media in smoothing Funar's rise in an interview to the Bucharest daily, *Cotidiánul*, on 19 March 1992.
65. Favourable assessments of Ceauşescu by Funar were given in interviews carried by *22* (24 April 1992), *NU* (22 July 1992), and *Baricada* (13 July 1992). The most considered statement on Ceauşescu, which was carried in *Baricada*, included some elements of criticism, but they did not appear to tarnish his overall image as 'a good Romanian':

> The things achieved in the 'Golden Epoch' or the 'Epoch of Ceauşescu' were ones that the Romanian people are proud of today. They are things which it was not easy for the Romanian people to accomplish in a short period. Unfortunately as a dictator who humiliated the Romanian people in various ways: hunger, human rights, promoting wrong values, closing frontiers, cold dwellings. But from the perspective of investment, of buildings, of attitudes relating to independence and sovereignty, he was able to be admired in my view as a good Romanian.

66. *22* (18 September 1992).
67. Shafir in Joseph Held (ed.), *Democracy and Right-Wing Politics in Eastern Europe in the 1990s*, Columbia University Press, Boulder CO and New York 1993, p. 153.
68. *România Mâre* (6 November 1992).
69. Mihai Ungheanu, *Natiunea* (November 1991); for the Hungarian claim, see *România Mâre* (13 December 1992). In July 1994, a report issued by the Romanian Information Service (successor to the Securitate) claimed that the forces of 'Hungarian irredentism' had played a role in the 1989 events; by now, Ungheanu was a member of the government which controlled the RIS. See Rompres, Bucharest, 25 July 1994, SWB EE/2057 B/6 (26 July 1994).
70. *România Mâre* (13 December 1992).
71. Romanian radio, 23 July 1992, SWB EE/1443 B/16 (27 July 1992).
72. The mayor had been disqualified after discrepancies had been found in the list of signatures supporting his candidature.
73. Romanian radio, 17 May 1992, SWB EE/1386 B/12 (21 May 1992).
74. Shafir, 'Romania: The Rechristening . . .', p. 27.
75. ARPRESS, Selective Daily Bulletin, 674 (28 May 1993).
76. See n. 74.
77. *România Liberă International*, No. 27 (25 September 1992).
78. *Mesagerul Transilvan* (17 September 1992).
79. *România Liberă International*, No. 27 (25 September 1992).

80. *Tinerama* (18 September 1992).
81. Rompres, 30 May 1991, SWB EE/1093 B/11 (8 June 1991).
82. Private source.
83. Hungarian state radio, 12 June 1992, SWB EE/1410 B/13 (18 June 1992).
84. Interview with Mrs Smaranda Enache, July 1991. See also Tom Gallagher, 'Romania: A Democrat Under Fire', *END News* (Autumn 1991).
85. *GM, Saptaminal Transilvan* (19 July 1993).
86. *Adevârul de Cluj* (16 January 1990).
87. Rompres, 11 December 1992, SWB EE/1570 B/11 (22 December 1992).
88. Transstar Press, Cluj, July 1993 report.
89. *RM* (7 February 1992).
90. *RM* (25 October 1991).
91. *Cuvîntul Liber* (3 October 1991). See also *Expres* (30 October 1991).
92. *RM* (24 January 1992).
93. *Tribuna Ardealului* (28 August 1993).
94. For details, see *România Liberă International* (15 October 1992); ARPRESS, Selected Daily Bulletin (6 October 1992).
95. *Politica* (26 February 1993).
96. In February 1993, Ion Hristu, a GRP deputy, had been expelled for criticising a style of leadership that 'had transformed each party member into the leader's personal footman': ARPRESS, Selected Daily Bulletin, 585 (6 February 1993). Months earlier, Radu Theodoru, the GRP's vice-president, had withdrawn from the party accusing Tudor of practising dictatorship, as well as many other sins: ARPRESS, Selected Daily Bulletin, 529 (26 November 1992).
97. *22* (25 September 1992).
98. *România Liberă International*, No. 27 (25 September 1992).
99. *22* (25 September 1992).
100. *Cuvîntul* (15 September 1992).
101. *RM* (4 September 1992).
102. *Socialistul* (23 September 1992).
103. Dan Ionescu, 'Romanian Corruption Scandal Implicates Top Officials', *RFE-RL Research Report*, Vol. 2, No. 30 (23 July 1993), pp. 23–4, 28.
104. ARPRESS, Selected Daily Bulletin, 688 (14 June 1993).
105. *The Economist* (18 December 1993).
106. *Cuvîntul* (2 February 1993).
107. ARPRESS, Selected Daily Bulletin, 732 (2 August 1993).
108. ARPRESS, Selected Daily Bulletin, 693 (18 June 1993).
109. *The Economist* (18 December 1993).
110. Adrian Bridge, *The Independent* (20 October 1993); Alfonso Rojo, *El País* (17 October 1993).
111. *România Liberă* (12 November 1993).
112. *Cuvîntul* (26 October 1993).
113. Information from Carol Harsan of Transstar Press, Cluj.
114. *Tineretul Liber* (7 November 1993).
115. David Kertzer, *Ritual, Politics and Power*, Yale University Press, New Haven CT and London 1988, p. 181.
116. *22* (4 April 1993).

Romania Five Years On

In 1989–90, hope returned to Romania. There appeared to be a possibility that the country would break free of the recurring cycles of unrepresentative government which had been the norm since independence, a period in which there had been regression from oligarchical rule to totalitarian dictatorship. The popular uprising at the end of 1989 offered grounds for believing that Romanians, at least in the cities, were overcoming their submissive mentality and that the gulf between state and society might be overcome. Early co-operation with Hungary suggested that frontiers between neighbouring states would also be less restrictive, and the cooperation between majority and minority in ousting the dictator suggested that Romanian-Hungarian relations were not as damaged as many had thought.

But the legacy of the communist era proved strong enough to slam shut the Romanian window of opportunity before the winter of 1989–90 was even over. Multi-ethnic political alliances failed to materialise except in the city of Timisoara. Mutual suspicion and sensitivity became more noticeable than a receptivity to different points of view and a capacity for dialogue. The climate of suspicion and frenetic competition for limited resources that had grown up under communism created a sense of social atomisation which well-placed officials in the state administration at national and local level were able to exploit so as to manage change on their own limited agenda.

Tirgu Mureş was where the optimism that Romania was capable of escaping from the vortex of ethnic strife was shattered in March 1990. But there has been an unexpected twist in the story of that city in the first half of the 1990s. Despite strenuous efforts being made to block a Hungarian ethnic from being elected mayor, a moderate HDFR member, Victory Nagy, was elected in May 1992; after the previous mayoral election had been declared null and void on a technicality, there had been an attempt to prevent any HDFR candidate from standing. It had taken the intervention of Premier Stolojan to make the contest an open and free one. The PRNU-dominated

Stolojan to make the contest an open and free one. The PRNU-dominated alliance received less than forty per cent of the vote on a seventy per cent turnout, a sign that a not insignificant number of ethnic Romanians had spurned the nationalist appeal to vote along ethnic lines. But it would take a year before the Mureş county council was able to convene: PRNU and pro-government councillors took advantage of a law requiring two-thirds of newly-elected members to attend a council's first session in order for it to commence its activities, by boycotting the council. It was only in February 1993, after four previous attempts, that enough members turned up for the council to convene.

The outcome of the protracted electoral struggle in Tirgu Mureş was a small victory for the forces of reason against a background of escalating nationalist tension both within and beyond Romania's borders. It showed that the advance of extreme nationalism being witnessed in Cluj was not inexorable.

Overall, it may be the case that the only real chance that forces untarnished by the communist era, or else the remnants of the historic parties, had of playing a directing role after 1989 might have arisen if the transition away from Marxism-Leninism had been externally driven. Foreign intervention would only have been remotely likely if Ceauşescu loyalists had waged stiffer resistance against their opponents, leading to a state of civil war. But this was always a distant prospect, and the emergence of the National Salvation Front reflected the balance of forces in the country: only ex-communist insiders around Iliescu and Roman could claim to be familiar with the workings of the state; they showed that they knew how to appeal to popular psychology; and they were able to acquire control over the security forces.[1]

Critics have described the NSF as 'neo-communist', but this description may be of limited usefulness; it should be recalled that before Ceauşescu turned the Romanian Communist Party into his personal instrument,it often appeared to stand less for ideology and more for the advancement of well-placed elements at local and national level who could exploit the ruling system for their own sectional ends. Once it was clear that liberal democrats were not prepared to join a platform of national unity, Iliescu did not hesitate to marginalise them. The tradition whereby the state became a source of private benefit for those in charge of it, re-emerged in the 1990s, especially as state assets began to be privatised under doubtful criteria. The NSF chose to monopolise resources and offices in its gift right down to village level. It seems to have inherited the view prevalent under communism that the dictates of political survival require power to be monopolised by a tight-knit group conforming to a restricted political agenda. Staunch conservatives whose political careers were shaped during the authoritarian era have modified the political system to allow important elements of pluralism such as a free press, competitive elections and a lifting of isolation. But many of their actions and statements suggest that they are reluctant democrats who have bowed to prevailing circumstances rather than voluntarily dropping authoritarian behaviour and embracing pluralism.

Against such a background, a case could be made for describing the NSF as essentially a non-ideological grouping which had emerged from the party apparatus with the aim of protecting a set of caste interests in new conditions. Those leading the NSF were motivated by a desire for survival which enabled them to secure the loyalties of political functionaries used to being directed from above. The requirements of survival, rather than any deep-seated loyalty to the communist system which Iliescu publicly admitted had been a failed experiment, helps to explain important features of NSF behaviour. Thus, the NSF's desire to retain a political monopoly reflects deep-seated trends in political history. Henry Roberts, who in 1946 talked of 'the unbroken continuity of Rumanian policy, which was not only in the hands of a definite caste, but which in many essential respects was altogether the exclusive business of a few privileged families' could not have predicted the 'socialism in one family' era of the Ceauşescus, but he was aware of the long-term character of Romanian government.[2]

As Romania has lurched from fragile and inadequate democratic rule to long periods of dictatorship, most citizens seem to have grown very sceptical about the ability of political institutions to improve their lives. This means that political expectations are low, which can be a boon in a transition process where rulers can offer few economic rewards in the short term. However, it also means that many citizens may be predisposed to believe in personalities as agents of salvation rather than parties or programmes. The name assumed by Ceauşescu's successors, the National Salvation Front, perhaps revealed that their instinct was to appeal to voters on populist grounds rather than on more orthodox criteria. 'Salvation' was not dropped from the title until July 1993, when the party was renamed the Party of Romanian Social Democracy.

Iliescu lacks most of the hallmarks of a populist leader but he has created a political system that can easily be exploited by demagogues, who are plentiful in the nationalist camp. Clearly, Romania is not moving in the direction of the west European political systems, where adherence to the rule of law and respect for civil society and individual rights are combined with encouragement for private economic enterprise and transnational co-operation. Dozens of NGOs and EU delegations have arrived in Romania since 1989 to promote aspects of west European governance. Not one such delegation has come from Latin America, but Romania seems to be adopting a brand of politics not so different from that seen in parts of Latin

America. A large rural population hungry for land and an even larger urban proletariat uprooted from the countryside gives Romania a clear affinity with countries like Brazil today and Argentina in the Peronist era. The state regulates economic activity, and a primary goal of citizens is to obtain its benevolent co-operation or neutrality in large and small transactions. Despite strong ideological divisions on the surface of politics, personality matters more than political doctrines, and parties are often organised around charismatic individuals who hold out the promise of preferential treatment from the state in return for unconditional loyalty. A populist party lacking a clear identity and strong roots in the population is usually the dominant political force. The opposition is weak and divided. The absence of mechanisms for regulating conflict and sharing power means that politics is highly partisan. Accordingly, there is an important role for the army, which may be expected to fill any political vacuum left by the collapse of civilian authority; other traditional forces such as the church do not lack influence. The intelligentsia expresses the alienation of vocal elements of society from the state, but the majority of university graduates direct their energies to obtaining secure and lucrative state employment.

The absence of checks and balances, intense competition for limited state resources, and a strongly nationalist political culture means that there is a real possibility that Romania will become sucked into a cycle of military coups and weak civilian government. The instability of 1990–1 could easily return if Iliescu vacates the presidency or if he suffers a severe loss of popularity. Governing arrangements whereby he has no responsibility for day-to-day policies but is nevertheless able to oversee all effective decision-making have been devised to suit his individual tastes and are not a recipe for long-term stability.

It should be noted that Romania's external standing has slowly improved mainly because the country remained relatively stable as neighbours like the former Yugoslavia, Soviet Union and Czechoslovakia broke up in an acrimonious manner. France's President Mitterrand was the first western leader to break the embargo on high-level contacts with Romania – adopted after the June 1990 riots in Bucharest –when he paid a visit in April 1991. Soon after, the EU made Romania eligible for aid to promote economic and social reconstruction. Then, following Iliescu's 1992 re-election, visits from the British foreign secretary and the heads of NATO and the West European Union were not long in following, recognition of Romania's regional importance in light of the Yugoslav conflict and the need to enforce sanctions on the main Serb aggressor.

Ion Iliescu has promoted to senior posts ultra-nationalists whose counterparts in the Yugoslav conflict zone have been responsible for terrible misdeeds. However, the expectations that west European policymakers had for eastern Europe – never high to begin with – have been scaled down in the past five years so that high-level recognition of Iliescu no longer seems incongruous. Besides, now as in the past, the emphasis has been on promoting political conditions that do not upset the general balance of European security. More often than not, this did not coincide with promoting democracy as a core objective, and it is clear from the external recognition that he has gradually won, that western leaders are generally satisfied with Iliescu. He may be a reluctant democrat and his style of rule may not always warrant close examination, but he has turned out to be less troublesome than initially anticipated and generally he has made a show of acquiescing in western bids to control the fall-out from the Yugoslav conflict.

With Romania politically calm in 1994 despite declining living standards, and the Yugoslav war an issue of relative unimportance, it was ties with Hungary and Moldova which focused attention on Romania's position in a region shaken by numerous internal and inter-state disputes. Relations with both countries evolved in new directions in 1994. In Hungary, elections in May led to the ruling Hungarian Democratic Forum, being evicted from office by the ex-communist Hungarian Socialist Party. Its leader, Gyula Horn, had been foreign minister at the time of Ceauşescu's overthrow and had taken some bold initiatives designed to improve bilateral relations. The electoral manifesto of the HSP had called for 'a historic reconciliation' with Hungary's neighbours, Slovakia and Romania, by means of confidence-building state treaties that would confirm the inviolability of the present borders and also guarantee minority rights in conformity with European norms.[3] Foreign and defence ministers of both states soon exchanged visits in preparation for treaty negotiations. But it remains to be seen if historic suspicions can be overcome by two ruling parties which derive their origins from the communist past. The nationalist bloc in Romania is dependent upon frosty relations with Hungary in order to maintain its political relevance. It may have been no coincidence that the election of Gyula Horn in Hungary was quickly followed by the release of a report in Bucharest by the RIS (ex-Securitate) which claimed that Hungary (along with the Soviet Union) had carried out 'destabilising activities' in Romania during the last days in office of Ceauşescu.[4] This may be an attempt to depict Horn as someone following an anti-Romanian agenda who is merely playing a more subtle game than his predecessors in office.

But perhaps most alarm at the arrival of the HSP in office has emanated from the Transylvanian Hungarian party, the HDFR. In a letter to Horn, Lászlo Tökés insisted that 'conditions for a historic reconciliation' between Hungary and Romania were not ripe.[5] Meanwhile, the HDFR was threatening civil disobedience over education policy in May 1994 and demanding 'special status' for the Hungarian community in educational and cultural matters, demands that were bound to complicate the conclusion of a basic treaty between Hungary and Romania.[6]

The behaviour of HDFR radicals suggests that they feel that protection from Hungary is a substitute for consensus in Romania. It remains to be seen if Budapest will continue to insist on the provision of collective ethnic rights for its co-ethnics in Romania. Sober minds in the new Hungarian leadership may well conclude that a worsening of ethnic tensions may result from the impression of favouritism based on ethnicity provided by the idea that distinct communities ought to have special political requirements. Gyula Horn is unlikely to push any proposition that would strengthen the hand of Romanian chauvinists and divert him from his domestic concerns.

Protection for the Hungarian minority in Transylvania is bound to make the completion of a basic treaty of friendship a complicated business. Until relations with Moldova suddenly deteriorated in the spring of 1994, it might have been expected that Romania could be persuaded to examine the policy towards minorities of another largely Romanian-speaking nation to see if there was room to apply elements of it in its own affairs.

Careful monitoring of the human-rights situation in Moldova by the USA, the CSCE and the Council of Europe has generally led to praise for the Chisinau authorities' readiness to protect minority interests. Moldova defines itself as a multi-ethnic country rather than as a national state. The concept of equal citizenship is supplemented by collective rights whereas, for instance, instruction in the mother tongue in monolingual schools is allowed (with the official language as a curricular subject). The rights of ethnic minorities have also been incorporated into bilateral agreements with their respective mother countries; finally, it is worth noting that the climate of ethnic tolerance makes Moldova one of the few parts of eastern Europe where anti-Semitism is largely absent (Israel and US Jewish bodies having expressed satisfaction with the position of Moldova's 65,000 Jews, whose numbers have increased in recent years).[7]

But it is unlikely that Moldova can prove a model to emulate for majority-minority relations in Romania. One commentator has pointed out that the Bessarabian tradition of accepting linguistic and ethnic diversity as natural, contrasts with Romania, where the prevalent outlook promotes ethnocultural uniformity.[8] Besides, relations between the two states deteriorated sharply in March 1994 as pro-Romanian parties gained less than seventeen per cent of votes in the Moldovan election of that month and Mircea Snegur, leader of the victorious Agrarian Democratic Party, used his endorsement to join the Commonwealth of Independent States. Romanian foreign minister Meleşcanu publicly warned the Moldovans against 'distorting [the facts of] our ethnic . . . linguistic and cultural

unity', while the new Romanian defence minister Gheorghe Tinca criticised Moldova's leaders for being unfriendly to Romania and for refusing
integration of the two countries.[9]

The Moldovan authorities, in joining the CIS, were acknowledging the
fact that geo-political realities and the presence of large Russian and
Ukrainian minorities meant that relations with their powerful eastern
neighbours were bound to be close ones. Romania had reacted in a similar
manner in the spring of 1991 when Bucharest had signed a defence pact
with the Soviet Union – then under the control of hardline communists
– which permitted Moscow a latitude in Romanian foreign policy which
it did not enjoy in any other Warsaw Pact state. This contentious treaty
lapsed with the collapse of the Soviet Union several months later, but
it revived speculation that those who had emerged on top in the 1989
Romanian uprising in fact possessed pro-Soviet leanings which were
bound to be reflected in some of the decisions they made.

Leaving this aside, the underlying threat that Russia has posed to
Romanian independence since the 1850s should not allow common
elements in the political culture of both countries to be overlooked. Orthodoxy, autocracy and nationalism, which at least one distinguished historian
suspects have been primary influences on the development of eastern
Europe, have arguably exercised more sway in Romania and Russia than in
other countries of the region, where it is western Christianity and capitalism
that have gained more of a foothold.[10] Initially denounced for its Protes-
tant heresy or Catholic attachments, the West has latterly been criticised
for its atheism and unbridled materialism. 'The tolerant, democratic but
individualistic societies that elevate technical rationality, social autonomy
and pluralism of values' are seen as wrong models for countries like Russia
and Romania.[11] But Orthodoxy which is seen as superior to western
Christianity on account of the spiritual powers and organic values which
it represents, has been weakened and compromised in the communist era.
It is unlikely to be strong enough for many years to come to orchestrate
an anti-western *Kulturkampf* which would be the equivalent of the clash
of civilisations that American political scientist Samuel P. Huntington
suspects will replace national and ideological quarrels as a primary source
of international conflict.[12] The fastest-growing religion in both Romania
and Russia has been evangelical Protestantism, often North American in
origin, which is arguably the only force to rival nationalism in its appeal to
emotional solidarity in today's Romania.

Romanian nationalism lacks original thinkers or convincing ideologues.
Instead, it has vulgar impresarios and indifferent poets like Vadim Tudor
and Păunescu to give it expression. The spread of nationalism in Europe
and Latin America in the first half of the nineteenth-century depended also

mainly on second-rate thinkers who influenced people through romantic historiography, cultural festivals, the theatre, and political calls to action.[13]

The arts permit the emotions to be pitted against reason, and it is not surprising that in both Romania and Russia it is restless or unscrupulous figures from the world of letters who have been among the best-known promoters of nationalism. The social bases of nationalism in both countries also display important similarities: 'members of the lower echelons of the party and state administration . . .people who had a position, however modest, in the old system which they had either lost or feared to lose'.[14]

Nationalists have benefited from the existence of a submissive mentality in which there is a widespread acceptance of the state as a supervisor of individual behaviour. The lack of a democratic tradition of resistance to despotism, and the survival of rural-based values which render the individual dependent upon group authority, have made sizeable social groups susceptible to the nationalist appeal in Romania. Here, industrialisation came much later than in Russia and was far less complete. A patriarchal morality which celebrates group values and demeaned individual ones was able to survive the transfer of population from the countryside to the big city. The communist regime prevented autonomous values from replacing a collectivist outlook by suppressing the status of the individual as a free subject. Individuals remained unaware of their rights as citizens even following the restoration of some basic liberties in 1990, and were open to manipulation from above.[15] Large sectors of the peasantry, exploited, used to an unfulfilling life, dependent upon agrarian bosses, instinctively looked to the state and its local agents for guidance. It explains why, in Tirgu Mureş in 1990, it apparently did not prove difficult for unscrupulous local officials to whip up peasants into a vengeful mob whose actions further disfigured the halting transition towards democracy being attempted.

In both Russia and Romania, belief in the necessity of strong centralised power is widespread. It will not necessarily result in the triumph of extremist ideologies or lead to the complete rejection of economic and social reform, but the bias in favour of authoritarian rule is obvious. However, in Russia there has been a much stronger critique of nationalism from intellectuals. Dmitri Likhachev, the leading Russian historian, has described nationalism in terms that even a liberal-minded Romanian might hesitate to use. As Likhachev see it, nationalism as a sentiment stems from a lack of confidence and from inadequacy. It is the manifestation of a nation's weakness, not of its strength. Usually only weak nations are infected by nationalism; they try to maintain themselves with the help of nationalist passion and ideology.[16] François Fejtö, the veteran historian, echoes Likhachev in describing nationalism as an enemy of the healthy patriotism that is comfortable with the idea of unity in diversity.[17]

Perhaps it is not surprising that Romanian ultra-nationalists have generally remained fairly tight-lipped about the Russian demagogue Vladimír Zhirinovsky, even though he has cast aspersions on Romania, a land he believes to be inhabited by 'Italian gypsies'. To make a fuss about this Russian neo-fascist leader might only result in emphasising uncomfortable parallels in language, ideas and domestic objectives that make Romanian and Russian nationalists kindred spirits.

The rejection of individualism and pluralism as political and moral guidelines means that Romania has a pre-democratic political culture. Doctrines like social democracy and liberalism are not shunned, but the emphasis is usually on adapting them to specific Romanian conditions. The grafting of western forms over traditional practices has created a dualism which means that a chasm often exists between political and constitutional forms and actual practices (also a feature in Latin America, where progressive laws have often masked domestic tyranny).[18]

Throughout its history as an independent state, there have been Romanians who have been keen to promote the country's integration into the international system and expose it to modernising and reformist trends usually from the direction of the west. But names like Take Ionescu, Nicolae Titulescu and Adrian Severin have not been the foremost ones in Romanian political history. A fragile and antagonistic relationship between the state and society, as well as Romania's disadvantageous geo-political location, have instead given the initiative to authoritarian-minded politicians who pit emotion against reason and demand internal uniformity in order to keep at bay external enemies real or imagined. In their different ways, the National Liberals in the 1920s, the Iron Guard one decade later, Ceauşescu between 1965 and 1989, and his nationalist heirs today, each blamed foreign interests or their local surrogates – the Jews in the 1930s – for the ills afflicting the country. Deep-seated economic problems were explained in nationalist terms. To overcome them, economic self-reliance was the answer, the agent of salvation being a strong state that imposed its will on society without being constrained by democratic mechanisms. Romania was finally to try this nationalist escape-route from dependency in the last two-thirds of communist rule. The result was a colossal series of policy failures which burdened Romania with useless, pollutant industries and sapped the physical and psychological strength of the people, leaving the country back at square one – increasingly dependent upon external interests.

But the nationalist values which sustained Ceauşescu have proven more durable than his failed regime. Its successor has failed to break with the past or devise new rules in politics which will reduce the likelihood of gross exploitation of the people in the future by their rulers. A flawed bid to create an economy with market mechanisms from the debris of the command economy has resulted in GNP falling by around thirty per cent in the space of four years along with a collapse in income and health standards for large swathes of the population.

Against such a gloomy background, it is not hard for anti-democratic intellectuals to do what they have always been good at in modern Romania – romanticise the past and create a set of scapegoats from groups who are marginal to the definition of what it is to be Romanian and who can be blamed for current ills. The appearance of western products and life-styles helps to create a sense of relative deprivation which ultra-nationalists can exploit. Fascination with western gadgetry, media products and life-styles exists alongside understandable resentment that such features of modern living are beyond the reach of all but those in the new post-communist oligarchy. It may well be that future nationalist challengers will combine high technology and modern music with traditional Romanian motifs to capture a youthful following. Adrian Păunescu, deployed rock music in the service of pro-Ceauşescu nationalism in the 1980s and in 1992 it was clear that aides around Iliescu were ready to exploit Michael Jackson's Bucharest concert to boost Iliescu's re-election bid.[19] Needless to say, Serbia provides the most chilling examples of how rock and folk themes have been combined by nihilist adventurers searching for a youthful urban following.

If there is one disenchanted group that nationalists already appeal to, it is the new class which emerged from the forced industrialisation of the Stalin type. By encouraging massive migration to the cities, the communists may have ended the chronic problem of rural overpopulation, but they created a social group dependent upon forms of heavy industry that were obsolete even at the point of construction, workers who would find it difficult to obtain a place in a more diversified economy except on poor terms. Unskilled workers uprooted from the land and with uncertain prospects are to be found all over eastern Europe. In Slovakia, a heavy-industry drive, approaching Romania's in intensity, created the social constituency that resulted in the electoral triumph of Vladimir Měciár, a minority-baiting populist, in September 1994.

Romanian political culture is likely to be influenced by forced industrialisation for another generation at least, and it may well only be a matter of time before a Měciár-style challenge is mounted by an ambitious populist. Mayor Funar has shown how a large city like Cluj with civic traditions dating back a long way can be taken over via the ballot-box by ex-nomenklatura officials who use nationalism to appeal to the newer inhabitants living on the large housing estates on the city's edge. It is likely that Funar will be re-elected mayor in 1996 – if he stands – but his presidential ambitions may have been wrecked by his identification with the Caritas racket that impoverished multitudes of gullible investors from all parts of the country in 1993. The existence of well-placed nationalists like Funar ready to exploit popular neuroses at a low point in the country's fortunes suggests that the biggest threat to Romania comes from within. However much a country like Romania has been subjected to foreign intervention in the past, it is the decisions which its rulers take about the political direction of the state and the extent to which they will encourage the strengthening of democratic values, even at the expense of their own power, which will determine the future.

Nationalism was necessary for the creation of the Romanian state. But the longer the Romanian elites cling to it as a guiding principle above all others, the more difficult it will be to tackle fundamental problems of political and economic organisation which have prevented the state from serving the needs of its citizens. The long-term prospects of the Romanian state will be better served by conciliating different ethnic interests rather than pretending that they do not exist. It is short-sighted to see minority demands for cultural autonomy in education as subversive. If granted they will lead to a redefinition of the state, but it will be small adjustment compared to the challenge which the traditional nation-state faces from the globalisation of capital or communications or the need to replace the command economy.

An honest recognition of the authenticity of different cultural traditions is just as likely to strengthen the state as to fragment or weaken it. Important national and transnational actors from the United States to the Council of Europe can do much to encourage the pacification of majority-minority disputes like the one in Romania. If the Council of Europe manages to agree on a common platform of minority rights, with implementation overseen by neutral third parties, it could be an important reference-point for Balkan states. But until now, the internecine disputes that have blighted relations between west European states since the end of the Cold War have hardly given Balkan countries a positive role model to follow. West European quarrels, from fish quotas to the proper course of action in the Yugoslav conflict, to the choice of a new president of the European Commission, in their different ways provide powerful ammunition to unapologetic nationalists in eastern Europe. If western states pursue their national interests at the expense of collective economic and security arrangements, just why should eastern states be any different?

Western Europe would be mindful of its own interests (as well as of the need to pay restitition for the decades of peace and prosperity it enjoyed largely at the expense of eastern Europe) if it were to provide a range of incentives to encourage East European governments to abandon hardline attitudes in dealing with minority issues and inter-state relations. Greater access to western markets, a faster timetable to European integration, or security arrangements that include the Balkans within a pan-European defence framework, could enormously strengthen those Balkan interests committed to a civic order rather than an ethnic state. The west could also, without any loss to itself, discreetly encourage the revival of pre-war attempts at Balkan co-operation which led to the signing of various pacts in the 1930s between Greece, Turkey, Yugoslavia and Romania. But there is little concerted push in this direction from Paris, London or Bonn. Instead, it has been left to isolated if wealthy individuals like the philanthropiost George Soros or the late Turkish President Ozal to link political co-operation between estranged ethnic groups or states with projects for mutually-sustaining economic expansion.

Through their diplomatic representatives, the countries of the west could also show their disapproval of politicals like Cluj's Mayor Funar by purposefully ignoring them or, perhaps even better, by making it clear how negatively their inflammatory actions were regarded beyond Romania's borders. Similarly, the west could do a lot to prevent the rise of funda-mentalism within frustrated minority groups, Hungarians in Romania not being immune from this temptation, although moderate and responsible leaders outnumber the firebrands.

Real differences of interest will continue to place apart Romanians and Hungarians who speak a different language and have been shaped by con-flicting histories. But if easy solutions to questions such as a state-financed Hungarian university or the provision of Hungarian education in second-ary schools do not exist, compromises ought to be arranged to draw the heat from them and prepare the ground hopefully for lasting settlements of these issues in the future. Conflict-resolution efforts sponsored by a well-known US foundation resulted in tangible progress in 1993, but it was the intransigence of hardline Hungarians around Bishop Tokes that ultimately foiled a breakthrough.

Great advantages could flow from a breakthrough in Romanian-Hungarian relations in Transylvania that was combined with an inter-state treaty regularising those between the two historically estranged Danubian states of Hungary and Romania. It would show that compromises arranged in western Europe by bitter historic rivals – France and Germany over Alsace-Lorraine, Italy and Austria over the South Tyrol – are equally possible in the east. Those Balkan politicians who contend that there are no circumstances permitting such breakthroughs are condemning south-eastern Europe to permanent isolation and a bleak future scarred by ethnic strife. They make it all too easy for west European leaders to press ahead with economic and political arrangements that may affect a new partition of the continent on a north-west to south-east axis; Greece, by its belligerent nationalism over Macedonia and Albania, is already condemning itself to increasing isolation even though officially a member of the EU.

If central European countries succeed in drawing closer to the west while the Balkans become a shunned, outer Europe seen as contaminated by the release into the atmosphere of toxic nationalism, Transylvania will have an uncertain future. It remains a transitional territory straddling the Balkans and central Europe. It is still one of the most individual corners of Europe. Like war-ravaged Bosnia, it has been a meeting-place, interesting and challenging because of the mingling of religions, cultures and languages that have emerged there. Like Bosnia, it was also ill-suited for the rise of nationalism which, during periods of Hungarian and Romanian rule, imposed the straitjacket of conformity on a region whose identity cannot be reduced to one single national state tradition. How majority-minority relations in Transylvania are dealt with is bound to affect the stability of both east-central Europe and the Balkans. Similarly, the prospects for inter-ethnic progress will depend upon events beyond the Danube basin that determine whether east-central Europe achieves some economic uplift as well as guarantees about its security. It remains to be seen whether narrow nationalism, ascendant now in western as well as eastern Europe, can be supplanted by a form of identity that emphasises partnership and trust across tribal and cultural boundaries. Given the weapons of total destruction that are within the grasp of ethnic warriors, Europe's prospects are deeply uncertain if this challenge is evaded in the way that occurred after the 1914–18 war.

NOTES

1. The American political scientist, Ken Jowitt, reckons that 'owing to the lack of anything better, the FSN was compelled to lead' at the end of 1989, there being no other elites waiting in the wings. See the interview with Ken Jowitt in *22* (10 July 1992).
2. Roberts, *Rumania*, p. 338.
3. Alfred Reisch, 'Hungarian Parties' Foreign Policy Electoral Platforms', *RFE-RL Research Report*, Vol. 3, No. 19 (13 May 1994).
4. Rompres news agency, Bucharest, 18 July 1994, SWB EE/2052 B/4 (20 July 1994).
5. Hungarian radio, Budapest, 3 August 1994, SWB EE/2066 B/2 (5 August 1994).
6. *The Independent* (11 August 1994).
7. The information used in this paragraph was derived from Socor, 'Moldova', *RFE-RL Research Report*, Vol. 3, No. 16 (22 April 1994), pp. 17, 19.
8. Vladimir Socor, 'Moldova's Political Landscape: Profiles of the Parties', *RFE-RL Research Report*, Vol. 3, No. 10 (11 March 1994).
9. *RFE-RL News Briefs*, Vol. 3, Nos 30 and 25 (1994).
10. See the Introduction by Stephen Fischer-Galati to *Nation, Man and State in Eastern Europe*, Pall Mall, London 1970, which he edited.

11. Eugene Kamenka, 'Nationalism: Ambiguous Legacies and Contingent Futures', *Political Studies*, Vol. 41, No. 4 (1993), p. 79.
12. Samuel P. Huntington, 'The Clash of Civilizations', *Foreign Affairs* (Summer 1993).
13. Kamenka, op. cit., p. 80.
14. Laqueur, *Black Hundred*, p. 257.
15. These insights are derived from Gulubovic, 'Nationalism and Democracy', p. 70.
16. Laqueur, op. cit., p. 272.
17. François Fejtö, 'Naciones y Minorías de Europa', *Diário 16* (Madrid), 9 November 1994.
18. Roberts, op. cit., pp. 20, 338.
19. For Paunescu's manipulation of rock music, see Judith Ingram, 'Smaranda Enache: A Transylvanian Life', *Uncaptive Minds*, Vol. 4, Part 2 (1991), p. 121.

Bibliography

NEWS AGENCIES

ARPRESS (Bucharest)
BBC World Service, Survey of World Broadcasts for Eastern Europe

NEWSPAPERS AND PERIODICALS CONSULTED

Adevârul de Cluj
Baricada
Cotidiánul
Cuvîntul
Cuvîntul Liber
Desteapte-Te Romane
Diário 16
Dimineátă
Dreptátea
East European Reporter
The Economist
Evenimentul Zilei
Expres
Expres Magasin
Gazeta de Mureş
GM, Saptaminal Transilvan
The Free Romanian
In faţa alegatorilor
In These Times
Mesagerul Transilvan
Natiunea
New Statesman and Society
NU
The Observer
Politica
Pro-Minoritate
Puntea
România Liberă
România Liberă International
România Mâre

Socialistul
The Times
Tinerama
Tineretul Liber
Tribuna Ardealului
22
Viaţa Crestina
Zig Zag

BOOKS AND ARTICLES CONSULTED

Almond, Mark, *The Rise and Fall of Nicolae and Elena Ceauşescu*, Chapmans,
    London 1992.
Arachelian, V. C., *Corneliu Coposu, Dialoguri*, Editura Anastasia, Bucharest 1992.
Ardealanu, Ion et al. *Horthyist Fascist Terror in North-Western Romania, September
    1940–October 1944*, Meridiane Publishing House, Bucharest 1986.
Arguments in Favour of Reviving Hungarian Higher Education in Romania,
    The Bolyai Society, Kolozsvar 1991.
Bacon, Walter, 'Security as Seen from Bucharest', in Daniel Nelson (ed.),
    Romania After Tyranny, Westview Press, London and San Francisco
    CA 1992.
Banac, Ivo, *The National Question in Yugoslavia*, Cornell University Press,
    Itheca NY 1992.
Beck, Sam and John W. Cole, *Ethnicity and Nationalism in South Eastern
    Europe*, University of Amsterdam, Amsterdam 1981.
Beck, Sam and Marilyn McArthur, 'Ethnicity, Nationalism and Development',
    in Sam Beck and John W. Cole, *Ethnicity and Nationalism in South
    Eastern Europe*, University of Amsterdam, Amsterdam 1981.
Behr, Edward, *'Kiss the Hand You Cannot Bite': The Rise and Fall of the
    Ceauşescus*, Hamish Hamilton, London 1991.
Berend, Ivan T., 'The Cultural Identity of Central and Eastern Europe',
    New Hungarian Quarterly, Vol. 28, No. 107 (Autumn 1987).
Biro, Sandor, *The Nationalities Problem in Transylvania, 1867–1940*, East
    European Monographs Series, Columbia University Press, New
    York 1992.
Bloom, Solomon, 'The Peoples of My Home Town Before Nationalism
    Crushed Romania's Design for Living', *Commentary* (April 1947).
Borsody, Stephen, *The New Central Europe: Triumphs and Tragedies*, East
    European Monographs, Boulder CO 1993.
Brett, Rachel, *The Challenges of Change*, Human Rights Centre, University
    of Essex 1992.
—— *The Development of the Human Dimension Mechanism of the Conference for
    Security and Co-operation in Europe*, Human Rights Centre, University
    of Essex 1992.
Brown, J. F., *Surge To Freedom: The End of Communist Rule in Eastern
    Europe*, Duke University Press, Durham NC and London 1991.
—— 'The Resurgence of Nationalism', *Report on Eastern Europe* (14 June 1991).
—— *Nationalism, Democracy and Security in the Balkans*, Rand Books, Santa
    Monica CA 1992.
—— 'Extremism in eastern Europe and the Former Soviet Union', RFE-RL
    Research Report, Vol. 3, No. 16 (22 April 1994).

Brucan, Sylviu, *The Wasted Generation: Memoirs of the Romanian Journey from Capitalism to Socialism and Back*, Westview Press, Boulder CO 1993.

Burks, R. V., 'The Rumanian National Deviation: An Accounting', in Kurt London (ed.), *Eastern Europe in Transition*, Johns Hopkins University Press, Baltimore MD 1967.

Cadzow, John F., Andrew Ludanyi and Louis J. Elteto (eds), *Transylvania: The Roots of Ethnic Conflict*, The Kent State University Press, Kent OH 1983.

Calinescu, Matei and Vladimir Tismaneanu, 'The 1989 Revolution and Romania's Future', in Daniel Nelson (ed.), *Romania After Tyranny*, Westview Press, London and San Francisco CA 1992.

Campbell, John, *French Influence and the Rise of Roumanian Nationalism*, Arno Press, New York 1970 (Ph.D. originally submitted to the History Department of Harvard University in 1940).

Campeanu, Pavel, 'National Fervor in Eastern Europe: The Case of Romania', *Social Research*, 58, No. 4 (1991).

Castellan, Georges, 'The Germans of Rumania', *Journal of Contemporary History*, Vol. 6, No. 1 (1971).

—— *A History of the Romanians*, East European Monographs, Boulder CO 1989.

Chirot, Daniel, *Social Change in a Peripheral Society: The Creation of a Balkan Colony*, Academic Press, New York 1976.

—— 'Social Change in Communist Romania', *Social Forces*, 57, No. 2 (1978).

Cioranescu, George, 'Vlad the Impaler – Current Parallels with a Medieval Romanian Prince', *Radio Free Europe Research*, Vol. 2, No. 5 (31 January 1977).

Cole, J. W., 'Reflections on the Political Economy of Ethnicity: South Tyrol and Transylvania', in H. Vermeulen and J. Boissevain (eds), *The Ethnic Challenge: The Politics of Ethnicity in Europe*, Herodot, Göttingen 1984.

Connor, Walker, *Ethnonationalism: The Quest for Understanding*, Princeton University Press, Princeton NJ 1994.

Cornea, Doina, *Scrisore Deschise si Alte Texte*, Humanitas, Bucharest 1992.

Deletant, Dennis, 'The Role of Vatra Romaneasca in Transylvania', *Report on Eastern Europe*, Vol. 2, No. 5 (1 February 1991).

Diamandouros, P. Nikiforos, 'Politics and Culture in Greece, 1974–91: An Interpretation', in R. Clogg (ed.), *Greece 1981–89: The Populist Decade*, St Martin's Press, London 1993.

Eddison, Elaine, *The Protection of Minorities at the Conference on Security and Co-operation in Europe*, Human Rights Centre, University of Essex 1993.

Eyal, J., 'A Framework for Handling Ethnic Minority Issues in Eastern Europe,' Memorandum submitted to the House of Commons Foreign Affairs Cttee (4 December 1991).

Fischer, Mary Ellen, *Nicolae Ceaușescu: A Study in Political Leadership*, Reinner, Boulder, CO 1989.

Fischer-Galati, Stephen (ed.), *Nation, Man and State in Eastern Europe*, Pall Mall, London 1970.

—— 'Introduction', in Joseph Held (ed.), *Democracy and Right-Wing Politics in Eastern Europe in the 1990s*, Columbia University Press (East European Monographs Series), Boulder CO and New York 1993.

—— *20th Century Romania* (2nd edn), Columbia University Press, New York 1993.

Gallagher, Tom, 'Romania: A Democrat Under Fire', END *News* (Autumn 1991).

—— 'Ultra-Nationalists Take Charge of Transylvania's Capital', RFE-RL *Research Report*, Vol. 1, No. 13 (27 March 1992).

—— 'Vatra Romaneasca and Resurgent Nationalism', *Ethnic and Racial Studies*, Vol. 15, No. 4 (1992).

—— 'Time to Build Bridges in Romania', *Studies* (Autumn 1992).

—— 'Ethnic Tension in Cluj', RFE-RL *Research Report*, Vol. 2, No. 9 (26 February 1993).

Georgescu, Vlad, *A History of the Romanians*, IB Tauris, London 1990.

—— *Politică Şi Istorie*, Humanitas, Bucharest 1991.

Geron Pilon, Juliana, *The Bloody Flag: Post-Communist Nationalism in Eastern Europe*, Transaction Publishers, New York 1992.

Gilberg, Trond, 'Ethnic Minorities in Romania under Socialism', *East European Quarterly*, 7 (1974).

—— Modernisation in Romania since World War II, Praegar, New York 1975.

—— 'State Policy, Ethnic Persistence and Nationality Formation in Eastern Europe', in Peter Sugar (ed.), *Ethnic Diversity and Conflict in Eastern Europe*, ABC-Clio, Santa Barbara CA 1980.

—— *Nationalism and Communism in Romania*, Westview Press, Boulder CO and Oxford 1990.

—— 'Romanians and Democratic Values: Socialization After Communism', in Daniel Nelson (ed.), *Romania After Tyranny*, Westview Press, London and San Francisco CA 1992.

Giurchescu, Anca, 'The National Festival "Song to Romania": Manipulation of Symbols in the Political Discourse', in C. Arvidsson and L. Blomqvist (eds), *Symbols of Power*, Almqvist & Wiskell, Stockholm 1987.

Graham, Lawrence, *Romania: A Developing Socialist State*, Westview Press, Boulder CO 1982.

Gulubovic, Zagorka, 'Nationalism and Democracy: The Yugoslav Case', *Journal of Area Studies*, 3 (1993).

Gyimesi, Eva Cs., 'The Ethnic Excuse', *Hungarian Quarterly*, Vol. 34 (Summer 1993).

Harsanyi, Doina and Nicolae, 'Romania: Democracy and the Intellectuals', *East European Quarterly*, Vol. 27, No. 2 (June 1993).

Hausleitner, Mariana, 'Women in Romania: Before and After the Collapse', in N. Funk and M. Mueller (eds), *Gender Politics and Post-Communism: Reflections from Eastern Europe and the Former Soviet Union*, Routledge, London 1993.

Held, Joseph (ed.), *Democracy and Right-Wing Politics in Eastern Europe in the 1990s*, Columbia University Press (East European Monographs Series), Boulder CO and New York 1993.

Hennessy, A., 'Latin America', in G. Ionescu and E. Gellner (eds), *Populism: Its Meaning and National Characteristics*, Weidenfeld & Nicholson, London 1969.

Hessell, Tiltman H., *Peasant Europe*, Jarrolds, London 1936.

Hitchins, Keith, *Conştiinţa Naţională Şi Actiune Politică La Romanii Din Transilvania, 1868–1918*, Editura Dacia, Cluj 1992.

—— *Rumania 1866–1947*, Oxford University Press, Oxford 1994.

Hockenos, Paul, 'Bloodletting in Transylvania', *In These Times*, New York (4–10 April 1990).

—— 'Romania's ultra-right gathers political might', *In These Times*, New York (24 July 1991).

—— *Free to Hate: The Rise of the Right in Post-Communist Eastern Europe*, Routledge, London 1993.

Human Rights in Romania since the Revolution, Helsinki Watch Report, New York 1991.

Huntington, Samuel P., 'The Clash of Civilizations', *Foreign Affairs* (Summer 1993).

Ignatieff, Michael, *Blood and Belonging: Journeys into the New Nationalism*, BBC/Chatto, London 1993.

Illyés, E., *National Minorities in Romania: Change in Transylvania*, Columbia University Press, Boulder CO and New York 1982.

Ingram, Judith, 'Smaranda Enache: A Transylvanian Life', *Uncaptive Minds*, Vol. 4, Part 2 (1991).

Ioanid, Radu, 'Nicolae Iorga and Fascism', *Journal of Contemporary History*, Vol. 27 (1992).

Ionescu, Dan, 'Religious Elements in the Glorification of Ceauşescu', *Radio Free Europe Research*, Vol. 13, No. 4 (28 January 1988).

—— 'Rewriting History', *Radio Free Europe Research*, Vol. 13, No. 38 (19 September 1988).

—— 'Violence and Calumny in the Election Campaign, *Report on Eastern Europe*, Vol. 1, No. 18 (25 May 1990).

—— 'The NSF's Anti-Opposition Campaign Escalates Following Elections', *Report on Eastern Europe*, Vol. 1, No. 30 (10 August 1990).

—— 'Marshall Antonescu Honored by Old and New Admirers', *Report on Eastern Europe*, Vol. 1, No. 32 (24 August 1990).

—— 'Concern over the Yugoslav Crisis', *Report on Eastern Europe*, Vol. 1, No. 29 (19 July 1991).

—— 'Government Moves to Recentralize Local Administration', *Report on Eastern Europe*, Vol. 1, No. 33 (7 September 1990).

—— 'Countdown for Romania's Germans', *Report on Eastern Europe*, Vol. 2, No, 36 (13 September 1991).

—— 'Riots Topple Petre Roman's Cabinet', *Report on Eastern Europe*, Vol. 2, No. 41 (18 October 1991).

—— 'Striving for a Better Image', *Report on Eastern Europe*, Vol. 2, No. 49 (20 December 1991).

—— 'Romania Straddles the Fence on the Yugoslav Conflict', *RFE-RL Research Report*, Vol. 1, No. 35 (4 September 1992).

—— 'Romania's Liberals', *RFE-RL Research Report*, Vol. 2, No. 22 (28 May 1993).

—— 'Romanian Corruption Scandal Implicates Top Officials', *RFE-RL Research Report*, Vol. 2, No. 30 (23 July 1993).

—— 'Has Romania's Ruling Party Become Stronger or Weaker?' *RFE-RL Research Report*, Vol. 2, No. 34 (27 August 1993).

Ionescu, Dan and Alfred A. Reisch, 'Still No Breakthrough in Romanian-Hungarian Relations', *RFE-RL Research Report*, Vol. 2, No. 42 (22 October 1993).

Ionescu, Ghita, *Communism in Rumania, 1944–1962*, Oxford University Press, Oxford 1964.

Jászi, Oscár, *The Dissolution of the Hapsburg Monarchy*, University of Chicago Press, Chicago IL 1958.

Jelavich, Barbara, *History of the Balkans, Volume 1: Eighteenth and Nineteenth Centuries*, Cambridge University Press, Cambridge 1983.

—— *History of the Balkans, Volume 2: Twentieth Century*, Cambridge University Press, Cambridge 1983.

Jeszenszky, Geza, 'Hungary's Foreign Policy Dilemmas', *Hungarian Quarterly*, Vol. 34 (Summer 1993).

Jowitt, Kenneth, *Revolutionary Breakthroughs and National Development: The Case of Romania, 1944–65*, University of California Press, Berkeley and Los Angeles CA 1971.

Kamenka, Eugene, 'Nationalism: Ambiguous Legacies and Contingent Futures', *Political Studies*, 41 No. 4 (1993).

Karnoouh, Claude, *L'Invention du Peuple: Chroniques de Roumanie*, Editions Arcantère, Paris 1990.

Kedourie, Elie, *Nationalism*, Hutchinson, London 1961.

Kertzer, David, *Ritual, Politics and Power*, Yale University Press, New Haven CT and London 1988.

King, Charles, 'Moldova and the Bessarabian Question', *The World Today* (July 1993).

King, R. R., *Minorities Under Communism: Nationalities as a Source of Tension among Balkan Communist States*, Harvard University Press, Cambridge MA 1973.

—— *The Romanian Communist Party*, Hoover Institution Press, Stanford CA 1980.

—— 'Romania', in R. Staar (ed.), *1991 Yearbook of International Communist Affairs*, Hoover Press, Stanford CA 1991.

Kohn, Hans, *Nationalism: Its Meaning and History*, Van Nostrand, New York 1971.

Kolarz, Walter, *Myths and Realities in Eastern Europe*, Lindsay Drummond, London 1946.

Kurti, Lászlo, 'Transylvania, Land Beyond Reason: Toward An Anthropological Analysis of a Contested Terrain', *Dialectical Anthropology*, 14 (1989).

Laqueur, Walter, *Black Hundred: The Rise of the Extreme Right in Russia*, Harper Collins, New York 1993.

Lendvai, P., *Eagles in Cobwebs: Nationalism and Communism in the Balkans*, Macdonald, London 1970.

Linden, Ronald, 'After the Revolution: A Foreign Policy of Bounded Change', in D. Nelson (ed.), *Romania After Tyranny*, Westview Press, London and San Francisco CA 1992.

Linscott Ricketts, Mac, *Mircea Eliade: The Romanian Roots, 1907–1945*, Columbia University Press, East European Monographs Series, Boulder CO 1988.

Longworth, Philip, *The Making of Eastern Europe*, Macmillan, London 1992.

Maccartney, C. A., *Hungary and Her Successors: The Treaty of Trianon and Its Consequences, 1919–1937*, Oxford University Press, London [1937] 1965.

Mack Smith, Denis, 'Regionalism', in E. R. Tannenbaum and E. P. Noether

(eds), *Modern Italy: A Topical History since 1861*, New York University
Press, New York 1974.

Madzar, Ljubomir, 'The Roots of Nationalism', *Balkan Forum*, Vol. 2, No.
1 (March 1994).

Manolescu, Nicolae, *Dreptul la Normalitate: Discursul politic şi realitate*,
Editura Litera, Bucharest 1991.

Markham, Reuben H., *Rumania under the Soviet Yoke*, Meador, Boston
MA 1949.

The May 1990 Election in Romania, International Delegation Report,
NDIIA/NRIIA, Washington DC 1991.

Michelson, Paul E., 'The Master of Synthesis: Constantin C. Giurescu
and the Coming of Age of Romanian Historiography, 1919–1947', in
Stephen Fischer-Galati (ed.), *Romania between East and West*, Columbia
University Press (East European Monographs Series), Boulder CO and
New York 1982.

Mihailescu, Ioan, 'Mental Stereotypes in Post-Totalitarian Romania',
Government and Opposition, Vol. 28, No. 3 (1993).

Misztal, Barbara, 'Must Eastern Europe Follow the Latin American Way?',
European Journal of Sociology, 33 (1992).

Mitrany, D., *Greater Rumania: A Study of National Ideas*, Hodder & Stoughton,
London and New York, n.d.

—— *The Land and the Peasant in Roumania*, Oxford University Press,
Oxford 1930.

Montias, J. M., *Economic Development in Communist Rumania*, MIT Press,
Cambridge MA and London 1967.

Moynihan, Daniel Patrick, *Pandaemonium: Ethnicity in International Politics*,
Oxford University Press, Oxford 1993.

Mungiu, Alina and Andrei Pippidi, 'Letter from Romania', *Government
and Opposition*, Vol. 29, No. 3 (1994).

Nedelea, Marin, *Prim-Miniştrii României-Mari*, *Viaţa Românească*, Garell
Poligraphis, Bucharest 1991.

Nelson, Daniel, *Romanian Politics in the Ceauşescu Era*, Gordon and Breach,
New York 1988.

—— (ed.), *Romania After Tyranny*, Westview Press, London and San
Francisco CA 1992.

Neuberger, Benyamin, 'National Self-Determination: Dilemmas of a
Concept', in *Nationalism in Europe, Past and Present*, University of
Santiago de Compostela 1994.

Nevers, Renee de, 'Democratization and Ethnic Conflict', *Survival*, 35,
No. 2 (Summer 1993).

Newman, Bernard, *Danger Spots of Europe*, The Right Book Club, London 1939.

—— *Balkan Background*, Robert Hale, London 1944.

Obrman, Jan, 'Havel Challenges Czech Historical Taboos', *RFE-RL Research
Report*, Vol. 2, No. 24 (11 June 1993).

Oltay, Edith, 'Anniversary of 1848 Revolution Celebrated', *Report on Eastern
Europe*, Vol. 2, No. 13 (5 April 1991).

—— 'Minority Rights Still an Issue in Hungarian-Romanian Relations',
RFE-RL Research Report, Vol. 1, No. 12 (20 March 1992).

—— 'Minorities as Stumbling Block in Relations with Neighbours', *RFE-RL
Research Report*, Vol. 1, No. 19 (8 May 1992).

Pasca-Harsanyi, Doina, 'Women in Romania', in N. Funk and M. Mueller (eds), *Gender Politics and Post-Communism: Reflections from Eastern Europe and the Former Soviet Union,* Routledge, London 1993.

Paşcu, Ioan Mircea, 'Romania's Response to a Structured World', in Daniel Nelson (ed.), *Romania After Tyranny,* Westview Press, London and San Francisco CA 1992.

—— 'Romania and the Yugoslav Conflict', in Charles L. Barry (ed.), *The Search for Peace in Europe: Perspectives From NATO and Eastern Europe,* National Defense University Press, Fort Lesley J. McNair, USA 1994.

Paşcu, Ştefan, *A History of Transylvania,* Wayne State University Press, Detroit MI 1982.

Patacki, Judith, 'A History of Transylvania: A Book with Its Own History', *Radio Free Europe Research,* Vol. 12, No. 13 (3 April 1987).

—— 'Free Hungarians in a Free Romania: Dream or Reality', *Report on Eastern Europe,* Vol. 1, No. 8 (23 February 1990).

Pearson, Raymond, *National Minorities in Eastern Europe, 1848–1945,* Macmillan, Basingstoke 1983.

Pearton, Maurice, 'Nicolae Iorga as Historian and Nation-Builder', in Dennis Deletant and Harry Hanak (eds), *Historians as Nation-Builders,* Macmillan, London 1988.

Pippidi, Andrei, 'Nation, Nationalisme et Démocratie en Roumanie', *L'Autre Europe,* part 26–27 (1993).

Rady, Martin, *Romania in Turmoil,* IB Tauris, London and New York 1992.

Reisch, Alfred, 'Hungary's Foreign Policy Reorientation a Success', *Report on Eastern Europe,* Vol. 2, No. 51 (20 December 1991).

—— 'Hungarian Parties' Foreign Policy Electoral Platforms', *RFE-RL Research Report,* Vol. 3, No. 19 (13 May 1994).

Rezler, Julius, 'Economic and Social Differentiation and Ethnicity: The Case of Eastern Europe', in Peter Sugar (ed.), *Ethnic Diversity and Conflict in Eastern Europe,* ABC-Clio, Santa Barbara CA 1980.

Roberts, Henry L., *Rumania: Political Problems of an Agrarian State,* Yale University Press, New Haven CT 1951.

Romania: A Case of Dynastic Communism, Freedom House, New York 1989.

Romanian Research Group, 'On Transylvanian Ethnicity', *Current Anthropology,* 20 (1979).

Rothschild, Joseph, *East-Central Europe between the Two World Wars,* University of Washington Press, Washington DC 1974.

—— *Return to Diversity: A Political History of East-Central Europe since World War II,* Oxford University Press, New York and Oxford 1989.

Rupnik, Jacques, 'Europe's New Frontiers: Remapping Europe', *Daedalus,* Vol. 123, No. 3 (Summer 1994).

Rura, Michael J., *Reinterpretation of History as a Method of Furthering Communism in Rumania,* Georgetown University Press, Washington DC 1961.

Safran, Alexandre, *Resisting the Storm: Romania, 1940–47: Memoirs* (edited and annotated by Jean Ancel), Yad Vashem, Jerusalem 1987.

Schmitter, Philippe C., 'Reflections on Mihail Manoilescu and the Political Consequences of Delayed Development on the Periphery of Western Europe', in K. Jowitt (ed.), *Social Change in Romania, 1860–1940,* California University Press, Berkeley CA 1977.

Schöpflin, G., 'National Minorities under Communism in Eastern Europe', in Kurt London (ed.), *Eastern Europe in Transition*, Johns Hopkins University Press, Baltimore MD 1967.

—— 'Rumanian Nationalism', *Survey*, Vol. 20 (Spring-Summer 1974).

—— 'Nationalism, Politics and the European Experience', *Survey*, Vol. 28, No. 4 (Winter 1984).

—— 'Transylvania as a Political Question', *Planet*, 62 (December-January 1988–9).

—— 'The Political Traditions of Eastern Europe', *Daedalus* (Winter 1990).

—— *Politics in Eastern Europe*, Blackwell, Oxford 1993.

Schöpflin, G., and Hugh Poulton, *Romania's Ethnic Hungarians*, Minority Rights Group, London 1991.

Seton-Watson, H., *Eastern Europe, 1918–41*, Cambridge University Press, Cambridge, 1945.

—— *The East European Revolution* (3rd edn), Methuen, London 1961.

—— *Nationalism and Communism* Camelot Press, London 1964.

—— *Nations and States: An Enquiry into Nationalism*, Weidenfeld & Nicholson, London 1975.

Seton-Watson, R. W., *A History of the Roumanians: From Roman Times to the Completion of Unity*, Cambridge University Press, Cambridge 1934.

—— *Transylvania: A Key Problem*, The Claric Press, Oxford 1943.

Shafir, Michael, *Romania, Politics, Economics and Society*, Pinter/Reinner, London and Boulder CO 1985.

—— 'The Provisional Council of National Unity: Is History Repeating Itself?' *Report on Eastern Europe*, Vol. 1, No. 9 (2 March 1990).

—— 'The Romanian Authorities' Reactions to the Violence in Tirgu Mureş', *Report on Eastern Europe*, Vol. 1, No. 15 (13 April 1990).

—— 'Government Encourages Vigilante Violence in Bucharest', *Report on Eastern Europe*, Vol. 1, No. 26 (6 July 1990).

—— 'Oppositional Regrouping: The Democratic Antitotalitarian Front and the Civic Alliance', *Report on Eastern Europe*, Vol. 1, No. 50 (14 December 1990).

—— 'Schopflinian Optimism and Romanian Reality', *Report on Eastern Europe*, Vol. 2, No. 6 (15 February 1991).

—— 'Public Opinion One Year After the Elections', *Report on Eastern Europe*, Vol. 2, No. 23 (14 June 1991).

—— 'Romania's New Institutions: The Draft Constitution', *Report on Eastern Europe*, Vol. 2, No. 37 (20 September 1991).

—— 'Romania: Constitution Approved in Referendum', *RFE-RL Research Report*, Vol. 1, No. 2 (10 January 1992).

—— '"War of the Roses" in Romania's National Salvation Front', *RFE-RL Research Report*, Vol. 1, No. 3 (24 January 1992).

—— 'Romania: National Liberal Party Quits Democratic Convention', *RFE-RL Research Report*, Vol. 1, No. 24 (12 June 1992).

—— 'Transylvanian Shadows, Transylvanian Light', *RFE-RL Research Report*, Vol. 1, No. 26 (26 June 1992).

—— 'The Movement for Romania: A Party of "Radical Return"', *RFE-RL Research Report*, Vol. 1, No. 29 (17 July 1992).

—— 'Romania: Main Candidates in the Presidential Elections', *RFE-RL Research Report*, Vol. 1, No. 35 (4 September 1992).

—— 'Romania's New Electoral Laws', RFE-RL *Research Report*, Vol. 1, No. 36 (11 September 1992).

—— 'Romania's Elections: Why the Democratic Convention Lost', RFE-RL *Research Report*, Vol. 1, No. 43 (30 October 1992).

—— 'Romania's New Government', RFE-RL *Research Report*, Vol. 1, No. 47 (27 November 1992).

—— 'The HDFR Congress: Confrontations Postponed', RFE-RL *Research Report*, Vol. 2, No. 9 (26 February 1993).

—— 'Growing Political Extremism in Romania', RFE-RL *Research Report*, Vol. 2, No. 14 (2 April 1993).

—— 'Romanians and the Transition to Democracy', RFE-RL *Research Report*, Vol. 2, No. 18 (30 April 1993).

—— 'Romania: The Rechristening of the National Salvation Front', RFE-RL *Research Report*, Vol. 2, No. 27, (2 July 1993).

—— 'Romanian Prime Minister Announces Cabinet Changes', RFE-RL *Research Report*, Vol. 2, No. 38 (24 September 1993).

Shoup, Paul, 'The National Question and the Political Systems of Eastern Europe', in S. Sinanian et al., *Eastern Europe in the 1970s*, Praegar, New York 1972.

Sislin, John, 'Revolution Betrayed? Romania and the National Salvation Front', *Studies in Comparative Communism*, Vol. 24, No. 4 (1991).

Socor, Vladimir 'Forces of Old Resurface in Romania: The Ethnic Clashes in Tirgu Mureş', *Report on Eastern Europe*, Vol. 1, No. 15 (13 April 1990).

—— 'The New President', *Report on Eastern Europe*, Vol. 1, No. 23 (8 June 1990).

—— 'Foreign Policy in 1990', *Report on Eastern Europe*, Vol. 1, No. 50 (28 December 1990).

—— 'Moldovan-Romanian Relations Are Slow to Develop', RFE-RL *Research Report*, Vol. 1, No. 26 (26 June 1992).

—— 'Moldova's Political Landscape: Profiles of the Parties', RFE-RL *Research Report*, Vol. 3, No. 10 (11 March 1994).

—— 'Moldova', RFE-RL *Research Report*, Vol. 3, No. 16 (22 April 1994), special issue on 'Intolerance'.

Solzhenitsyn, Aleksander, *Rebuilding Russia: Reflections and Tentative Proposals*, Farrar, Strauss, and Giroux, New York 1991.

Sozan, M., 'Ethnocide in Rumania', *Current Anthropology*, 18 (1977).

—— 'A Reply', *Current Anthropology*, 20 (1979).

Stefanescu, Crisula, 'The Romanian Academy Adrift', *Radio Free Europe Research*, Vol. 13, No. 29 (22 July 1988).

—— '"Free Romanian Television" Loses Its Credibility', *Report on Eastern Europe*, Vol. 1, No. 8 (23 March 1990).

Sturdza, Michel, *The Silence of Europe*, Watchtower Books, Boston MA 1968.

Sturdza, Mihai, 'Distortions Mark 70th Anniversary of Romanian Unification', *Radio Free Europe Research*, Vol. 13, No. 52 (30 December 1988).

—— 'Worldwide Indignation at the Miners' Rampage in Bucharest', *Report on Eastern Europe*, Vol. 1, No. 25 (6 July 1990).

—— 'The President and the Miners: The End of a Privileged Relationship', *Report on Eastern Europe*, Vol. 1, No. 37 (28 September 1990).

—— 'The Politics of Ambiguity: Romania's Foreign Relations', *Report on Eastern Europe*, Vol. 2, No. 13 (5 April 1991).

—— 'The Files of the State Security Police', *Report on Eastern Europe*, Vol. 2, No. 35 (13 September 1991).

Sugar, P. (ed.), *Ethnic Diversity and Conflict in Eastern Europe*, ABC-Clio, Santa Barbara CA 1980.

Sugar, P. and I. Lederer, *Nationalism in Eastern Europe*, University of Washington Press, Seattle WA 1969.

Szabo, Adam T., 'A Hungarian University in Transylvania', *New Hungarian Quarterly*, No. 123 (Autumn 1991).

Szajkowski, Bogdan, 'Romania', *New Political Parties of Eastern Europe and the Soviet Union*, Longman, London 1991.

Tannenbaum, Edward R. and Emiliana P. Noether (eds), *Modern Italy: A Topical History since 1961*, New York University Press, New York 1974.

Tismaneanu, Vladimir, 'Ceauşescu's Socialism', *Problems of Communism* (January-February 1985).

—— 'Byzantine Rites, Stalinist Follies: The Twilight of Dynastic Socialism in Romania', *Orbis* (Spring 1986).

—— 'Personal Power and Political Crisis in Romania', *Government and Opposition*, Vol. 24, No. 2 (1989).

—— 'The Tragicomedy of Romanian Communism', *Eastern European Politics and Societies*, Vol. 3, No. 2 (Spring 1989).

—— *Reinventing Politics: Eastern Europe from Stalin to Havel*, The Free Press, New York 1992.

—— 'The Quasi-Revolution and Its Discontents: Emerging Political Pluralism in Post-Ceauşescu Romania', *East European Politics and Societies*, Vol. 7, No. 2 (Summer 1993).

Tismaneanu, Vladimir and M. Mihaies, *East European Reporter* (January–February 1992).

Topor, Gabriel, 'The National Salvation Front in a Crisis', *Report on Eastern Europe*, Vol. 2, No. 35 (16 August 1991).

Varkonyi, Agnes R., 'Pro quiete regni – For the Peace of the Realm', *Hungarian Quarterly*, Vol. 34 (Summer 1993).

Veiga, Francisco, *La mística del ultranacionalismo (História de la Guardia de Hierro Rumania, 1919–41)*, Univ. Autonomia de Barcelona, Barcelona 1989.

—— *Els Balcans: La desfeta d'in somni*, Eumo Editorial, Girona 1993.

—— 'Por Que Yugoslavia. Hipotese socio-economicas para el origen de la guerra: 1948–91', *L'Avenc*, 173 (September 1993).

—— '"Ceauşescu Tenia Razon": Ultranacionalismo y radicalismo en Rumania, 1989–93', paper presented at a conference on nationalism in eastern Europe at the East European Institute, University of Complutense, Madrid (9–10 December 1993).

Verdery, Katherine, *National Ideology Under Socialism: Identity and Cultural Politics in Ceauşescu's Romania*, University of California Press, Berkeley CA 1991.

—— 'Nationalism and National Sentiment in Post-socialist Romania', *Slavic Review*, Vol. 52, No. 2 (Summer 1993).

Volovici, Leon, *Nationalist Ideology and Anti-Semitism: The Case of Romanian Intellectuals in the 1930s*, Pergamon Press, Oxford, 1991.

Voltan, Peter M. E. (ed.), *Bound to Change: Consolidating Democracy in East-Central Europe*, Institute for East-West Studies, New York and Prague 1992.

Walters, E. Garrison, *The Other Europe: Eastern Europe To 1945*, Dorset Press, New York 1988.

Watts, Larry, 'The Romanian Army in the December Revolution and Beyond', in Daniel Nelson (ed.), *Romania After Tyranny*, Westview Press, London and San Francisco CA 1992.

Weber, Eugen, 'Romania', in H. Rogger and E. Weber (eds), *The European Right: A Historical Profile*, University of California Press, Berkeley CA 1974.

Welsh, David, 'Domestic Politics and Ethnic Conflict', *Survival*, Vol. 35, No. 1 (Spring 1993).

Wolff, Robert Lee, *The Balkans in Our Time*, Harvard University Press, Cambridge MA 1974.

Zidaru-Barbulescu, Aurel, 'Romania Seeks Admission to the Council of Europe', *RFE-RL Research Report*, Vol. 2, No. 2 (8 January 1993).

Acronyms

CADA	Committee for Action to Democratise the Army
CAP	Civic Alliance Party
CIS	Commonwealth of Independent States
CNM	Council of National Minorities
CSCE	Conference on Security and Co-operation in Europe
DAF	Democratic Anti-Totalitarian Forum
DC	Democratic Convention
DNSF	Democratic National Salvation Front
DPRF	Democratic Party of Romanian Farmers
EC	European Community
EU	European Union
FRY	Federal Republic of Yugoslavia
GRP	Greater Romania Party
GSD	Group for Social Dialogue
HAR	Hungarian Autonomous Region
HDFR	Hungarian Democratic Forum in Romania
HSP	Hungarian Socialist Party
MFR	Movement For Romania
Miszsz	Federation of Hungarian Youth Organisations from Romania
NATO	North Atlantic Treaty Organisation
NGO	Non-Governmental Organisation
NLP	National Liberal Party
NPP	National Peasant Party
NPP-CD	National Peasant and Christian Democratic Party
NSF	National Salvation Front
PNUC	Provisional National Unity Council
PRNU	Party of Romanian National Unity
PSDR	Party of Social Democracy of Romania
RCP	Romanian Communist Party
RDC	Romanian Democratic Convention
RIS	Romanian Information Service
RNP	Romanian National Party
RWP	Romanian Workers Party
SLP	Socialist Labor Party
UN	United Nations
WEU	West European Union

Index